BRITISH LIBERAL LEADERS

Leaders of the Liberal Party, SDP and Liberal Democrats since 1828

EDITED BY
Duncan Brack, Robert Ingham & Tony Little

Biteback Publishing

First published in Great Britain in 2015 by
Biteback Publishing Ltd
Westminster Tower
3 Albert Embankment
London SE1 7SP
Selection and editorial apparatus copyright © Duncan Brack,
Robert Ingham and Tony Little 2015

ISBN 978-1-84954-197-8

10 9 8 7 6 5 4 3 2 1

A CIP catalogue record for this book is available from the British Library.

Set in Bulmer MT Std

Printed and bound in Great Britain by
CPI Group (UK) Ltd, Croydon CR0 4YY

MIX
Paper from
responsible sources
FSC
www.fsc.org   FSC® C020471

BRITISH LIBERAL LEADERS

CONTENTS

PREFACE

This book is the sixth in the series of Liberal history source books produced by the Liberal Democrat History Group; the others are *Dictionary of Liberal Biography* (1998), *Dictionary of Liberal Quotations* (1999, revised edition 2013), *Great Liberal Speeches* (2001), *Dictionary of Liberal Thought* (2007) and *Peace, Reform and Liberation: A History of Liberal Politics in Britain 1679–2011* (2011).

Given the critical importance of party leadership in British politics, for some time we had thought that an analysis of Liberal leaders and their strengths and weaknesses would provide a valuable addition to this range; we developed a set of criteria against which to measure their effectiveness (summarised in Chapter 1) and commissioned authors to write chapters on individual leaders. Completely separately, Charles Clarke, Toby James and colleagues began their studies of Conservative and Labour leaders, and in due course Biteback Publishing decided to publish all three books as a set.

Leaders in the other two books were assessed by slightly different criteria, so the first three chapters in this book present three contrasting ways of judging Liberal leaders. There is of course no single way of doing this, and we hope that this book will contribute to a debate about the characteristics of effective political party leadership in general, and Liberal leadership in particular.

After the three introductory chapters, the next twenty-four cover every leader of the Liberal Party, SDP and Liberal Democrats from Lord Grey in 1828 to Nick Clegg's resignation in 2015. Lord Hartington and Lord Granville, who led the Liberals in the Commons and Lords during Gladstone's first retirement in 1875–80, are given a joint chapter. As in the other two books, the authors we approached are, in general, admirers of the leaders they have written about, but we asked them to assess their subjects objectively against the criteria we provided. For readers interested in learning more about particular individuals, we have included a list of further reading. (The book does not include the leaders of the various Liberal breakaway factions – the Liberal Unionists of 1886–1912 and the Liberal Nationals of 1931–47.)

The final three chapters are transcripts of interviews with three Liberal and Liberal Democrat leaders – David Steel, Paddy Ashdown and Nick Clegg – on the general topic of Liberal leadership and their particular experiences of it.

•   •   •

The support and encouragement of the History Group's executive has been vital to the successful completion of this book, and we place on record our thanks to them. We have enjoyed cooperating with Charles Clarke and Toby James in aligning our book with theirs, and thank them for their chapters. We thank David Steel, Paddy Ashdown and Nick Clegg for their interviews, and Sophie Moxon and Esperanza Galera Suarez, at the University of East Anglia, for excellent transcriptions of the recordings. Melissa Bond, Olivia Beattie and Iain Dale at Biteback Publishing have been consistently encouraging and patient. Above all, the authors of the chapters on the leaders have written, and in many cases rewritten, their chapters to a high quality and to tight deadlines. Our warmest thanks go to them all.

Duncan Brack, Robert Ingham and Tony Little
July 2015

AUTHOR BIOGRAPHIES

PETER BARBERIS is emeritus professor at Manchester Metropolitan University. He has written extensively on British government and politics and is the author of *Liberal Lion – Jo Grimond: A Political Life* (2005). He is a fellow of the Royal Historical Society and of the Joint University Council.

CHRIS BOWERS is a freelance writer and broadcaster on sport and current affairs. His *Nick Clegg: The Biography* was published by Biteback Publishing in 2011 (paperback update 2012), and among his other books is *The Sporting Statesman* (2014), about how the tennis champion Novak Djokovic is rehabilitating the reputation of Serbia.

DUNCAN BRACK is the editor of the *Journal of Liberal History*, and has co-edited and contributed to all the Liberal Democrat History Group's previous books. He has been director of policy for the Liberal Democrats, chair of the party's conference committee, and special advisor to Chris Huhne MP, Secretary of State for Energy and Climate Change. He is currently vice-chair of the party's Federal Policy Committee.

DAVID BROWN is professor of modern history at the University of Southampton. He has published widely on nineteenth-century British history, and his books include *Palmerston: A Biography* (2010) and *Palmerston and the Politics of Foreign Policy, 1846–55* (2002).

JIM BULLER is a senior lecturer in politics at the University of York. He has a PhD from the University of Sheffield and has previously worked in the department of political science and international studies at the University of Birmingham. He has written widely on the subject of British politics and public policy, including recent articles in the *New Political Economy*, *British Journal of Politics and International Relations*, *West European Politics*, *Contemporary European Politics and British Politics*. He has recently co-edited a special issue of *Parliamentary Affairs* on 'Assessing Political Leadership in Context – British Party Leadership During Austerity'. He is also chair of the PSA Anti-Politics and Depoliticisation Specialist Group.

JOHN CAMPBELL is a freelance political biographer. His books have included *Lloyd George: The Goat in the Wilderness* (1977), *Nye Bevan and the Mirage of British Socialism* (1986), *Edward Heath* (1993, NCR Prize 1994), *Margaret Thatcher: The Grocer's Daughter* (2000), *The Iron Lady* (2003), and, most recently, *Roy Jenkins: A Well-Rounded Life* (2014), which was shortlisted for the Samuel Johnson and Costa book prizes and won the Paddy Power Political Biography award for 2015.

CHARLES CLARKE was Member of Parliament for Norwich South from 1997 to 2010. He served as Education Minister from 1998 and then in the Home Office from 1999 to 2001. He then joined the Cabinet as Minister without Portfolio and Labour Party chair. From 2002 to 2004, he was Secretary of State for Education and Skills, and then Home Secretary until 2006. Charles was previously chief of staff to Leader of the Opposition Neil Kinnock. He now holds visiting professorships at the University of East Anglia, Lancaster University and King's College London, and works with educational organisations internationally. He edited *The 'Too Difficult' Box* and co-edited *British Labour Leaders* and *British Conservative Leaders*.

MATT COLE is a teaching fellow in history at the University of Birmingham. He is the author of *Richard Wainwright, the Liberals and Liberal Democrats: Unfinished Business* (2011) and worked in the SDP's general election unit in 1987.

DAVID DUTTON taught at the University of Liverpool for thirty-five years before retiring in 2010 as Ramsay Muir professor of modern history. His books include *A History of the Liberal Party since 1900* (2013) and *Liberals in Schism: A History of the National Liberal Party* (2008).

DR RICHARD A. GAUNT is associate professor in British history at the University of Nottingham. He is the author of *Sir Robert Peel: The Life and Legacy* (2010) and the editor of *Peel in Caricature: The 'Political Sketches' of John Doyle ('HB')* (2014).

DAVID HOWARTH is professor of law and public policy at the University of Cambridge, where he also directs the MPhil in public policy. From 2005–10, he was the Member of Parliament for Cambridge, serving in the Liberal Democrat shadow Cabinet as shadow Secretary of State for Justice. Before that he was leader of Cambridge city council. His research mainly concerns the relationship between law and politics and the design of legal institutions, but he also writes occasionally on Liberal and Liberal Democrat history.

GREG HURST spent fifteen years as a political journalist at Westminster, first with Southern Newspapers, and, from 2000–07, with *The Times*. He is the author of *Charles Kennedy: A Tragic Flaw* (2006, updated edition 2015). He was editor of *The Times Guide to the House of Commons 2010* and, since 2009, has been the newspaper's education editor.

ROBERT INGHAM is a historical writer who has contributed to many of the Liberal Democrat History Group's publications as well as the *Journal of Liberal History*.

TOBY S. JAMES is a senior lecturer in British and comparative politics at the University of East Anglia. He has a PhD from the University of York and has previously worked at Swansea University and the Library of Congress, Washington DC. He is the co-convenor of the Political Studies Association's Political Leadership Group and has published on statecraft theory/political leadership in journals such as *British Journal of Politics and International Relations*, *Electoral*

Studies and *Government and Opposition*. He has co-edited a special issue of *Parliamentary Affairs* on 'Assessing Political Leadership in Context – British Party Leadership During Austerity', is the author of *Elite Statecraft and Election Administration*, and co-edited *British Labour Leaders* and *British Conservative Leaders*.

DR TUDOR JONES is honorary research fellow in history of political thought at Coventry University. His publications include *Remaking the Labour Party: From Gaitskell to Blair* (1996), *Modern Political Thinkers and Ideas: An Historical Introduction* (2002), and *The Revival of British Liberalism: From Grimond to Clegg* (2011).

TONY LITTLE is chairman of the Liberal Democrat History Group and a former Liberal Democrat council group leader. Before retiring, he was head of corporate governance with a fund management company. He jointly edited the Liberal Democrat History Group's *Great Liberal Speeches* (2001), and contributed to the *Dictionary of Liberal Thought* (2007) and *Peace Reform and Liberation* (2011).

DR HENRY MILLER is lecturer in nineteenth-century British history at the University of Manchester. He previously worked on the history of Parliament's House of Commons 1832–68 project. He has published widely on nineteenth-century politics, including *Politics Personified: Portraiture, Caricature and Visual Culture in Britain, c. 1830–1880* (2015).

KENNETH O. MORGAN was fellow and tutor at Queen's College, Oxford, 1966–89; vice-chancellor at the University of Wales, 1989–95, and visiting professor at King's College London, since 2011. He was made a fellow of the British Academy in 1983 and a life peer (Labour) in 2000. An honorary fellow of Queen's and Oriel colleges, Oxford, he received a parliamentary award for lifetime achievement in 2014. His thirty-four books on modern British history include *The Age of Lloyd George* (1971), *Consensus and Disunity: The Lloyd George Coalition*

Government 1918–1922 (1980), *Ages of Reform: Dawns and Downfalls of the British Left* (2010), and *The Oxford Illustrated History of Britain* (1983).

TONY MORRIS is emeritus professor at the University of Ulster. His books include *C. P. Trevelyan: Portrait of a Radical* (1977) and *The Scaremongers: The Advocacy of War and Rearmament 1896–1914* (1984).

DR JAIME REYNOLDS has written extensively on Liberal history. He studied politics at the LSE and was awarded a PhD for research on east European history. He has worked for many years in international environmental policy, first in the UK public administration, and, for the past decade, as an official of the European Union.

DR IAIN SHARPE completed a University of London PhD thesis in 2011 on 'Herbert Gladstone and Liberal Party revival, 1899–1905'. He works as an editor for the University of London International Academy and has served as a Liberal Democrat councillor in Watford since 1991.

GREG SIMPSON worked for the Liberal Democrats between 1997–2009 in various roles including foreign affairs and defence advisor, deputy head of the press office, speechwriter to Charles Kennedy, and head of policy and research. Since leaving the party, he has worked for the Ministry of Defence and the Department of Energy & Climate Change.

DAVID TORRANCE is a freelance writer, broadcaster and journalist. He was educated at Leith Academy, the University of Aberdeen and the Cardiff School of Journalism. He writes a regular column for the *Herald* newspaper and has written or edited more than a dozen books on Scottish and UK politics, including *David Steel: Rising Hope to Elder Statesman* (2012).

ELLIS WASSON was educated at Johns Hopkins and Cambridge Universities, and teaches at the University of Delaware. He is the author of six books on

British and European history, including *A History of Modern Britain: 1714 to the Present* (2009, 2015).

DR ALUN WYBURN-POWELL is the author of *Clement Davies – Liberal Leader* (2003) and *Political Wings*, a biography of William Wedgwood Benn, 1st Viscount Stansgate (2015). He received his PhD from the University of Leicester for his research into political defections, which was published as *Defectors and the Liberal Party 1910 to 2010* (2012). He is a visiting lecturer in the department of journalism at City University, London.

PART I

FRAMEWORKS FOR ASSESSING LEADERS

CHAPTER 1

INTRODUCTION: LIBERAL LEADERS AND LEADERSHIP

DUNCAN BRACK, ROBERT INGHAM AND TONY LITTLE

The purpose of this book is to analyse the leaders of the British Liberal Party, Social Democratic Party and Liberal Democrats from the era of the Great Reform Act to 2015: were they good leaders, bad leaders or somewhere in the range between adequate and barely adequate? This chapter provides a brief summary of the history of the parties, discusses the criteria used throughout this book in assessing Liberal leaders, and concludes by ranking them against five key criteria.

•   •   •

Political debate in Britain, as in many other countries, often revolves around the characters of political party leaders. Elections are portrayed as contests between leaders, voters are often asked to say which leader they will be voting for – even though they can't, unless they happen to live in a leader's constituency – and the media, during elections, party conferences and day-to-day politics, generally focus on the leader, sometimes, in small parties, to the exclusion of all other figures. Within their parties, even in relatively democratic institutions like the Liberal Democrats, the leader exercises considerable influence over party policy and strategy.

Classical political writers have often highlighted the role of and the need for political leadership. Machiavelli, in *The Prince*, listed the attributes that a prince needed to possess at some stage in his career to be able to win and hold on to power: above all, he needed to be 'a most valiant lion and a most cunning fox; he will find him feared and respected by everyone'.[1] In the nineteenth century, the Scottish writer Thomas Carlyle claimed that 'the history of the world is the history of great men'.[2] This focus on the leader continued into democratic politics, with the German sociologist Max Weber pointing to the way in which party members 'expect that the demagogic effect of the leader's *personality* during the election fight of the party will increase votes and mandates and thereby power, and, thereby, as far as possible, will extend opportunities to their followers to find the compensation for which they hope', whether it be office, the achievement of the political programme or 'the satisfaction of working with loyal personal devotion for a man'.[3]

More recently, Archie Brown has pointed to the way in which:

> Leaders everywhere operate within historically conditioned political cultures. In the way they lead, they cannot rely on reason and argument alone, but must be able to appeal to emotion, sharing in the sense of identity of their party or group. In government, the minority of leaders who come to be revered and who retain the admiration of posterity are those who have also fostered a sense of purpose within their country as a whole, who have provided grounds for trust and have offered a vision that transcends day-to-day decision-making.[4]

This again suggests the need for strong leadership – but in fact this is an extract from Brown's *The Myth of the Strong Leader*, which stressed the shortcomings of dominant leadership. Brown suggested that in parliamentary democracies there is a tendency for the public to believe that the top leader counts for more than they actually do; thanks to the media's focus on the leader, policy outcomes or

---

1   Niccolo Machiavelli, *The Prince (Il Principe)* [1513], Harmondsworth, Penguin Classics edition, 1975, p. 110.

2   Thomas Carlyle, 'The Hero as Divinity', in *Heroes and Hero-Worship*, London, Chapman & Hall, 1840.

3   Max Weber, *Politics as a Vocation*, 1919, available at http://anthropos-lab.net/wp/wp-content/uploads/2011/12/Weber-Politics-as-a-Vocation.pdf, p. 14.

4   Archie Brown, *The Myth of the Strong Leader*, London, Bodley Head, 2014, p. 61.

election victories are often attributed to the leader even when there may be many others who should take more of the credit. Brown concluded by pointing to the dangers of leaders bypassing their colleagues, surrounding themselves with personal supporters and ignoring advice with which they disagree, all leading to poor decision-making and, potentially, a loss of trust in the political system itself.

What qualities, then, are required for effective political leadership? Who is a good leader and who a bad? Biographies of the leaders of British political parties are legion. Studies of political *leadership*, like those cited above, are much fewer in number and are either theoretical in nature or tend to focus on a small number of examples, often drawn from presidential systems like the United States. Studies of British political leadership over time and within the context of a single political party are non-existent. It is this gap which this series of books on leadership in the three main British parties seeks to address. This book considers leaders and leadership in the Liberal Party, the Social Democratic Party (SDP) and the party into which they merged, the Liberal Democrats.

LIBERALS, SDP AND LIBERAL DEMOCRATS

While the SDP and the Liberal Democrats have clear organisational histories, it is impossible to make the same claim for the Liberal Party. It developed in an age when politics was primarily the responsibility of a small aristocratic elite in which family and patronage, as much as policy and ideology, defined political groupings. The term 'Liberal', borrowed from the Spanish '*liberales*' at the time of the Napoleonic Wars, only gradually attached itself to British politicians and, in particular, to those professing the primacy of the people in Parliament over the monarchy, or executive, and to those who promoted free trade in the products of industry in preference to the privileges of the land-owners from whom the elite were drawn. These liberal beliefs allowed the formation of shifting alliances between the Whigs – a collection of aristocratic families, their clients and fellow travellers, who were the foremost in professing the supremacy of Parliament and tolerance of disparate Christian denominations

– free-trade Tories, whether followers of Canning in the 1820s or of Peel in the 1840s, and various radical groups committed to widening the franchise as a means of increasing the accountability of the elite to the people. This conglomeration transformed British politics through the passage of the Great Reform Act in 1832 – and this is the starting point for our selection of Liberal leaders, with Charles, Earl Grey the first in the book.

The modestly enhanced electorate produced by the first reform act required the development of constituency organisations to fight elections, and the beginnings of central co-ordination to provide the candidates, funding and policy commitments which modern political activists could recognise as the building blocks of a party. But while the components of the party were being developed, it was not always obvious to the participants what they were building. Leaders saw themselves as primarily directing the monarch's government, secondly as builders of parliamentary followings, and only gradually as figureheads of national movements.

The Great Reform Act alliance gradually disintegrated over the 1830s, though Lord Melbourne implemented further cautious reforms until 1841. When the Whigs were returned to power in 1846 under Lord John Russell, it was more by courtesy of Tory difficulties over the Corn Laws (import duties on grain) than because of any increased tendency to cooperate among those professing Liberal beliefs. The break-up of the Conservative Party over the Corn Laws, however, was of long-term significance, as it saw the gradual detachment of the Peelites (free-trade followers of the Tory leader Sir Robert Peel), including Gladstone, who were to become important recruits to the Liberal Party. It also helped to align the rising industrial and commercial interests (who preferred free trade for their products and cheap bread for their workers) with the Liberals as against the land-owning and agricultural interests behind the Tories.

Despite Russell's record as the architect of the Great Reform Act, he struggled to hold his government together. The second attempt to create the fusion of Liberals, the 1852 Aberdeen coalition, was unable to withstand the strains of the Crimean War, and it was not until Palmerston's government of 1859 that the factions settled enough of their differences to sustain unity. The famous meeting of

6 June 1859 in Willis's Rooms, St James's, between Whigs, radicals and Peelites, is generally held to mark the foundation of the Liberal Party.

Palmerston, and after him Gladstone, were the dominant figures in Victorian politics, in competition with the Tories' Disraeli and Salisbury. If Palmerston created the space in which senior figures learned to work together in extending free trade and Russell forced the pace for the creation of a second reform act, it was Gladstone who exploited the opportunity to present himself as a popular leader with a mission to change the nation. In the 1850s he established his reputation for prudent financial innovation by sweeping away tariffs in the interests of free trade, replacing taxes on goods and customs duties with income tax, and by modernising parliamentary accountability for government spending. He won strong support from Nonconformists for his attitude to religious questions, which at that time deeply affected basic liberties and education. His first government, between 1868 and 1874, represents the pinnacle of Victorian reform, introducing the secret ballot, a national system of primary education, disestablishment of the Church of Ireland and reform of trade unions, the army, civil service and local government. 'Peace, retrenchment and reform' became the watchwords of the Victorian Liberal Party.

Yet the pace of reform itself caused strain. In some cases Gladstonian compromises disillusioned the radicals, while for many Whigs Gladstone was too advanced. While disagreements over domestic policies were the most frequent, disputes about Ireland were critical. Gladstone's solution in 1886 – home rule – resulted in the permanent loss of many of the Whigs and some of the radicals who, as Liberal Unionists, forged an alliance with the Conservatives to defeat Gladstone and end his third government. A second failure to carry home rule through the House of Lords after 1892 ended Gladstone's career.

Gladstone's successor, Lord Rosebery, proved to be weak and indecisive. Neither Rosebery nor his short-lived successor Harcourt could provide firm direction, and the party split over the empire and the Boer War. At the same time, the 'New Liberal' ideas of state intervention to help the poorer sections of society, which were to provide the agenda for twentieth-century politics, were slowly developing. From 1899, however, Campbell-Bannerman – perhaps one of the most effective party managers in Liberal history – helped heal the rifts in the party, and led it to the spectacular electoral landslide of 1906, exploiting Conservative splits over free trade and education. A further factor, secret at the time, was an electoral pact with the new Labour Party, which ensured that the impact of the progressive vote was maximised.

The Liberal government of 1906–15 was one of the great reforming administrations of the twentieth century. Led by towering figures such as Asquith (Prime Minister after Campbell-Bannerman's death in 1908), Lloyd George and Churchill, it laid the foundations of the modern welfare state, created the national insurance system, introduced old-age pensions and established labour exchanges. This was the realisation of the New Liberal programme – removing the shackles of poverty, unemployment and ill-health to allow individuals to be free to exercise choice and realise opportunity. From the outset the Liberals had difficulty passing legislation through the Tory-dominated House of Lords. The crunch came when the Lords rejected Lloyd George's 1909 'People's Budget', which introduced a supertax on high earners to raise revenue for social expenditure and naval rearmament. Two elections were fought in 1910 on the issue of 'the peers versus the people'. The massive majority of 1906 was destroyed, but the Liberals remained in power with the support of Labour and Irish Nationalist MPs. In 1911, with the King primed to create hundreds of new Liberal peers if necessary, the Lords capitulated and the primacy of the House of Commons was definitively established.

After 1910, however, the government faced increasing difficulties over rising trade union militancy, the campaign for women's suffrage, a renewed attempt to grant home rule to Ireland, and the international tensions within the European power system which led ultimately to the outbreak of war in 1914. What would have happened in the absence of war has been the subject of extensive speculation, but in reality the once-productive partnership between Asquith and Lloyd George broke down, leaving the party divided and demoralised; Liberal factions led by each of them fought each other in the 1918 and 1922 elections. The party's grass-roots organisation fell apart, allowing the Labour Party to capture many of the votes of the new working-class and women voters enfranchised in 1918; many of those, who could later be identified as Social Democrats, left the

Liberals for the more evidently successful progressive alternative, the Labour Party; others, fearful of the growth of socialism, joined the Conservatives.

The Liberals reunited around the old cause of free trade to fight the 1923 election, which left them holding the balance of power in the Commons. Asquith's decision to support a minority Labour government, however, placed the party in an awkward position and effectively polarised the political choice between Conservatives and Labour; the disastrous 1924 election relegated the party to a distant third place as the electorate increasingly opted for a straight choice between the other two parties.

Despite a renewed burst of energy under Lloyd George, which saw the party fight the 1929 general election on a radical platform of Keynesian economics, the Liberals were by then too firmly established as the third party to achieve much influence on government. They split again in the 1930s, in the wake of the upheaval brought by the Great Depression, and continued to decline, although the party participated in Churchill's wartime coalition. Successive leaders – Samuel in 1935, Sinclair in 1945 – lost their own seats on election day. By the time of the 1951 election the party was facing extinction and if its leader, Clement Davies, had accepted Churchill's invitation to join his Cabinet its independence might have ended. By 1957, there were only five Liberal MPs left, and just 110 constituencies had been fought at the previous general election. Despite the political irrelevance of the party itself, however, the huge impact of the Liberal thinkers Keynes and Beveridge, whose doctrines underpinned government social and economic policy for much of the post-war period, showed that Liberalism as an intellectual force was still alive and well.

Revival came with the election of Jo Grimond as party leader in 1956. His vision and youthful appeal were well suited to the burgeoning television coverage of politics, and he was able to capitalise on growing dissatisfaction with the Conservatives, in power since 1951. The party learned how to concentrate its resources on by-elections, culminating in the sensational by-election victory at Orpington in 1962. Although the upswing receded under Wilson's Labour government in the 1960s, a second revival came in the 1970s under Jeremy Thorpe, peaking in the two general elections of 1974, with 19 and 18 per cent of the vote (though only fourteen and thirteen seats, respectively, in Parliament). The breakdown of class-based voting and disillusionment with the inability of the other two parties to halt Britain's seemingly inexorable economic decline were major factors behind the Liberal revival, but a further reason was the development of community politics, in which Liberal activists campaigned intensively to empower local communities. This strategy – which was a grass-roots rather than leadership initiative – was formally adopted by the party in 1970, and contributed to a steady growth in local authority representation, and a number of parliamentary by-election victories.

Following Labour's defeat in the 1979 election, the growing success of the left within the party alienated many MPs and members. Moderate Labour leaders had worked with the Liberal Party during the 1975 referendum on membership of the European Community, and during the Lib–Lab pact which kept Labour in power in 1977–78. In 1981, a number of them broke away from Labour to found the SDP under former Labour deputy leader Roy Jenkins. The new party attracted members from both the Labour and Conservative parties and also brought many people into politics for the first time. It agreed with the Liberal Party, now led by David Steel, to fight elections on a common platform with joint candidates; some argued that this represented the revival of the pre-1914 progressive tradition, where liberals and social democrats were to be found together in the Liberal Party, before the break-up of the party forced its more progressive members out towards Labour.

The Liberal–SDP Alliance won 25 per cent of the vote in the 1983 general election, the best third-party performance since 1929, only just behind Labour, but only twenty-three seats. In the 1983–87 parliament, however, tensions between the leaders of the two parties became apparent. David Owen, SDP leader from 1983, was personally less sympathetic towards the Liberals than his predecessor, and was also more determined to maintain a separate (and in practice more right-wing) identity for his party; differences emerged, most notably on defence. After the Alliance's share of the vote fell in the 1987 election, the two parties agreed to merge – though the decision was opposed by Owen, who left to form his own short-lived 'continuing SDP', leaving Robert Maclennan to lead the SDP into merger.

After a difficult birth, the Liberal Democrats suffered a troubled infancy. Membership, morale and finances all suffered from the in-fighting over merger; but under its first leader, Paddy Ashdown, slowly the party recovered; by-election wins and local authority gains followed, and ruthless targeting of resources on winnable constituencies enabled the party to double its number of MPs in the 1997 election despite a fall in its vote. Ashdown saved the party from oblivion; but the more controversial part of his legacy was 'the project', his attempt to work with Labour to defeat the Conservatives' seemingly endless political hegemony. The scale of Labour's triumph in 1997 made any coalition impossible, but a pre-election agreement on constitutional reform helped ensure that the Blair government introduced major changes to the governance of Britain.

Ashdown and his two successors, Charles Kennedy and Menzies Campbell, positioned the Liberal Democrats as a centre-left party, benefiting from New Labour's shift to the right, especially after the Iraq War of 2003. The 2005 election saw the party win sixty-two seats, the highest number of Liberal MPs since 1923, and 22 per cent of the vote. Yet, as in previous post-war revivals, much of this support in reality came from unaligned protest voters and was vulnerable once the party lost its appeal. The election of Nick Clegg in 2007 was followed by a deliberate attempt to shift the party's image to the right. Disillusionment with the Labour government and the Conservative opposition left the Liberal Democrats holding the balance of power after the 2010 election, and on 11 May 2010 the first peacetime coalition government since the 1930s was formed, between the Liberal Democrats and the Conservatives. The following five years was to show just how perilous coalition can be for the junior partner. Despite a number of Liberal Democrat achievements, the party's support crashed in the 2015 election: it lost two-thirds of its vote and 85 per cent of its MPs. Probably the fact of entry into coalition with the party's historic enemy caused most of the damage, but this was not helped by a number of crucial errors in government and a poor centrist-focused election campaign.

The story of the Liberal Party, the SDP and the Liberal Democrats over the 180 years covered by this book is a remarkable one – from the dominant political force in the mid- and late nineteenth century to division, decline and near

disappearance by the mid-twentieth, to successive waves of recovery leading ultimately to entry into government once more – followed by the most catastrophic
election result in the party's history. This book is the story of the leaders of those
parties, what they did and how they performed, from 1828 to 2015.

SELECTING THE LEADER

I n 1976, the Liberal Party became the first major British party to open its leadership election to its entire membership, and a 'one member, one vote' (OMOV)
system has always been an accepted feature of Liberal Democrat leadership
elections. Before 1976, however, there was no formal system for appointing the
leader, and the practice changed and evolved over time.

From the earliest days of political parties, the choice of leader when the party
was in power was effectively in the hands of the monarch who, after consulting
trusted advisors, would send for a senior member of the party and ask him to
form a government. The monarch's choice then generally became both Prime
Minister and party leader; Grey, Melbourne, Russell and Asquith all assumed
the leadership in this fashion. The monarch, however, had no duty to consult
the party; in 1894, for example, Queen Victoria chose Rosebery as Gladstone's
successor without asking Gladstone, who would have preferred Lord Spencer. But the monarch did not enjoy complete freedom of choice. In 1859, in an
attempt to avoid both Russell and Palmerston, those 'two terrible old men', Victoria invited Lord Granville to form a government; he failed, and Palmerston
proved that he enjoyed the confidence of his party. In 1880, very much against
her wishes, Victoria was obliged to accept Gladstone; she would have preferred
Hartington, but Gladstone's contribution to the unexpectedly decisive Liberal
election victory was so clear as to make him the only plausible choice.

The position was more confused when the Liberals were out of power. The
party in the House of Commons and the party in the House of Lords each had
a leader (sometimes formally appointed as 'chairman') with no obvious mechanism suggesting that one enjoyed any preference over the other. With the steady

widening of the franchise throughout the nineteenth century, however, the expectation grew that the leader of the Liberals in the Commons would be the leader in the country overall as, increasingly, he would bear the weight of campaigning at election time. Rosebery was the last Liberal peer to lead the party, but he had been appointed Prime Minister for the previous year before election defeat in 1895.

Sometimes the leader in the Commons was obvious without any identifiable process of nomination. After the defeat of Melbourne, Russell assumed the post, as did Harcourt after the fall of Rosebery; in neither case was this disputed. Russell did not formally retire from leading the party after his government was defeated in 1866, but Gladstone was leader in the Commons and headed the 1868 election campaign, and the Queen appointed him Prime Minister when the election result became clear. Between 1852 and 1859 the leadership was disputed between Russell and Palmerston and, while Palmerston became Prime Minister in 1855, Russell did not concede defeat until 1859, conspiring to bring his rival down in 1858. After Gladstone's temporary resignation in 1875, it was not clear who should succeed him in the Commons: Lord Hartington and W. E. Forster were both plausible candidates, and the choice was resolved in Hartington's favour by soundings among MPs; Granville continued as leader in the Lords. When Harcourt abandoned the leadership in 1898, no one was prepared to stand against Campbell-Bannerman, although Asquith and Grey were potential candidates; a formal meeting of the party's MPs at the Reform Club confirmed 'CB' in the post.

Lloyd George became the last Liberal to hold the office of Prime Minister, effectively through a parliamentary coup against Asquith organised with the help of leading Conservatives, but Asquith retained the leadership of the party, and the two leaders fought each other at the head of separate factions in the 1918 and 1922 elections. After reunion in 1923, Asquith remained leader, retaining the post even after he lost his seat in the 1924 election debacle; he only resigned after suffering a stroke in 1926. Lloyd George took over as the only plausible successor, though this was not welcomed by those still loyal to Asquith, and prompted calls for Liberal activists to have a say in the selection of their party's chief. Ramsay Muir, appointed chairman of the National Liberal Federation in 1931, was particularly critical of the parliamentary party's role in appointing the leader, arguing that the much reduced number of Liberal MPs no longer represented the views of the rank and file.[5]

Despite this pressure from the grass roots, in practice there was generally little real choice of personnel. In 1931, Lloyd George's sudden illness thrust his deputy Samuel into the leadership; on his defeat in 1935, no one opposed the succession of the Chief Whip, Sinclair. In 1945, the twelve surviving Liberal MPs adopted the procedure of asking each possible candidate to leave the room while they discussed their merits; in the end Clement Davies was chosen. On his standing down in 1956, again there was only one plausible contender, Jo Grimond; the four other MPs, excluding Davies, either owed their seats to arrangements with the Conservative Party, or were heavily committed to non-parliamentary work, or both.

Grimond's appointment, which was popular, dampened the grass-roots demands for change, but the question remained of whether a small group of MPs could legitimately select a leader on behalf of the party as a whole. The furore surrounding the hasty election of Jeremy Thorpe in 1967, who was supported by just six out of twelve Liberal MPs, only days after Grimond's retirement, ensured that the old system could not continue (the other two candidates each received three votes, and stood down in favour of Thorpe).[6] Thus, in July 1976, David Steel became the first leader of the Liberal Party to be elected by a vote of its entire membership – a groundbreaking move for a major political party in the UK. Reflecting the concerns of the activists that the votes of the armchair members would swamp their own – supposedly more politically aware – voices, the system was not a simple OMOV arrangement. An electoral college was effectively created, in which ten votes were allocated to each Liberal association, with a further ten votes if the association had existed for more than a year, and an additional vote for each 500 votes won by the Liberal candidate for the constituency at the last general election. Thus, campaigning activity and hard work were rewarded with a greater say over the leadership. It was left to local associations to decide how to ballot their membership; some did so by a postal vote of

5   J. S. Rasmussen, *The Liberal Party: A Study of Retrenchment and Revival*, London, Constable, 1965, p. 21.

6   Ibid., p. 36.

the entire membership, others by allocating votes to members who turned up to the association meeting held to conduct the vote.

In 1981, the founders of the SDP were determined to create a structure which would avoid the kind of left-wing militant takeover which had helped to drive many of them out of the Labour Party. The principle of one member, one vote was enshrined throughout the party; members had the right to vote for the party leader, president and other leading positions. Despite this democratic principle, the SDP faced the same problem as the Liberals, a shortage of plausible candidates. Although the party's first leader, Roy Jenkins, was elected in a straight fight with David Owen in 1982, after Jenkins stood down in 1983 Owen was the only candidate to succeed him. Similarly, in 1987, after Owen resigned after losing the ballot on entering negotiations for merger, Bob Maclennan was the only possible successor after the only other pro-merger SDP MP, Charles Kennedy, ruled himself out.

Of all the many issues that occupied the time of the Liberal and SDP negotiators for merger in 1987–88, the question of the leadership was not one of them: one member, one vote was accepted without disagreement and has applied to the five Liberal Democrat leadership elections held to date (Steel and Maclennan acted as interim leaders of the merged party until its first leadership election was concluded). The party has so far avoided the old problem of a lack of plausible candidates, with two MPs contesting the first leadership election, in 1988, five in 1999, three in 2006, two in 2007 and – even at the party's lowest ebb, with just eight MPs remaining after the 2015 election – two in 2015.

ASSESSING THE LEADERS

How does one assess the effectiveness of a party leader? Max Weber, in arguing that the development of campaigning among a large electorate required a political machine in which power, at first in the hands of the elite, became concentrated in the hands of the leader, chose the example of Gladstone: 'What brought this machine to such swift triumph over the notables was the fascination of Gladstone's "grand" demagogy, the firm belief of the masses in the ethical substance of his policy, and, above all, their belief in the ethical character of his personality.' Gladstone, he argued, had 'mastered the technique of apparently "letting sober facts speak for themselves".'[7] The other key characteristics emphasised by Weber also related to the charisma of the leader, possessed in abundance by Gladstone. 'If he is more than a narrow and vain upstart of the moment, the leader lives for his cause and "strives for his work." The devotion of his disciples, his followers, his personal party friends is oriented to his person and to its qualities ... Men do not obey him by virtue of tradition or statute, but because they believe in him.'[8]

Personal charisma can be vital in communicating the party's message, winning elections and driving through reform in government, but it can also create tensions and divisions within the party. Charismatic leaders – Gladstone and Lloyd George are obvious Liberal examples; in other parties, Margaret Thatcher and Tony Blair both qualify too – can damage their own parties, leaving them in much worse shape than they found them. Furthermore, charisma by itself may help to win elections, but if the leader has no underlying vision or agenda to follow, electoral victory may mean little in terms of advancing the cause of Liberalism.

Accordingly, this book attempts to assess the quality of each Liberal, SDP and Liberal Democrat leader against a roughly common template. The chapters on each leader that form the main part of the book are not simply biographical; we asked our authors to write about the following:

- The individual's background: a short biography; their record before becoming leader; the strengths and weaknesses of the party at the time; their ideological position in it; how they became leader; why they stopped.

- An assessment of their record in power and/or opposition: personal abilities (drive, energy, stamina, charisma, integrity etc.) and flaws; communication ability; achievements in projecting the party and themselves; development of a vision and a party position in ideological

7   Weber, op. cit., p. 16.
8   Ibid., p. 2.

or strategic terms; parliamentary ability and record; record in party management, Parliament and among the party in the country, both in government and in opposition; achievements, both legislative and non-legislative; the distinctiveness of their record and message.

- In conclusion, an overall assessment: main strengths and weaknesses; achievements for the country, for Liberalism and the party; given where they started from, how did they leave the party – better or worse?

Based on the assessments of the twenty-four leaders that follow (seventeen Liberal, three SDP and four Liberal Democrat), we consider that there are five key criteria against which the performance of Liberal leaders can be judged. Clearly, the way in which these factors are expressed and operate varies significantly over the period covered by this book, from the fluid parliamentary politics of the Great Reform Act to the disciplined mass parties of the mid-twentieth century to today's fractured party system. The expression of leadership also differs markedly between those leaders who were or who could hope to be Prime Minister (Liberal leaders up until Lloyd George) and those who, following the disintegration of the party in the 1920s and 1930s, could at best hope to influence the political debate on specific issues or perhaps participate in coalition government.

The first key criterion is *communication and campaigning skills*, including the ability to win, or at least perform well in, elections. This is clearly essential to any leader at any time, though the context in which it is expressed has changed markedly throughout the period covered by this book. In the early nineteenth century, Parliament was the key arena in which this skill was expressed, as the leader needed to attract and retain a stable following of MPs and peers. As the century wore on and the electorate expanded under successive reform acts, the ability to appeal to mass audiences became of increasing importance. One factor underlying Gladstone's impressive political achievements was his propensity for placing his great political causes before large gatherings of ordinary people, often in speeches lasting three or four hours; among other rewards, this earned him the sobriquet of 'the People's William'. During the twentieth century the ability to perform well on radio and television, and coin memorable soundbites, became steadily more important, as exemplified most strikingly by 'Cleggmania', the Liberal Democrat surge in the opinion polls following Nick Clegg's performance in the first televised debate of the 2010 election campaign.

The second, and closely related, criterion is the leader's *ability to develop and articulate a vision* of what their party stands for. To a certain extent, this was easier in the nineteenth century, when the Liberal Party was the main (usually the only) anti-Conservative Party and also clearly the party most likely to represent the interests of the rising manufacturing and commercial classes, and to a certain extent the working class, against the landed elite. The Liberal Party was never, however, class-based, and tended to express its appeal more in terms of principles, such as 'peace, retrenchment and reform', and specific policies. This posed more of a problem as the electorate expanded and government took on responsibility for the management of the economy and the welfare state; in the political contest of working class versus middle class it was not obvious which side the Liberals were on.

In turn the breakdown of class-based politics in the late twentieth century offered new opportunities to the party. With the Liberals, SDP and Liberal Democrats by then firmly established as the third party, the party leader had to offer something distinctive that would attract voters and inspire members. For party activists this could be a coherent ideological approach, appealing, for example, to 'freedom' or 'liberty'; for ordinary voters it was more likely to focus on specific policies, like Campbell-Bannerman's opposition to tariff reform and 'Chinese slavery', Asquith's appeal to the people versus the peers or Paddy Ashdown's support for a penny on income tax for education. The leader can also attempt to put forward a vision of the party not through specific policies but through general positioning, as in David Steel's presentation of the Liberal–SDP Alliance as a moderating force on the extremes of left and right in the 1983 election. This can be, however, a difficult path to follow, risking a loss of any clear positive reason to vote for the party – as Nick Clegg discovered to the party's cost in 2015.

The third key criterion is the leader's *ability to manage their party*. By conviction independently-minded and inherently suspicious of authority, Liberals have never been an easy party to lead; as Paddy Ashdown put it in June 1999:

Our beloved Lib Dems, who are, bless them, inveterately sceptical of authority, often exasperating to the point of dementia, as difficult to lead where they
don't want to go as a mule, and as curmudgeonly about success as one of those
football supporters who regards his team's promotion to the premier league
as insufficient because they haven't also won the FA Cup![9]

Before democratic politics, the key task was to manage the leader's supporters in
Parliament; as the experience of leaders such as Grey, Russell and Palmerston show,
this was never an easy task in the era of shifting political allegiances. As mass party
memberships emerged, management of party members became more important;
Gladstone and Campbell-Bannerman proved adept at this, at times proving more
popular with the party in the country than with their parliamentary colleagues. Yet
relations with the parliamentary party remained important, as in the breakdown of
Liberal Democrat MPs' belief in Charles Kennedy as an effective leader, for example. The historic propensity of the party to split into competing factions – as with
the Liberal Unionists of 1886, Coalition Liberals in 1918 or Liberal Nationals in
1931 – underlines the difficulty of managing Liberal politicians, though it is to Nick
Clegg's credit that, despite the evident strains of coalition in 2010–15, the Liberal
Democrats never split or became seriously factionalised. Leaders do not always
have to manage their party directly; they can choose able subordinates to do it for
them – but of course the choice of those subordinates is itself an aspect of party
management. The fourth key criterion is the extent to which the leader *achieved
the objectives of Liberalism*. This is most obviously measured by achievements in
government – legislation passed, crises contained, wars avoided or won. As their
individual chapters show, many of the Liberal prime ministers included here –
Grey, Melbourne, Russell, Palmerston, Gladstone, Asquith, Lloyd George – have
solid records of achievement to their credit, though some of them, particularly
Lloyd George, had perhaps more lasting successes in earlier ministerial positions
before they became Prime Minister. In other cases – Campbell-Bannerman, and
most clearly, Rosebery – the record is less impressive.

---

9   Paddy Ashdown, open letter to leadership contenders, *The Guardian*, 11 June 1999.

Most of the leaders included in this book never became Prime Minister; but this is not to say that they achieved nothing for Liberal aims. Jo Grimond revived the party after its long mid-century decline; he gave it a profile and self-confidence it had lacked for decades. Roy Jenkins managed at least to crack, if not to break, the mould of British politics in founding the SDP. Through the Cook–Maclennan agreement with the Labour Party, Paddy Ashdown helped to provide an agenda for constitutional reform implemented by Tony Blair's government.

Our final criterion is simpler than the first four. Did the leader *leave the party in better or worse shape* than they found it? The extent to which leaders could pass or influence legislation, win elections or gain seats is of course critically affected by the political context within which they operated, including the electoral system. No Liberal leader since Lloyd George, for example, could possibly hope to win a general election (in the sense of gaining a majority in the House of Commons), but any of them could aim to win more seats, to expand the party's representation in local government or to strengthen the party's organisation, finances and policy agenda. It is notable that several of the Liberal leaders with the most glittering record of achievement, including Gladstone, Asquith and Lloyd George, in the process created serious stresses within their parties and in each case left them in worse shape than they found them.

ALTERNATIVE APPROACHES

Our approach to assessing Liberal leaders is only one of several that could possibly be taken, and is rather different to those adopted in the book's companion volumes on the Conservative and Labour parties, reflecting the different genesis of the books. Consequently, Chapters 2 and 3 apply the systems of assessments presented in these two books to Liberal leaders.

Chapter 2, by Toby S. James from the University of East Anglia and Jim Buller from the University of York, redevelops the 'statecraft' approach to assess Liberal leaders in terms of whether they take their party towards power, which includes five criteria: electoral strategy; governing competence, especially in economic policy;

party management; winning the battle of ideas; and managing the constitution, or 'bending the rules of the game'. There is obviously considerable overlap between these criteria and those we describe above, though in our view the statecraft approach applies most satisfactorily to prime ministers or potential prime ministers. Leaders of third parties generally have no opportunity either to demonstrate achievements in government or to change the rules of political combat through modifying the electoral system, and can only hope to win the battle of ideas on a few specific issues, at best. The ability simply to get the party noticed – as Paddy Ashdown did, for example, over his support for passports for Hong Kong citizens – was often a key aim for Liberal leaders, and is not wholly reflected in the statecraft approach.

Chapter 3, by Charles Clarke, adopts a somewhat blunter approach to assessing party leaders, purely in terms of their ability to win votes and seats at election time. This is obviously a key characteristic, even for third parties, though the first-past-the-post system means that there may be little relationship between votes won and seats gained. The chapter also summarises the assessments of prime ministers that have been produced from time to time by academics and journalists.

CONCLUSIONS

The following tables rank all of the twenty-four leaders included in this book by the five criteria we have outlined above, in each case judged as 'good', 'poor' or 'mixed'. The final table aggregates these rankings into an overall assessment. Within each table cell, the leaders are listed in chronological order.

A few points are worth bearing in mind when reading the tables. First, we assess the leaders on their period in the leadership; some of them, perhaps most notably Lloyd George, had far more impressive records in politics before they became leader. Second, the external environment is crucial. In Table 1.5, for example, note the long list of leaders who left the party in worse shape than they found it; although in some cases this was a direct effect of their actions (Gladstone, Lloyd George), in others there was little they could realistically have done to stem the party's decline, however hard they struggled (Samuel, Sinclair, Davies). Third, leaders' ability to achieve objectives depends crucially on their starting point – Ashdown's main achievement, for example, was to save his party from extinction, a very real possibility in 1989; his successors as Liberal Democrat leaders started from a higher base and had different opportunities. Finally, some leaders were in post for too short a time to have been able to make much of a difference (Harcourt, Campbell), and although this marks them down in our assessment, it does not mean that they were devoid of accomplishment in the rest of their careers. Finally, of course, this is the opposite of an exact science; these ratings are almost entirely subjective and you may well disagree with them!

TABLE 1.1: COMMUNICATION AND CAMPAIGNING SKILLS.

Good	Mixed	Poor
Palmerston	Grey	Rosebery
Gladstone	Melbourne	Harcourt
Lloyd George	Russell	Samuel
Grimond	Granville / Hartington	Sinclair
Steel	Campbell-Bannerman	Davies
Ashdown	Asquith	Maclennan
Kennedy	Thorpe	Campbell
	Jenkins	
	Owen	
	Clegg	

TABLE 1.2: ABILITY TO DEVELOP AND ARTICULATE A VISION.

Good	Mixed	Poor
Grey	Melbourne	Granville / Hartington
Russell	Palmerston	Rosebery
Gladstone	Campbell-Bannerman	Harcourt
Lloyd George	Asquith	Samuel
Grimond	Steel	Sinclair
Jenkins	Maclennan	Davies
Owen	Kennedy	Thorpe
Ashdown	Clegg	Campbell

TABLE 1.3: PARTY MANAGEMENT.

Good	Mixed	Poor
Melbourne	Russell	Grey
Palmerston	Gladstone	Rosebery
Granville / Hartington	Sinclair	Harcourt
Campbell-Bannerman	Grimond	Asquith
Ashdown	Jenkins	Lloyd George
	Maclennan	Samuel
	Campbell	Davies
	Clegg	Thorpe
		Steel
		Owen
		Kennedy

TABLE 1.4: ACHIEVED THE OBJECTIVES OF LIBERALISM.

Good	Mixed	Poor
Grey	Campbell-Bannerman	Granville / Hartington
Melbourne	Lloyd George	Rosebery
Russell	Sinclair	Harcourt
Palmerston	Davies	Samuel
Gladstone	Thorpe	Campbell
Asquith	Steel	
Grimond	Owen	
Jenkins	Maclennan	
Ashdown	Kennedy	
	Clegg	

TABLE 1.5: LEFT THE PARTY IN BETTER OR WORSE SHAPE THAN FOUND IT.

Better	Mixed	Worse
Palmerston	Grey	Melbourne
Campbell-Bannerman	Russell	Gladstone
Grimond	Granville / Hartington	Rosebery
Thorpe	Harcourt	Asquith
Steel	Campbell	Lloyd George
Ashdown		Samuel
Kennedy		Sinclair
Maclennan		Davies
		Jenkins
		Owen
		Clegg

TABLE 1.6: OVERALL ASSESSMENT.

Good	Mixed	Poor
Russell	Grey	Rosebery
Palmerston	Melbourne	Harcourt
Gladstone	Granville / Hartington	Samuel
Campbell-Bannerman	Asquith	Sinclair
Grimond	Lloyd George	Davies
Ashdown	Thorpe	Campbell
	Steel	
	Jenkins	
	Owen	
	Maclennan	
	Kennedy	
	Clegg	

Over nearly two centuries, Liberals have provided examples of success and failure and of different styles of leadership. The achievements and disasters of party leaders may often be dictated by circumstances, trends and events outside their control, by the actions of their competitors and by the desires of the electorate, yet those successes and failures are personalised in the leader as both figurehead and ultimate decision-maker within the party. Some are renowned and others damned. It is impossible to avoid making comparisons – and also impossible to believe that the conclusions we make will be accepted by all of our readers, or even by all of our contributors, who have made their own conclusions independently of us and of each other. Through this book we seek to promote debate on the significance of leadership – and, in particular, of Liberal leadership – and to provide evidence that will improve future comparisons.

CHAPTER 2

TOWARDS POWER: A FRAMEWORK FOR ASSESSING LIBERAL LEADERS?

TOBY S. JAMES AND JIM BULLER

Assessing party leaders is not an easy task. In this chapter Toby S. James and Jim Buller[10] discuss the challenges that we face in trying to do so and some of the alternative approaches that can be taken. They consider the case for evaluating Liberal leaders in terms of whether they win office for their party, or move their party in that direction, and evaluate the tasks that leaders need to achieve in order to move towards winning power.

•   •   •

The British Liberal Party has a long history. It is so long that it is often difficult to trace a beginning.

For many, the party began in 1859 as a loose collection of free-trade Peelite, radical and Whig Members of Parliament who sought to overthrow Benjamin Disraeli and Lord Derby.[11] Others go further and claim a continuity dating back to the Whigs of 1679.[12] It is no surprise that this history therefore includes many highs and lows.

---

10   The authors are very grateful to the editors for helpful comments on an earlier version of this chapter.

11   See: Andrew Russell and Edward Fieldhouse, *Neither Left nor Right? The Liberal Democrats and the Electorate*, Manchester, Manchester University Press, 2005, p. 16.

12   Conrad Russell, *An Intelligent Person's Guide to Liberalism*, London, Duckworth, 1999.

William Gladstone's general election victory of 1880 over incumbent Prime Minister Benjamin Disraeli is undoubtedly one of the greatest of moments. Gladstone gave rallying speeches across Britain, criticising what he termed 'Beaconsfieldism' – the foreign and colonial policies of Disraeli (Lord Beaconsfield). Nearly 87,000 people were said to have witnessed one of his eighteen major speeches, which were surrounded by triumphant processions and were roundly reported on in the press. *The Times* alone printed 250,000 of his words.[13]

The Liberal Party won over 1,800,000 votes, a surge of over half a million since the previous election in 1874, ending up with 352 seats in the House of Commons.[14] As a proportion of the electorate (albeit not universal suffrage), this was the greatest that a Liberal leader has yet achieved, although Henry Campbell-Bannerman won more seats in 1906 (see Figure 2.1).[15] It was a 52-seat majority, and the result was a great surprise to many contemporaries. One Conservative minister described it as like 'thunder ... from a clear sky'.[16]

And the lowest of moments? Within minutes of the closing of the polling stations for the general election on 7 May 2015, exit polls forecast that the Liberal Democrats would lose the vast majority of the seats they had been gradually accumulating since 1988. The former Liberal Democrat leader Paddy Ashdown suggested that the forecast was so unnecessarily gloomy for his party that he would eat his hat if they proved correct. They weren't quite correct, but the actual final outcome was worse. The party lost forty-nine of the fifty-seven seats it won in 2010, and received votes from 5.2 per cent of the

---

13   Figures from: Ian St. John, *Gladstone and the Logic of Victorian Politics*, New York and London, Anthem Press, p. 246–7. Also see: Tony Little, 'The Liberal Heyday (1859–1886)', in Duncan Brack and Robert Ingham, *Peace, Reform and Liberation: A History of Liberal Politics in Britain 1679–2011*, London, Biteback Publishing, 2011, pp. 96–100; Robert Kelley, 'Midlothian: A Study in Politics and Ideas', *Victorian Studies*, 4(2), 1960, pp. 119–40.

14   Data source as used in Figure 2.1. It should be noted that, in nineteenth century elections, it was common for significant numbers of seats to go uncontested, particularly when one party was facing political and financial difficulties; thus, voting figures can underestimate support for the stronger party. In 1880, forty-one Liberal MPs were elected uncontested; in fact, this was a relatively low number for the period.

15   Note that the Whigs won 68.3 per cent in 1832.

16   Cited in T. A. Jenkins, 'Gladstone, the Whigs and the Leadership of the Liberal Party, 1879–1880', *The Historical Journal*, 27(2), 1984, p. 338.

registered electorate. Not since October 1959 had the Liberal Party received a lower vote share – an era when the party had only just survived extinction. Nick Clegg resigned the next day saying that the results were 'immeasurably more crushing' than he had feared.

Ashdown did eat his own hat, a chocolate one anyway, when presented with it on the BBC's *Question Time* the day after the election.[17]

As Figure 2.1 shows, the electoral history in long-term perspective has an undulating, but markedly downward trend. The Liberals sank from periods of hegemony in British politics in the second half of the nineteenth century to near extinction by the middle of the twentieth century. There was a significant revival from the 1970s, as the two-party system seemed to be coming to an end, which culminated in a position in coalition government in 2010. But significant political uncertainty followed after the 2015 result.

FIGURE 2.1: THE LIBERAL PARTY'S VOTE SHARE AND SEAT SHARE IN THE HOUSE OF COMMONS AT GENERAL ELECTIONS, 1832–2015.

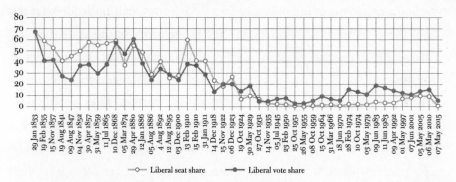

Data is authors' calculations based on information in Rallings and Thrasher, British Electoral Facts (London, Total Politics, 2009) – Liberal vote (pp. 61–2); electorate (pp. 85–92); Liberal MPs (p. 59); total MPs (pp. 3–58) – and information for the 2010 and 2015 general elections is calculated from information provided by the BBC: (http://news.bbc.co.uk/1/shared/election2010/results/ and http://www.bbc.co.uk/news/election/2015/results).

*The data therefore provided by Rallings and Thrasher includes: the Liberals and National Liberals, 1922; Independent Liberals, 1931; Liberal–SDP Alliance, 1983–87; Liberal Democrats 1992 onwards.

17   Charlotte Krol, 'General election 2015: Paddy Ashdown "eats hat" following Conservative win', *Daily Telegraph*, 9 May 2015, accessed 28 June 2015 (http://www.telegraph.co.uk/news/general-election-2015/11594442/General-election-2015-Paddy-Ashdown-eats-hat-following-Conservative-win.html).

PARTY LEADERS MATTER

I t is natural for observers to blame or credit the party leader of the time for
changing fortunes. Britain has a parliamentary system of government in which
citizens vote for a local parliamentary candidate to represent their constituency
in the House of Commons. They do not directly vote for a president. Knowing little about their local candidates, however, voters commonly use the party
leaders as cues for whom to vote for. Moreover, as time has passed, the powers of party leaders have grown. As Prime Minister, Leader of the Opposition
or leader of any other party, leaders have played an increasing role in shaping the direction of the party. They have become more important in shaping
policy, making appointments within the party or articulating the party's key
message.

Assessing party leaders is therefore important. A party leader without the
communication skills necessary to present their vision could mean vital public policies are never implemented. A leader who fails to end party divisions
could leave their party out of power for a generation. A leader who makes key
strategic errors could see national interest hindered or damaged.

THE DIFFICULTIES OF ASSESSING
POLITICAL LEADERS

A ssessing political leaders, however, is not easy. There are at least three
problems that must be faced.

Firstly, it is just a subjective process, in which we will all have our favourites.
Can even the most detached observer really claim to make objective, scientific
judgements about who was 'best', or will our own political views and values
prevent us making a fair assessment? For example, would contemporary members of the Liberal Democrats have the same views as those who are active in
another political party about who the best Liberal leader was? Does it depend
entirely on our own particular interests, affiliations and values? The benchmarks

for success and failure are not clear unless we nail down some criteria; ideological disagreement will always get in the way.

Secondly, who is the leader in question anyway? Thinking about leaders implies that the focus should be on assessing one single person. British party leaders rarely make substantive decisions on their own, even if they don't consult their entire Cabinet/shadow Cabinet team on every matter. As a general election approaches, they will devise a broader team to steer on strategy. Leaders will also seek out and receive crucial guidance from their advisors, and this contribution needs to be taken into account when evaluating political leadership. As noted in Chapter 1, there has not always been a formal post of 'leader' in the Liberal Party. A further complication is that, over time, the Liberal Party has taken many organisational forms. In the 1980s, the Liberal Party fought elections as part of the Liberal–SDP Alliance and then merged with the SDP to form the Liberal Democrats in 1988. At times, various factions have also split away from the official party – the Liberal Unionists in the late nineteenth century, Lloyd George's Coalition Liberals after the First World War, and the Liberal Nationals in the 1930s. So who should be the focus of our analysis?

Thirdly, aren't leaders' fortunes influenced by whether they have to govern in difficult or favourable times? The political scientist James MacGregor Burns claimed that some US presidents were capable of transformative leadership: a great President could redesign perceptions, values and aspirations within American politics.[18] But is this always possible during times of economic crisis, party division or war? Leaders who are establishing new political parties may have their fortunes shaped by the popularity of their competitors. What impact can we really expect leaders of small opposition parties to have on society? Do leaders really steer events or are they casualties of them? No two leaders are in power at the same time, so direct comparison is impossible.

Certainly, closer analysis of Gladstone's victory forces us to re-assess him, at least a little. His return to politics and Midlothian campaign was situated in fortuitous circumstances for his leadership prospects. As David Brooks

18   James Macgregor Burns, *Leadership*, New York, Harper and Row, 1978.

has noted, the murder of a British envoy in Afghanistan revived concerns about Disraeli's foreign policy. Britain was also in an economic depression in the 1870s, which worsened close to the election. The harvest of September 1879, the worst since 1816, threatened the livelihoods of many farmers. Rising prices also threatened consumption, increased pauperism and reduced governing revenue.[19]

Closer analysis of the 2015 general election result also requires a different assessment of Nick Clegg. It was Clegg, after all, who had brought the Liberal Democrats into power for the first time, and the 2015 result was widely seen as being the price of being in government. Clegg also had at his disposal a party with a much lighter institutional machine and experience of being in power than his senior partners, the Conservatives, who had been particularly astute at creating a narrative of the economic crisis that suited them.[20]

POTENTIAL APPROACHES TO ASSESSING LIBERAL LEADERS

A clear framework is necessary to assess leaders. There are a few alternative approaches that can be taken. One approach is to assess the leader in terms of their *personal characteristics*. A keen interest in the attributes of the leader is a common starting place for public discussion about leaders, especially in an age where the media is increasingly focused on them, and many scholars talk of the personalisation of politics.[21] Such a line of thought has a rich tradition in academic scholarship on political leadership. The characteristics that are often thought to make a great American President are: communication skills; organisational capacity; political aptitude; public policy vision;

---

19   David Brooks, 'Gladstone and Midlothian: The Background to the First Campaign', *Scottish Historical Review*, 1985, 64(177), pp. 53–4. See Chapter 6.

20   Andrew Gamble, 'Austerity as Statecraft', *Parliamentary Affairs*, 68(1), January 2015, pp. 42–57.

21   Maja Simunjak and John Street, 'Media portrayals: from leadership cults to celebrity politicians', in J. Storey, J. Hartley, J-L Denis, P. T. Hart, and D. Ulrich eds, *The Routledge Companion to Leadership*, London: Routledge, forthcoming, Chapter 39.

cognitive style; and emotional intelligence.[22] In Britain, the distinctiveness of Margaret Thatcher's personal approach to government led many to reflect on the significance of her personality as a cause for her electoral success, but also her demise as leader of the Conservatives. Some have suggested that the criteria deemed important to be a good American President could be useful benchmarks for British prime ministers too.[23] Duncan Brack, elsewhere, has argued that communication skills and personal ability are among the characteristics that Liberal Democrat leaders need.[24]

There are risks on focusing on personality, however. Different personal traits might be needed in differing contexts, times and places. It is unclear whether the traits needed to be a good US President are the same as those required to be a good British leader. And there might be differences again between being a Prime Minister and being the leader of a smaller party. Are the characteristics required in 2015 the same as in 1915? Or 1815? A more substantial problem when evaluating leaders in terms of the pre-made characteristics that have made a leader successful in another time is that we might relegate a focus on the leader's imprint on their own contemporary society. Defects in leaders' personalities, after all, can also be 'fixed' by complementing them with other members of their team, if leadership is a collective process.

A second approach would be to evaluate political leaders in terms of whether they have aims, use methods and bring about outcomes that are principled and morally good. In one of the sister volumes to this book, *British Labour Leaders*, this is defined as *conscience leadership*.[25] This involves an ethical and normative judgement about whether a leader's imprint on the world is positive, and whether they achieved their ends via means that were not unethical.

22 Fred I. Greenstein, *The Presidential Difference: Leadership Style from FDR to Barack Obama*, Princeton and Oxford, Princeton University Press, 2009.

23 Kevin Theakston, 'Gordon Brown as Prime Minister: political skills and leadership style', *British Politics*, 2011, 6(1), pp. 78–100.

24 Duncan Brack, 'Liberal Democrat Leadership', *Journal of Liberal History*, Vol. 83, summer 2014, pp. 34–45.

25 See: Toby S. James, 'Introduction: The British Labour Party in search of the complete leader', in Charles Clarke and Toby S. James eds, *British Labour Leaders*, London, Biteback Publishing, 2015.

There are a variety of ends that Liberal leaders have achieved, or sought to achieve, which might fall under this category. These include: the passage, while in government, of laws with ethically good ends (such as the land reform in Ireland, which ended oppression by landlords); blocking legislation that is 'morally wrong' or 'true liberal'; or acting as a party of principled opposition during times when the party has had little chance of outright power itself.

There are many reasons for adopting this approach, and it is naturally the more attractive one, but it is difficult, because agreement about what constitutes 'morally right' policy or law is, in many circumstances, often disagreed upon, even among Liberals.

A third approach is to appraise leaders in terms of whether they are successful in winning power, office and influence. This forces us to introduce a degree of political realism into our evaluations. Leaders operate in a tough, cut-throat environment, where the costs of electoral defeat are usually their job and their party's prospects of power. This can be considered *cunning leadership*.[26]

No doubt, many leaders will want to achieve more than this. They may be concerned about their legacy – how they are viewed by future generations – or driven by a desire to implement policies that they think will improve the good of their party and people. Most leaders will lay claim to be motivated to enter politics for reasons of conscience, not just cunning.[27] However, nothing is possible without office, power and influence first. Moreover, without electoral progress, they may not remain as party leader for long, due to the cut-throat nature of politics. General election results where the leader has underperformed against expectations have, increasingly during the course of British history, brought about leadership challenges and expectations of resignation.[28]

For many more recent Liberal leaders, the prospects of winning an election

---

26   Ibid.

27   On the difference, see ibid.

28   For an extended discussion, ibid.

have not been realistic, of course. David Steel told his party members in the autumn of 1981 that they should 'go back to [their] constituencies and prepare for government'.[29] But, apart from that moment of optimism, Liberal leaders have not recently been thought of as likely majority (or even minority) partners in government. Yet, we can still evaluate Liberal leaders in terms of whether they move their party in that direction. While political parties come in different forms, with different origins and initially divergent objectives,[30] they all require seats, power and influence to obtain their objectives. The exception to this might be single-issue parties. But the Liberal Party has never seen itself as a single-issue party, and single-issue parties soon broaden their appeal as they gain electoral success.

So how can we assess Liberal leaders' success in winning office, or moving in that direction? The approach offered here is that we identify the tasks that leaders, to a greater or lesser extent, need to achieve in order to win office.[31] Each of these, we suggest, can be used as criteria to evaluate leaders. Below, we set out the five main tasks leaders need to accomplish: devise a winning electoral strategy; establish a reputation for governing competence; govern their party effectively; win the battle of ideas over key policy issues; and manage the constitution so that their electoral prospects remain intact.

Before they are introduced, two important points need to be made. First, the nature and viability of different strategies for achieving these tasks, and the relative importance of each task, will vary according to the stage of a party's historical development. Figure 2.2 outlines five basic stages of electoral development that a party may have in a parliamentary majoritarian democracy. Each of these could be considered a progressive step towards office. A party might take each step in turn, as the Labour Party did in the twentieth

---

29   David Denver and Mark Garnett, *British General Elections since 1964: Diversity, Dealignment and Disillusion*, Oxford and New York, Oxford University Press, 2014, p. 76.

30   For example, see: Richard Gunther and Larry Diamond, 'Species of Political Parties: A New Typology', *Party Politics*, 9(2), pp. 167–99.

31   The chapter therefore adapts the statecraft approach, outlined in the sister volumes to this book and in Jim Buller and Toby S. James, 'Statecraft and the Assessment of National Political Leaders: The Case of New Labour and Tony Blair', *The British Journal of Politics & International Relations*, 14(4), 2012, pp. 534–55.

and early twenty-first century. Parties might also miss out steps, however, through a sudden rush of electoral progress. The Liberals' post-war history saw them missing Stage 2 to become a partner in coalition government with the Conservatives in 2010, before moving back to Stage 1 in the aftermath of the 2015 general election.

FIGURE 2.2: A LINEAR PATHWAY TO POWER FOR PARTIES IN PARLIAMENTARY DEMOCRACIES.

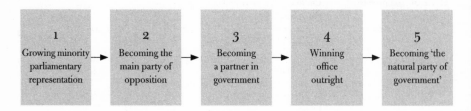

Secondly, some leaders are gifted more fortunate circumstances than others when trying to achieve these tasks. We have argued elsewhere that the context in which leaders find themselves must be factored into our assessments of them. This is not an easy task either, however. Can we realistically, for example, compare William Gladstone's context to, say, Nick Clegg's? Can we realistically quantify our judgements and say that Sir Archibald Sinclair's circumstances were twice as hard as David Steel's? Given that leaders operate in different historical moments, which are *qualitatively* different in kind, quantitative measurement is difficult. The circumstances that leaders face are also different for each individual.[32]

In-depth historical studies are therefore needed to understand the circumstances in which leaders lead their office, and this is why this volume rightly invites individual biographers to provide detailed portraits of each leader. Nonetheless, some form of comparison is possible. To aid discussion, Table 2.1 lists some of the contextual factors that might be important and these will be unpacked under each statecraft task considered next.

---

32   For an extended discussion, see: Jim Buller and Toby S. James, 'Integrating Structural Context into the Assessment of Political Leadership: Realism, Gordon Brown and the Great Financial Crisis', *Parliamentary Affairs*, 68(1), 2015, pp. 77–96.

TABLE 2.1: CONTEXTUAL FACTORS TO BE CONSIDERED WHEN ASSESSING LEADERS.

Leadership task	Contextual factors
Winning electoral strategy	Party resources and campaign infrastructure Unfavourable electoral laws (constituencies, election administration, electoral system, party finance) Partisan alignment of the press Ability to call election when polls are favourable
Governing competence	Party reputation Conditions for successful economic growth Foreign policy disputes
Party management	Presence of credible rival leaders Rules for dethroning Levels of party unity Available mechanisms for party discipline
Political argument hegemony	Ideological developments at the international level Alignment of the press Available off-the-shelf strategies in the 'garbage can' Developments in the party system
Bending the rules of the game	Presence of policy triggers or favourable conditions to enact (or prevent) change

'WINNING' ELECTORAL STRATEGY

Firstly, leaders need to develop an electoral strategy by crafting an image and policy package that will help the party achieve the crucial impetus in the lead-up to the polls. When the Liberals have a chance of winning office, it delivers them sufficient votes and seats. When the party is a smaller opposition party in a two-party system, the challenge for the Liberals is often to establish their distinctiveness in the eyes of the public.

Opinion polls, and, to some extent, local/European election and by-election results, give a very good indication of how a party is faring in the development of a winning strategy and allow a party leader's fortunes to be charted over time, although this information is not always as readily available for the earlier Liberal leaders, when polling was more infrequent or did not take place at all. It is also notable that, in most post-1945 elections, the Liberal standing in the polls has been prone to rise in the immediate heat of the election campaign, as the party receives greater exposure.

In developing a winning strategy, the leader will need to pay close attention to the interests of key segments of the population, whose votes might be important for electoral progress. This may involve differentiating their party from the others on key issues on which they think they can win support. Leaders may need to respond to transformations in the electoral franchise, demography or the class structure of society, and build new constituencies of support when necessary. These changes can often disadvantage a leader. The extensions of the franchise in the Great Reform Acts, for example, fundamentally altered the structure of the electorate and had the potential to turn electoral politics upside down in favour of the Liberal Party. However, they also created the conditions for new political competition in the form of the emergent Labour Party. From 1832 onwards, Britain experienced a growth in the urban working class, from which trade unions emerged. The founding of organisations like the Fabians developed the intellectual basis of social democracy in Britain, while the Labour Party gave parliamentary representation to the movement. This created new competition for the Liberal Party.[33]

A winning electoral strategy is not just a matter of getting votes, but getting votes in the right places: the geographical distribution of support matters. Modern times have twice (1951, February 1974) delivered election results where the party with the most votes did not win the most seats. Vote efficiency is also a critical problem for 'smaller' parties in the UK where an even spread of support across the country, in a first-past-the-post system, will deliver very few seats. As Figure 2.1 illustrates, the Liberal seat share has been lower than their vote share in every general election since 1923. The 1983 result was particularly disproportionate:

---

33   There is an extensive debate about whether the Liberals could have held on to the working-class vote after 1910, and whether it was the war and the division of the party in 1918 that allowed Labour to grow. For a review of the arguments, see Martin Pugh, 'The Triumph of the New Liberalism', in Duncan Brack and Robert Ingham eds, *Peace, Reform and Liberation: A History of British Liberalism, 1679–2011*, London, Biteback Publishing, 2011.

18.4 per of registered votes brought the party only 3.5 per cent of seats in the Commons. There is, therefore, a need to strategically concentrate resources to build support in specific areas. Winning seats in local government first can help to alleviate 'the credibility gap' – a perception among the public that the Liberals are unlikely to win and that a vote for them in parliamentary elections is therefore a wasted vote.[34] Developing a winning electoral strategy therefore takes this into consideration.

This point highlights how electoral laws can make it easier or more difficult for leaders to win power. Since 1945, the first-past-the-post electoral system has significantly advantaged the main two parties and shut out competitors. This has, therefore, made it difficult for contemporary Liberal leaders to win seats. The laws on party funding and electoral administration will also directly affect a leader's chances of a winning election. Having money to spend does not guarantee success, but it helps. To some extent, leaders can build electoral resources by developing electoral momentum and credibility, and courting appropriate prospective funders. However, party resources and electoral war chests will also depend on other factors, such as the historical relationships between parties and business, and the unions. These resources can be vital in financing a sophisticated media campaign and building a party machine. Although it is not just money that matters: internal organisation is crucial, and it undermined the Liberal–SDP Alliance campaign in 1983.[35] Electoral administration can matter, too. The procedures used to compile the electoral register and the methods by which citizens are allowed to vote can also disadvantage some parties and candidates.[36]

When the incumbent leader can decide the timing of an election, in the absence of fixed parliamentary terms, (s)he may have some advantage. Leaders do not always get this right, though. Harold Wilson's Labour Party overtook the Conservative opposition in the opinion polls for the first time in three years in May

---

34   Russell and Fieldhouse, 2005, Chapters 1 and 7.

35   Andrew Russell and Edward Fieldhouse, *Neither Left nor Right? The Liberal Democrats and the Electorate*, Manchester, Manchester University Press, 2005, p. 5.

36   Toby S. James, 'Electoral Administration and Voter Turnout: Towards an International Public Policy Continuum'. *Representation*, 45(4), 2010, pp. 369–89.

1970 and he called a snap election. However, support for Labour quickly collapsed again and the Conservatives won the election.[37] The act of timing an election has therefore been called 'the most important single decision taken by a British Prime Minister.' [38] The Fixed-Term Parliaments Act 2011 made this strategic option obsolete for future leaders. Liberal leaders, of course, have not had the opportunity to set the date of an election since Lloyd George, but they have often faced the risk of being at a disadvantage from this. It does show, however, how leaders will not try to achieve a winning electoral strategy on a level playing field. They have unevenly distributed constraints and opportunities.

During the long life of the Liberal Party, the media has become increasingly important, with the rising circulations of newspapers and the increased prevalence of TV and then, of course, of the internet. The media, however, is rarely neutral. Although broadcast television has remained relatively unbiased in Britain, newspapers will openly support or show hostility to individual parties and their leaders. Some outlets will be particularly influential and this will benefit some leaders and disadvantage others.[39] In more recent times, the press has often been argued to have a pro-Conservative bias.[40] The last wholly pro-Liberal paper, the *News Chronicle*, ceased publication in 1960. But the emergence of the printing press in the nineteenth century was originally thought to be a voice for liberal politics and therefore an advantage for Liberal leaders.

GOVERNING COMPETENCE

S econdly, a leader seeking office outright must cultivate a reputation for governing competence. Achieving this requires careful thought about the policies the leader chooses to support and the viability of their implementation.

---

37   Alistair Smith, 'Election Timing in Majoritarian Parliaments', *British Journal of Political Science*, 33(3), 2003, p. 399.

38   Kenneth Newton, 'Caring and Competence: The Long, Long Campaign', in Anthony King ed., *Britain at the Polls 1992*, Chatham NJ, Chatham House, 1993.

39   John Street. *Mass Media Politics and Democracy*, Basingstoke, Palgrave, 2001.

40   See Nick Clegg on this issue in Chapter 27.

Leaders in office and motivated to promote and protect an image of governing competence would not normally be wise to introduce policies that are likely to face substantial opposition or significant obstacles, which may lead to their failure or reversal. Considerations of governing competence normally dictate that leaders will not try to introduce risky policies in the first place. However, if they can change the structural context within which they are operating to make it easier to implement their policies, then they might succeed. Governing competence is therefore a broad concept that applies to nearly any policy area, across the whole period of Liberal history.[41]

The importance of governing competence is illustrated by contemporary theories of voter behaviour. Political parties can often collect a considerable number of votes by being the party closest to the electorate on a particular issue – what psephologists often call 'positional issues'. Many psephologists also think, however, that the public does not see many issues on left/right terms. Instead, it simply votes for the party and leader it thinks is the most competent on a problem that it considers to be pressing. There is a broad agreement about the ends that voters want: the paramount question for them is which leader and party will deliver it.[42] In modern elections, the problem that is usually most pressing is, in the words of Bill Clinton's campaign strategist, the 'economy, stupid'. However, during the course of the nineteenth century, when Liberal prime ministers were common, other issues may have been of more importance. The economy could impact on their fortunes, nonetheless. Understood in this way, the fortunes of many leaders, those seeking office at least, will be the result of their ability to generate a perception of being competent in managing the economy.

A leaders' ability to achieve governing competence is hindered or helped by a number of factors. Political leaders take charge of a party with a reputation

41   See: Jim Bulpitt, 'The discipline of the New Democracy: Mrs. Thatcher's Domestic Statecraft', *Political Studies*, 34(1), p. 22; Jim Buller, 'Conservative Statecraft and European Integration in Historical Perspective', in Kai Oppermann ed., *British Foreign and Security Policy: Historical Legacies and Current Challenges*, Augsburg, Wissner Verlag, 2012.

42   Harold D. Clarke, David Sanders, Marianne C. Stewart and Paul Whiteley. *Political Choice in Britain*, Oxford and New York, Oxford University Press, 2004; Harold D. Clarke, David Sanders, Marianne C. Stewart and Paul Whiteley. *Performance Politics and the British Voter*, Cambridge, Cambridge University Press, 2009.

for being 'strong' or 'weak' on the economy or defence, for example. Once in office the ability of a leader to develop a reputation for competence is strongly influenced by the state of the economy. A new Prime Minister may inherit an economy with a balance-of-payments deficit, sluggish growth and a high public deficit. Responsibility for slow growth can sometimes be shifted to predecessors or other factors. However, this strategy becomes increasingly implausible the longer the party is in office. A leader of an opposition party may find developing a reputation for competence difficult when a strong economy boosts perceptions of competence for the incumbent government.

Importantly for the Liberal Democrats, a third-placed party in opposition may struggle to develop a reputation for competence, especially on the economy. First, they will not have the media exposure that the leaders of the largest two parties will have. Second, without a recent experience of governing themselves, demonstrating such a reputation is difficult. Third, they will be reliant on the party of government losing their reputation, as the Conservatives did in the early 1990s and Labour did after the 2007/08 financial crisis. It is therefore perhaps no surprise that the party has failed to break through in this area. Polling data exists for most of the Liberal Democrat's history as to whether they were considered to be the best party in managing the economy. As Figure 2.2 illustrates, the party had between 3 and 12 per cent of respondents name them first – the figure was higher during the 1992 recession and 2007/08 financial crisis, but relatively low (6 per cent) going into the 2015 general election. It might therefore be more astute for a party at Stages 1, 2 and 3 in its development (Figure 2.2) to focus on pursuing popular 'protest' policies that enable it to appear radical and distinctive. A leader will need to consider valence issues, however, if the party is to progress beyond these stages.[43] Whatever approach is taken, a key task of a Leader of the Opposition is to attack and dismantle the reputation of the occupants of Nos 10 and 11 Downing Street if they are to be unseated.

Gaining support on valence issues, however, is not impossible. Since the

---

43   On the conundrum, after 2015, see: David Howarth and Mark Pack, *The 20% Strategy: Building a Core Vote for the Liberal Democrats*, London, July 2015.

financial crash of 2007/08, a very strong proportion of voters have thought that neither of the main two political parties, who both adopted strong neo-liberal economic outlooks, will manage the economy well.[44] Smaller opposition parties can therefore be given space to articulate arguments for alternative ways of managing the economy. It is noticeable in Figure 2.2 that the Liberals' peaks were higher when the incumbent government lost its own reputation. During the 2007/08 crisis, Vince Cable was widely praised for 'predicting' the economic crisis, and enhanced his personal reputation. Yet, opposition parties are often left waiting for such critical moments to make their own breakthrough – and they need to use such moments opportunistically.

FIGURE 2.3: PERCEPTIONS OF THE BEST PARTY TO MANAGE THE ECONOMY, 1990–2015.

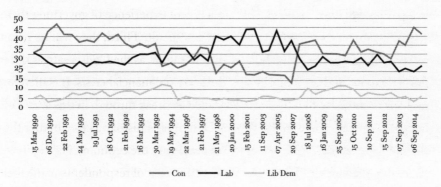

Source: Ipsos MORI, 'Best Party on Key Issues: Managing the Economy', updated 20 April 2015, accessed 18 June 2015 (https://www.ipsos-mori.com/researchpublications/researcharchive/22/Best-Party-On-Key-Issues-Managing-the-Economy.aspx).

As mentioned above, the economy is not the only issue of importance. Foreign policy, among others, matters too. Here, some incumbent governments may inherit pressing international crises, such as an ongoing war, terrorist attack or a diplomatic conflict with a potential aggressor. The international political system is also increasingly interlinked with the divide between 'domestic' and 'foreign' policy disappearing, especially for members of the EU.

---

44   Paul Whiteley, Harold D. Clarke, David Sanders and Marianne C. Stewart, 'The Economic and Electoral Consequences of Austerity Policies in Britain', *Parliamentary Affairs*, 68(1), January 2015, pp. 4–24.

This integration of the internal and external realms may in itself present opportunities and constraints. There may even be times when political leaders utilise international institutions to help them manage or solve national problems, or use them as scapegoats for their own mistakes. For opposition leaders, they can present opportunities to criticise the incumbent, as Charles Kennedy did of Tony Blair on Iraq, to create political momentum.

PARTY MANAGEMENT

Thirdly, leaders need to successfully manage their party. Party leaders do not always fall from office at election time. For example, pressure from MPs pushed Charles Kennedy from office. Leaders therefore have to ensure that members of the (shadow) Cabinet, parliamentary party and grass roots are content enough with their performance to allow them to continue. This does not mean the relationship between leaders and their party need always be harmonious. Leaders might deliberately harbour an antagonistic relationship in order to prove to the wider public that they are above party and to establish a broad appeal. They will, however, need to fend off any potential leadership challenges and ensure sufficient unity: images of divisions will have a deleterious impact on a party's ability to deliver its legislative programme, and its reputation for competence in office. The importance of party management was accentuated during the nineteenth century. As Robert Saunders notes in a sister volume to this book, *British Conservative Leaders*, during this time, governments won and lost power more through the management of the floor of the House of Commons than the ballot box.[45]

Party management will be more difficult when ties to a party are looser, as parliamentarians need to be carefully managed so that they do not form splinter groups like the Liberal Nationals or Liberal Unionists. A leader will also be able to bring

---

45   See: Robert Saunders, 'Benjamin Disraeli', in Charles Clarke, Toby S. James, Tim Bale and Patrick Diamond eds, *British Conservative Leaders*, London, Biteback Publishing, 2015.

about substantial growth in their party's fortunes if they take an astute position on merging with other parties, or agree cross-party agreements. In effect, a leader might be able to skip some of the early steps identified above. The party could quickly become part of a coalition, as the Ashdown–Blair project might have and the Clegg–Cameron deal did, or provide rapid growth in support, as the SDP–Liberal collaboration did. These strategies will have consequences for future winning electoral strategies, however, as the Liberal Democrats experienced in 2015.

Party management will also be more difficult for some leaders than others. Some leaders will face credible rivals equipped with the political skill and courage to challenge them; some will not. In some circumstances, the rules for dethroning a leader will make a challenge from a rival relatively cost-free, in others, less so. It is in no party's interests to undertake long and protracted internal leadership battles because they may affect the party's political standing. A failed attempt to oust a leader can also have negative consequences for the careers of the instigators. If a rival needs a significant amount of the parliamentary party to trigger a contest, many will be deterred.

Party dissent can undermine the authority of a leader and lead to such leadership challenges. The ability of leaders to resolve dissent can be influenced by the rewards or sanctions they have available to appeal to or discipline errant party members, the degree to which there is greater homogeneity of preferences within the party, whether there are strong traditions of party loyalty and whether there are specialist committee systems and established spokesmen on particular issues.[46]

The emergence of new issues can threaten to split a party. For example, the question of home rule at the end of the nineteenth century and the prospect and conduct of the Great War at the start of the twentieth century split the Liberal Party decisively. These divisions offer challenges but also opportunities. They can provide the opportunity for new leaders to emerge (as they did for Lord Hartington and Joseph Chamberlain) or they can split the opposition, as the Corn Laws, tariff reform and Europe have done for the Tories.

---

46   Rudy B. Andeweg and Jacques Thomassen, 'Pathways to party unity: sanctions, loyalty, homogeneity and division of labour in the Dutch Parliament', *Party Politics*, 17(5), 2011, pp. 655–72.

POLITICAL ARGUMENT HEGEMONY

Fourthly, leaders will need to win 'the battle of ideas' so that the party's arguments about policy solutions and the general stance of government become generally accepted among the elite, and perhaps even the general public. In more grand terms, this has been coined 'political argument hegemony'. A party leader who is successful in these terms might find that political opponents adopt their policies as manifesto commitments in the run-up to an election, or their ideas become the hallmark of government policy in future years.

Winning the 'battle of ideas' might involve victories over particular policy issues, such as health care, nuclear disarmament, home rule or immigration. It might also, however, involve victories over more deep-rooted questions, such as the role of government in society. It is often thought, for example, that Margaret Thatcher was successful in generating a new discourse during the 1980s that moved the electorate towards the right and helped her win three consecutive elections. There is some evidence that Thatcher was less successful in achieving political argument hegemony among the public than was widely thought,[47] but subsequent Labour Party politicians certainly came to accept many of her Conservative government's policies during the 1990s, suggesting some success at the elite level.[48]

Some factors may make winning the battle of ideas more or less difficult for leaders. There have been major ideological changes across all western democracies since the formation of the Liberal Party. Industrial societies have undergone a 'cultural shift' since the 1970s, as new post-material issues like the environment and human rights have arisen, and old left/right politics are no longer applicable.[49] The rise of these issues and the changing nature of British society – of course, in part – owes much to the actions of past leaders themselves. They also have profound implications for a party seeking to develop a winning electoral strategy.

---

47   Ivor Crewe, 'Has the Electorate Become Thatcherite?', in Robert Skidelsky ed., *Thatcherism*, Oxford, Blackwell, 1988, pp. 25-49.

48   Buller and James, op. cit., 2012.

49   Ronald Inglehart, *Culture Shift in Advanced Industrial Society*, Princeton NJ, Princeton University Press, 1990.

Leaders will be better able to win the battle for political argument hegemony if they are given a credible set of policy ideas. Leaders may be reliant on think tanks or their party to develop a new narrative to win over political support. The partisan bias of the media is important for this task too.

BENDING THE RULES OF THE GAME

Lastly, leaders may need to maintain or change the constitutional rules of the game to make winning elections easier to achieve.[50] Those leaders who only serve in opposition need to place constitutional reforms that will help their party onto the political agenda and, if they become a coalition partner, negotiate and implement such reforms. The importance of constitutional rules has already been noted above. Achieving a more proportional electoral system for elections to Westminster would therefore be a considerable achievement for Liberal Democrat leaders – one yet to be realised. But nineteenth-century Liberal leaders would have been wise to defend electoral rules that gave them a disproportionate number of seats for their votes (see Figure 2.1). It is not just electoral laws that might matter, however; other aspects of the constitution can be important too. For example, a House of Lords that is packed with opposition peers can make it difficult for a leader to pass legislation. This legislation might be essential for developing a winning electoral strategy or achieving governing competence. Maintaining any constitutional rules that advantage the party, and reforming those that do not, therefore equates to good statecraft.

Leaders will have other reasons to take a strategic approach to the constitution. They might want to back reforms that are popular with the public to win over voters, even if the direct consequences of this for their party hinder their statecraft strategy. They might also promise reforms to other parties in order to entice them to form coalitions over legislation or government formation. David

---

50   This task was added to the statecraft terms in Toby S. James, *Elite Statecraft and Election Administration: Bending the Rules of the Game*, Basingstoke and New York, Palgrave, 2012.

Cameron's promise to Nick Clegg to hold a referendum on electoral system reform in 2011 was probably good, albeit risky, statecraft for him. Even though a reformed electoral system might have disadvantaged the Conservatives at future elections, it was a 'deal-breaker' in forming the coalition and bringing Cameron to power. The 1832 Great Reform Act inspired a political narrative that the Whigs and Liberals were the progressive parties and the Tories were opposed to popular politics. Disraeli's pursuit of a Conservative Reform Bill in the 1860s could therefore be understood to be an attempt to recast his party as 'the friends of the people', but it also divided the opposition.[51]

Changing the rules of the game will be easier to achieve when there are few checks on executive power, as there traditionally have been in Britain's Westminster system. It is also easier when there are high levels of public support for change. Since universal suffrage was established, these moments have tended to be uncommon, as constitutional reform rarely features highly on the public's radar. An incident or scandal can, however, quickly put constitutional reform on the agenda. Pressures for electoral reform, for example, often follow unusual election results – when the party with the most votes did not win – or a scandal, like the parliamentary expenses incident of 2009. Exploiting these opportunities is important. For leaders seeking to maintain the status quo, the public's indifference is an advantage.

In other aspects of the constitution, the public have been more animated, however. The most obvious exception to public indifference has been the Union. The issue of home rule dominated politics at the end of the nineteenth century and the early twentieth century. Welsh, but more notably Scottish, nationalism re-emerged in the 1960s, accelerated in the 1990s, and brought forward demands for devolution and independence that continue with new force. Consecutive waves of devolution left 'the English question' behind for subsequent leaders to contemplate. The approach leaders take to this issue will have significant consequences for their electoral strategy and party management.

---

51   Robert Saunders, *Democracy and the Vote in British Politics*, London, Ashgate, 2011. See: James, ibid., for a further discussion.

Constitutional management is, therefore, a task that all party leaders must confront. Even those leaders who only serve in opposition, knowingly or otherwise, will be developing policy positions that might help to consolidate the status quo in their party's (dis)advantage, and woo potential coalition partners and voters. It will have important consequences for their prospects of achieving a winning electoral strategy, party management and even governing competence.

CONCLUSION

This chapter has considered the difficulties involved in evaluating political leaders and has outlined some of the available approaches that can be used. These have included a focus on the personal characteristics of a leader and a judgement in terms of whether they were led by *conscience* leadership or *cunning* leadership – the latter involving an assessment as to whether they have successfully won power and influence for themselves and their party. The main part of the chapter has unpacked what successful leadership might look like, in terms of political cunning, by discussing the tasks that Liberal leaders must achieve in order to obtain the ultimate goal of office. This means that we should praise in our assessment those who do well in achieving the tasks, and criticise those who do not. But we should also bear in mind that achieving these tasks is much easier for some than it is for others. This means that we should also 'reward' those leaders who did well in difficult circumstances, and 'punish' those who did not in more favourable times.

CHAPTER 3

MEASURING THE SUCCESS OR FAILURE OF LIBERAL LEADERS: THE GENERAL ELECTION TEST

CHARLES CLARKE

In this chapter, Charles Clarke examines whether or not the success or failure of Liberal leaders can be measured, particularly by their general election results. He provides tables that show the increase or decrease in the number of seats in Parliament, and the increase or decrease in the Liberal/Liberal Democrat share of the vote. On this basis, he develops a 'league table' of Liberal leaders since 1834, divided into two phases: 1835–1931, and 1950–2015. From this, he analyses the performances of the leaders and draws some conclusions about the reasons for relative successes and failures.

• • •

The premise of this book is that the quality of political leadership is important. History is not driven only by inevitable forces, important though they are. The decisions and actions of political leaders make a difference and can change outcomes, with big consequences for people's lives.

That said, the mechanisms of leadership are difficult to describe and even more difficult to measure. This chapter offers one means of measuring the success or failure of Liberal leaders over time, though the parties' complicated history does not make this straightforward, and so the result is not entirely satisfactory.

The history of the Liberal and Liberal Democrat parties, and their leaderships, is set out in Chapter 1. It divides into two quite distinct periods. The first lasted from the 1832 Great Reform Bill until the rise of the Labour Party in the early part of the twentieth century. Asquith was the last truly Liberal Prime Minister, appointed in 1908 and serving until 1916, though the Liberal Lloyd George led a coalition government from 1916 to 1922, dividing the Liberal Party in the process. During this period, the Liberal Party (and its Whig predecessor) was a consistent contender for government, and its leaders included some of the greatest prime ministers in British political history. The second period lasted from the 1920s until the present day, and, for much of this period, the Liberal Party has been an entirely marginal, even residual, political force, often with tiny numbers of MPs. The Liberal collapse between these two eras, say from 1924 until 1935, was rapid and spectacular.

The Liberals participated as minor coalition partners in government in 1931–32 and 1940–45, and in 1977–78 they formed a pact to support the Labour government, though without any ministers. In 2010–15, the Liberal Democrats formed a formal coalition government with the Conservatives, with Liberal Democrats holding the role of Deputy Prime Minister and a number of other ministerial posts. In February 1974, they had decided not to support the Conservatives, when Ted Heath, in order to sustain himself in power, made an offer that was judged inadequate.

However, despite this occasional and marginal participation in government since 1931, the Liberals have not seriously challenged to form a government since the 1920s, and their post-1945 engagement with government has simply been a residual outcome of parliamentary arithmetic. In this era, they have never really been a significant force, though the steady decline of Conservative/Labour two-party dominance since 1951 has given the Liberals/Liberal Democrats an increasing role in politics, at least until 2015.

Of the twenty Liberal leaders since 1834, only three leaderships (Granville/Hartington, Harcourt and Menzies Campbell) failed to lead their party into a general election.[52] The circumstances in which these twenty became leaders are difficult to compare, as the political and social environments shifted so strongly over the 180-year period. Of the seventeen who did contest general elections, the first eight, until 1926, all became Prime Minister. Since then, none did, or got anywhere near – or even became Leader of the Opposition.

The twelve leaders after 1926 were engaged in quite a different political game from their predecessors. The first two, Samuel and Sinclair, were doing their best to ensure that their party contributed positively to the momentous events of the years from 1931 to 1945. The ten thereafter were trying to maintain a small foothold in British politics. Until 2015, the party retained some strength in its Celtic heartlands,[53] but otherwise gained support by being neither Labour nor Conservative and pursuing an oppositionist stance towards the government of the day. Government was never a realistic ambition or strategic preoccupation, except as the consequence of a possible alliance with other parties. And, of course, the one substantive venture into government, the 2010–15 coalition, turned out to be an electoral disaster for the Liberal Democrats. The Liberals had also done pretty badly in 1979, after the Lib–Lab pact.

Two of the three SDP leaders – Roy Jenkins in 1983 and David Owen in 1987 – led their party in general elections. They were in alliance with the Liberals but returned significantly fewer MPs. In the tables below, I treat David Steel as the effective leader. The third SDP leader, Robert Maclennan, did not lead his party into a general election, and his main contribution was to facilitate the formal party merger that created the Liberal Democrats.

---

52   I do not include Grey, who led in 1832. The comparisons in this chapter measure performance between general elections, so the comparison between the 1832 reformed parliament and its unreformed 1831 predecessor is not really valid.

53   Sir Herbert Samuel in 1931 was the last Liberal leader until Nick Clegg not to represent a parliamentary seat in Scotland, Wales or the West Country.

Despite the undoubted fact that the contexts and circumstances for the twenty Liberal leaders are all very different, it is worth considering how well each performed given the hands they were dealt. It is certainly the case that the personality, style and leadership quality of each individual contributed – whether positively or negatively – to the fortunes of the Liberal Party.

For example, it is a major issue in modern history to wonder how Liberal fortunes would have differed had Asquith and Lloyd George been able to sort out their leadership of the party in a non-divisive way between 1916 and 1926, or had Gladstone not decided to pursue the cause of Irish home rule in the 1880s.

There are a number of possible numerical measures of success in leadership. These include: changes in the number of party members; opinion-poll ratings; and performances in other votes, for example, in local government or European Parliament elections. And a number of more individual assessments of performance ('key performance indicators' in modern management jargon) could be developed on a pretty subjective basis, as discussed in Chapters 1 and 2. For example, Chapter 1 contains a subjective ranking of all Liberal and SDP leaders based on the criteria this book's editors set for the chapter authors. Occasional comparisons of prime ministers have been generated in this way, though so far not of party leaders. I consider some of these below.

However, in a parliamentary democracy, the most authoritative measure must surely be performance in general elections. This is, in truth, what drives both political parties and their leaders. It is not always the absolutely definitive determinant of behaviour – political leaders, particularly in government, will sometimes take actions that they believe to be in the national interest, even if such actions don't favour their party support. This trade-off between governmental responsibilities and party performance was certainly a permanent characteristic of the conduct of Liberal leaders before 1924. However, no political leader will ever forget their party interest, and they will always take into account the impact of their actions upon their party's results at the forthcoming general election.

This chapter consists principally of a simple statistical measurement of the general election performance of the leaders since Lord Melbourne, in the form of an overall 'league table' of those leaders who have contested general elections.

For these, there are reasonably objective measures of success in the form of the number of parliamentary seats won or lost in a general election, and the increase or decrease in the share of the vote. Other general election performance measures could have been chosen, but the simplest seem most appropriate.

This does mean, however, that three Liberal leaderships (the Granville/ Hartington combination, Harcourt and Menzies Campbell) do not appear, since, as mentioned, they didn't lead in general elections.

From 1875 to 1880, the leadership was shared between Lord Granville, leader in the Lords, and the Marquess of Hartington, leader in the Commons. Their joint leadership was, effectively, simply a pause in Gladstone's leadership. After standing down as leader in 1875, Gladstone began his comeback in 1876, concluding with his famous Midlothian campaign in 1879–80. After the Liberal election victory of 1880, both Granville and Hartington were offered the premiership, but Gladstone would serve under neither of them, and again became Prime Minister himself. Granville became his Foreign Secretary and Hartington his Secretary of State for India and then Secretary for War.

Sir William Harcourt became leader, unenthusiastically, in 1896, after the 1895 election defeat that had deeply divided the Liberal Party. His position was not stable and he continued until 1898, before the party's internal divisions again came to a head and he decided to resign.

Menzies Campbell was leader of the Liberal Democrats from March 2006 (after Charles Kennedy had stood down in January) until October 2007, when it had become clear that Gordon Brown would not be calling an early general election. Campbell lost the confidence of his fellow Liberal Democrats and he was eventually forced to accept that he could not continue.

Despite these three absences, and some weaknesses in this form of measurement, general election performance does provide an interesting basis of comparison between Liberal leaders. The overall results for the Liberals/Liberal Democrats are shown in the following tables. Tables 3.1 to 3.6 relate to the changes from election to election in parliamentary seats and share of the vote, and rank the leaders. Because of the very different political natures of the two periods for the Liberals, I have divided each of Tables 3.4, 3.5 and 3.6 into sub-tables for 1835–1931 and 1950–2015. This makes analysis far clearer. The elections of 1935 and 1945 were a transitional phase between the two eras, and I have not included them in the sub-tables.

The Liberals have a rather complicated history of party splits and divisions, and so in these tables I have followed the approach followed by Rallings and Thrasher in their authoritative statistical analysis of general election results,[54] from which the main tables are drawn. On this basis the general election figures in the tables are as follow below.

The Liberal Unionists, who fought elections in alliance with the Conservatives from 1886 to 1910 before merging into them, are not included in the Liberal figures.

In 1918 and 1922, the total figure comprises the MPs elected for the official Liberals (led by Herbert Asquith), and the Coalition Liberals[55] (led by David Lloyd George).[56] Similarly, in 1931, the total figure comprises the thirty-three MPs elected for the official Liberals (led by Sir Herbert Samuel), and the four independent Liberals (mainly Lloyd George and his family). In 1931, 1935 and 1945, the total Liberal figures do *not* include the Liberal Nationals, who, like the Liberal Unionists before them, were Conservative allies and eventually merged into the Conservative Party.

---

54   Colin Rallings and Michael Thrasher eds, *British Electoral Facts 1832 –2012*, London, Biteback Publishing, 2012.

55   'National Liberals' in 1922.

56   Thirty-six official Liberals and 127 Coalition Liberals in 1918; sixty two official Liberals and fifty-three National Liberals in 1922.

In 1983, the total figure comprises both the seventeen elected Liberal MPs, led by David Steel, and the six SDP MPs, led by Roy Jenkins. In 1987, it is formed of the seventeen Liberal Party MPs, still led by Steel, and five Social Democrat MPs, then led by David Owen. From 1992, after the Liberals and the SDP had merged, the figure in the table is the number of MPs elected as Liberal Democrats.

Fort the reasons described earlier, I have treated the Liberal leader in 1880 as Gladstone, although Hartington and Granville were technically joint leaders (in the Commons and the Lords).

I have treated the Liberal leader for all the elections from 1910 to 1924, including 1918 and 1922, as Asquith, despite the fact that Lloyd George and the Coalition Liberals were an important component of the overall Liberal electoral performance in those years. I have treated Lloyd George as the leader for the 1931 election, as well as 1929. In 1931, he was suffering from a prolonged illness, but was consulted by the deputy leader Samuel and his colleagues on key decisions, though he strongly opposed the calling of the general election and then opposed the official Liberal line. I set out my approach clearly in case any feel it to be an inappropriate over-simplification.

For the 1983 and 1987 elections, I treat Steel as the leader, though the respective roles as SDP leader of Jenkins in 1983 and Owen in 1987 should be noted.

Through all the tables, I have marked with an asterisk the years 1880, 1918, 1922, 1931, 1983 and 1987 where there is some complication in considering who should most appropriately be considered the leader of the Liberals. The issues are discussed above.

TABLE 3.1: LIBERAL PERFORMANCES IN EACH OF THE FORTY-FIVE GENERAL ELECTIONS, 1835–2015.[57]

Year	Leader	Seats change	Vote percentage change	Leader's cumulative seat change	Leader's cumulative vote percentage change	Term of Office
2015	Clegg	-49	-15.2	-54	-14.2	7yr,5m
2010	Clegg	-5	+1.0			
2005	Kennedy	+10	+3.7	+16	+5.2	6yr,5m
2001	Kennedy	+6	+1.5			
1997	Ashdown	+26	-1.0	+24	-5.8	11yr,1m
1992	Ashdown	-2	-4.8			
1987*	Steel	-1	-2.8	+9	+4.3	12yr,0m
1983*	Steel	+12	+11.6			
1979	Steel	-2	-4.5			
1974 Oct	Thorpe	-1	-1.0	+1	+9.8	9yr,4m
1974 Feb	Thorpe	+8	+11.8			
1970	Thorpe	-6	-1.0			
1966	Grimond	+3	-2.7	+6	+5.8	10yr,2m
1964	Grimond	+3	+5.3			
1959	Grimond	0	+3.2			
1955	Davies	0	+0.1	-6	-6.3	11yr,3m
1951	Davies	-3	-6.5			
1950	Davies	-3	+0.1			
1945	Sinclair	-9	+2.3	-9	+2.3	9yr,7m
1935	Samuel	-15	-0.3	-15	-0.3	4yr,0m
1931*	Lloyd George	-23	-16.5	-4	-10.8	5yr,0m
1929	Lloyd George	+19	+5.7			
1924	Asquith	-118	-11.9	-359	-31.6	18yr,6m

57 Data from Rallings and Thrasher, op. cit., 2012, Tables 2.01 and 2.03 for the UK. Note that the time served as leader is sometimes ambiguous, particularly in the early period, and figures for both Gladstone and Asquith include the overall period of their leadership, despite some intervals.

1923	Asquith	+43	+0.9			
1922*	Asquith	-48	+3.2			
1918*	Asquith	-109	-18.6			
1910 Dec	Asquith	-2	+0.7			
1910 Feb	Asquith	-125	-5.9			
1906	Campbell-Bannerman	+216	+4.4	+222	+3.7	9yr,2m
1900	Campbell-Bannerman	+6	-0.7			
1895	Rosebery	-95	+0.6	-95	+0.6	2yr,7m
1892	Gladstone	+80	+0.1	-97	-15.1	25yr,3m
1886	Gladstone	-127	-2.4			
1885	Gladstone	-33	-8.0			
1880*	Gladstone	+110	+2.7			
1874	Gladstone	-145	-8.8			
1868	Gladstone	+18	+1.3			
1865	Palmerston	+13	-5.5	+45	+1.8	10yr,8m
1859	Palmerston	-21	+0.6			
1857	Palmerston	+53	+6.7			
1852	Russell	+32	+4.5	+53	+11.5	15yr,5m
1847	Russell	+21	+7.0			
1841	Melbourne	-73	-4.8	-170	-19.8	8yr,3m
1837	Melbourne	-41	-5.7			
1835	Melbourne	-56	-9.3			
1832	Grey	–				

TABLE 3.2: LIBERAL PERFORMANCES IN EACH OF THE FORTY-FIVE GENERAL
ELECTIONS, 1835-2015, RANKED BY SEATS GAINED OR LOST.

Year	Leader	Seats change	Vote percentage change
1906	Campbell-Bannerman	+216	+4.4
1880*	Gladstone	+110	+2.7
1892	Gladstone	+80	+0.1
1857	Palmerston	+53	+6.7
1923	Asquith	+43	+0.9
1852	Russell	+32	+4.5
1997	Ashdown	+26	-1.0
1847	Russell	+21	+7.0
1929	Lloyd George	+19	+5.7
1868	Gladstone	+18	+1.3
1865	Palmerston	+13	-5.5
1983*	Steel	+12	+11.6
2005	Kennedy	+10	+3.7
1974 Feb	Thorpe	+8	+11.8
2001	Kennedy	+6	+1.5
1900	Campbell-Bannerman	+6	-0.7
1966	Grimond	+3	-2.7
1964	Grimond	+3	+5.3
1959	Grimond	0	+3.2
1955	Davies	0	+0.1
1987*	Steel	-1	-2.8
1974 Oct	Thorpe	-1	-1.0
1992	Ashdown	-2	-4.8
1979	Steel	-2	-4.5
1910 Dec	Asquith	-2	+0.7
1951	Davies	-3	-6.5
1950*	Davies	-3	+0.1
2010	Clegg	-5	+1.0

1970	Thorpe	-6	-1.0
1945	Sinclair	-9	+2.3
1935	Samuel	-15	-0.3
1859	Palmerston	-21	+0.6
1931*	Lloyd George	-23	-16.5
1885	Gladstone	-33	-8.0
1837	Melbourne	-41	-5.7
1922*	Asquith	-48	+3.2
2015	Clegg	-49	-15.2
1835	Melbourne	-56	-9.3
1841	Melbourne	-73	-4.8
1895	Rosebery	-95	+0.6
1918*	Asquith	-109	-18.6
1924	Asquith	-118	-11.9
1910 Feb	Asquith	-125	-5.9
1886	Gladstone	-127	-2.4
1874	Gladstone	-145	-8.8

TABLE 3.3: LIBERAL PERFORMANCES IN EACH OF THE FORTY-FIVE GENERAL
ELECTIONS, 1835–2015, RANKED BY SHARE OF VOTE GAINED OR LOST.

Year	Leader	Seats change	Vote percentage change
1974 Feb	Thorpe	+8	+11.8
1983*	Steel	+12	+11.6
1847	Russell	+21	+7.0
1857	Palmerston	+53	+6.7
1929	Lloyd George	+19	+5.7
1964	Grimond	+3	+5.3
1852	Russell	+32	+4.5
1906	Campbell-Bannerman	+216	+4.4
2005	Kennedy	+10	+3.7
1959	Grimond	0	+3.2
1922*	Asquith	-48	+3.2
1880*	Gladstone	+110	+2.7
1945	Sinclair	-9	+2.3
2001	Kennedy	+6	+1.5
1868	Gladstone	+18	+1.3
2010	Clegg	-5	+1.0
1923	Asquith	+43	+0.9
1910 Dec	Asquith	-2	+0.7
1859	Palmerston	-21	+0.6
1895	Rosebery	-95	+0.6
1892	Gladstone	+80	+0.1
1955	Davies	0	+0.1
1950	Davies	-3	+0.1
1935	Samuel	-15	-0.3
1900	Campbell-Bannerman	+6	-0.7
1997	Ashdown	+26	-1.0
1974 Oct	Thorpe	-1	-1.0
1970	Thorpe	-6	-1.0

1886	Gladstone	-127	-2.4
1966	Grimond	+3	-2.7
1987*	Steel	-1	-2.8
1979	Steel	-2	-4.5
1992	Ashdown	-2	-4.8
1841	Melbourne	-73	-4.8
1865	Palmerston	+13	-5.5
1837	Melbourne	-41	-5.7
1910 Feb	Asquith	-125	-5.9
1951	Davies	-3	-6.5
1885	Gladstone	-33	-8.0
1874	Gladstone	-145	-8.8
1835	Melbourne	-56	-9.3
1924	Asquith	-118	-11.9
2015	Clegg	-49	-15.2
1931*	Lloyd George	-23	-16.5
1918*	Asquith	-109	-18.6

TABLE 3.4: OVERALL CUMULATIVE LIBERAL LEADERS' PERFORMANCES IN THE FORTY-FIVE GENERAL ELECTIONS, 1835–2015, RANKED BY SEATS GAINED OR LOST.

No. elections	General elections for this leader	Leader	Leader's cumulative seats change	Leader's cumulative vote percentage change	Term of office as leader
2	1900, 1906	Campbell-Bannerman	+222	+3.7	9yr, 2m
2	1847, 1852	Russell	+53	+11.5	15yr, 5m
3	1857, 1859, 1865	Palmerston	+45	+1.8	10yr, 8m
2	1992, 1997	Ashdown	+24	-5.8	11yr, 1m
2	2001, 2005	Kennedy	+16	+5.2	6yr, 5m
3	1979, 1983*, 1987*	Steel	+9	+4.3	12yr, 0m
3	1959, 1964, 1966	Grimond	+6	+5.8	10yr, 2m
3	1970, 1974 Feb, 1974 Oct	Thorpe	+1	+9.8	9yr, 4m
2	1929, 1931*	Lloyd George	-4	-10.8	5yr, 0m
3	1950, 1951, 1955	Davies	-6	-6.3	11yr, 3m
1	1945	Sinclair	-9	+2.3	9yr, 7m
1	1935	Samuel	-15	-0.3	4yr, 0m
2	2010, 2015	Clegg	-54	-14.2	7yr, 5m
1	1895	Rosebery	-95	+0.6	2yr, 7m
6	1868, 1874, 1880*, 1885, 1886, 1892	Gladstone	-97	-15.1	25yr, 3m
3	1835, 1837, 1841	Melbourne	-170	-19.8	8yr, 3m
6	1910 Feb, 1910 Dec, 1918*, 1922*, 1923, 1924	Asquith	-359	-31.6	18yr, 6m

Table 3.4 shows the cumulative performance of the seventeen Liberal leaders over the total number of general elections for which they were leader (left-hand column). These are then ordered by total number of seats gained or lost over their period of leadership.

TABLE 3.4A: OVERALL CUMULATIVE LIBERAL LEADERS' PERFORMANCES IN THE
TWENTY-FIVE GENERAL ELECTIONS, 1835–1931, RANKED BY SEATS GAINED OR LOST.

No. elections	General elections for this leader	Leader	Leader's cumulative seats change	Leader's cumulative vote percentage change	Term of office as leader
2	1900, 1906	Campbell-Bannerman	+222	+3.7	9yr, 2m
2	1847, 1852	Russell	+53	+11.5	15yr, 5m
3	1857, 1859, 1865	Palmerston	+45	+1.8	10yr, 8m
2	1929, 1931*	Lloyd George	-4	-10.8	5yr, 0m
1	1895	Rosebery	-95	+0.6	2yr, 7m
6	1868, 1874, 1880*, 1885, 1886, 1892	Gladstone	-97	-15.1	25yr, 3m
3	1835, 1837, 1841	Melbourne	-170	-19.8	8yr, 3m
6	1910 Feb, 1910 Dec, 1918*, 1922*, 1923, 1924	Asquith	-359	-31.6	18yr, 6m
17	All 1835–1906	—	-42	-17.3	71yr
25	All 1835–1931	—	-405	-59.7	96yr

Table 3.4a is a part of Table 3.4 and shows the cumulative performance of the
eight Liberal leaders until Lloyd George over the total number of general elections for which they were leader (left-hand column). These are then ordered
by total number of seats gained or lost over their period of leadership. I have
added two summary rows at the bottom for the periods 1835–1906 and 1835–1931.

TABLE 3.4B: OVERALL CUMULATIVE LIBERAL LEADERS' PERFORMANCES IN THE
EIGHTEEN GENERAL ELECTIONS, 1950–2015, RANKED BY SEATS GAINED OR LOST.

No. elections	General elections for this leader	Leader	Leader's cumulative seats change	Leader's cumulative vote percentage change	Term of office as leader
2	1992, 1997	Ashdown	+24	-5.8	11yr, 1m
2	2001, 2005	Kennedy	+16	+5.2	6yr, 5m
3	1979, 1983*, 1987*	Steel	+9	+4.3	12yr, 0m
3	1959, 1964, 1966	Grimond	+6	+5.8	10yr, 2m
3	1970, 1974 Feb, 1974 Oct	Thorpe	+1	+9.8	9yr, 4m
3	1950, 1951, 1955	Davies	-6	-6.3	11yr, 3m
2	2010, 2015	Clegg	-54	-14.2	7yr, 5m
18	All 1945–2015	—	-4	-1.1	70yr

Table 3.4b is a part of Table 3.4 and shows the cumulative performance of the
seven Liberal leaders since 1950 over the total number of general elections for
which they were leader (left-hand column). These are then ordered by total
number of seats gained or lost over their period of leadership. The bottom row
summarises the whole period.

TABLE 3.5: OVERALL CUMULATIVE LIBERAL LEADERS' PERFORMANCES IN THE FORTY-
FIVE GENERAL ELECTIONS, 1835–2015, RANKED BY SHARE OF VOTE GAINED OR LOST.

No. elections	General elections for this leader	Leader	Leader's cumulative seats change	Leader's cumulative vote percentage change	Term of office as leader
2	1847, 1852	Russell	+53	+11.5	15yr,5m
3	1970, 1974 Feb, 1974 Oct	Thorpe	+1	+9.8	9yr,4m
3	1959, 1964, 1966	Grimond	+6	+5.8	10yr,2m
2	2001, 2005	Kennedy	+16	+5.2	6yr,5m
3	1979, 1983*, 1987*	Steel	+9	+4.3	12yr,0m
2	1900, 1906	Campbell-Bannerman	+222	+3.7	9yr,2m
1	1945	Sinclair	-9	+2.3	9yr,7m
3	1857, 1859, 1865	Palmerston	+45	+1.8	10yr,8m
1	1895	Rosebery	-95	+0.6	2yr,7m
1	1935	Samuel	-15	-0.3	4yr,0m
2	1992, 1997	Ashdown	+24	-5.8	11yr,1m
3	1950, 1951, 1955	Davies	-6	-6.3	11yr,3m
2	1929, 1931*	Lloyd George	-4	-10.8	5yr,0m
2	2010, 2015	Clegg	-54	-14.2	7yr,5m
6	1868, 1874, 1880*, 1885, 1886, 1892	Gladstone	-97	-15.1	25yr,3m
3	1835, 1837, 1841	Melbourne	-170	-19.8	8yr,3m
6	1910 Feb, 1910 Dec, 1918*, 1922*, 1923, 1924	Asquith	-359	-31.6	18yr,6m

Table 3.5 shows the cumulative performance of the seventeen Liberal leaders
over the total number of general elections for which they were leader (left-hand
column). These are then ordered by total share of vote gained or lost over their
period of leadership.

TABLE 3.5A: OVERALL CUMULATIVE LIBERAL LEADERS' PERFORMANCES IN THE
TWENTY-FIVE GENERAL ELECTIONS, 1835–1931, RANKED BY SHARE OF VOTE GAINED
OR LOST.

No. elections	General elections for this leader	Leader	Leader's cumulative seats change	Leader's cumulative vote percentage change	Term of office as leader
2	1847, 1852	Russell	+53	+11.5	15yr, 5m
2	1900, 1906	Campbell-Bannerman	+222	+3.7	9yr, 2m
3	1857, 1859, 1865	Palmerston	+45	+1.8	10yr, 8m
1	1895	Rosebery	-95	+0.6	2yr, 7m
2	1929, 1931*	Lloyd George	-4	-10.8	5yr, 0m
6	1868, 1874, 1880*, 1885, 1886, 1892	Gladstone	-97	-15.1	25yr, 3m
3	1835, 1837, 1841	Melbourne	-170	-19.8	8yr, 3m
6	1910 Feb, 1910 Dec, 1918*, 1922*, 1923, 1924	Asquith	-359	-31.6	18yr, 6m
17	Whole 1835–1906	–	-42	-17.3	71yr, 0m
25	Whole 1835–1931	–	-405	-59.7	96yr, 0m

Table 3.5a shows the cumulative performance of the eight Liberal leaders until
Lloyd George over the total number of general elections for which they were
leader (left-hand column). These are then ordered by total share of vote gained
or lost over their period of leadership.

TABLE 3.5B: OVERALL CUMULATIVE LIBERAL LEADERS' PERFORMANCES IN THE
EIGHTEEN GENERAL ELECTIONS, 1950–2015, RANKED BY SHARE OF VOTE GAINED OR
LOST.

No. elections	General elections for this leader	Leader	Leader's cumulative seats change	Leader's cumulative vote percentage change	Term of office as leader
3	1970, 1974 Feb, 1974 Oct	Thorpe	+1	+9.8	9yr,4m
3	1959, 1964, 1966	Grimond	+6	+5.8	10yr,2m
2	2001, 2005	Kennedy	+16	+5.2	6yr,5m
3	1979, 1983*, 1987*	Steel	+9	+4.3	12yr,0m
2	1992, 1997	Ashdown	+24	-5.8	11yr,1m
3	1950, 1951, 1955	Davies	-6	-6.3	11yr,3m
2	2010, 2015	Clegg	-54	-14.2	7yr,5m
18	Whole 1945-2015	-	-4	-1.1	70 yr,0m

Table 3.5b is a part of Table 3.5 shows the cumulative performance of each Liberal leader since 1950 over the total number of general elections for which they were leader (left-hand column). These are then ordered by total share of vote gained or lost over their period of leadership. The bottom row summarises the whole period.

TABLE 3.6: LIBERAL LEADERS' 'LEAGUE TABLE', RANKED BY SEATS.

Ranking by seats	Leader	Ranking by share of vote	Prime Minister
1	Campbell-Bannerman	6	Yes
2	Russell	1	Yes
3	Palmerston	8	Yes
4	Ashdown	11	No
5	Kennedy	4	No
6	Steel	5	No
7	Grimond	3	No
8	Thorpe	2	No
9	Lloyd George	13	Yes
10	Davies	12	No
11	Sinclair	7	No
12	Samuel	10	No
13	Clegg	14	No
14	Rosebery	9	Yes
15	Gladstone	15	Yes
16	Melbourne	16	Yes
17	Asquith	17	Yes

Table 3.6 is a reworking of Table 3.4 as a summary 'league table'. It orders the Liberal leaders by the number of seats won or lost. The figure in the third column is their position in the 'share of vote' league table. The final column indicates which Liberal leaders became Prime Minister.

TABLE 3.6A: LIBERAL LEADERS' 'LEAGUE TABLE' FOR 1835 TO 1931, RANKED BY SEATS.

Ranking by seats	Leader	Ranking by share of vote	Prime Minister
1	Campbell-Bannerman	2	Yes
2	Russell	1	Yes
3	Palmerston	3	Yes
4	Lloyd George	5	Yes
5	Rosebery	4	Yes
6	Gladstone	6	Yes
7	Melbourne	7	Yes
8	Asquith	8	Yes

Table 3.6a is the part of Table 3.6, covering the general elections from 1835 to 1931.

TABLE 3.6B: LIBERAL LEADERS' 'LEAGUE TABLE' FOR 1950 TO 2015, RANKED BY SEATS.

Ranking by seats	Leader	Ranking by share of vote	Prime Minister
1	Ashdown	5	No
2	Kennedy	3	No
3	Steel	4	No
4	Grimond	2	No
5	Thorpe	1	No
6	Davies	6	No
7	Clegg	7	No

Table 3.6b is the part of Table 3.6, covering the general elections from 1950 to 2015.

A number of observations can be made about these tables, particularly 3.4, 3.5 and 3.6 and their sub-tables.

The pattern of the overall performances for 1835–2015 is far less clear than that for either the Conservatives or Labour. However, clear patterns emerge when considering the separate periods 1835–1931 and 1950–2015:

- First, they demonstrate the importance of major contextual issues. The dominant performance before 1931 is that of Herbert Asquith, which, of course, includes the First World War. The story might have been very different had Asquith proved an effective war leader. However, in the end, he lost 359 parliamentary seats and 31.6 per cent of the share of the vote over six general elections, from 1910 to 1924. These are utterly enormous figures, and describe graphically the decline of the Liberals from their central position in British politics to near irrelevance. The split with Lloyd George was a further symptom of the destruction of the party and was a direct consequence of the national disaster of the First World War. Of course, the fundamental causality is a critical matter of debate. Was Asquith simply the victim of these momentous events? To what extent were the events the consequences of Asquith's own failures of leadership? Nevertheless, the context is essential to understanding Asquith's performance. The same can be said of the way in which Melbourne oversaw the decline of the Liberals after the triumph of the Great Reform Act, as the Conservatives were able to reassert and redefine themselves with the new electorate. Of course, he was up against Peel – the Conservatives' most successful ever leader in terms of general election results. And the Irish context of Gladstone's leadership certainly had a major impact upon his electoral performance. He faced great challenges in considering how best to address the demands for Irish home rule, and the difficulties he faced, including party division, were a direct result of the choices he exercised within that overall context. After 1950, Clegg's comparatively disastrous performance is a direct consequence of the precise contextual arithmetic of the 2010 general election. This created a situation within which Clegg had few good options in terms of maximising his performance at the subsequent election. However, though his strategic choices in May 2010 were very constrained (and – in my opinion, at any rate – he made the right big decision), he made a significant number of tactical errors then, and later on in the parliament.

- Second, it helps if your opposition is weak. Melbourne, Gladstone and Rosebery all faced very strong Conservative opposition in Peel, Disraeli and Salisbury. Derby and Balfour were not strong opponents for Russell, Palmerston and Campbell-Bannerman. Of course, Asquith's strong opposition came from Lloyd George – within his own party! The challenges for the post-1950 Liberal leaders were different. They were not facing one pretty clearly defined enemy, as the leaders of both the Conservatives and Labour were. They

therefore had to improve their party's performance on that basis,
and attempt to carve out a position for their party, distinct from both
the other main parties. This led to difficult tactical choices, though,
in general (with important exceptions), they tended to default to
opposing the government of the day.

- Third, these tables serve to suggest that those doing better were more
successful at one of Toby James and Jim Buller's criteria:[58] *devising
a winning electoral strategy*. Campbell-Bannerman, Ashdown,
Kennedy and, to an extent, Steel, with his SDP merger, were all
effective at doing this; Asquith, Melbourne, Rosebery, Davies and
Clegg were totally unsuccessful.

- Fourth, another of Toby James and Jim Buller's criteria, *party
management*, was better handled, albeit with much smaller
parliamentary parties, which were easier to handle, by the later
leaders than it was by Gladstone, Asquith and Lloyd George – all of
whom, to some extent or another, left a legacy of deep party
division.

- Fifth, there are some striking divergences between the change in
share of the vote and the change in the number of seats. In the early
period, Campbell-Bannerman and Palmerston did significantly
better in gaining seats than in increasing the share of the vote,
whereas Rosebery did significantly worse in seats than vote share.
In the case of the 1906 Liberal landslide, part of the credit must go
to the electoral pact agreed between Herbert Gladstone and Ramsay
MacDonald, which reduced the conflict between Labour and the
Liberals. Since 1950, Ashdown did significantly better in gaining
parliamentary seats, despite a decrease in share of the vote in both

---

58   See Chapter 2.

1992 and 1997, which probably reflected a better strategy of electoral
targeting, together with a significant level of anti-Conservative tactical
voting between Labour and Liberal Democrat supporters in 1997.
In contrast, Grimond, Thorpe, Steel and Kennedy all performed
extremely well in increasing the share of the vote, but failed to secure
significant gains in seats. The main reason for these divergences is
the impact of the vagaries of the British voting system, which can
encourage minor parties with a clear geographical basis of support
and exacerbate inner-party divisions. Different leaders probably had
different aptitudes in fighting within this framework.

On top of these general assessments, some fairly strong conclusions emerge
from this statistical analysis of Liberal leaders' election performances in the
two eras, based on general election performance.

Between 1835 and 1931, three Liberal leaders do significantly better than
all of the others. In terms of both increased vote share and increased parliamentary seats. Campbell-Bannerman, Russell and Palmerston are the top
three on both measures.

It is similarly clear that the bottom three on both measures are Asquith,
Melbourne and Gladstone. Probably the performances of Gladstone (fifteenth
in both tables overall) and Asquith (seventeenth) will be particularly surprising, since they are both, in general, ranked so high as great Liberal leaders
and prime ministers. These are also the two longest-serving Liberal leaders,
and so they each dominated the party for a long time. Nevertheless, neither
of them has an overall electoral record to be proud of.

Lloyd George and Rosebery are mid-table in that league, with Lloyd George
doing very badly in reduced vote share and Rosebery in reduced parliamentary seats.

Between 1950 and 2015, there is similar clarity at the bottom. Davies and
Clegg fare worst on both counts. Clegg's defence has to be the particular
circumstances of the 2010 result, though many will argue that he had better
options than he in fact took. Davies's poor performance over three general

elections illustrates the difficulties of delivering a clear Liberal message when the Conservatives and Labour so dominated the political agenda.

At the top, the picture is slightly more confused. Ashdown and Kennedy certainly did most strongly in the number of seats gained, but Thorpe, Grimond, Kennedy and Steel (in that order) all did well in increasing vote share, where Ashdown did almost as badly as Davies in reducing share of the vote.

It is interesting to compare the rankings in this Liberal leaders' league table, based on general election results, with other assessments. In recent years, there have also been some subjective assessments of prime ministers. Some cover only post-war prime ministers, which clearly doesn't include any Liberals. Kevin Theakston and Mark Gill from Leeds University have written a fairly full and substantial analysis of twentieth-century prime ministers, published in 2005.[59]

There have been the following 'league table' exercises (listed chronologically in Table 3.7, with their ranked order of Liberal prime ministers).

59   Kevin Theakston and Mark Gill, 'Ranking Twentieth-Century British Prime Ministers', *British Journal of Politics and International Relations*, Vol. 8, 2006, pp. 193–213.

TABLE 3.7: LIBERAL LEADERS IN PREVIOUS RANKINGS OF BRITISH PRIME MINISTERS.

Date	Survey organiser	Ranking in order
1999	BBC Radio 4, based on twenty historians	Lloyd George, Asquith, Campbell-Bannerman
2000	BBC Politics Group, from twenty-two academics[60]	Lloyd George, Asquith, Campbell-Bannerman
2004	Leeds University/MORI, 139 academics[61]	Lloyd George, Asquith, Campbell-Bannerman
2006	BBC *History Magazine*, by Francis Beckett[62]	Campbell-Bannerman, Asquith, Lloyd George
2010	*The Times*, from Phil Collins, Ben Macintyre, Matthew Parris, William Rees-Mogg, Peter Riddell and Phil Webster[63]	Lloyd George, Gladstone, Asquith, Palmerston, Russell, Campbell-Bannerman, Melbourne, Rosebery
2015	*The Times*, from Danny Finkelstein, Lucy Fisher, Oliver Kamm, Patrick Kidd, Damian MacBride, Tim Montgomerie, Jenni Russell, Rachel Sylvester, Phil Webster and Giles Whittell[64]	Lloyd George, Asquith, Campbell-Bannerman

60   Churchill "greatest PM of twentieth century", BBC News, last updated 4 January 2000, accessed 19 February 2015 (http://news.bbc.co.uk/1/hi/uk_politics/575219.stm).

61   Theakston and Gill, op. cit.

62   'Thatcher and Attlee top PM list', BBC News, last updated 29 August 2006, accessed 19 February 2015 (http://news.bbc.co.uk/1/hi/uk_politics/5294024.stm).

63   'The Times's Top 50 Prime Ministers', *The Times*, last updated 5 May 2010, accessed 19 February 2015 (http://www.timesonline.co.uk/tol/news/politics/article7116855.ece).

64   http://www.thetimes.co.uk/redbox/topic/2015-election-campaign/interactive-who-is-britains-greatest-modern-day-prime-minister

n 2010, Stephen Bray, for Iain Dale's Diary,[65] produced an amalgamation of these judgements, which suggested that the ranking of Liberal prime ministers was: Gladstone, Lloyd George, Grey, Palmerston, Asquith, Russell, Melbourne, Campbell-Bannerman and Rosebery.

Clearly the criteria for these assessments vary: they are about prime ministe-rial and governmental leadership rather than party leadership; they use different measures and timescales for the assessments; and they involve different tech-niques to come to the judgement.

Nevertheless, what is striking about these assessments, subjective though they are, is that they all[66] grade Lloyd George, Asquith, Campbell-Bannerman in that order. Lloyd George and Asquith are in the very top group of prime ministers from any party, and Campbell-Bannerman is rated pretty highly.

These ratings are different from those generated by this analysis of election performance, and the divergence is interesting.

Campbell-Bannerman does perform well on this basis, and, indeed, is the only Liberal Prime Minister since 1900 to have a strong electoral record. How-ever, Asquith and Lloyd George do not and it is worth considering why their poor electoral records are seen by historians as of such relatively little account.

The reasons for the general high rating of Lloyd George in assessments that focus on national prime ministerial performance are fairly straightforward. He was eventually a successful war leader with an absolutely dominant personality, and many commentators will consider his electoral performance, like his per-formance as Prime Minister from 1918 to 1922, as a secondary consideration. Similarly, his contribution to the great Liberal collapse may be seen by some as less significant than his national achievements. All that said, for me, there remains an important question as to whether different conduct by him after 1918 would have reduced the extent of the Liberal decline, and what that might have meant.

Asquith is a different case. Before 1914, it is quite understandable that his

---

65   Stephen Bray, 'Guest Post: The Greatest Prime Ministers of All Time', Iain Dale's Diary, last updated 5 August 2010, accessed 19 February 2015 (http://iaindale.blogspot.co.uk/2010/08/guest-post-greatest-prime-ministers-of.html).

66   Except Francis Beckett's analysis for the BBC *History Magazine*, which puts them in the reverse order.

premiership would be highly rated. Leading a highly talented team, including both Lloyd George and Churchill, he brought about transformational constitutional change in relation to both the House of Lords and the welfare state. He had also been Chancellor in Campbell-Bannerman's government. Few prime ministers have done as much. However, after 1914, the case is much less clear. He was not a great war leader. Had he been, Lloyd George would not have been able to oust him. And, from 1918 to 1926, Asquith's leadership of the Liberals, who were facing existential challenges and deep personal divisions, seems to have been desultory at best. His overall electoral record for the Liberals is nothing short of disastrous. These factors should be given some weight, as well as his 1908–14 performance, in considering his contribution.

The one subjective ranking that includes pre-1900 Liberal leaders follows the others in giving Lloyd George and Asquith top ranking, despite their poor electoral record. To that, they understandably add Gladstone – again, despite his poor electoral record. After that, the ranking follows the electoral record, except it puts Rosebery below Melbourne.

The correlation between these subjective assessments and the general election result methodology of this chapter should not be overstated. As indicated at the beginning of this chapter, any system for measuring the quality of leadership cannot be at all precise, as circumstances vary so greatly. Nevertheless, a rating based on general election performance does have some value, and, from the point of view of party leadership, can be extended to leaders who did not become Prime Minister, which is now essential for the Liberals, who have no prime ministerial pretensions.

At the very least, general election performances should be considered as a contributory criterion when assessing how Liberal leaders have done.

PART II

ASSESSMENTS OF LIBERAL LEADERS

CHAPTER 4

CHARLES (EARL) GREY

HENRY MILLER

Charles Grey, 2nd Earl Grey, is perhaps best known in the popular mind today for giving his name to a flavour of tea. Yet Grey was the first Liberal Prime Minister. His 'reform' government of 1830–34 brought Whigs and Liberal Tories together in a lasting coalition that paved the way for Victorian liberalism. The landmark Great Reform Act of 1832, which Grey helped to pilot through stormy waters, fundamentally reshaped the representative system and ushered in an era of Liberal dominance. Grey was, however, a transitional figure, whose style of aloof aristocratic leadership looked back to the eighteenth century, rather than forwards to the era of modern political parties. Even one admiring biographer has characterised his style as 'cold and shadowy'.[67] An indifferent, indolent and often absentee opposition leader, Grey was decisive and masterly as Prime Minister in handling the reform question, justifying his description as 'one of the most skilled politicians of the nineteenth century'.[68]

- Charles Grey (13 March 1764 – 17 July 1845), born in Northumberland, the first surviving son of Charles Grey, 1st Earl Grey.
- Educated at Eton and Trinity College, Cambridge, followed by a Grand Tour of Europe.
- Married in 1794 Mary Elizabeth, daughter of William Brabazon Ponsonby, 1st Baron Ponsonby.
- Sixteen children, two of whom became MPs.

---

67   G. M. Trevelyan, *Lord Grey of the Reform Bill*, London, 1920, p. 212.

68   E. A. Wasson, 'Whigs and the Press, 1800–50', *Parliamentary History*, Vol. 25, 2006, p. 68.

- MP for Northumberland 1786–1806, then both Appleby and Tavistock in 1807, shortly before succeeding his father as 2nd Earl Grey.
- First Lord of the Admiralty 1806; Foreign Secretary 1806–07; leader of the Whig Party 1807–34; Prime Minister 1830–34.

H ailing from a family of Northumberland landowners, Grey's father, General Sir Charles Grey, was a distinguished soldier. Soon after his election for Northumberland in 1786, however, Grey broke with his family's Tory politics and associated himself with the Whig opposition led by Charles James Fox. At this time, parties were gradually shifting from being aristocratic parliamentary factions, based on personal connections and familial links, to being bound by principle. In the late eighteenth century, the Foxite Whigs styled themselves as defenders of the people from the excessive power of the crown, were sympathetic to the early stages of the French Revolution, and identified themselves with religious tolerance and civil liberties. The Foxites were not democrats or radicals, but presented themselves as aristocratic tribunes of the people. Their opponents, the government and the supporters of William Pitt the Younger – often called Tories – firmly opposed any constitutional reform. They resisted the extension of civil rights to Protestant Dissenters and Catholics, and waged a long war against revolutionary and Napoleonic France abroad, and radicalism at home.

Grey's lifelong association with parliamentary reform began with his formation of the Society of the Friends of the People in April 1792 – a Whig attempt to steer a middle course between popular radicalism and the reactionary stance of Pitt's government. The society sought to arrest the influence of Edmund Burke's alarmist interpretation of the French Revolution over Whig grandees, and to push the party in a more progressive and reformist direction. Ultimately, the Society of the Friends of the People was a failure, due to the polarisation of opinion over the French Revolution. The society was too moderate to appeal to an increasingly radical popular movement outside Parliament, but sufficiently progressive to scare many leading Whig grandees into drifting towards Pitt's

Tories. The society was the trigger for the break-up of the Whig Party and its reconstitution as an avowedly Foxite rump.[69] For much of the following decade, the Foxites stood for peace with France, and opposed Pitt's repressive measures. Following Pitt's death, the Foxites briefly took office in 1806–07 as part of the coalition 'Ministry of All the Talents'. After a brief spell at the admiralty, Grey served as Leader of the House of Commons and Foreign Secretary following Fox's death in 1806. He succeeded his father as 2nd Earl Grey the next year. Grey's formative political years gave him a strong attachment to Foxite principles, but the failure of the Society of the Friends of the People made him wary of seeking popular support outside Parliament. The daring of his radical youth gave way to a 'strange fatality' and an unwillingness to offer a strong lead without a shift in public opinion towards his principles.[70]

Between the fall of the 'Ministry of All the Talents' and the formation of the reform ministry in December 1830, Grey was the leader of the Whig opposition. Writing in 1816, Grey defined his principles as retrenchment, a liberal foreign policy, extending civil rights to Catholics, and a 'moderate and gradual reform of Parliament'. This document shows that Grey had identified many of the key tenets of the later Liberal Party before it had been formed. Yet Grey despaired of seeing these principles carried into policy, noting: 'I feel very much below the mark, and … I have no spirit or power left.'[71] Grey was absent from Westminster for long periods and made little secret of his preference for private life at Howick, his Northumberland estate. Although contemporaries often regarded Grey as aloof, arrogant and cold, privately he was plagued by self-doubt and melancholy, which contributed to his indolence and ineffectiveness as a leader at this time. However, while Grey's lacklustre leadership added to the Whigs' problems, their fortunes were largely dictated by circumstances beyond their control.

With the exception of the Ministry of All the Talents, Britain was governed by Tory governments between 1783 and 1830. The monarch held the ultimate power

69   L. G. Mitchell, *Charles James Fox and the Disintegration of the Whig Party, 1782–1794*, Oxford, Oxford University Press, 1971, pp. 177–201.

70   *Newcastle Journal*, quoted in *Gentleman's Magazine*, xxiv, September 1845, p. 303.

71   Grey to Lord Holland, 8 December 1816, quoted in Trevelyan, op. cit., p. 179.

to appoint and dismiss governments, and George III had excluded the Whigs from office – a policy continued by his son, who ruled as Prince Regent and then as George IV. Grey rejected overtures to join the government, and, in 1820, confirmed the new King's hostility to him by opposing his attempt to divorce Queen Caroline. The attempt to institute proceedings against Caroline, which was hugely unpopular in the country, was eventually abandoned by government. Although Grey kept above the radical-led, pro-Caroline popular campaign, he spoke against the bill and was severe in his criticism of the government.[72]

The Whig opposition's position in the Commons, the Lords and within the wider public was far from strong. This added to Grey's difficulties, although he did little to solve them. Parliamentary politics was generally polarised into two camps – ministers and opposition, or Whig and Tory – but these were not really disciplined parties in the modern sense, and both sides were internally divided on key issues. Within this fluid and loose system of parliamentary politics, the Whigs were a large minority – but a minority nonetheless – in both the Commons and the Lords.

Having been burnt by his experience of the Society of the Friends of the People, Grey had an ambivalent attitude towards popular support. His party defended civil liberties and freedom of the press and assembly from the repressive legislation introduced after the Peterloo Massacre of 1819, but Grey resisted closer cooperation with radicals outside Parliament. It was left to others such as Henry Brougham to pioneer new relations between the Whigs, the rapidly expanding newspaper press and the provincial middle classes. The most recent historian of the Whig opposition years has concluded that the party 'consistently failed to establish their standing as an alternative source of leadership', and, for this, Grey must bear much of the responsibility.[73]

Why did Grey remain leader during the opposition years, given the lack of success and his own unwillingness to lead? Firstly, alternative leaders were incapable, unwilling or mistrusted by the party.

---

72 Hansard, 1746–7, 10 November 1820.

73 W. A. Hay, *The Whig Revival, 1808–1830*, Basingstoke, Palgrave, 2005, p. 10.

Secondly, Grey possessed a number of qualities that were valued in early nineteenth-century political leadership, not least his aristocratic pedigree. He was a parliamentary orator of the first rank, which counted for much at this time. A parliamentary reporter noted that, in debate, Grey's 'language was beautifully correct ... his style united simplicity with vigour in no ordinary degree'.[74] He saved his speeches for the most important occasions, but really excelled in his replies to opponents. Grey avoided making conversation in the Lords, and instead closely followed the debate. This watchfulness, and his talent for anticipating the line his opponents would take, allowed him, 'on a moment's notice', to 'triumphantly demolish the positions of an adversary'.[75] His handsome appearance contributed to this attractiveness as a parliamentary speaker. 'There was dignity in his looks and in every movement he made. It was still more visible when he rose to speak,' one contemporary noted.[76] The painter Benjamin Haydon recalled Grey as 'tall in figure, refined in look, and noble in principle'.[77] His dignified and statesmanlike public persona would prove a valuable asset during the reform crisis.

Thirdly, Grey could be decisive on occasions, and his most important achievement as opposition leader was a negative one. He preserved the independent identity of the Whig Party and gained a reputation for integrity by refusing to join coalitions with the Tories in 1809 and 1812. Uninterested in power and place for their own sake, Grey declined to join George Canning's Liberal Tory government in 1827, unless it introduced Catholic emancipation. Grey refused to join coalitions except on the grounds of principle and agreed policy. When Grey was told that his refusal would lead to the resumption in office of the old Tory government, he responded: 'There certainly is one evil greater, much greater, in my estimation, and that is the dissolution of the Whig Party and the total destruction of its consequence and character.'[78]

---

74   J. Grant, *Random Recollections of the House of Lords*, London, Smith, Elder & Co., 1836, p. 275.

75   Ibid., p. 269.

76   Ibid., p. 266.

77   Willard Bissell Pope ed., *The Diary of Benjamin Robert Haydon*, Cambridge MA, Harvard University Press, (five volumes) 1960–63, Vol. 4, p. 211.

78   Earl Grey to Lord Holland, 16 September 1827, quoted in Trevelyan, op. cit., p. 375.

As an opposition leader, Grey had many failings, but, by preserving the identity of the Whig Party, he played an important part in the emerging idea that parties were bound together by principle rather than just personal and family connections. His persistent refusal to accept office, except on grounds of principle, gave him a reputation as a high-minded statesman of integrity, who refused to sacrifice his party's principles for office. His high standing and prestige proved to be invaluable as the political scene changed out of all recognition between 1827 and 1830.

Three factors transformed the fortunes of Grey and the Whigs.

Firstly, the Tory Party broke up after Lord Liverpool's stroke in 1827 brought latent divisions between Liberal Tories and High Tories over economic policy and Catholic relief out into the open. After Canning's death and the failure of his successor, these differences were apparently patched up in the Duke of Wellington's government, but unity proved to be short-lived. Liberal Tories including Lord Melbourne and Lord Palmerston, who were increasingly coming to the view that parliamentary reform was unavoidable, resigned in 1828. The following year, Wellington alienated High Tories by taking the momentous decision to introduce Catholic emancipation to avert unrest in Ireland, leaving his government without stable support in the Commons.

Secondly, the death of George IV in June 1830, and the succession of his brother William IV, finally ended the long proscription on the Whigs taking office as a party.

Thirdly, Wellington's position was further weakened by the general election of 1830, in which many of the constituencies with larger electorates returned pro-reform MPs.

Casting off years of indecisiveness, Grey argued strongly for parliamentary reform when Parliament met in November 1830, noting: 'Through my whole life I have advocated reform, and I have thought that, if it were not attended to in time, the people would lose all confidence in Parliament.'[79] His

---

79 Hansard, 37–8, 2 November 1830.

speech drew Wellington into unwisely declaring his opposition to any constitutional changes.[80] When Wellington's ministry, which had long lost control over the Commons, resigned a few weeks later, William IV invited Grey to form a government.

On taking over as Prime Minister, Grey wrote: 'I feel appalled at the difficulties with which I am surrounded' – but he proved to be an effective Cabinet maker.[81] His government was a coalition of Whigs, Liberal Tories and one High Tory (the Duke of Richmond), which agreed on little except that parliamentary reform was necessary. Grey's government contained some formidable egos and difficult personalities, including his radical son-in-law Lord Durham. An important appointment was Grey's choice of Palmerston as Foreign Secretary, with whom he steered British policy in a new direction, encouraging constitutional government in Europe.[82] Another excellent appointment was his brother-in-law Edward Ellice, who proved to be a popular and effective Chief Whip in the Commons. If Lord Althorp was an indifferent Chancellor of the Exchequer, he was a respected and trusted Leader of the Commons.

Grey entrusted the drafting of the English Reform Bill to a committee of four Whigs. The resulting reform scheme contained three elements: a redistribution of seats from depopulated 'rotten boroughs', controlled by patrons, to newer towns; a reform of the franchise; and the redrawing of constituency boundaries.[83] Grey favoured a bold scheme that would provide a final settlement and restore public confidence in Parliament. However, he was not against alterations that 'would not destroy its character and efficiency', thus displaying his pragmatism as well as principle.[84]

---

80 Hansard, 52–3, 2 November 1830.

81 Earl Grey to Princess Lieven, 16 November 1830, in G. Le Strange ed., *Correspondence of Princes Lieven and Earl Grey*, London, R. Bentley, (three volumes) 1890, Vol. 2, p. 121.

82 J. Parry, *The Politics of Patriotism: English Liberalism, National Identity and Europe, 1830–1886*, Cambridge, Cambridge University Press, 2006, p. 47.

83 For the details of the reform bills and the changes, see P. Salmon, 'The English Reform Legislation, 1831–1832', in D. R. Fisher ed., *History of Parliament: The House of Commons, 1820–32*, Cambridge, Cambridge University Press, (seven volumes) 2009, Vol. 1, pp. 374–412.

84 Grey to Lieven, 28 February 1831, in Le Strange, op. cit., p. 176.

Shortly before the first English Reform Bill was introduced in March 1831, Grey confidently wrote: 'I have strength enough for this fight, and with the support of the King and the people, I cannot but think I have a good chance of victory.'[85] His skill in dealing with both the monarch and the people was to be a major factor in getting the Reform Bill through an unreformed Parliament, and, some historians have suggested, averting a revolution.[86] The first Reform Bill was defeated on a wrecking amendment in the Commons in April 1831. Grey moved swiftly to persuade William IV to dissolve Parliament in person, and the following general election was essentially a referendum on reform – a 'revolutionary' move, according to one historian.[87] The election results strengthened Grey's hand and gave him a two-to-one majority in the Commons in favour of reform.

While Grey did not actively stoke public support for reform, there is no doubting his popularity during the reform agitation. Caricatures, portraits, medals, banners and political ceramics presented him and other Whig leaders as the 'invincible champions' of reform.[88] His government did nothing to suppress the pro-reform political unions that had been formed across the country, provided they stayed within legality. The battle now shifted to the House of Lords, which rejected the second Reform Bill in October 1831, sparking riots in Derby, Nottingham and Bristol. In the Lords, Grey reiterated his willingness to accept reasonable amendments and hinted that the country would not be at peace until the measure was passed.[89] To circumvent the Lords' opposition, Grey extracted a secret pledge from the reluctant King that he would create sufficient peers to enable the bill to be passed. At the same time, Grey faced pressure from moderates within the Cabinet to water down the third and

85   Grey to Lieven, 3 March 1831, ibid., p. 181.

86   E. Royle, *Revolutionary Britannia? Reflections on the Threat of Revolution in Britain, 1789–1848*, Manchester, Manchester University Press, 2000, pp. 74–9.

87   Ibid., p. 69.

88   H. Miller, *Politics Personified: Portraiture, Caricature and Visual Culture in Britain, c. 1830–1880*, Manchester, Manchester University Press, 2015, p. 36.

89   Hansard, 867–8, 26 March 1832; Hansard, 26, 9 April 1832.

final Reform Bill and come to a compromise with the 'waverers' – Tory peers who sought a settlement.

In the event, when the Lords passed a wrecking amendment against the third Reform Bill in May 1832, the King refused to create sufficient peers, and Grey's government resigned. Grey refused to let the Reform Bill be 'cut, carved, mutilated, and destroyed'.[90] Amid rumours of mounting popular unrest, Wellington failed to form a government to pass a compromise reform measure, and Grey's ministry was restored. Pressing home his advantage, Grey resumed office with a written guarantee from William IV to create peers to secure the passing of the bill, with the precise number to be determined by the Cabinet. This proved enough to face down the Lords, who passed the bill without further amendment. Although the creation of peers was unnecessary, the pledge was used as a precedent by Asquith's Liberal government during the debates on the 1911 Parliament Bill in the Lords.

Radicals at the time, and historians since, have argued that the 1832 Reform Act was a conservative measure. In an influential study, Norman Gash argued that the post-reform electoral system differed little from the unreformed period.[91] Another popular critique is that the act enfranchised the middle classes but not the working classes. Yet Grey's Cabinet, one of the most aristocratic of the nineteenth century, never claimed to be introducing democracy. The act was not intended to simply extend the franchise. Although £10 householders were given the vote in towns, existing non-resident voters lost their votes, and others who did not pay local taxes were also disenfranchised. The act intended to purify and, to a degree, standardise the franchise to ensure that voters had a real stake in their constituency. In focusing on the franchise clauses, historians have missed the wider significance of the 1832 Reform Act.[92] By disenfranchising rotten boroughs, enfranchising new towns and dividing geographically large constituencies, the act made the political system more responsive, representative

90   Hansard, 766, 9 May 1832.
91   N. Gash, *Politics in the Age of Peel*, London, Longmans, 1949, p. x.
92   Salmon, op. cit., p. 411.

and legitimate. The result was to reinvigorate parliamentary government and, as Grey intended, strengthen the attachment between the people and the constitution.[93] No less importantly, the accompanying Boundary Act of 1832 reshaped the electoral geography of Britain. The 1832 English Reform Act, and its Scottish counterpart, ended the Tory monopoly and ushered in an era of Liberal hegemony, leading to a permanent shift in power away from the crown and House of Lords to the Commons.

Grey remains something of a hero in popular accounts of the Reform Bill, but a number of historians have argued that he was increasingly conservative and an impediment to the development of a more constructive and progressive social and religious agenda by younger Whigs like Lord John Russell.[94] Once reform had been passed, Grey's main aim was to preserve Cabinet unity, and he offered little direction. Although important reforms followed, such as the abolition of slavery in the British colonies in 1833, Grey had little to do with them. In truth, his aloof, aristocratic style of leadership was increasingly outdated in the post-reform political climate. For example, Grey continually sought to appease the conservative Lords and King, failing to recognise that power had shifted decisively to the Lower House. The first general election under the Reform Act in December 1832 produced a crushing defeat for the old Tory Party, but Grey now had to deal with a reformed Commons that included many radicals, reformers, Liberals and an Irish party led by Daniel O'Connell. These groups all had their own agendas for the post-reform era, which Grey's government needed to address to retain their support. The government became increasingly divided over religious issues. A number of moderates resigned from the Cabinet in April 1834 over the issue of using the surplus revenues of the Church of Ireland for secular purposes, leaving Grey increasingly isolated. When it was leaked that a junior minister had offered, without higher approval,

---

93   J. Parry, *The Rise and Fall of Liberal Government in Britain, 1830–1886*, New Haven CT, Cambridge University Press, 1993, pp. 78–84.

94   P. Mandler, *Aristocratic Government in the Age of Reform*, Oxford, Clarendon Press, 1990, p. 71; R. Brent, *Liberal Anglican Politics: Whiggery, Religion and Reform, 1830–1841*, Oxford, Clarendon Press, 1987, p. 74.

to amend the Irish Coercion Bill in negotiations with O'Connell in July 1834, a weary Grey resigned.

Grey lived long enough to experience a transformation in his party's fortunes. From being a permanent party of opposition, the Whigs became leaders of a broader Liberal Party that would go on to dominate the Victorian period. As an opposition leader, Grey was frequently absent, lazy, cautious and unwilling to take a lead. However, he preserved the integrity and independence of the Whigs and prevented them from being swallowed up by their Tory opponents through coalition. He also established that the Whig Party rested on fundamental principles, such as constitutional reform, religious tolerance, civil liberty and a foreign policy that encouraged constitutionalism in Europe. All of these ideas and policies provided an important intellectual legacy for the Victorian Liberal Party. Although the founding of the Liberal Party is usually dated to the 1859 meeting at Willis's Rooms, Grey's reform ministry can be seen as the first liberal government, bringing together Liberal Tories and Whigs. There was a strong continuity in personnel between Grey's Cabinet and the Liberal governments of the 1850s. The post-reform period also saw the emergence of a broad Liberal Party consisting of reformers, radicals, and Whigs.[95]

If Grey contributed little to the creation of a post-reform agenda for the party, which was largely left to Russell and other more dynamic, younger Whigs, his achievement in securing the passage of reform should not be forgotten. He skilfully managed the Cabinet, King and public expectations, and, although he was carried along by events, he provided clear, decisive leadership and refused to water down the bill. Reform reinvigorated the representative system, strengthened the attachment between people and Parliament, and paved the way for the formation of modern political parties. Despite his lack of sympathy with the direction of Liberal politics after his leaving office, Grey's public reputation stood very high and was closely associated with the values that were prized in political leaders at the time. As one commentator wrote of Grey in 1836:

95   J. Coohill, *Ideas of the Liberal Party: Perceptions, Agendas and Liberal Politics in the House of Commons, 1832–52*, Oxford, Wiley, 2011; Parry, op. cit., 1993, p. 131.

His high family connections, his great talents, his unimpeachable integrity, his stainless consistency of public conduct, and his known determination and energy of purpose, all concur to invest him with an importance, and give him a weight of character, such as no man of the present day possesses.[96]

96   Grant, op. cit., p. 264.

CHAPTER 5

LORD JOHN (EARL) RUSSELL

TONY LITTLE

'The Last Doge of Whiggism', as William Harcourt described him, Lord John Russell saw himself as the heir to Charles James Fox; he epitomised Whiggism in office for almost thirty-five years. Scion of one of the most powerful aristocratic families, he achieved greatness through his indefatigable battles in Parliament over the years on behalf of the expansion of liberty: he was the principal architect of the Great Reform Act of 1832. A man with a clear vision of the purpose of his class, he proved an effective reforming minister and politician, who facilitated the transition from the Whigs to the Liberal Party; but his two terms as Prime Minister cannot be accounted as a success, and, on each occasion, his government was followed by a Tory administration.

- Lord John Russell (18 August 1792 – 28 May 1878), Earl Russell from 1862, was a younger son of the 6th Duke of Bedford.
- Schooled mostly at home before attending university in Edinburgh.
- Married: (1) Adelaide Lister (1807–38), widow of Lord Ribblesdale, in 1835 (she died in childbirth); (2) Lady Fanny Elliot (1815–78), daughter of Lord Minto, in 1841.
- Two children from first marriage, four from second.
- MP for Tavistock 1813–17, 1818–20, 1830–31, Huntingdonshire 1820–26, Bandon Bridge 1826–30, Devon 1831–32, Devon South 1832–41, London 1841–61.
- Paymaster General 1830–34; Home Secretary 1835–39; Colonial Secretary 1839–41, 1855; Foreign Secretary 1852–53, 1859–65; Cabinet member without office 1853–54; Lord President of the Council 1854–55; special mission to Vienna 1855; Prime Minister 1846–52, 1865–66.
- Publications included a play, a novel, and biographies of Charles James Fox and Lord Russell.

Russell was born prematurely, and, as a result, was slight (shorter than 5ft 5) and frequently in delicate health. His health was the reason he was largely taught by private tutors; it would prove, at times, to be a handicap to his career, but it did not prevent him from attending university in Edinburgh or travelling to the Iberian Peninsula during the Napoleonic Wars. As a teenager, he came under the influence of Lord and Lady Holland, who ran a Whig salon and preserved the legacy of Charles James Fox, Holland's uncle. Russell became an MP early – for a family-controlled borough – but, for the first seventeen years of his political career, the Whigs were in opposition. This provided him with the opportunity for a literary career, which included a biography of his ancestor William, Lord Russell (a protagonist of the exclusion crisis from which the Whigs derived their origins), *An Essay on the History of the English Government and Constitution*, and works of European history.

This combination of influences allowed the development of a coherent political philosophy based on the contemplation of the risks of inflexible authoritarian government. A propertied aristocratic class, such as the Whigs, was, in this view, required to have the standing and the vested interest to hold the executive to account through Parliament. However, their purpose must be to promote civil and religious freedom and responsibility, rather than themselves seeking to monopolise power, even in a good cause. The role of government was to improve or reform institutions to allow this moral purpose to be achieved, and to educate and guide public opinion, which, as the French Revolution had demonstrated, could otherwise be diverted into destructive passions.

As Russell argued as early as 1822, when introducing an unsuccessful Reform Bill:

> History here, too, tells us, that if great changes accomplished by the people
> are dangerous, although sometimes salutary, great changes accomplished
> by an aristocracy, at the desire of the people, are at once salutary and safe.
> When such revolutions are made, the people are always ready to leave in

the hands of the aristocracy that guidance, which tends to preserve the balance of the government and the tranquillity of the state.[97]

He argued for limited change at a time when – as he pointed out – because
of the small electorates in the rotten boroughs, 'a majority of the members of
this House are returned by a body of electors not fully 8,000 in number'.[98]

From this creed, a series of policies flowed. Parliament should be reformed
to prevent it acting solely in the interests of the landed or commercial interests,
and a reformed Parliament should create a framework for more efficient local
government. Education should be provided for all, so that all could understand their moral purpose in society. Toleration was required for Catholics,
Nonconformists and Jews, to prevent the Church of England taking a narrow, monopolistic view of its place in the nation (when Russell first entered
Parliament, those not conforming to Anglicanism could not enter the ancient
universities or certain official occupations, and neither Catholics nor Jews
could sit in the House). The British had a responsibility to spread Liberalism to their neighbours around the world, starting, of course, with Ireland
– joined in union to Great Britain, but suffering even more than England from
discrimination against Catholicism – and then with the colonies.

The period of Russell's political apprenticeship was frustrating for the Whigs,
who were weakly led, poorly organised and lacking a coherent alternative to
Liverpool's repressive Tory government. The passing of Liverpool in 1827,
and, shortly afterwards, of George Canning, opened the way for change; Russell was on hand to exploit it and build his reputation. After Lord Goderich's
brief administration, wracked by divisions over reform and religious policy,
the Duke of Wellington, assisted by Sir Robert Peel, indicated a willingness to
accept some of Russell's proposals to reallocate the worst of the rotten-borough
seats to new expanded industrial towns. These proposals were insufficient for
the Canningite wing of the party, who refused to serve under Wellington, and,

---

97   Hansard, HC deb., 25 April 1822, vol. 7, col. 85–6.
98   The full speech is in Hansard, HC deb., 25 April 1822, vol. 7, col. 51–88.

in due course, Canningites such as Melbourne and Palmerston joined forces with the Whigs.

Having forced electoral reform on to the political agenda, Russell turned to religion. Lord Holland facilitated meetings with politically organised Nonconformists to provide Lord John with the ammunition to propose, in 1828, the abolition of the Test and Corporation Acts. Though frequently ignored in practice, the acts technically restricted official positions to Anglicans. The motion was carried with the unexpected help of some Tories, and, with some modification, repeal was taken over and passed by the government. Shortly afterwards, Wellington's administration passed legislation to emancipate Catholics, in response to Daniel O'Connell's success in securing election in Clare, despite his religious disqualification. Emancipation heightened division among the Tories, while the Whigs utilised parliamentary debates on reform to facilitate alliances with both Canningites and radicals.

As the political elite worried about the overthrow of the French monarchy in 1830, poor harvests, and campaigns by the political unions (which brought together middle-class and working-class supporters of reform), the death of George IV precipitated a general election. Russell narrowly lost his seat and was out of Parliament when Wellington unwisely provoked the defeat of his government by refusing further electoral reform. A Whig government was formed under Lord Grey, including Palmerston and Melbourne. Lord John was offered office as Paymaster General, and his family organised his election for Tavistock. Although a junior minister, outside the Cabinet, Russell was co-opted onto the committee to draft the government's Reform Bill, and his proposals were ultimately preferred by the Cabinet.

Although the Great Reform Act of 1832 was to pave the way to full democracy over the next century, this was by no means Lord John's intention. As Russell had already declared in the Commons in 1822: 'The spirit of Whiggism is to require for the people as much liberty as their hands can safely grasp at the time when it is required.' The country should be given 'what we cannot much longer refuse, without danger to ourselves and ruin to our country', but on the condition that, 'if it could be proved we should obtain the advantages we desire by a lesser change, it would be unwise to attempt a greater'.

The principal focus of the bill introduced by Russell in 1831 was consequently the elimination of the seats with the smallest electorates and their redistribution to Birmingham, Manchester and other more populous areas. Qualifications to vote were regularised and electoral registers introduced; the consequent procedures for securing or objecting to the inclusion of individuals on the register helped to accelerate the formation of party organisation. The secret ballot, however, was rejected, and was not secured until 1872, after Russell's retirement. The Reform Act was only finally passed after a further general election, riots in Derby, Nottingham and Bristol, and government threats to create enough peers to overwhelm the Tory majority in the Lords.

The huge majority bequeathed by the 1832 election, and the licence this gave the Whigs to introduce further reforms, created opportunities for Russell to demonstrate both his skills as a leader, energising the government and managing the measures through the Commons, and his deficiencies, unnecessarily creating crises through ill-chosen words.

Throughout the century, Ireland was to create difficulties for Whig and Liberal governments in their attempts to reconcile the Irish to union with the mainland. In the 1830s, the problem they sought to tackle was the Church of Ireland. It was estimated that the Irish population were 80 per cent Catholic, 10 per cent Presbyterian and 10 per cent (Anglican) Church of Ireland; yet all were obliged to support the established Church. The government agreed that the resources available to the Church exceeded its needs, but differed over the disposition of these funds.

Russell, who was under-occupied as Paymaster General, visited Ireland in 1833 to familiarise himself with its problems, and came to the view that surplus Church funds should be used for Irish education or the payment of Catholic priests. Lord Stanley, the Colonial Secretary previously responsible for Ireland, did not share his views, and threatened to resign. The Cabinet postponed a decision, but, in the Commons, Russell impetuously replied to a hypothetical question confirming his own personal view and publicly revealing the differences between ministers – in Stanley's words, upsetting the coach. Stanley and three other ministers resigned, Stanley joined the Conservatives, and, eventually, as Lord Derby, became their leader. These resignations led, not long afterwards, to Grey's retirement. His replacement Lord Melbourne appointed Russell to succeed Lord Althorp as Leader of the Commons, when Althorp was elevated to the Lords as Earl Spencer, which, in turn, precipitated Melbourne's dismissal by King William IV.

The King's choice of replacement, Sir Robert Peel, did not survive long after Russell negotiated the Lichfield House Compact for the support of the radicals and O'Connell's Irish MPs against the Conservatives. When Melbourne returned to office in 1835, he appointed Russell as Home Secretary, as well as Leader of the Commons, giving him the scope to contrast his humanitarian administration with that of previous repressive Tory governments. Lord John limited the range of crimes to which the death penalty applied, instituted a prison inspectorate, and separated youthful offenders from adults. He obtained a pardon for the Tolpuddle Martyrs, who had been transported to Australia for trade union activity, and responded calmly to the first wave of Chartist activity, rather than resorting to emergency legislation.

The principal domestic legislation – the Municipal Corporations Act, introduced by Russell in 1835 – rationalised local government as a counterpart to the Reform Act, establishing ratepayer-elected councils, with powers, for example, to set up police forces, install drainage or undertake street-cleaning. Although, like the Reform Act, this was a moderate measure dealing mainly with the worst abuses, and leaving considerable room for further improvement in local government, like that act, it was highly partisan – designed to undermine a Tory near-monopoly of local corporations. Russell was proving himself a polarising politician, energising not just his own side but also the opposition.

The Conservatives continued to meddle in most of Russell's reforms, principally through the Lords; few proposals reached the statute book without amendment. Tory peers proved particularly obstructive over Ireland, where Russell was unable to appropriate Church revenues for alternative uses. Nevertheless, he continued to ameliorate the Catholic position through administrative adjustments, such as the appointment of Irish Catholic magistrates and police-men, through which he retained the loyalty of O'Connell. He did rather better for the English Nonconformists, commencing the reform of tithes, legalising mar-riage ceremonies in Nonconformist chapels, and instituting a national register of births, marriages and deaths to replace the purely Anglican parish registers. He attempted to initiate a national system of primary education but was defeated by the vested interests of the Anglican schools, consoling his supporters with the first centralised government committee to oversee the distribution of the then modest government funds for schools. This committee of the Privy Council grew into a Cabinet committee, and, serviced by energetic senior civil servants, became the predecessor to an education ministry and introduced school inspectors.

When another election was required in 1837, following the death of William IV, the government's achievements were insufficient to maintain the scale of its majority, and, since parliamentary support continued to erode over the next four years, the radicalism of the government, though not of Lord John, continued to wane. For Lord John, there was a greater tragedy when his wife died follow-ing the birth of his second daughter, and, for some months, he withdrew from politics. In 1839, Russell transferred to the Colonial Office; he annexed New Zealand, ended the role of New South Wales as a penal colony, and steered the union of Upper and Lower Canada through Parliament.

Political parties during the period were very far from cohesive; it has been estimated that, between 1835 and 1837, 'nearly three-quarters of the govern-ment's supporters voted against it on more than 10 per cent of occasions'.[99] Russell was to play a key role in the slow transition to a more disciplined party system through a protracted period of confusing debate and realignment. As the Lichfield House Compact had demonstrated, he was conscious of the need to conciliate the other forces of what was to become the Liberal Party, alongside the Whigs. He was also clearly aware of the perpetual tendency of progres-sive parties to shake loose their supporters: 'That very old difficulty of Whig

---

99 T. A. Jenkins, *The Liberal Ascendancy, 1830–1886*, London, Macmillan, 1994, p. 36 (citing the work of Ian Newbould).

administrations that their friends expect them to do more than is possible; so that if they attempted little, their friends grow slacker, and if they attempt much, their enemies grow strong.'[100] But he was not necessarily the man best equipped for the task. His shyness and taciturnity could easily be seen as aloofness and aristocratic hauteur. If, as he frequently demonstrated, he was prepared to act without consulting Cabinet colleagues, what contribution could more distant allies expect to make? Nevertheless, Russell's service in Melbourne's government clearly established him as the successor to the leadership of the Whigs. Furthermore, he had put down a marker for the future when he reached out to those radicals who followed Cobden and Bright – the founders of the Anti-Corn Law League – by tabling proposals on the corn duty as one of the final acts of the Melbourne government.

A few weeks before the Melbourne ministry fell, in 1841, Russell remarried. Lady Fanny Elliott took on the four children from Adelaide Lister's first marriage and the two daughters Adelaide bore to Lord John, while she and Lord John added four more children to the family. Despite an age difference of more than twenty years, the marriage was happy, although she was not considered by contemporaries to be a political asset. Critics thought her family was too greedy for the government posts at the disposal of a Prime Minister, and even she described herself as too willing to say what she thought. In the absence of a department to run, Russell resumed his literary career, and, while Lord John and Fanny were happy entertaining fellow authors, Lady Russell could not compete with Lady Waldegrave or, more particularly, Lady Palmerston as a political hostess at a time when such entertaining was vital for gathering intelligence, flattering potential allies and neutralising internal enemies.

Russell was obliged to wait for Peel's Tory government to run into trouble; almost inevitably, that trouble originated in Ireland. Peel was nothing like as conciliatory as Lord John had been to the Irish majority, but, in 1845, he proposed an increase in the grant for the Catholic Maynooth seminary, leading to a major rebellion in his own ranks; the grant could only be carried with Whig

---

100   Cited in Ian Newbould, *Whiggery and Reform*, Stanford, Stanford University Press, 1990, p. 212.

votes. Coming after what had been seen as Peel's U-turn in 1829 over Catholic emancipation, Maynooth permanently alienated a section of his followers.

His treachery was completed later in the year. By 1845, the Anti-Corn Law League had won the intellectual argument among Liberals and a significant element of Conservative ministers, though, naturally, not among the farmers or their representatives in the Conservative Party. When news of the failure of the Irish potato crop began to arrive in London in autumn 1845, Peel's Cabinet was divided over reducing duties on corn to help meet the emergency. Russell pre-empted them in a letter from Edinburgh – written without consulting any of his colleagues – advocating immediate repeal. When this precipitated Peel's resignation, Russell's failure to consult his colleagues in fact proved providential: he could not persuade enough of them to serve together and was forced to give up the attempt to form a government. Peel was obliged to return to office and, with Liberal votes, reformed the Corn Laws against the opposition of his own party, led by Disraeli and Bentinck. The resultant fracturing of the Tories kept them mostly out of power for a generation and was instrumental in the formation of the Victorian Liberal Party, which eventually absorbed its Peelite free-trade component.

Shortly after Peel's bill was enacted, Tory rebels combined with the Liberals and the Irish to defeat the Irish Coercion Bill, bringing Peel down. By then, Russell had conferred with his colleagues and was able to construct a Cabinet including Palmerston and Charles Grey – the source of his earlier problems. Russell took office for the first time as Prime Minister in June 1846.

Russell's first government has not had a good press. In part, this is because the Conservative break-up proved permanent, and the fate of its components proved a more attractive subject for investigation than the more mundane activities of Peel's successor. In part, economic circumstances turned unfavourable, with a financial crisis in 1848, against the background of a resurgence of Chartism, and revolutionary activity on the continent and in Ireland. But it is also, in part, because Russell's administration never had a majority or the scope for heroic action. Alongside the Whigs, Russell could only hope for the intermittent support of the independent Liberals and a variety of radicals, who did not always agree among themselves. Ireland elected 105 MPs – some of whom represented Conservative or O'Connellite positions, and, some, the many varieties of Liberalism found in England. In addition, there were the Peelites, who theoretically held the balance of power, but whose leader gave no clear sense of direction beyond his desire to prevent the protectionist Tories from taking office; Russell was unable, at this stage, to persuade the Peelites to join him.

Consequently, Russell's government had to be opportunist, tailoring its proposals to whatever Parliament would tolerate, and, as with legislation limiting factory hours for women and children in 1847, taking advantage of bills put forward by backbenchers. In education, Russell was able to negotiate some state funding for Catholic and Nonconformist schools, and grants towards the funding of teachers (rather than just buildings) and improved teacher-training arrangements. The government completed the abolition of the Corn Laws, rationalised the sugar duties, and, in 1849, abolished the Navigation Acts (which had restricted the use of foreign shipping for British trade), extending further the country's commitment to free trade. Central control over the administration of the Poor Law was rationalised, though it was never made as humanitarian as its critics would like, or as cheap as economists hoped. Similarly, the government established a central board of health in 1848, and encouraged the establishment of local boards with powers to provide paving, water and drainage and to inspect food quality and lodging houses. This prepared the way for future action, but the legislation was only permissive, and few local authorities seized the opportunity, since no central funding was available.

Russell's government can be cleared of the exaggerated claims by some US politicians of genocide in Ireland, but its response to the famine was inadequate. Peel's actions in 1845 had provided short-term relief, but the repeated failure of the potato crop in the following years meant starvation on a mass scale. Accurate figures are not available, but estimates suggest that possibly one million people died, and a further million emigrated. Russell's intention was to provide relief without creating dependency, to ensure that the better-off Irish landlords fulfilled their responsibilities, and to guarantee that reforms would prevent any future recurrence of famine. But different parts of the government took different views of how this could be achieved; Parliament vetoed parts of the programme, and inadequate administration within Ireland, in both the public and charitable sectors, thwarted even the best of intentions.

Initially, the primary focus was on paid job-creation programmes, though it was recognised that the scale could not be adequate while Parliament frustrated proposals that might have been valuable, but would have benefited private interests. This was followed by the extension of the English Poor Law arrangements to Ireland, but the qualification for relief left the poor with no prospects of future recovery. Direct food relief through soup kitchens was provided – only on a temporary basis – but inadvertently helped to spread disease. Efforts to make the better-off Irish pay for poor relief through the rates were only partially successful. Land reform was intended to bring in new capital to farming, but, inevitably, respect for property rights frustrated the radicalism of the proposals, and, predictably, the approach was too long-term to deal with the immediate problem of starvation.

Russell's biographer criticises his 'inability to apply himself regularly and steadily to the problem at hand'. He 'tried to guide his colleagues by hasty judgements, whose limitations were exposed by the first objection', though he 'handled his Cabinet as a committee of friends and equals, and good humour predominated'.[101] Such traits left him vulnerable if mistakes were made.

Although the 1847 election improved the Liberal position, the government still enjoyed no reliable majority, and, even after Peel died in 1850, the Peelites did not resolve to take a side. Russell and his colleagues needed to increase their popularity. In the 1850 Don Pacifico debate, Palmerston's oratorical assertion of Britain's right to protect its citizens anywhere in the world positioned the Whigs well to capitalise on pride in nation and empire, but reinforced Palmerston's tendency to act independently of colleagues or convention.[102]

In the same year, Lord John sought to reinforce the government's Protestant popularity, writing a letter to the Bishop of Durham attacking the decision of the Pope to restore a geographical-based diocesan structure in England. Although

---

101   John Prest, *Lord John Russell*, London, Macmillan, 1972.

102   'Civis Romanus Sum', Viscount Palmerston on foreign policy, House of Commons, 25 June 1850, in Duncan Brack and Tony Little eds, *Great Liberal Speeches*, London, Politico's, 2001.

reinforced by the Ecclesiastical Titles Act, carried with Tory assistance, Russell's move was a mistake, appalling his own latitudinarian colleagues (whom he had not consulted), the high-minded High Church Anglicans among the Peelites, and the Irish Catholic MPs. His next mistake, though an unavoidable one, was to sack Palmerston in the autumn of 1851 for officially recognising Louis Napoleon's coup in France without consulting either Russell or the Queen. In February 1852, Palmerston had his revenge by arranging Russell's defeat on an amendment to the Militia Bill. The government resigned, and Lord Derby formed a short-lived minority Conservative administration, which was destroyed by the Peelite Gladstone's attack on Disraeli's Budget.

Thanks to the Durham letter, Russell found himself poorly placed to form a government that needed to include the Irish and the Peelites. Persuaded by his brother, he consented to accept office as Leader of the Commons under the premiership of the Peelite Lord Aberdeen, initially also taking the Foreign Office, while Palmerston was berthed safely away from the Queen in the Home Office. Although the Aberdeen coalition brought together the forces that were to form the Liberal Party in 1859, the fusion of 1852 proved premature and unable to withstand the strains of a European war. The government drifted into war against Russia in the Crimea in 1854, in alliance with France and Austria, but its objectives were unclear, and the military administration and leadership incompetent. By the time the ministry's military failings had been exposed in *The Times*, and the radical MP Roebuck had tabled a critical motion in Parliament, Russell had been rebuffed in his attempts to remove the senior Peelite Newcastle from the War Office, and, since he was unwilling to defend the government against Roebuck, he resigned. Again, Russell had been right in his intentions, but exceedingly clumsy in his actions. His desertion of the ministry made it impossible for him to construct a replacement government from the same colleagues, and made it unavoidable for the more belligerent Palmerston to become Prime Minister.

For the next few years, the rivalry between Russell and Palmerston persisted, with Palmerston holding the upper hand, but Russell retaining the capacity to undermine him. After accepting Cabinet office under Palmerston in February 1855, Russell was forced to resign five months later, finding himself caught in the political cross-currents of negotiating the Crimean peace settlement. Embittered and hostile, he nursed a lingering resentment against his former colleagues. When Palmerston gagged his education reform proposals in April 1856, Russell became, one Whig observed, 'a concentrated essence of lemon'.[103] Russell had his revenge, combining with the Manchester radicals and the Peelites to defeat Palmerston's government over the Second Opium War in 1857, helping to force its resignation the following year and colluding to prolong the life of Derby's second minority government.

The 1859 general election saw an improvement in Derby's position, however, and underlined the necessity for a reunion of the liberal forces. The outbreak of war between France and Austria over the future of Italy, and Derby's apparent sympathy for Austria's position against Italian nationalism, provided the pretext. After negotiations, Russell and Palmerston declared to the famous meeting of Whigs, Peelites and radicals in Willis's Rooms on 6 June 1859 their mutual willingness to serve under the other in order to bring down Derby; the meeting is generally held to mark the formation of the Liberal Party.

The Queen attempted to avoid the choice between the 'two terrible old men' by sending for Lord Granville, but, in the end, selected Palmerston as the lesser evil. Russell served as Foreign Secretary until Palmerston's death in 1865. It was during this period that he was elevated to the House of Lords as Earl Russell, to relieve the stresses to his health inherent in the Commons. During the 1859–65 government, Palmerston and Russell worked together surprisingly well, consulting each other and using government despatches to preach Whiggish virtues to the world. Together, they just about avoided the calamity of backing the wrong side in the American Civil War – though neither was blameless for Britain's impotent posturing over Prussia's invasion of Schleswig-Holstein in 1864.

Russell took office as Prime Minister for the second time in October 1865. His career ended as it had begun: with electoral reform. In Melbourne's government, Russell had defended the 1832 Reform Act with such vigour that he

---

103   Holland to Brougham, 14 July 1856 (Brougham Mss. 16295), cited in Angus Hawkins, *Parliament, Party and the Art of Politics, 1855–59*, Stanford, Stanford University Press, 1987, p. 34.

had earned the nickname 'Finality Jack', but, by 1865, he had long since conceded that further expansion of the electorate would be both safe and desirable.
Unsuccessful attempts to bring in new reform bills were made in 1851–52, 1854
and 1859–60. So, when Russell formed his second government, with Gladstone
as Leader of the Commons, it was no surprise that he again committed himself
to reform as his prime task. However, it was to take a politician more Machiavel-
lian than either Russell or Gladstone to navigate the bill through the Commons
– a politician such as Disraeli.

In the 1865 election, Palmerston had bequeathed Russell an increased majority, and, although many Liberals had espoused reform in their election addresses,
not all meant it or were prepared to sacrifice themselves in the consequent redistribution of constituencies. A group of Whiggish MPs joined the Tories to defeat
Russell's bill and bring an end to his government, just eight months after he had
taken office.

In the end, the Whig rebels were betrayed by Disraeli, whose own Reform
Act of 1867 was more radical than Russell's – though this attempt at 'Tory
democracy' did not prevent the Liberals decisively winning the 1868 election.
Russell did not officially retire and may have been disappointed not to have
been included in Gladstone's first Cabinet. He remained active in the Lords,
proposing universal primary education and discussing reforms to the Church
of Ireland with Gladstone – both issues taken up by the new premier after 1868.
Russell died in 1878.

In 1869, the magazine *Vanity Fair* carried a cartoon portrait of Earl Russell
after he had retired. It was captioned: 'The greatest liberal statesman of modern times' – a worthy tribute to his vision and successes under Melbourne, but
Russell was too impulsive and impractical in judging what was achievable for
it to be a fair verdict.

Rev. Sydney Smith – the Whig cleric and fellow protégé of Holland House
– left two verbal pictures of Russell that better capture his courage and his
commitment to the Liberal cause, but also the impatience and disregard for
his colleagues that often frustrated his ambitions. In a speech, Smith played on
Russell's diminutive stature:

Before this reform agitation commenced, Lord John was over 6ft high. But engaged in looking after your interests, fighting the peers, the landlords and the rest of your natural enemies, he has been so constantly kept in hot water that he is boiled down to the proportions in which you now behold him.[104]

Later, Smith wrote:

There is not a better man in England than Lord John Russell; but his worst failure is that he is utterly ignorant of all moral fear; for there is nothing he would not undertake. I believe he would perform the operation for the stone, build St Peter's, or assume (with or without ten minutes' notice) the command of the Channel Fleet; and no one would discover by his manner that the patient had died, the church tumbled down, and the Channel Fleet had been knocked to atoms. I believe his motives are always pure, and his measures often able; but they are endless, and never done with that pedetentous[105] pace and pedetentous mind in which it behoves the wise and virtuous improver to walk. He alarms the wise Liberals; and it is impossible to sleep soundly while he has command of the watch. Do not say, my dear Lord John, that I am too severe upon you. A thousand years have scarce sufficed to make our blessed England what it is; an hour may lay it in the dust; and can you with all your talents renovate its shattered splendour, can you recall back its virtues, can you vanquish time and fate? But alas! You want to shake the world, and be the Thunderer of the scene![106]

---

104 Cited in D. Englefield et al., *Facts about the British Prime Ministers*, London, Mansell, 1995, p. 161.
105 Proceeding step by step or cautiously.
106 Second letter to Archdeacon Singleton, 1838.

CHAPTER 6

LORD MELBOURNE

ELLIS WASSON

William Lamb began his political apprenticeship in the House of Commons between 1806 and 1828. He accomplished little. His disastrous marriage with the tempestuous Lady Caroline Ponsonby undermined his confidence. A protective mask of indifference and flippancy slipped over his public persona. This has led some historians to underestimate his considerable achievements as Home Secretary (1830-34) and Prime Minister (1834-41) after he succeeded to the title Viscount Melbourne. During the later 1830s, by both happenstance and design, he became the father of the Liberal Party.

- William Lamb, 2nd Viscount Melbourne (15 March 1779 - 24 November 1848), probably the son of the 3rd Earl of Egremont and the wife of the 1st Viscount; born into a Whig family of comparatively recent origins.
- Educated at Eton, Cambridge and the University of Glasgow.
- Married, disastrously, Lady Caroline Ponsonby in 1805 (she died 1828).
- MP Leominster 1806, Haddington Burghs 1806–07, Portarlington 1807–12, Peterborough 1816–19, Hertfordshire 1819–26, Newport (Isle of Wight) 1827, Bletchingley 1827–28.
- Succeeded to the House of Lords 1828. Chief Secretary for Ireland 1827–28, Home Secretary 1830–34, Prime Minister 1834 and 1835–41.

Melbourne was born into a family of little lineage. A mid-eighteenth-century barrister and a successful moneylender between them built up a huge fortune. The latter's son gained a peerage, and his son became Prime Minister. The Whig elite embraced the Lambs.

Melbourne attended Eton and Cambridge. Later, he was sent to a Scottish university to hone his brain. For the rest of his life he was a serious reader, with wide-ranging intellectual interests. His most influential mentor was Charles James Fox. The Whigs saw themselves as trustees of the people and protectors of liberty against the crown. They believed in progress and the march of the mind, although Melbourne was never in a hurry.

Given Melbourne's formidable defence mechanisms, the great question has always been: did he have *any* political principles? He was, by nature, undogmatic – perhaps a little afraid, even contemptuous, of the passion that some men brought to the arena of ideas. However, he respected sincerity and instinctively moved to the centre when he could. At the same time, he had imbibed the fundamental Whig notion that reactionaries who drew red lines to defend positions that had lost the support of the political nation were not only fools, but also endangered the fabric of the constitution and the country. What justification was there for an aristocracy unless it was useful and disinterested, active on behalf of everyone?

Although many of the positions espoused by the Liberal Tory George Canning in the 1820s made sense to Lamb, he was never a Canningite, nor did he ever consider himself a Conservative.[107] He was somewhat closer to William Huskisson after the latter took the lead among 'centrists' upon Canning's death in 1828, but no formal allegiance existed. Along with a number of moderate Whigs, Lamb took office in the coalition government in 1827, but he resigned after Wellington became Prime Minister.

Lord Melbourne accepted Earl Grey's offer to join the reform administration in 1830. The Prime Minister needed ballast in a Cabinet that contained a Tory,

---

107   Peter Mandler, *Aristocratic Government in the Age of Reform: Whigs and Liberals, 1830–1852*, Oxford, Oxford University Press, 1990, p. 106.

mercurial radicals such as Henry Brougham and Lord Durham, and liberal men of substance, who had no office-holding experience, like Viscount Althorp, the new Leader of the House of Commons.

The ministry was a coalition, but two men made the key decisions – Grey and Althorp. Their resignations were the only ones that could cause its dissolution. Both were Whigs. Grey was deeply rooted in the Rockingham/Fox tradition of the previous century; Althorp came from a younger generation scarred by years of Tory reaction. Melbourne fell somewhere in between. He was not an enthusiast for wholesale parliamentary reform, espousing a Burkean preference for piecemeal change. However, he shared his friend Lord Palmerston's opinion that constitutional reconstruction was necessary. To join the party of resistance with Wellington and Peel was 'to jump off Westminster Bridge'.[108]

The Whigs are often seen as too aristocratic and conservative. They understood, however, that commercial and intellectual changes had taken place. The 1830s and 1840s were years of disruption and economic dislocation. The question that divided those who remained 'Whigs' and those who began to call themselves 'Liberals' was about the pace of change, not about accommodating 'progress' and 'improvement'.[109]

Melbourne is best known in these years for his involvement with two issues. The first was his resolute response to serious rural disturbances in southern England. The Home Secretary supported local magistrates in maintaining order. He had no interest, however, in framing coercive measures or calling out the army, which Tory governments had resorted to in the years after the French Revolution. Destroyers of property were treated harshly, which one would expect from a regime dominated by landowners. He was also aware, however, that the support of both the King (William IV was never an enthusiastic reformer) and the majority of landowners (parliamentary reform had to pass through the House of Lords to become law) were necessary for the Grey government to accomplish its

---

108   Michael Brock, *The Great Reform Act*, London, Hutchinson, 1973, p. 108.

109   For the term 'Liberal', see: Parry, op. cit., 1993, pp. 1 (n. 1), 353 (n. 11); Norman Gash, *Reaction and Reconstruction in English Politics 1832–1852*, Oxford, Clarendon Press, 1965, pp. 165–6.

aims. Criminal charges were brought against machine breakers, but Melbourne also requested farmers to hire more labourers in the winter months and called on landlords to help their tenantry.

The second issue Melbourne confronted was the Reform Bill itself. He did not like it. Yet, when the more radical members of the Cabinet constructed what conservatives regarded as a revolutionary measure, he did not resign. When confrontations in both Houses rocked Parliament to its foundations, and the quailing King was forced to promise, if necessary, to flood the upper chamber with a mass creation of Whig peers, Melbourne stayed loyal to the Prime Minister. He told Queen Victoria in 1839: 'I saw it was unavoidable.'[110]

Near the end of his tenure at the Home Office, Melbourne was again confronted with threatening developments in rural districts. His name is associated with the Tolpuddle Martyrs of 1834. Recent research shows that Melbourne's involvement was modest. The prosecutions stemmed not from a governmental initiative, but from the determination of local magistrates to stamp out trade unionism among agricultural workers in Dorset. The Home Office was at first lukewarm. Finally, Melbourne endorsed the crackdown. What eventually persuaded him to take notice of the magistrates' pleas for support was the administration of secret oaths. These violated existing law, not, he warned the JPs, the trades unions themselves.[111]

In 1834, Lord Grey's insistence on harsh coercive measures to maintain order in Ireland precipitated a Cabinet crisis fatal to his government. The Prime Minister retired and recommended Melbourne to the King as his successor. The liberal Lord Althorp was a more natural choice as leader of a ministry sanitised by the removal of its right-wing and centre-right members. William IV, however, asked Melbourne to open discussions with Peel and Wellington about forming a coalition government. The Home Secretary's reply to the King was a rap over the royal knuckles. 'Would it be fair in V[iscoun]t Melbourne', he wrote,

110 Brock, op. cit., pp. 208–9.

111 Roger Wells, 'Tolpuddle in the Context of English Agrarian Labour History, 1750–1850', in John Rule ed., *British Trade Unionism, 1750–1850: The Formative Years*, London, Longmans, 1988; Malcolm Chase, *Early Trade Unionism: Fraternity, Skill, and the Politics of Labour*, Ashgate, Aldershot, 2000.

'to offer to these distinguished individuals the appearance of a negotiation, in which V[iscoun]t Melbourne would have everything to demand, and nothing to concede?'[112] There was no common ground to be occupied. The unhappy monarch had to shuffle towards a Whig administration with Melbourne in the lead, but 'cautioning him against the admission of persons with visionary, fanatical or republican principles'.[113]

It is true that Melbourne became Prime Minister because he was not Althorp, who the King feared was too radical. What is important to note is the firmness of his rejection of a coalition. Melbourne was no 'movement' man (a term used to describe the far left in the Commons), but he was ready to work with radicals and even the Irish nationalists, led by Daniel O'Connell. Unlike Grey, his lips did not curl with distaste when O'Connell's name was mentioned. More than that, Melbourne believed in progressive government and further reform. He chose Althorp as his second in command, and Althorp became a loyal lieutenant. 'I consider [Melbourne's] judgement', he said, 'better than that of all the rest of us put together.'[114]

The new government was hardly afloat when it sank. The death of Althorp's father removed the Leader of the Commons to the Lords. The King claimed that Melbourne had told him Althorp was the rock upon which the ministry rested. The last dismissal of a government by a monarch in British history unfolded. The reason for precipitate royal action was the news that Melbourne's nominee to replace Althorp was Lord John Russell, who supported secular appropriation of surplus revenues of the Irish Church – in the eyes of conservatives, a step towards the subversion of not only Anglicanism in Ireland, but also the religious establishment in England as well. Melbourne made it clear to the King at his dismissal interview that he also fully supported the lay appropriation measure.

The King made arrangements for Sir Robert Peel and the Duke of Wellington to form an administration and hold an election. The Tories failed to gain

112   Melbourne memorandum to William IV, 10 July 1834 (Peel MS, BL, Add. MS 40404 f. 201).

113   E. A. Smith, *Lord Grey, 1764–1845*, Oxford, Clarendon Press, 1990, p. 308.

114   Althorp to Palmerston, 15 January 1834 (Broadlands MS, Southampton UL, consulted unfoliated in West Sussex RO).

sufficient seats in the Commons to retain office. In April 1835, Peel resigned in the face of a challenge over Irish Church appropriation. The desperate King once more tried to construct a coalition government. He claimed appropriation might violate his coronation oath. Melbourne told him it was non-negotiable, and he would not take office without authorisation to proceed. After much further wriggling, William surrendered.

Lord Melbourne was given to gloomy predictions of disaster. These laments have often misled historians. Although he was by nature slow and cautious, a broad Liberal agenda was enacted by 1841. He had the guts, which Grey lacked, to fire Lords Brougham and Durham, not on political grounds (he appointed men more radical than them to office and chose the more left-leaning Russell, not the more centrist Palmerston, as Leader of the Commons), but because their uncontrolled egos disrupted government business and antagonised the Cabinet. A more productive ministry was the result.

Melbourne began his career as an indifferent speaker, and he was never one to deliver oratorical masterpieces of the kind in which Grey specialised. During his premiership, however, he gave speeches that were effective, and he enjoyed debating his Tory opponents in the House of Lords, winning accolades from his supporters in the Commons and the country. Moreover, Melbourne's fearlessness in confronting the King was essential to the success of the ministry, while his gentle tutelage of the young Victoria after her accession in 1837 won the government support from the first Whig monarch since George II. Melbourne was softer than the brittle Russell, harder than the gentle Althorp, more human and humane than the cerebral Lansdowne, and steadier than the unstable Brougham. He lacked the assurance of Grey and Palmerston, but he had substance, intelligence and judgement.

The crucible of Victorian Liberalism, Jonathan Parry suggests, was the moment Lord Melbourne decided that lay appropriation of Irish Church revenues was the *sine qua non* of his ministry. This commitment in 1834 'was probably the most important single step in the formation of the Liberal Party'.[115] Melbourne made

---

115   Parry, op. cit., 1993, p. 108.

the decision out of conviction, not just to garner Irish MP votes. He asserted that
Parliament had the right to redistribute Church property on behalf of the whole
people, not a sectional group. It symbolised the responsiveness of the reformed
Parliament to Irish needs. It showed the ministry was committed not only to
maintaining order, but also to 'liberty and brotherhood'. Whigs such as Edward
Stanley (later the Tory Prime Minister Lord Derby) were obliged by this policy
to flee to the opposition benches, and all conservatives fiercely resisted the proposal.[116] Lay appropriation also liberated Melbourne from the dead weight of
the King's restraining hand. Within reason, the Prime Minister could now do
what he wished. He commanded a majority in the Commons that lasted seven
years and, after a brief hiatus under Peel, his would become the predominant
party in politics for decades to come.

As John Phillips has demonstrated: 'Reform, act and era, transformed informed
voters into nationally oriented partisans.'[117] The assumption that the aristocratic
Whigs remained separated from radicals and bourgeois Liberals as members
of the exclusive Brooks's Club, mired in outmoded methods of doing business
and ancient family relationships, has been undermined by recent research.[118]
Melbourne rarely led the charge in implementing Liberal reforms, but his methods were inclusive. His conception of party and progress was the antithesis of
Toryism.

It was under Melbourne that the traditional assumption that parliamentary
government was largely executive and administrative was replaced by a more
activist approach. It is true that Melbourne himself said in 1836: 'The duty of a
government is not to pass legislation but to rule.'[119] But legislation flowed from
his administration in an unprecedented stream. His first task was to address
items already in the pipeline, most notably the revisions to the Poor Laws and

116 Ibid., pp. 108–9, 111.

117 John A. Phillips, *The Great Reform Bill in the Boroughs: English Electoral Behaviour 1818–1841*, Oxford, Clarendon Press, 1992, p. 106.

118 Seth Alexander Thévoz, 'The Political Impact of London Clubs, 1832–1868', PhD thesis, University of War-wick, 2013; 'The MPs of Brooks's, 1832–68', in Charles Sebag-Montefiore and Joe Mordaunt Crook eds, *Brooks's 1764–2014*, London, Paul Holberton Publishing, 2013, pp. 39–49.

119 Oliver MacDonagh, *Early Victorian Government, 1830–1870*, London, Holmes & Meier, 1977, p. 5.

municipal corporations' reform. Both were among the most important pieces of legislation of the nineteenth century, and Melbourne was intimately involved in their origins, as Home Secretary, and enactment, as Prime Minister. The first embodied liberal economic theory. The second ended self-electing oligarchic town governments and was, according to Boyd Hilton, 'the supreme achievement of Melbourne's second government'.[120] The Municipal Corporations Act of 1835 went beyond ending oligarchies. It also required borough councils to establish police forces, and the County Police Acts of 1839–40 empowered JPs to establish them as well, and place the cost on the rates.

Reduction of the stamp tax on printed materials by three-quarters took place in 1836. In 1835, there were 35 million stamped newspapers. Fifteen years later, the number was close to 100 million, many of them with a Liberal stance. The ministry also accelerated the spread of news through the introduction of the penny post. Proposals to reform education foundered on the rocks of fierce sectarian rivalries, but the government did succeed in setting up a new education committee of the Privy Council, empowered to make grants and regulate schools, receiving such funding, through inspectors. For the first time, a rival authority to the Church of England in matters of educational policy was established. Legal reforms also included dismantling the old criminal code. Melbourne used the innovative mechanism of royal commissions to investigate social problems, and, in the later 1830s, the management of prisons and children's employment in mines and factories came under review. The idea of a centralised inspectorate established by the 1833 Factory Act was implemented in a variety of other areas. This was a key moment in the use of restrictive legislation to intervene in the economy and relieve injustice.

It is almost impossible to think of any major reform Melbourne left undone that could have passed through the Lords. Even appointment of Treasury clerks by examination was begun in 1838, presaging the revolution in the civil service enacted later in the century. Parry argues:

---

120 Boyd Hilton, *A Mad, Bad, and Dangerous People? England 1783–1846*, Oxford, Oxford University Press, 2006, p. 499.

By 1841, the structural groundwork of Victorian social policy had been laid. Inspectors were reporting, the public mind was exercised [by evidence collected by commissions relating to sanitation, health, education, crime, mines, factories etc.], and elected urban and rural authorities were in place to mirror and capitalise on local interest.[121]

Pressure was imposed on the Church of England to reform itself. In 1835, Melbourne commissioned his ministers to come up with measures to relieve the grievances of Dissenters. This produced a number of bills establishing civil registration of births, deaths and marriages. The attempt to abolish church rates, however, failed. The *Westminster Review* described 'an outbreak of episcopal fury almost unparalleled in the modern annals of ecclesiastical turbulence'.[122] Legislation to admit Dissenters to Oxford and Cambridge was also scuttled. The government then turned to support the foundation of the University of London, where non-Anglicans were admitted.

Melbourne made several important contributions to constitutional development. He helped harden the existing but infrequently tested principle that a government was not obliged to resign upon the passage of a vote of censure in the House of Lords so long as the King and Commons continued to give their support. He was the first Prime Minister publicly to assert the position in 1836.[123] A rebellion in Canada in 1837 prompted the Prime Minister to send Lord Durham out as governor, perhaps as much to remove him from the country as to ameliorate conditions in North America. The end result, however, was the Durham Report, which established a template for self-government in the dominions that helped hold the empire together for another century.

It is claimed the Whigs eschewed efficient organisational management of the Liberal Party in the 1830s.[124] In fact, Melbourne had close and effective

---

121   Parry, op. cit., 1993, p. 127.

122   Gash, op. cit., 1965, p. 72.

123   Hansard, 961, 27 June 1836; Hansard, 478–83, 25 July 1836; Abraham D. Kriegel ed., *The Holland House Diaries, 1831–1840*, London, Routledge, 1977, pp. 343, 394.

124   Ian Newbould, *Whiggery and Reform, 1830–41*, Basingstoke, Macmillan, 1990, p. 24.

working relationships with Althorp and Russell as leaders of the Commons. He appointed Edward 'Ben' Stanley, an able manager, Chief Whip. Perhaps the most celebrated event in the early life of the ministry in 1835 was a meeting held to seize the political initiative before the parliamentary session began. The Prime Minister was not the originator or organiser of the Lichfield House Compact, in which radicals and Irish MPs agreed to support the government. However, he was fully appraised and supportive of the plan. He had already held a much less well known meeting of senior Liberal leaders at his country house in Hertfordshire, including Russell, Hobhouse, Duncannon, Poulett Thomson and the radical Joseph Hume, to make plans and form a committee to organise support for co-ordinated action. He also corresponded directly with O'Connell.

Melbourne understood the crucial importance of the post-1832, more politicised electorate. He put the exceptionally able Joseph Parkes, a radical solicitor from Birmingham, in charge of co-ordinating registration of voters under the reformed system. In May 1835, a Central Reform Association was formed for this purpose. Parkes worked with Ben Stanley on registration and discussed progress with Melbourne. The newly reformed municipalities provided centres of support for Liberalism, which, in the long term, proved invaluable. In addition, the Melbourne administration began to appoint substantial numbers of manufacturers and Dissenters as JPs in urban areas.

Melbourne has been criticised of doing too little to manage the press.[125] In fact, he cultivated relations with various publications and got on well with the radical, hypersensitive editor of the *Morning Chronicle*, John Black, who was made a welcome visitor at Downing Street. The Prime Minister ensured government documents were put at Black's disposal, and influenced the tone of articles. Melbourne also socialised with Sir John Easthope (owner of the *Chronicle*), and he maintained a connection with the editor of the great Whig organ the *Edinburgh Review*.[126]

125 Newbould, op. cit., p. 34.

126 Ellis Wasson, 'The Whigs and the Press, 1800–1850', in Karl Schweizer ed., *Parliament and the Press, 1689–c.1939*, Edinburgh, Edinburgh University Press, 2006, pp. 80–82.

Melbourne's ministry ended in 1841, when the Liberals lost the general election. A serious depression and poor harvests had brought free trade in corn to the fore. The Prime Minister recognised the need to move, but was, as always, inclined to take cautious and incremental steps. He correctly feared the Corn Law issue would hurt the party at the polls, where the landed interest and farmers were still potent. The administration had been making a general assault on high tariffs and announced plans to modify the Corn Laws. Parry argues:

> This strategy marked a seminal development in Liberal politics. To place so directly before the electors a question of direct financial significance to them was a great constitutional innovation. Peel, disgusted, saw it as an open bribe and an incitement to class hatred. But for Liberals, it was not only legitimate but necessary in order to guide agitation and demonstrate government responsiveness. It highlighted Liberals' self-perception as rational defenders of popular rights and interests.

This sent a message to both anti-Corn Law leaguers and Chartists: the government was listening. 'Melbourne did not fall in 1841 because of internal division or government incoherence. He fell because Liberalism was in advance of opinion among the electors who mattered, those who dictated the result in county and small-town seats.'[127] The year 1841 also marked the end of Melbourne's career as a politician. By the time the Liberals returned to power in 1845, he had suffered a stroke and was in serious physical decline, so there was no question of his resuming office.

Some historians see Whig aristocrats like Melbourne as merely defending their own interests or as 'anachronistic survivors, clinging to power for power's sake, without views of their own'.[128] What innovation there was in the party is attributed to Russell, not Melbourne. Others argue that Melbourne and Russell, though old fashioned, transformed an inchoate, unorganised collection

---

127 Parry, op. cit., 1993, pp. 128, 147–8.

128 Donald Southgate, *The Passing of the Whigs, 1832–1886*, New York, St Martin's Press, 1962, pp. 66–8, 72–3, 78, 194; Newbould, op. cit., pp. 8, 316.

of Whigs and Liberals into a unified, organised, more ideologically consistent Liberal Party in the later 1830s and 1840s.[129]

Boyd Hilton points to the core issue of Whig Liberals wanting 'a more inclusive society and less privilege'. In this, the Tories were not with the Whigs, and the radicals were. Both the Whig and radical labels gradually merged into Liberal, whether consciously or unconsciously, or perhaps merely for convenience – but it worked. By embracing the change in the Corn Laws, Melbourne left the Liberal Party 'facing in the right direction'.[130]

Melbourne had many weaknesses. He lost his feel for compromise and conciliation over time. He became out of touch with party sentiment when he spent hours tutoring Queen Victoria. Yet, throughout his premiership, he showed firmness, discretion and good judgement. He did not provide passionate or inspiring leadership. He was very good at getting things done.

T. B. Macaulay noted in April 1834 that the strongest party in the country 'beyond all comparison' was 'the *centre gauche*, the party that goes further than the majority of the present ministry, and yet stops short of the lengths to which [radicals] go. That party is a match for all the other parties in the state together.'[131] Melbourne took the lead of that party and ruled for nearly eight years as its head. When he became Home Secretary in 1830, no such thing as the Liberal Party existed. At his resignation from the premiership in 1841 it was in being. Liberal voters viewing Westminster from a distance saw Melbourne as a 'Whig radical' in the battle against corruption, inefficiency, entrenched privilege and injustice.[132] Sometimes leading, sometimes merely facilitating, Melbourne was the father of Victorian Liberalism.

---

129   Richard Brent, *Liberal Anglican Politics: Whiggery, Religion, and Reform, 1830–1841*, Oxford, Clarendon Press, 1987, p. 16.

130   Hilton, op. cit., pp. 506, 518–19.

131   Thomas Pinney, *The Letters of Thomas Babington Macaulay*, Cambridge, Cambridge University Press, (six volumes) 1974–81, Vol. 3, p. 74.

132   Phillips, op. cit., p. 45.

CHAPTER 7

LORD PALMERSTON

DAVID BROWN

Palmerston dominated early Victorian politics, holding high office, as Foreign Secretary, Home Secretary and Prime Minister for around thirty years between 1830 and 1865. This might, in many ways, be termed the 'Age of Palmerston'. His significance lies not simply in his longevity, however, but in the perception of him as a national, patriotic, hero who, while no enthusiast for democracy, won the hearts of large numbers of the 'people'. A forceful and sometimes divisive figure at Westminster, he drew on this perception of wider support to affirm his continuing relevance. Yet beneath the jaunty image and flamboyant rhetoric lay a serious politician who also did much to secure the ascendancy of liberal principles and values and, as a prominent leader in Parliament and the country at large, did much to lay out and secure the foundations of a Liberal Party.

- Henry John Temple, 3rd Viscount Palmerston (20 October 1784 – 18 October 1865), born in London to Henry Temple, 2nd Viscount Palmerston (1739–1802), a Whig politician, and his second wife, Mary, Viscountess Palmerston (née Mee, 1754–1805).
- Educated at home in Hampshire (the family seat at Broadlands, near Romsey) and London by private tutors until sent to Harrow School in 1795, from where he went on to study at the Universities of Edinburgh (1800–03) and Cambridge (St John's, 1803–06).
- Married Emily Cowper (née Lamb, 1787–1869) in 1839 and is popularly believed to have been the father of three of the five children from her first marriage, to the 5th Earl Cowper (1778–1837).
- Entered Parliament in 1807 as MP for Newport, Isle of Wight, and subsequently sat for the University of Cambridge 1811–31, Bletchingley 1831–32, South Hampshire 1832–35, and finally Tiverton 1835–65.

• Served as Junior Lord of the Admiralty 1807–09, Secretary at War 1809–28, Foreign Secretary
   1830–34, 1835–41, 1846–51, Home Secretary 1852–55, and Prime Minister 1855–58, 1859–65.

enry John Temple, 3rd Viscount Palmerston, defied easy categorisa-
tion. In 1855, one essayist complained:

> The difficulty of daguerreotyping Proteus would be comparable with the
> perplexity of a biographer in attempting a sketch of the career of Henry John
> Temple, Viscount Palmerston. For, though the individuality is, at all stages,
> identical, there are four different personages to deal with – Palmerston, who
> was the raging young Pittite; Palmerston, the adolescing Canningite; Palm-
> erston the juvenile Whig; and Palmerston the attaining-years-of-discretion
> coalitionist. There is none of the Ciceronian symmetry in the career – begin-
> ning, middle, and end; it is all beginning.[133]

Yet when, a decade later, Gladstone observed of Palmerston's passing that 'death
has indeed laid low the most towering antlers in all the forest',[134] there was little
doubt these were the antlers of the Liberal leader. Palmerston's rise to the top
of the Liberal Party, however, is a problematic one: he did not identify himself
as such, nor indeed for much of his career was there obvious agreement about
who or what constituted the Liberal Party.[135] He spent much of his career at
odds with those who were (or have subsequently been seen to be) the heroes of
the party's history, and, while somehow popular, he has not attracted the levels
of widespread interest and attention so often lavished on that apparently arche-
typal Victorian Liberal, William Gladstone.

133   Edward M. Whitty, *The Governing Classes of Great Britain*, London, Trübner and Co., 1854, p. 129.

134   W. E. Gladstone to Sir Anthony Panizzi, 18 October 1865 (Palmerston Papers [hereafter PP], University of
       Southampton, BR22ii/22/6). I am grateful to the University of Southampton Library for permission to repro-
       duce material from these papers.

135   See, for example, David Brown, 'Reform, Free Trade and the Birth of the Liberal Party (1830–1859)', in Dun-
       can Brack and Robert Ingham, eds, *Peace, Reform and Liberation: A History of Liberal Politics in Britain
       1679–2011*, London, Biteback Publishing, 2011, pp. 41–75.

Palmerston's father, the 2nd Viscount Palmerston, had been a well-travelled and well-connected Whig MP, but was always more of a dilettante than a politician, and Palmerston did not grow up in any sort of ideologically charged, or even especially intellectual, household. He was schooled in languages and the classics, first at home by private tutors and later at Harrow School, but – not being descended from a great Whig family or able to lay claim to a recognisable political heritage – he was probably regarded as being destined for a distinguished, if essentially unremarkable diplomatic career, much as his brother William would go on to enjoy. If there was a turning point in Palmerston's early life, it was the decision to send him to the University of Edinburgh, ahead of his anticipated Cambridge career, by way of extending his intellectual development beyond what Harrow could offer. Palmerston's father described sending his son north of the border as offering 'some intermediate situation between school and an English university',[136] yet it was to be much more than that. As Palmerston himself later remembered, it was in Edinburgh at the turn of the century where he had been 'furnished by able hands with charts and compasses, which taught me how to steer my course, to avoid many of the dangers to which the voyage of life is exposed, and to pursue in safety the career I was destined to fill'.[137]

As a student of, and lodger with, Dugald Stewart, the eminent professor of moral philosophy at Edinburgh, Palmerston learned what Stewart called the 'science of the legislator' and, from Stewart's lectures on political economy, Palmerston learned the principles of government, inspired by Scottish (Whig) Enlightenment thought. Government, he was taught, was legitimate only if it accommodated itself to the 'tide of public opinion' and, while this was no recipe for democracy, Palmerston was encouraged to see his privileged position as carrying with it an obligation, and indeed a patriotic duty, to govern his 'fellow creatures' in a manner designed to maximise their happiness. This was, in essence, a prescription for a benevolent compact between governors and

---

136   2nd Viscount Palmerston to Dugald Stewart, 19 June 1800, in Brian Connell, *Portrait of a Whig Peer*, London, André Deutsch, 1957, p. 426.

137   From Palmerston's speech at the University of Edinburgh, April 1863, printed in the *Edinburgh Evening Courant*, 2 April 1863 (PP, BR206/2).

governed, but one founded not only on a sense of moral justice, but also flexibility – acknowledging that society was not static, but, indeed, that it was moving
at a rapid rate.[138]

Although Palmerston's early career did not give formal or overt expression
to these ideals – dependent as he was, following his father's death in 1802, on
the Tory patrons, such as Lord Malmesbury, to whom his father had entrusted
his son's entrée into public life – this is not to say that Palmerston was without political substance. Entering Parliament in 1807 as MP for Newport, Isle
of Wight – on the strict understanding that he 'should never, even for the election, set foot in the place; so jealous was the patron lest any attempt should be
made to get a new interest in the borough'[139] – Palmerston's career developed
in steady if unspectacular fashion. Between 1807 and 1809, he served, as had his
father, as a Junior Lord of the Admiralty, before moving to the War Office as Secretary at War – a post he held until 1828. The Secretary at War was an inferior
post to that of Secretary for War, and brought Palmerston a largely bureaucratic
workload (such as preparing the annual estimates of the army's financial require-
ments and presenting them to Parliament), but, in this role, he proved himself
a conscientious and effective administrator, and learned how to master detail
amid large quantities of paperwork. Though offered the Chancellorship of the
Exchequer in 1827 – an offer Palmerston refused – this was not necessarily a
sign that Palmerston had finally established himself as a politician of the front
rank (the Chancellorship of the Exchequer was not yet the heavyweight office
it has since become), but he was, in that same year, brought into the Cabinet.

Palmerston's elevation to the government front bench, however unremarkable in many respects, brought him forward just as the Tory Party, which had
dominated British politics for so long, was beginning to fracture. Divided over
religious and economic policies, the government was increasingly split between

---

138   On Palmerston's education see: David Brown, *Palmerston: A Biography*, New Haven and London, Yale Uni-
      versity Press, 2010, pp. 1–39; Kenneth Bourne, *Palmerston the Early Years, 1784–1841*, London, Allen Lane,
      1982, pp. 1–47.

139   Palmerston, 'Autobiography', in H. L. Bulwer, *The Life of Henry John Temple, Viscount Palmerston*, London,
      Richard Bentley, (three volumes) 1870–74, Vol. 1, p. 370.

ultra, or traditional, Tories, firm in their loyalty to the established institutions of Church and state, and more liberal elements, led variously by figures such as George Canning, William Huskisson and Robert Peel. With these, and particularly Canning and Huskisson, Palmerston felt an affinity as they spoke of religious toleration (Palmerston had long sat awkwardly with many traditional Tories with his sympathy for the cause of Catholic emancipation and the relaxing of religious bars to public office) and policies to promote free trade. Significantly, it was at this time that Palmerston began to see direct links between what he had been taught by Dugald Stewart and the political climate of the day; or, more specifically, he saw what might be termed Edinburgh answers to some Westminster problems. Entries in his notebooks at this time show Palmerston addressing important questions of political identity, with references to free trade, commerce, religion and politics, liberty, freedom and constitutional government, alongside pieces on Ireland and on slavery, drawing frequently on ideas taken from Stewart's lectures. And in his first major speech on foreign policy, in the summer of 1829, Palmerston highlighted the importance of engaging with public opinion in directing public affairs:

> Those statesmen who know how to avail themselves of the passions, and the interests, and the opinions of mankind, are able to give an ascendancy, and to exercise a sway over human affairs, far out of all proportion greater than belong to the power and resources of the state over which they preside; while those, on the other hand, who seek to check improvement, to cherish abuses, to crush opinions, and to prohibit the human race from thinking, whatever may be the apparent power they wield, will find their weapon snap short in their hand, when most they need its protection.[140]

While some biographers have been tempted to paint Palmerston's switch from Tory to Whig at this time as evidence of opportunism, in fact this was the moment at which the real Palmerston emerged. Two decades of service in Tory

---

140   Hansard, 1643–70, 1 June 1829.

governments represented largely that: an extended period of public service, and not an absence or abnegation of political principle. In the more febrile political atmosphere of the late 1820s, however, Palmerston was obliged to show his hand more openly, and he revealed a set of Whig liberal cards. Palmerston's career from 1830, now harnessed to the Whig carriage, brought him much more clearly into the political limelight. As Foreign Secretary three times between 1830 and 1851 – and for more than fifteen of those twenty-one years, he was in office (1830–34; 1835–41; 1846–51) – Palmerston was able to bring his liberal instincts to bear directly on government policy.

At the Foreign Office, Palmerston aimed to develop a genuinely liberal foreign policy; that is, one that would promote constitutionalism abroad, free trade, peace and stability. In August 1832, for example, he had told the House of Commons that he considered constitutional states 'to be the natural allies of this country',[141] thereby significantly making an explicit connection between policy and ideology. In part, of course, this was also practical: constitutional government, argued Palmerston, was stable government, while the forces of conservatism and reaction were 'the immediate causes of all the revolutions that happen from time to time'.[142] Thus, Palmerston welcomed the ideological division of Europe in the early 1830s, which saw Britain, France, Spain and Portugal drawn into an alliance against Russia, Prussia and Austria. This was, he said, 'western against eastern Europe; the liberal and constitutional against the despotic states', and the rise of a liberal West, he added, would produce 'many results favourable to the civilisation and happiness of mankind ... in due course of time'.[143] And so Palmerston's support for, *inter alia*, constitutionalists in the Iberian Peninsula in the 1830s and 1840s, Poles in the 1840s, Italians in the 1850s and Danes in the 1860s was presented as part of a narrative of liberal progress and the advance of freedom.

---

141 Palmerston, House of Commons, 2 August 1832, in *Opinions and Policy of the Right Honourable Viscount Palmerston*, London, Colburn and Co., 1852, p. 208.

142 Palmerston to Sir Frederick Lamb, 6 April 1833 (Beauvale Papers, British Library [hereafter BL], Add Ms 60464, ff. 81–3).

143 Palmerston to Sir Frederick Lamb, 14 November 1833 (Beauvale Papers, BL, ff. 182–91).

Of course, the rhetorical justifications of policy could hide the pragmatic concessions that were also being made to *realpolitik* interests. The Quadruple Alliance of 1834, which had apparently bound the four western allies into a liberal pact against eastern autocracy, was only something Palmerston sought to promote once it became clear that his attempts to establish a link with Metternich's Austria (one of his 'despotic' states) failed. And one might identify other examples of Palmerston's apparent inconsistency or willingness to privilege strategic interests over liberal idealism; to take but three: if making sure that Russia did not gain ground in the Ottoman Empire meant ignoring demands for partition and reform from within Ottoman territory, then such was a price to pay in the interests of avoiding war. Palmerston's support for Italian independence in the later 1850s was as much about building up a barrier to Austrian power in south-central Europe as any high-minded commitment to Italian independence and freedom. And, later, Palmerston's vacillation in the US Civil War over whether Britain should support the north or south was viewed largely in economic terms; it was, after all, important for trade that Britain be on good terms with whichever side won. This, however, could be presented as a liberal support for states' rights and self-determination when the south appeared to have the upper hand, and as opposition to slavery when the north gained ground later in the conflict, and especially so once Abraham Lincoln had made his Emancipation Proclamation. But whatever concessions were being made to *realpolitik* calculations, Palmerston was arguably sincere in his belief that, in so far as it was possible, it was desirable to encourage liberal government in place of autocratic forms, and give weight to the opinions of those who lived within various states, rather than simply consolidating dynastic and oligarchic interests.

This construction of a narrative of liberal progress in which Britain played a prominent role as a champion of progressive reforms was also intended to appeal to domestic audiences. In advance of democracy at home, Palmerston could cultivate a feeling in the country at large that the people were represented by enlightened ministers and lived within a constitutional state themselves. Thus, Palmerston paid careful attention to journalists and newspapers, seeing in their ever-widening reach a valuable means to reinforce his liberal message. Many of Palmerston's speeches, particularly those that elucidated the (liberal) principles upon which he based his foreign policy, were often disseminated as pamphlets, in hustings performances and in speaking tours around the country. His repeated references to the promotion of constitutional freedom, to free trade and to states' rights, as well as moral causes such as the suppression of slavery and the slave trade, created a powerful image. It made Palmerston popular in the country at large, where audiences increasingly recognised in him a defender of freedoms and a champion of good causes, while at Westminster it gave him considerable political ballast. Rivals such as the Queen and Lord John Russell would find that they could not easily dislodge the 'most English' minister.

Yet, while Palmerston's foreign policy achievements, or actions, have frequently attracted most interest among his biographers, in accounting for his rise to leadership of the Liberal Party, it is important to give just as much weight to his domestic record. While for some he was easily dismissed as pursuing little more than 'crude belligerence abroad and class fear at home',[144] there was a good deal more to Palmerston than this might suggest.

In December 1852, Palmerston was appointed to the Home Office in Lord Aberdeen's new coalition government. After years spent rubbing shoulders with the diplomatic elite, this new post was widely seen as representing a demotion.[145] And yet, while frequently overlooked or treated as relatively insignificant by many of his biographers, Palmerston's Home Office career was, in fact, central to any proper assessment of his political identity and make-up. It gave him a platform from which to demonstrate his commitment to principles of liberal progress in a manner directly relevant to the British people, and to further his claims to the leadership of liberal interests at Westminster.

Far from seeing the Home Office as an unimportant political backwater, Palmerston addressed himself to the work of that department with as much energy as had characterised his work at the Foreign Office. His achievements there,

---

144   John Vincent, *The Formation of the British Liberal Party, 1857–68*, London, Constable, 1966, pp. 141–9, esp. pp. 146–8.

145   D. Roberts, 'Lord Palmerston at the Home Office', *The Historian*, Vol. 31, 1958, p. 63.

however, speak of more than mere industry. He had told his constituents in Tiverton in January 1853 that he had accepted 'that office I was most desirous to fill'.[146] The time had come, he explained to his brother-in-law Laurence Sulivan, to cease playing the part of 'a reckless adventurer' and commit to the cause of 'the great Liberal Party, (not in the H[ouse] of C[om]m[on]s, nor at Brooks's, nor at the Reform Club, but in the United Kingdom'.[147] This professed commitment to 'the great Liberal Party' is important. As Joseph Coohill has demonstrated, these years witnessed the emergence of a coherent Liberal identity at Westminster, strengthened by an increasingly engaged electorate, and it was important for Palmerston to seek to harness those forces that had, increasingly, the character of party about them.[148]

During the life of the government, Palmerston endeavoured to improve working conditions (notably through the introduction of the Factory Act of 1853, which went some way towards improving industrial working conditions, especially for children) and employment rights (for example, bringing in the Truck Act, which entitled workers to payment in money, rather than goods or tokens for employers' own shops). Elsewhere, Palmerston sought to improve the condition of society, both environmentally and morally, with measures such as the Smoke Nuisance Abatement Act of 1853 and reform of the board of health in 1854. He was a supporter of temperance societies, and addressed himself to the problems of prison reform.[149] Even if in these things he was criticised (for example, by evangelical campaigners) for not going further, such measures were nonetheless important in re-directing and shaping government priorities and giving them a liberal tone.

Palmerston's attitude to questions of public health can be seen to have revealed his interest in 'improvement', underpinned by a rationalist view of welfare and science in which the government had an important role to play. When cholera

---

146 *Daily News*, 4 January 1853.

147 Palmerston to Sulivan, 31 December 1852 (PP, GC/SU/34/2).

148 See Coohill, op. cit.

149 On Palmerston's work at the Home Office, see Roberts, 'Palmerston at the Home Office'; Brown, op. cit., pp. 334–80.

struck Britain in the autumn of 1853, for example, Palmerston refused appeals
to address the problem through prayers and fasting, arguing instead this was
not a punishment for man's sins, but rather:

> An awful warning given to the people of this realm that they have too much
> neglected their duty in this respect and that those persons with whom it rested
> to purify towns and cities and to prevent or to remove the causes of disease
> have not been sufficiently active in regard to such matters.[150]

The remedy, then, was in public works, evidence of Palmerston's sense that
a centralised paternalist state could do more to improve the condition of the
people than faith and hope would (and that, for Palmerston, outweighed any
concerns about an overly powerful state). Though the sanitary and public health
reforms achieved during Palmerston's tenure at the Home Office may have been
ultimately unremarkable,[151] Palmerston's determination to tackle the cholera
epidemic at all, and to do so with drains and clean water rather than prayers, is
revealing; it spoke of a genuine commitment to address the 'condition of England' question by direct intervention.

In Parry's narrative of the 'rise and fall' of Liberal government in the Victorian period, it is Palmerston's domestic record, both at the Home Office and
subsequently as Prime Minister in the later 1850s and early 1860s, as much as
his popular ebullient foreign policy that helped establish his claims to leadership of Liberal politics. With Liberal forces in the mid-1850s in need of a
clear focus, Parry discerned three competing strategies: Russellite schemes
for a Liberal–radical coalition based on constitutional and religious reform; a
Peelite-inspired 'programme of economy and good administration'; or, the 'most
successful' in the event, a Palmerstonian third way.[152] The race was essentially
between Lord John Russell and Palmerston, but, as Parry argues, Russell fell

---

150   Henry Fitzroy to W. H. Tweedie, 19 October 1853 (TNA, HO 103/12, ff. 240–41).

151   Roberts, op. cit., pp. 74–5.

152   Parry, op. cit., 1993, p. 170.

at three separate fences: he was not 'sufficiently Prime Minister'; he continued
to embody Whiggish social exclusiveness; and he managed to alienate radical
support through his perceived 'impulsiveness'.[153] Palmerston seemed to offer a
compelling alternative. His bombastic nationalism of the 1840s and early 1850s
had endeared him to a broad cross-section of the population, and his willingness
to stand up to heads of state (including his own) suggested he had the spirit to
provide convincing leadership. He could build on this with a domestic record
that had elaborated on his view of society and government responsibility. It is
against this background that one should read Palmerston's rivalry with Lord
John Russell for the leadership of the Whigs and Liberals in the 1850s. The spats
with Russell, most famously Palmerston's dismissal from Russell's government
at the end of 1851 and his subsequent 'tit-for-tat' defeat of Russell a couple of
months later, were not simple matters of personal conflict, but means by which
two heavyweights separated themselves as Liberal leaders. When he resigned
from the government of Lord Aberdeen in late 1853, Palmerston did so as much
to show he was different from Russell – by allowing the impression to circulate
that the cause of his going was a disagreement over parliamentary reform, which
Russell championed in many ways – as anything else.[154]

It was because Palmerston believed that the state – enlightened, liberal, benevolent – could most effectively determine society's best interest that he never
warmed to arguments about increasing the political rights of the people. Palmerston had only ever been a lukewarm parliamentary reformer. The Reform
Act of 1832 had been a necessary concession, but a final one: thereafter he positioned himself as a stern opponent of further change. But while he was most
certainly not a democrat, that is not to say that he did not recognise a role for
the people in political life. During the winter of 1853/54, for example, Palmerston made quite clear his fear that reform proposals put forward to lower the
property qualification for voters would 'overpower intelligence and property by

---

153 Ibid., pp. 173–5.

154 David Brown, *Palmerston and the Politics of Foreign Policy, 1846–55*, Manchester, Manchester University
      Press, 2002, pp. 183–90.

ignorance and poverty'.[155] Ever suspicious of democratic tendencies, he asked the Prime Minister, Lord Aberdeen: 'Can it be expected that men who murder their children to get £9 to be spent in drink will not sell their vote for whatever they can get for it?'[156] He feared intimidation, manipulation and corruption would increase with the creation of a larger, and necessarily financially poorer and politically illiterate, electorate; but, more seriously, he worried that the stability of the existing, responsible system of representation, in which power was delegated to 'select councils', would be jeopardised by the proposed reforms, and this would undermine the liberal efforts to improve society, such as Palmerston was pursuing at the Home Office.

But if the people were not to be formally enfranchised, they did still have a role in public life, even if that was within a largely virtual sense. While public opinion did not dictate to government, Palmerston told the people of Glasgow in 1853, when ministers earned 'the approbation of their countrymen', they received 'the most ample encouragement to pursue that course, which they have thought for the benefit of the country'.[157] Government in the popular interest, and by a limited but benevolent and enlightened elite, was, therefore, both legitimate and efficient. This should serve as a qualification of simplistic assessments of Palmerston as simply a reactionary anti-democrat. In 1864, he wrote:

> The fact is that a vote is not a *right* but a *trust*. All the nation cannot by possibility be brought together to vote, and therefore a selected few are appointed by law to perform this function for the rest, and the publicity attached to the performance of this trust is a security that it will be responsibly performed.[158]

The argument came straight from Dugald Stewart's lectures, backed by Palmerston's years of parliamentary experience. Of course, that experience, particularly

---

155 Palmerston to Lansdowne, 8 December 1853 (PP, GC/LA/110).

156 Palmerston to Aberdeen, 12 February 1854 (PP, HA/G/10/1–2).

157 From the *Glasgow Constitutional*, September 1853 (PP, SP/B/3/2).

158 Memorandum by Palmerston, 15 May 1864 (PP, HA/N/13).

in the 1830s, had taught Palmerston, on a practical level, how divisive reform could be, and he had good reason to be wary of anything that risked government stability. But Palmerston was not being only pragmatic: there was a sincerity about his belief in careful progress. What would ensure that it was safe, he argued, was education.

In many respects, Palmerston's liberalism might be boiled down to this issue: it was by producing a more educated, informed and (politically) literate population that society could progress. Though this did not necessarily translate into particularly extensive legislative activity under Palmerston's own direction, he spoke eloquently about the need to promote education as a key to future progress. Addressing audiences in the north of England in November 1856 as Prime Minister, for example, Palmerston insisted that, by providing working people with the means of improvement, they were able to develop their 'moral and intellectual faculties' and be raised 'as citizens in the scale of civilisation'. A country that demonstrably promoted the 'intellectual advancement of the country' and 'welfare of all classes' was one that exercised a 'potent influence' in the world, Palmerston observed.[159]

If this was a *mentalité*, or an ethos, more than a prescription for (immediate) action, it is no less important as a signal of Palmerston's conception of government and approach to its execution. Education would improve men's minds, but it would also help harmonise society by giving its members a sense of their place within the wider scheme of things. What made Britain a more stable country than many others, he insisted in a speech in 1860, was that, by promoting an appreciation of 'order', 'every rank knows its own position; it is neither jealous of those above, nor does it treat without proper respect those who happen to be below it'.[160] Education, then, by which Palmerston meant personal improvement and social progress, would underpin stability by striking at the root of problems, not just addressing their effects.[161] As he said in October 1860:

---

159   *The Times*, 7 November 1856.

160   *The Times*, 27 October 1860.

161   *The Times*, 29 October 1860.

It is, indeed, a useful lesson to all who are disposed to read it; it shows how the progress of enlightenment, the progress of intellect, the diffusion of knowledge, the increase of civilisation, and the augmentation of civil and political liberty lead to personal and collective security – how that great aggregate, by increasing the security of property and affording a safe development for industry, tends to multiply the happiness of the people, to increase the wealth and power of the country, and to conduce to all those improvements in society, which more and more qualify man to fill the dignified position his creator destined for him in this world.[162]

Palmerston consolidated his reformist credentials, therefore, as Home Secretary (1852–55) and as Prime Minister (1855–58 and 1859–65), championing a range of progressive measures. He encouraged education reforms, for example, that would review school curricula and place greater emphasis on science, modern languages and mathematics, making the education provided more useful and relevant to the needs of the time. Elsewhere he oversaw modest reform and the opening-up of the civil service through the introduction of competitive entry and the establishment, in 1855, of the civil service commission. More broadly, the cultivation of an air of disinterested (even professional) government, by way of limited use of patronage – limited, at least, when compared with his predecessors' use of such privilege and the introduction to government of a body of more modern politicians, professional and skilled rather than simply high-born, weakened the aristocracy's hitherto hegemonic grip on power.

His was a government 'ethos' of efficient administration, rather than unchecked legislative innovation. Contrary to popular perception, the Palmerston governments were very active, but active in a careful manner: Palmerston guided the ship of state towards moderate change, but he made sure statutes were lasting and permanent.[163] His 1864 quip to Goschen that the government 'cannot go on

---

162　*The Times*, 29 October 1860.

163　Parry, op. cit., 1993, pp. 180–83.

adding to the statute book *ad infinitum*'[164] was less a signal of his reactionary intent, but rather a plain statement of his view that good government meant sound administration and not perpetual revolution.

Here, however, Palmerston's record has attracted considerable debate. Earlier commentators such as Philip Guedalla were content to take Palmerston at his word, and characterised his attitudes to government at home as one of 'less is more'.[165] More recently, however, closer examination of Palmerston's record as Prime Minister has prompted suggestions that he was not simply more progressive than historians, such as Guedalla, had allowed, but he positively encouraged a new, more modern (and democratic) era, and supervised the political education of future Liberal heroes such as Gladstone.[166] Historical fashion today, then, is to portray Palmerston as the quintessential mid-Victorian Liberal. As Parry concludes:

> In administrative, financial and foreign policy, Palmerston squared the circle. He presided over far-reaching change in the image of the state. To a much greater extent than before, its ministers seemed disinterested, its taxes justifiable, its fiscal stance neutral as between interests, its success in promoting liberal commercial, constitutional and religious values cheap at the price. The sting was drawn from radicalism; it sought increasingly to participate with dutiful aristocrats in sober administration. Liberalism came to look responsible. Again, much more than in the 1830s, the 'permanent interests' of the country could place trust in it. Where national and propertied interests were concerned, Palmerston seemed to have as safe a pair of hands as one could expect in a liberal age.[167]

At the beginning of March 1859, with the liberal groups at Westminster to be found searching for a rallying cry in the face of a minority Tory government

---

164 Quoted in M. E. Chamberlain, *Lord Palmerston*, Cardiff, University of Wales Press, 1987, p. 107.

165 P. Guedalla, *Palmerston*, London, Ernest Benn, 1926.

166 E. D. Steele, *Palmerston and Liberalism, 1855–1865*, Cambridge, Cambridge University Press, 1991 (for a very brief summary of the main arguments, see pp. 1–22, 367).

167 Parry, op. cit., 1993, p. 191.

led by Derby, Russell announced that he planned to call a meeting of the Liberal Party to consider reform. As two former prime ministers, and rivals for the leadership of Whig/Liberal politics, Palmerston and Russell met to discuss how best to achieve this, and to work out a broad platform on which they could both agree.[168] Yet, while both were keen to turn out Derby's government, neither wanted to hand the initiative within their own party to the other. Thus, Palmerston was anxious lest Russell use parliamentary reform as the grounds upon which to challenge Derby, knowing that any victory so gained would probably benefit Russell, who was more widely associated with this aspect of the Liberal programme, rather than Palmerston. It was not clear that Palmerston's claims to Liberal leadership had yet unequivocally overcome Russell's. By the same token, it was evident that Lord Derby's Tory government could disintegrate at any moment. Palmerston's sparring with Russell over party leadership risked appearing irresponsible if the Conservatives were indeed on the verge of collapse.

By May 1859, therefore, there was finally some evidence of Palmerston and Russell looking for genuine grounds for reconciliation and accord. It was clear that, while they could agree that they did not like Derby's plan for modest reform of Parliament, any attempt to devise a detailed scheme of their own would only aggravate tensions between them. To avoid splits among themselves, then, they decided to press a negative agenda – to go for a vote of want of confidence in the current government and leave it to fate to determine which of them should replace Derby in No. 10, should they triumph (they did, at least, agree that they would not work under a third party, so the Liberal choice was only ever between the two of them).

The parliamentary defeat for the government duly came, and Derby resigned and called a general election. It was clear that the liberal elements in Parliament needed a more stable base to try to move beyond the Palmerston–Russell contest. Palmerston proposed a meeting of the Liberal Party when he met Russell at the beginning of June, and Russell agreed to join him, while still nursing a

---

168   G. C. Lewis's diary, 3/4 March 1859 (Harpton Court Ms, National Library of Wales [hereafter NLW], Ms 3573); Palmerston's diary, 7 March 1859 (PP, D/19).

sense of personal rivalry, on 6 June, when the party was to gather at Willis's Rooms in St James's, London. At that meeting, Palmerston spoke first, outlining the need to step up to the challenge of replacing Derby's government, which had, he insisted, forfeited the confidence of the country. He told the audience of over 270 Liberals that it was the only 'manly and straightforward course' to accept the challenge to form a new government. Russell addressed the meeting next and, in speaking of the Liberal Party, laid emphasis on the need for 'the three great sections of that party – the old Whigs, the Peelites, and the advanced Liberals' – to be represented in any future Liberal government. Other speakers also took up the theme of recent Liberal discord, but, overall, the tone of the meeting was conciliatory, and Palmerston and Russell's public reconciliation seemed to be well received.[169]

At the election in June, the Liberals were returned with a majority and, contrary to expectations, the Queen turned first to Lord Granville to form a government. When it was apparent Granville did not possess enough parliamentary support, Victoria was obliged to acknowledge that leadership of the Liberals was really in the hands of Palmerston and Russell. Of the two, she charged Palmerston with forming his second government.

Palmerston would lead the Liberals in government until his death in October 1865. During the final six years of his life, there were no real challenges to his leadership of the party. Yet, by the same token, it might be said that Liberal heavyweights such as Russell and Gladstone – as well as those on the more radical wing, such as Richard Cobden and John Bright – were less than enthusiastic in their support for 'Old Pam'. Indeed, when he died in 1865, many commentators seemed almost to sense a collective intake of breath among the political classes as they consciously braced themselves for a new era of change and activity. Benjamin Disraeli, from the Conservative benches, foresaw 'tempestuous times, and great vicissitudes in public life',[170] while Palmerston's erstwhile colleague Charles Wood, Secretary of State for India, observed: 'Our quiet days

---

169   *The Times*, 7 June 1859; G. C. Lewis's diary, 6 June 1859 (Harpton Court Ms, NLW, Ms 3573).

170   Paul Smith, *Disraeli: A Brief Life*, Cambridge, Cambridge University Press, 1996, p. 136.

are over; no more peace for us.'[171] The suggestion that Palmerston had been a brake on change, or an obstacle to improvement, however, is unsatisfactory. While early historians of Palmerston's life and career, such as Philip Guedalla, might have seen him as little more than a throwback to the eighteenth century – and everything that connoted in terms of reactionaryism and backwardness – Palmerston could not have held his government and its broadly defined Liberal backers together without some sense of a more modern, liberal outlook than those early accounts allowed. And, thus, in more recent years, his governments have even been described as having offered a 'conscious introduction' to a new democratic era. While it is problematic to view Palmerston as a democrat, to argue that his liberal policies did create conditions in which later 'democratic' innovation was possible is plausible, and herein a key contribution made by Palmerston to liberal progress in this period.

That Palmerston led is indisputable. But what and who he led remain interesting questions, as does the issue of how he did so. Palmerston's governments left a sparse legislative record, and hopes of finding a clearly articulated liberal agenda in terms of its formal activities are likely to be disappointed. At the same time, this is not to say that his governments were without their domestic achievements, not least in their pursuit of efficiency and greater equality of opportunity in government and society. But, arguably, Palmerston's most significant contribution to the development of Liberal politics and the securing of a so-called 'Liberal ascendancy'[172] was his ability to develop a sense of a liberal ethos, and this is not negligible. Indeed, in many ways, Palmerston has some claims to be seen as the most successful of all early-to-mid-Victorian Liberal leaders, in the purest sense of his having provided clear leadership around which disparate groups and interests were able to coalesce.

Palmerston was undoubtedly a charismatic leader. When the mayor of Southampton called him the 'people's minister' in 1852, he captured an important element of Palmerston's political character. Palmerston was highly effective at

---

171   R. Blake, *Disraeli*, London, Eyre & Spottiswoode, 1966, p. 436.

172   See, for example, T. A. Jenkins, *The Liberal Ascendancy, 1830–1886*, London, Palgrave, 1994.

communicating a message, whether that be through his well-developed sense of how to manage the press, or through his ability to engage the attention, and command the respect, of a significant number of those 'bald-headed men at the back of the omnibus', who, for Walter Bagehot, defined public opinion in Palmerston's England.[173] Though not necessarily one of the century's great orators, Palmerston was an effective speaker, particularly as his career wore on. As Joseph Meisel has noted, by the later 1850s and early 1860s, 'when Gladstone was only just discovering audiences of "the people", Palmerston was successfully using the extra-parliamentary platform to maintain his base of popular support', not least in his tours in northern England during those years.[174] And, in Parliament, he was increasingly adept at winning over an audience, with his wit as much as his reasoning. In 1846, for example, an article in *Fraser's Magazine* noted that Palmerston:

> Possesses himself of considerable power of ridicule; and when he finds the argument of an opponent unanswerable, or that it could only be answered by alliance with some principle that might be turned against himself, he is a great adept at getting rid of it by a side-wind of absurd allusion. He knows exactly what will win a cheer and what ought to be avoided as calculated to provoke laughter in an assembly where appreciation of what is elevated in sentiment is by no means common.[175]

Palmerston seemed less distant and aloof than many of his contemporaries at Westminster. While Gladstone or Aberdeen studied the classics, Palmerston relished a good boxing match, a ride on his horse, and in the evening an entertaining soirée. And he was aided throughout by the important, though frequently

---

173   P. Smith ed., *The English Constitution* [Walter Bagehot, 1867], Cambridge, Cambridge University Press, 2001, p. 30.

174   Joseph S. Meisel, *Public Speech and the Culture of Public Life in the Age of Gladstone*, New York, Columbia University Press, 2001, pp. 233–4.

175   George Henry Francis, 'Contemporary Orators, No. VIII: Lord Palmerston', *Fraser's Magazine*, xxxiii, No. 195, March 1846, pp. 319–20, quoted in Joseph S. Meisel, 'Humour and Insult in the House of Commons: The Case of Palmerston and Disraeli', *Parliamentary History*, 28(2), 2009, p. 234.

underestimated, role of his wife as a leading society hostess. Lady Palmerston had her own rich network of political connections and a well-developed political sense that made her a valuable advisor and support to her husband. Palmerston, then, was accessible, clubbable and, to many, likeable. By these means, he was also able more effectively than most to convey a political message to different audiences, and particularly ones beyond Westminster. This was, therefore, an important part of the explanation of Palmerston's rise to leadership of the Liberals, alongside the consolidation of Liberal power in government.

Although election contests in the late 1850s and early 1860s, dominated by foreign affairs questions such as war with China, relations with France, or British policy over Schleswig-Holstein, were never, strictly speaking, exclusively judgements on Palmerston personally, many in the country were disposed to see them as such all the same. It seemed that a key political question in these years – and, by extension, an important determinant of political identity – was whether one was for or against Palmerston. It was, arguably, a recognition of the fact that he had established himself as a political leader. It was this that Lord Carlingford, who had been under-secretary for the colonies in Palmerston's governments, alluded to when, in later life, he reflected that 'the secret of Lord Palmerston's popularity lay in the fact that he was "understanded of the people"'.[176] Unlike twentieth-century political leadership, which demanded a command of parties and identities in rather formal ways, for Palmerston in mid-Victorian Britain, being a symbol of Liberalism was leadership in itself.

The message Palmerston concentrated on was one of patriotic duty, national progress and honour, but was also rooted in a philosophy of (moderate) liberal progress, which drew, for its inspiration, on the world of the Scottish Whig Enlightenment and its notions of a benevolent compact between governors and governed. While the Liberals were, throughout, a fractured, not to say fractious, grouping, Palmerston offered a sufficiently broad-church Liberal identity to encompass a variety of interests. His vision of a liberal, tolerant, constitutional Britain that everyone in Britain could feel part of – even if only, for

---

176   Henry Drummond Wolff, *Rambling Recollections,* London, Macmillan, (two volumes) 1908, Vol. 1, pp. 114-15.

some, in a virtual sense – combined with some tangible legislative achievements, designed to address aspects of the 'condition of England' question, offered to many a compelling idea of liberal politics around which they could gather. If Palmerstonian liberalism lacked radical bite, that was, in many ways, one of its attractions: Palmerston offered a notion of progress, but one safely contained within moderate bounds. Robert Lowe complained in 1865 that Palmerston had 'left his party without tradition, chart or compass, to drift on a stormy sea on which their only landmark was his personal popularity'.[177] This is both just and unfair: Palmerston might have left his party to navigate a 'stormy sea', and subsequent Liberal divisions over reform questions were indeed still apparent, but his 'personal popularity' remained a pretty useful landmark all the same.

177   A. Patchett Martin, *Life and Letters of the Right Honourable Robert Lowe, Viscount Sherbrooke*, London and New York, Longmans, Green & Co., (two volumes) 1893, Vol. 2, p. 243.

CHAPTER 8

WILLIAM EWART GLADSTONE

RICHARD A. GAUNT

William Ewart Gladstone (1809-98) represents the embodiment of British Liberalism in the popular imagination. He is arguably the most famous, recognisable and enduring of all the party's leaders. Though he was not the party's first leader, he was undoubtedly the first to establish himself securely in the popular imagination, to the extent that his name and example is still a matter of controversy over a century after his death. Yet Gladstone's long and tortuous journey to the leadership of the party, and the fact that scholars refer to 'Gladstonian Liberalism' as a particular brand of ideas and practices within the wider canon of British Liberalism, suggest that important distinctions need to be made in evaluating his long tenure at the head of the party (November 1868 to February 1874; April 1880 to March 1894), in order to separate the man from the myths that have grown up around him.

- Gladstone, William Ewart (29 December 1809 – 19 May 1898), born in Liverpool, the fifth child and fourth and youngest son of Sir John Gladstone and his second wife Anne, née Robertson.
- Educated at Eton and Christ Church, University of Oxford.
- Married Catherine Glynne (1812–1900) in 1839.
- Eight children, of whom one, Herbert John Gladstone, also entered politics.
- Initially elected as a Conservative MP, he was a Peelite from 1846–1859, entering the Liberal Party thereafter.
- Elected for Newark 1832–1846, University of Oxford 1847–1865, South Lancashire 1865–1868, Greenwich 1868–1880, and Midlothian Boroughs 1880–1894.

- Served as president of the board of trade 1843–45, Secretary of State for War and Colonies 1845–46, Chancellor of the Exchequer 1852–55, 1859–66, 1873–74, 1880–82, Lord Privy Seal 1892–94, Prime Minister 1868–74, 1880–85, 1886, 1892–94, leader of the Liberal Party 1868–74, 1880–94.

It has been fashionable, in recent years, to anchor Gladstone's mature political statecraft as Liberal Prime Minister (1868–74, 1880–85, 1886, 1892–94) to his Peelite heritage and, more particularly, his first experience of Cabinet office in the Conservative government of Sir Robert Peel. Gladstone's indebtedness to Peel has formed the keynote for one of his more recent biographers. However, there was nothing pre-ordained about this process, whatever the older Gladstone may have thought or felt, and his inheritance of the Peelite mantle was far from natural or self-assured.[178]

Gladstone entered Parliament after the passage of the Great Reform Act of 1832, sitting as a Conservative MP for the 'pocket' borough of Newark in Nottinghamshire, under the patronage of the Tory Duke of Newcastle. Gladstone's maiden speech (1833) expressed qualified opposition to the abolition of slavery, in deference to the views of his father John Gladstone, a Liverpool merchant plutocrat whose fortunes were founded, in part, on West Indian trade. The young Gladstone had been raised in a Protestant, Tory tradition, though one that embraced such issues as the repeal of the Test and Corporation Acts (1828) and Catholic Emancipation (1829), which enabled Nonconformists and Catholics to sit as MPs. It did not embrace parliamentary reform, which Gladstone memorably denounced during his undergraduate career at Oxford. Entering Parliament, like Peel, with a double first in classics and mathematics, Gladstone soon attracted attention and, in 1834, was given his first taste of junior office. By the late 1830s, Gladstone was regularly part of the circle of advisors and protégés around Peel, and, during the Conservative government of 1841–46, was twice appointed to the Cabinet (1843, 1846).

178   Richard Shannon, *Gladstone: Peel's Inheritor, 1809–1865*, London, Allen Lane, 1999. The book was originally published (Hamish Hamilton, 1982) without its significant subtitle. See also: Richard A. Gaunt, 'Gladstone and Peel's Mantle', in Roland Quinault, Roger Swift and Ruth Clayton Windscheffel eds, *William Gladstone – New Studies and Perspectives*, Farnham, Ashgate, 2012.

However, there is nothing in the two men's relations to suggest that Gladstone sought to gain (or Peel to bequeath) the mantle of 'Peel's inheritor'. Peel's sudden death in July 1850, as the result of a riding accident, and the confused state of mid-Victorian party politics made the future political allegiance of the Peelites – Gladstone prominent among them – a matter of continuing speculation. Their secession from the Conservative Party, following the repeal of the Corn Laws in June 1846, invested them with a moral and political power disproportionate to their numbers, which continued to decline steadily at the general elections of 1847, 1852 and 1857. Their adherence to the memory of Peel helped to inculcate a sense of political martyrdom, which called to mind older traditions of allegiance, organised around charismatic dead leaders like Pitt, Fox and Canning.

This was a position Gladstone was temperamentally suited to, having been raised as a Canningite by his father, who was one of George Canning's close political supporters. However, it was a politically frustrating position to be in a party that stood no realistic chance of securing power by itself. In 1857, Gladstone told Samuel Wilberforce that he 'greatly felt being turned out of office', and was 'losing the best years of my life out of my natural service'.[179] From Peel, Gladstone had learned the importance of a strong executive power, a directing hand over the business of government, and the primacy of financial policy as the means of achieving a legislative programme. However, these things had only been made possible by having a strong, organised party apparatus, supporting the executive in Parliament. During the final four years of Peel's life, Gladstone had been a notable private critic of Peel's technique of 'standing above party' while expecting unquestioning loyalty to his political ideals. Ten years later, after once again finding himself in opposition, and after three years' service as Chancellor of the Exchequer in the Whig–Peelite coalition of Lord Aberdeen (1852–55), Gladstone privately bemoaned the 'declining efficiency of Parliament', which he dated to the dissolution of party identity in the period immediately preceding the repeal of the Corn Laws.[180]

---

179 H. C. G. Matthew, *Gladstone, 1809–1874*, Oxford, Oxford University Press, 1988, p. 106.

180 Peter Ghosh, 'Gladstone and Peel', in Peter Ghosh and Lawrence Goldman eds, *Politics and Culture in Victorian Britain: Essays in Memory of Colin Matthew*, Oxford, Oxford University Press, 2006.

This was the mixed Peelite inheritance Gladstone took into the 1850s and 1860s, at a time when a number of younger claimants – notably the 5th Duke of Newcastle and Sidney Herbert – were unofficially vying with Gladstone for the Peelite crown. That Gladstone became the most successful, politically speaking, of the group during the 1850s, owed something to luck and political fortune. Despite being Chancellor during the Crimean War (1853–56), Gladstone suffered none of the political obloquy attached to those Peelite colleagues with departmental responsibility for the conduct of the campaign. Conversely, during the same period, Gladstone began to establish the Treasury as the principal department of state, and the organ through which contending parts of the legislative programme were mediated. The Treasury was given scrutiny of all aspects of departmental expenditure, while reforms to the civil service (stimulated by the Northcote–Trevelyan Report of 1854) encouraged the emergence of an Oxbridge-educated administrative class, susceptible to, and expressive of, the 'Treasury mind'. Gladstone's first two periods as Chancellor (1852–55, 1859–66) served to raise the profile of the office to the point where it vied with the older secretaryships of state – for foreign, home and colonial affairs – as the breeding ground of future prime ministers.[181]

The 1850s solidified Gladstone's reputation as a man of liberal economic principles – the raison d'être of the Peelites after 1846. In 1853, speaking at the unveiling of Manchester's statue to Sir Robert Peel, Gladstone self-consciously appropriated Peel's legacy for sound financial management, seeing in it an important means of connecting parliamentary politicians to popular extra-parliamentary sentiment. Gladstone's technique of reaching out to the masses, epitomised most famously by the Midlothian campaign in 1879, became his favoured mechanism for securing a political mandate as a counterweight to divisions in the Liberal Party.[182]

However, there were continuing and frequently voiced uncertainties as to

---

181   H. C. G. Matthew, 'Gladstone and the Politics of Mid-Victorian Budgets', *Historical Journal*, Vol. 22, 1979, pp. 615–43.

182   Eugenio Biagini, *Liberty, Retrenchment and Reform: Popular Liberalism in the Age of Gladstone, 1860–1880*, Cambridge, Cambridge University Press, 1991.

Gladstone's political allegiances during this period, which his own actions served to reinforce. On more than one occasion, the Conservatives seriously thought that Gladstone would return to his old party. Even Disraeli, whose first Budget as Chancellor had been demolished by Gladstone in December 1852, was prepared to make generous overtures in order to attract him.

Gladstone's eventual emergence as Liberal leader was, thus, anything but pre-ordained. Gladstone was not at the meeting at Willis's Rooms on 6 June 1859, at which the assorted representatives of liberalism, Whiggery, radicalism, the Irish and Peelites agreed to coalesce against Derby's minority Conservative government – the canonical moment in the foundation of the nineteenth-century Liberal Party. Nor did he vote against the Conservatives in the confidence debate on 10 June. Yet, days later, Gladstone accepted the Exchequer from Palmerston and served in his ministry for the following six years. Gladstone's biographers have interpreted this contradictory course of action as the triumph of his executive mind and service ethic, rather than seeing it as a moment of conversion to Liberalism. For John Morley, Gladstone was 'a liberal reformer of Turgot's type, a born lover of government', while Colin Matthew saw acceptance of office under Palmerston as Gladstone's best opportunity to put through 'the extensive and remarkable programme of Exchequer-led financial and administrative reform, which he had drawn up in 1856 in the post-Crimean doldrums'. In that respect, as Richard Shannon has argued, Gladstone became a Liberal the better to be a Peelite.[183]

Gladstone's Peelite heritage may be one of the more compelling reasons for his emergence as a Liberal politician after 1859, but there was no natural coming-together between him and the Liberal Party during the 1860s, more a slow and gradual accommodation of sentiment. His financial proposals as Chancellor (notably, the abolition of the paper duty) were highly contentious – leading to a clash with the Prime Minister, Lord Palmerston, as well as a stand-off between the Commons and the Lords. Gladstone's religious adherence to the Church

---

183   John Morley, *The Life of William Ewart Gladstone*, London, Macmillan, (three volumes) 1903, Vol. 1, p. 631; H. C. G. Matthew, 'William Ewart Gladstone', in *The Oxford Dictionary of National Biography* [online edition]; Richard Shannon, *Gladstone: God and Politics*, London, Hambledon Continuum, 2007, Chapter 7.

of England also put him at odds with the party's Nonconformist core, not least in his continuing (though gradually qualified) support for church rates. Similarly, Gladstone's declaration, on a tour of Tyneside in October 1862, that the Confederates in the American Civil War had 'made a nation' created a public furore, appearing, as it did, to position the British government as anything but impartial in the contest. Conversely, two years later, during the debate on Edward Baines's Reform Bill, Gladstone declared in favour of a more radical scheme of parliamentary reform than the Liberal leadership (especially Palmerston) was willing to accept.[184]

Gladstone had travelled some distance since seeing 'something of Antichrist' in the 1831 Reform Bill, and being castigated by Macaulay, after writing *The State in its Relations with the Church* (1838), as the 'rising hope of the stern, unbending Tories'. Gladstone was now christened 'the people's William' – an epithet coined by his favoured press organ the *Daily Telegraph* – and his face and image began to adorn a range of transfer-printed ceramic wares. Politically, the change was marked at the general election of 1865, when Gladstone was defeated as MP for the University of Oxford (which he had represented, as a Peelite, since 1847), and returned for industrial South Lancashire instead. Announcing his candidacy in Manchester's Free Trade Hall, the spiritual home of economic liberalism since the foundation of the Anti-Corn Law League in 1838, Gladstone observed that he was now 'unmuzzled'.[185]

Pronouncements of this sort were invested with unique significance – none more so than in the contemporary observation that Gladstone was 'Oxford on the surface and Liverpool underneath'. Yet it took a further six years before Gladstone discontinued the practice of describing himself as a 'liberal conservative' in *Dod's Parliamentary Companion*, and he only joined the Reform Club in 1869, after becoming head of a Liberal government and, by extension, of the Liberal Party.[186]

---

184 Morley, op. cit., Vol. 2, p. 126.

185 Ibid., p. 146.

186 Shannon, op. cit., 2007, pp. 182–5.

Gladstone became Prime Minister for the first time in November 1868, heading a party with a majority of 112 seats. He was almost fifty-nine years old and had been acknowledged as the leader of the party since Russell signified his unwillingness to serve as Prime Minister again. It was a remarkable resurgence for the party – and for Gladstone personally – after the bruising divisions to which both had been subjected during the parliamentary reform debates of 1866–68.

After the death of Palmerston in October 1865, Russell, as incoming Prime Minister, and Gladstone, as Chancellor and Leader of the House of Commons, introduced a relatively modest measure of parliamentary reform. Gladstone gained much of the ensuing opprobrium for the bill, as well as its less-than-skilful presentation in debate. Beset by internal divisions and an unexpected loss of authority, the government resigned in June 1866. Energised by these events, the incoming Conservative government of Lord Derby proceeded to introduce a far more extensive Reform Bill, which, by stratagem, daring and skill, Disraeli managed to pass through the House of Commons. Gladstone suspended his usual habit of addressing extra-parliamentary audiences during this period.

However, once the Reform Act was passed, Gladstone recovered his nerve and his authority, quickly facing down the new Conservative premier Disraeli with a series of measures that attacked the government's weakest point – its defence of Anglican privilege – and re-uniting the Liberals in the process. Gladstone carried a bill that abolished compulsory church rates (a measure on which his own views had now changed significantly) and passed a resolution to abolish the Anglican establishment in Ireland (the Church of Ireland). This provided him with the platform upon which to fight and win the first of his four general election victories in the autumn of 1868.

Gladstone brought to the leadership of the Liberal Party, and to the steadily increasing labours of ministerial office, a physical and mental temperament unequalled among former prime ministers. A voracious reader and bibliophile, who found leisure in his closely argued studies of the classical poets Homer and Dante, Gladstone was no mere academic. His spry physique and passion for physical labour found expression in walking, estate work at Hawarden (his wife's family home in north Wales), and tree-felling. It also found expression in the rescue of London prostitutes – a cause he had taken up from a sense of religious evangelism in the 1840s, but one that continued to expose him to moral and physical temptations; the more especially as he continued to pursue this work throughout his first two premierships.

In 1868, the principal doorkeeper of the House of Commons, William White, observed:

> Nature never made a countenance more sensitive, more perfectly an index and outward and visible sign of the inward emotions of the mind, than Gladstone's. He can no more hide his feelings than he can suppress his thoughts. His is, indeed, a most expressive face, and, when lighted up, as it always is when speaking with animation, or even when at rest in calm serenity, a handsome face, if beauty of countenance consisteth as much in expression as in correctness of features, as many hold it does.[187]

These were sentiments that were amply borne out in the increasing number of illustrations featuring Gladstone from this time onwards – whether in portraits, sketches, photographs or the cartoons of *Punch* magazine and Phil May. It was telling that Queen Victoria's commission for Gladstone to form his first ministry arrived while he was tree-felling at Hawarden. Receiving it, he intoned, 'with deep earnestness in his voice, and great intensity in his face ... "My mission is to pacify Ireland."'[188]

However, if Ireland was the central political topic of interest for Gladstone during his first ministry (1868–74), the government as a whole was dominated by a Peelite ethic of institutional and administrative reform. Indeed, in historical terms, the government ranks alongside Peel's 1841–46 administration as the most important, in point of domestic legislation, of the nineteenth century. In his own retrospective list of chief heads of legislative work, drawn up in 1896, Gladstone singled out for special mention the abolition of religious tests at Oxbridge

---

187 William White, *The Inner Life of the House of Commons* [two volumes, 1897], London, Richmond Publishing Company, (two volumes published in one) 1973, Vol. 2, p. 81.

188 Matthew, op. cit., 1988, p. 147.

(1871) and 'four other important measures ... two of which passed: 1. Education [1870], 2. Ballot [1872]'. The two other 'failed' bills named by Gladstone were a public house licensing act – for which an abortive bill was produced in 1871 and a modified act in 1872 – and the abolition of army purchase (1871), which had to be enacted by royal warrant before a legislative compromise was reached. Of both of these measures, Gladstone noted: 'They were not under my personal charge.'[189]

Gladstone's tendency to valorise the chief legislative measures for which he took responsibility, such as the Irish Church Act in 1869 and the Irish Land Act of 1870, is an understandable enough reflex judgement on his own government. However, it seriously underestimates the contribution of other measures – and other ministers – in Liberalism's assault on vested interests, including the Church, the universities, the armed services and the drink trade, during this period. The Elementary Education Act, which was the responsibility of the Lord President of the Council, Earl de Grey and the Vice-President of the Council, W. E. Forster, was undermined (from Gladstone's perspective) by the passage of the Cowper-Temple amendment, which provided for latitudinarian religious instruction in all schools, rather than Gladstone's preference for state-provided secular teaching and the funding of religious teaching by the Church. Gladstone was also more dubious of the virtues of the secret ballot than his later judgement would suggest. In so far as H. A. Bruce's Licensing Act is concerned, Gladstone's famous comment, after the Liberal Party's defeat in the 1874 general election, was clear: the party had been 'borne down in a torrent of gin and beer', as the drink trade punished the Liberals for their hostility to its interests.[190]

However, in spite of Gladstone's explanation, no single factor adequately accounts for the party's electoral defeat in 1874, after six years of reforming legislation. It was more the accumulated impact of a succession of episodes, focused around large issues (like drink and education), that, together, suggested a pervasive sense of Liberal malaise. The dangerous excesses of extreme energy on

---

189   John Brooke and Mary Sorensen eds, *Autobiographica* [W. E. Gladstone, 1894], London, HMSO, 1971, p. 137.

190   Morley, op. cit., Vol. 2, p. 495.

the one hand, and extreme latitude on the other, were presented, by a resurgent Conservative opposition, as equally damaging to national interests. In April 1872, Disraeli famously told his Conservative followers at Manchester that the government front bench resembled 'a range of exhausted volcanoes. Not a flame flickers on a single pallid crest ... there are occasional earthquakes, and ever and anon the dark rumbling of the sea.'[191]

The government's foreign policy also suggested that 'Gladstonian' Liberalism had changed direction since the heady, bellicose days of Lord Palmerston. A diplomatist in the spirit of Castlereagh (rather than his childhood idol, Canning), Gladstone used his first ministry to establish a reputation for personal involvement in foreign policy, which would increase over time. In spite of having two successful and accomplished foreign secretaries – Lord Clarendon, who died in 1870, and Lord Granville – Gladstone personally helped negotiate the settlement of the *Alabama* case. This involved compensating the United States for damages caused during the Civil War (1861–65) by a southern gunboat built on the Mersey and sold to the Confederacy by the British government. The final settlement of £3.2 million was regarded by many people as a 'sell-out', designed to atone for Gladstone's expressed sympathy for the American south during the conflict.

European policy also appeared, to some sectors of public opinion, unduly conciliatory, in that it prioritised diplomatic solutions over the sort of aggressive rhetoric that had characterised Palmerston's approach. In the face of a newly unified German nation, and the Franco-Prussian War of 1870–71, Gladstone published a putatively anonymous article on 'Germany, France and England' for the *Edinburgh Review*, the authorship of which was quickly established. The article's principal purpose was to assert the primacy of international law, in order, as much as anything, to secure the interests of Belgium. By the Treaty of London (1870), Britain helped to reinforce Belgium through a defensive treaty with France and Prussia, which later provided the grounds for Britain's entry into the First World War.

---

191   W. F. Monypenny and G. E. Buckle, *The Life of Benjamin Disraeli*, London, John Murray, (six volumes) 1910–20, Vol. 5, p. 191.

Gladstone's 'mission to pacify Ireland' was, in practical terms, the rock upon which his first government foundered. In 1873, a bill to reform university education by broadening the basis of Catholic attendance raised opposition from Irish MPs, the Catholic hierarchy and Liberal secularists. Gladstone made it a vote of confidence in the government and lost by three votes. Disraeli, relishing his opponent's discomfort, refused to form a minority Conservative government, and Gladstone continued in office for another ten months. His election manifesto, published on 24 January 1874, announced a plan to abolish the income tax. However, behind the scenes (and in an ominous prophecy of events twenty years later), there was Cabinet resistance to Gladstone's proposal to cut the army and navy budgets in order to achieve his financial plans.

On 16 February 1874, a day before resigning as Prime Minister, Gladstone resigned the leadership of the Liberal Party. The Conservative Party had achieved a stable majority for the first time since 1841, and Gladstone, who had served as Chancellor of the Exchequer as well as Prime Minister during the last year of the government, declared that he would 'no longer retain the leadership of the Liberal Party, nor resume it, unless the party had settled its difficulties'. The word 'resume' would turn out to have more significance than was realised at the time.[192]

Any assessment of Gladstone's leadership at this point would undoubtedly conclude that – despite much promise and six years of striking government intervention, especially in the domestic sphere – the party had given way to internal dissensions and factional disputes that Gladstone felt unable – or unwilling – to conciliate any further. It was not exactly 'a study in failure', but nor, at the level of statesmanship, had Gladstone's tenure ended with the kind of fanfare attending Peel in 1846.[193]

Though there is no reason to doubt the sincerity of Gladstone's stated reasons for resigning the party's leadership, nor to think that it was designed for rhetorical effect, it is clear that, much as with Peel's attitude towards party after 1846,

192   M. R. D. Foot and H. C. G. Matthew eds, *The Gladstone* Diaries (fourteen volumes), Oxford, Oxford University Press, 1968–1994, Vol. 8, pp. 461, 463.

193   Robert Rhodes James, *Churchill: A Study in Failure, 1900–1939*, London, Weidenfeld & Nicolson, 1970.

the prolonged experience of office and the daily compromises demanded in con-
ciliating competing interests had taken their toll on him. In 1868, as Gladstone
stood on the verge of leading the party, William White meditated thoughtfully
upon the compromises leadership demanded:

> In the conduct of a great party there is much to be done that the outer world
> does not see. All the outer world sees is the onward sweep of a party in a great
> fight like that in which the Liberals are now engaged. It knows nothing of the
> tact and the manoeuvrings and constant watchfulness necessary to keep this
> party together: how pride has to be flattered, vanity conciliated; how irrita-
> tions have to be soothed, differences reconciled, cherished impossible hopes
> not to be rudely dispelled, patronage to be judiciously distributed; aspiring,
> sucking [sic] statesmen, though modest, not to be too roughly discouraged;
> different subjects to be deftly avoided. All this the world does not see; and yet
> these inner movements are quite as important and require as much consider-
> ation and thought to keep the party together as are required to lead the party,
> when it is united, onward to the attack. Now, in this department of a leader's
> work, it is quite possible that Gladstone fails.[194]

White's point was that Gladstone lacked the sort of 'man management' skills all
successful leaders required. Much the same criticism had earlier been made of Peel.

In 1874, Gladstone retired to his scholarly studies at Hawarden, and the
leadership of the party passed to two impeccable Whigs, Lords Granville and
Hartington, who could be relied upon to maintain a socially conservative tone.
Partly in reaction to them, in May 1877, Joseph Chamberlain established a new
caucus organisation – the National Liberal Federation – as a means of exerting
pressure on the leadership and direction of the party. Gladstone, who was still
a major attraction at public events, accepted an invitation to address its inaugural meeting in Birmingham.

Gladstone's reasons for doing so relate to his re-emergence at the centre of

---

194   White, op. cit., Vol. 2, pp. 115–16.

public life. After 1874, he gave a typically quixotic performance of a politician 'in retirement', intervening prominently in theological debates, following the Papal declaration of infallibility, and opposing the ecclesiastical policy of the Disraeli government. But it was the sudden and dramatic confirmation of the Turkish massacre of Orthodox Christians in the Balkans during 1876 that brought Gladstone back to front-line political action. Gladstone published *The Bulgarian Horrors and the Question of the East* (1876), with its famous exhortation to remove the Turks 'bag and baggage' from the country, and, afterwards, he made a succession of barn-storming public speeches on the subject. This was a direct challenge to Britain's traditional policy of supporting the maintenance of the Ottoman Empire in Turkey and the Near East, for fear of aggrandising Russia. Gladstone's intervention was equally disruptive to the party's new leaders and to moderate Liberal opinion in the House of Commons, which opposed his views and his methods of advancing them. Had Gladstone faced the Bulgarian crisis as party leader, it is difficult to know how he would have maintained his position while simultaneously retaining the support of his followers.[195]

But, as events transpired, Gladstone was 'unmuzzled' in the full sense of the word. Freed from the ordinary dictates of party discipline, he intervened, with increasing ferocity, against the evils of 'Beaconsfieldism' – Disraeli having been elevated to the House of Lords as Earl of Beaconsfield in 1876. This was a wide-ranging assault not just on the practical and political, but on the moral basis of Conservative foreign policy. Energised by the prospect of fighting an election campaign on these issues, Gladstone accepted an invitation to contest the Scottish seat of Midlothian, in advance of the 1880 general election. The campaign, spearheaded by the prominent Scottish Liberal the Earl of Rosebery – who had witnessed American caucus-style campaigns first hand – utilised the full advantages of newspapers and the wireless telegraph. This ensured that Gladstone's election speeches were delivered, verbatim, to the nation at large. Gladstone topped the poll, defeating Lord Dalkeith (son of the Duke of Buccleuch) on 5 April 1880 in a general election that cast the Conservatives from office and

195   Richard Shannon, *Gladstone and the Bulgarian Agitation, 1876*, London, Nelson, 1963.

delivered another Liberal majority in the House of Commons. In spite of the marked reluctance of Queen Victoria – whose personal and political distaste for Gladstone only deepened with time – Lords Granville and Hartington advised her 'that it was most for the public advantage' to send for Gladstone.[196]

Gladstone resumed the leadership of the Liberal Party, and the premiership, not from any natural unity of sentiment between them, but because, as Colin Matthew argued, 'he was an essential link between factions within it, which were otherwise irreconcilable'. This does little to explain why Gladstone was any more capable of uniting them in 1880 than in 1875, considering the uneasiness felt at his views – and his opportunism – during the Bulgarian crisis. Gladstone maintained that his leadership of the party was temporary. The length and duration of his tenure would be determined by the settlement of outstanding problems, whether in correcting the consequences of Beaconsfieldism before 1885, or in the struggle to achieve home rule for Ireland after 1886. Gladstone's leadership was also determined by his colleagues' unwillingness to consider any serious alternative. This mutually supportive embrace between a dominant, charismatic leader and a party whose internal tensions he helped to keep in check increased Gladstone's indispensability to the party, but made it dangerously dependent upon his own reading of the political situation. In essence, Gladstone had 'made the party unleadable during his active lifetime, save by himself'.[197]

Moreover, in attempting, during the Midlothian campaign, to codify the six principles to which he would adhere in foreign policy, Gladstone set himself a high standard of moral and political rectitude in international affairs, which the subsequent history of his second ministry (1880–85) would do much to undermine.

Two episodes offered a marked contrast between the rhetoric and reality of Gladstonian foreign policy. Having initially expressed his support for the cause of Egyptian nationalism, Gladstone consented to the bombardment of Alexandria by a British fleet, following serious riots in the city in the summer of 1882.

---

196   H. C. G. Matthew, *Gladstone, 1875–1898*, Oxford, Oxford University Press, 1995, p. 101.

197   Matthew, 'William Ewart Gladstone', *Oxford Dictionary of National Biography*.

By the autumn, having failed to secure French backing for a joint intervention in the name of the Concert of Europe, Britain unilaterally invaded the country and established control. The country's strategic importance had increased ever since the opening of the Suez Canal (1869) provided an alternative sea route to India, while the investment of £4 million in canal shares by Disraeli's government made Britain a participant in Egyptian political affairs (in spite of Gladstone's reluctance) until well into the 1950s.

Closely related to events in Egypt was the case of General Charles Gordon, who had been despatched to the Sudan in order to counter a nationalist uprising under the leadership of the Mahdi. Gladstone was held personally responsible for the late despatch of a relief mission in support of Gordon, whose death at the hands of nationalist rebels caused a public outcry in Britain in 1885. Portraits and ceramics featuring Gordon's face vied with the growing market for Gladstone-related memorabilia, while a cruel inversion of Gladstone's popular sobriquet was introduced into the English language – 'Grand Old Man' became 'Murderer of Gordon'.[198]

If Gladstone found himself overruled by his Cabinet's determination for military intervention in foreign affairs – as was the case in Egypt, Afghanistan and southern Africa – then he asserted his authority in the realm of financial policy, and with respect to Ireland. Gladstone combined the role of Prime Minister and Chancellor of the Exchequer during the first two years of his government. His principal achievement, during his fourth and final period at the Exchequer, was the abolition of the malt tax – the eradication of which had been sought by English farmers since the age of Peel.

Meanwhile, the troubled state of Ireland had been further inflamed by the success of the Irish Land League, whose campaign for tenant rights was organised around the three 'f's – 'fair rent', 'fixity of tenure' and 'free sale'. Conscious of the inadequacies of his own Land Act of 1870, Gladstone established a royal commission under Lord Bessborough and introduced a new Land Bill in 1881,

---

198 Richard Joseph Scully, 'The origins of William Ewart Gladstone's Nickname "The Grand Old Man"', *Notes and Queries*, Vol. 61, 2014, pp. 95–100.

which legislated for court arbitrations in adjudicating the rights of landowner and tenant. Gladstone took personal control of the bill, rightly including it in his retrospective 'chief heads of legislation' at the end of his life.[199]

The Land League was proscribed on 20 October 1882, in the same period in which Gladstone began maturing a comprehensive political settlement for Ireland. This was designed to satisfy the growing demands for a system of Irish self-government, short of, or leading to, full home rule. Gladstone focused his attention on Charles Stewart Parnell, the charismatic leader of the Irish parliamentary party, utilising Katharine O'Shea (Parnell's lover) as an intermediary. The exposure of the O'Shea–Parnell relationship later in the decade caused a major internal division in the Irish parliamentary party. It cost Parnell the support of the Catholic hierarchy and the leadership of his party, and, on a political level, deprived Gladstone – who was, by then, in the midst of campaigning openly for home rule – of a useful ally. However, ultimately, Gladstone was prepared to sacrifice Parnell in order to preserve his Irish policy.

From the start, there were suspicions about the exact nature of the relationship between Gladstone and Parnell, starting with the terms of the Kilmainham Treaty, by which Parnell and other home-rule MPs were released from prison in 1882. At this stage, the Cabinet was engaged in considering possible alternative plans for the re-organisation of local government across the United Kingdom. However, no practical plan capable of securing support emerged during Gladstone's second ministry and events were overtaken by the re-emergence of parliamentary reform as the central focus of legislative activity.

In terms of domestic policy, it was the settlement of the franchise in 1884 and the redistribution of seats in 1885, in two separate bills covering the entire United Kingdom, for which Gladstone's second government was principally remembered. Contention between the two major parties centred on the extension of household suffrage to the counties. The House of Lords rejected the bill in July 1884 and Gladstone set out on a public-speaking tour in its favour. During the autumn, the leaders of the two main parties (Gladstone leading for the Liberals,

---

199   Brooke and Sorensen, op. cit. [Gladstone], p. 137.

Salisbury for the Tories) settled a compromise agreement by which the Conservatives agreed to the franchise changes in return for significant concessions in the Redistribution Bill – including the move to single-member constituencies.

Gladstone was seventy-five by the time his second government fell as the result of a hostile amendment to the Budget in June 1885. He had successfully held his party together through five turbulent years of domestic and foreign policy entanglement and in spite of three resignations from Cabinet – stimulated by the occupation of Egypt and the Land Act for Ireland. Gladstone showed no inclination to surrender the leadership of the party as he had ten years before, and still less to accept the terms of the recently issued radical Programme – inspired by the ideas of Joseph Chamberlain and Jesse Collings – which amounted, in his view, 'to socialism, which I radically disapprove [of]'.[200] Faced by Salisbury's incoming minority government, Gladstone took control of the party's election manifesto, prioritising land and local government reform. The party won the subsequent general election with 333 MPs – a majority of seventy-two seats over the Conservatives, who could only defeat them by uniting with all eighty-six home-rule MPs. Two months later, Gladstone kissed hands as Prime Minister for the third time.

Gladstone's third ministry (1886) was entirely dominated by his publicly announced conversion to home rule for Ireland. The news had broken shortly before Christmas 1885, when Gladstone's son Herbert 'flew the Hawarden Kite'. The news immediately shattered Gladstone's privately nurtured hopes for a bipartisan solution, after the fashion of the recent settlement on parliamentary reform. It immediately positioned him in relation to a specific set of proposals, which the Cabinet – and the party – had not had time to discuss or digest. Hartington, a crucial link to Whig sentiment, refused to join Gladstone's new Cabinet, which was formed with a view to considering various solutions for Irish self-governance, rather than in support of a specific proposal.

However, Gladstone had already matured such a proposal, after privately soliciting Parnell for his input in the weeks preceding the general election. The

200   Foot and Matthew, op. cit., Vol. 11, pp. 408–09.

measure offered the basis for the social and political re-settlement of Ireland. A Land Bill proposed the injection of £50 million of state funding, in order to effect the transfer of land ownership from the existing Protestant landowning class. The measure precipitated the resignation of two Cabinet ministers, including Joseph Chamberlain. Gladstone also proposed a Government of Ireland Bill to establish a two-chamber Parliament and return Irish political representation to Dublin. On 8 June 1886, the bill was defeated in the House of Commons by a majority of thirty (341–311), with ninety-three Liberal Unionists voting against it. The party had split over home rule, and Gladstone convinced a reluctant Cabinet to dissolve Parliament and fight a general election.

Gladstone's actions in 1886 contrast markedly with those of Peel, forty years earlier. Peel had steadfastly refused the notion that MPs, as representatives of their constituents, should seek a new mandate on the basis of a change of views. He had passed the repeal of the Corn Laws, with the help of a supportive opposition and an openly partial monarch, in the face of his internal party critics, from whom he became increasingly detached. By contrast, Gladstone lacked support from the opposition and the crown, and reached out to the political nation beyond Parliament with a flurry of speeches, letters and telegrams in a general election that attempted to compensate for the disruption of the party. According to Lord Randolph Churchill, Gladstone was an 'old man in a hurry', because public opinion had failed to keep pace with the fast-changing nature of events at Westminster. The election results appeared to bear him out: the Gladstonian Liberals returned just under 200 MPs (a loss of around 130 seats), with no party securing an overall majority. The government resigned without meeting Parliament, and Gladstone ceased to be Prime Minister at the end of July.

Gladstone retained the leadership of the Liberal Party for a further eight years, passing six of them in opposition. It was his longest period in the role of Leader of the Opposition. Gladstone spent most of the late 1880s trying to educate his party to the case for home rule. Perhaps wisely, he played no part in the Round Table Conference of 1887, which attempted to reunite the disaffected wings of the party. However, he addressed all but one of the annual meetings of the National

Liberal Federation between 1886 and 1892. At the 1891 meeting in Newcastle, Gladstone accepted that home rule was part of a wider programme of progressive reforms – quickly named the Newcastle Programme – which would form the basis for his next administration. The programme played to Gladstone's strengths in constitutional reform and free trade. Gladstone was less accommodating about social changes, refusing to consider female suffrage, but encouraging (in carefully circumscribed limits) the cause of labour representation.

Gladstone formed his fourth and final government on 15 August 1892 at the age of eighty-two. The Liberals had secured the largest share of the vote and 272 seats at the general election in July, which was insufficient to ensure the successful passage of home rule, by the 'doctrine of the mandate', through the House of Lords. Gladstone's second Government of Ireland Bill, stripped of any accompanying measure for land redistribution, was introduced into the House of Commons in February 1893. It consumed vast quantities of Gladstone's time over the course of the following six months, as he personally handled all aspects of its progress through the committee stages. It finally passed the Commons in September, only to receive a summary defeat in the House of Lords. The same fate befell most of the government's legislation in 1893, as the in-built Tory majority altered or rejected all the major bills of the session. The Cabinet was unmoved by Gladstone's pleas for a dissolution of Parliament and a general election fought on the future of the House of Lords. The man who had begun his parliamentary career as the nominee of a Tory peer, and who had enjoyed the company of aristocratic society throughout his life, was now animated by the desire to reform the prerogatives of the upper chamber.

On Tuesday 9 January 1894, 'in a speech of fifty minutes', Gladstone announced his resignation of the leadership of the party and premiership to the Cabinet. The immediate cause was his opposition to the draft defence estimates, which were designed to finance a major programme of naval expansion. The news was greeted with regret, but, in the days that followed, the Cabinet disagreed over whether it meant the immediate dissolution of the government. The Foreign Secretary Lord Rosebery, who eventually succeeded Gladstone (in deference to the views of Queen Victoria), argued:

Our breaking-up on Mr Gladstone's resignation would be so much the worse
that it would be proved that the Liberal Party would have to declare itself
unable even for a moment to carry on the government after the resignation
of a statesman in his eighty-fifth year; and that sooner than stomach such a
humiliation, I would serve in a government headed by Sir Ughtred Kay-Shut-
tleworth (the first name of a subordinate minister that came into my head)
or anyone else.[201]

Gladstone presided over his last Cabinet meeting on 1 March 1894. Kimberley and Harcourt broke down in tears, but 'the emotion of the Cabinet did not
gain [Gladstone] for an instant'. Indeed, he was 'obviously disgusted' by this
public display of emotion. The Cabinet dispersed 'like mourners coming out
of a vault after the conclusion of the funeral service' and Gladstone proceeded
to the House of Commons, where, after denouncing and declaring war on the
House of Lords, 'the enthusiasm of the party knew no bounds and they waved
their hats and cheered and cheered again'.[202]

What Lord Rosebery called Gladstone's 'great, though unconscious, tenacity of office' goes some way to explaining his hold over the British Liberal Party
after resuming its leadership in 1880.[203] By this point, according to Colin Matthew, Gladstone had:

Begun the process by which Liberalism and Gladstonianism became fused
into a political movement, which could be seen both as awkwardly over-per-
sonalised and as a unique and beneficent political crusade, whose character
derived from one person's remarkable capacity to absorb and resolve within
himself the self-contradictions of the Liberal movement.[204]

---

201 Robert Rhodes James, *Rosebery*, London, Weidenfeld & Nicolson, 1963, pp. 498-9.

202 John Morley's diary, 1 March 1894, quoted in Matthew, op. cit., 1995, p. 354; Rhodes James, ibid., p. 508;
     Patrick Jackson ed., *Loulou: Selected Extracts from the Journals of Lewis Harcourt (1880-1895)*, New Jersey,
     Fairleigh Dickinson University Press, 2006, pp. 219-20.

203 Rhodes James, op. cit., 1963, p. 499.

204 Matthew, 'William Ewart Gladstone', *Oxford Dictionary of National Biography*.

It was this combination of physical and moral earnestness, embodied in the personality of Gladstone himself, that imbued late-nineteenth-century British Liberalism with its 'Gladstonian' character. This was not the same as Liberalism itself. Gladstone was never as secure in his own Cabinet, let alone in the Liberal Party, as the subsequent mythology surrounding him implied. Gladstone certainly represented a very particular type of 'Liberal' – though whether he was a Liberal at all remains a matter of some controversy.[205]

Gladstone died on 19 May 1898. His life and legacy were soon re-fashioned for political use. John Morley's 'official' three-volume biography established Gladstone as a Liberal 'pilgrim' questing towards truth. It was an image that was remarkably impervious to revision throughout most of the twentieth century. The work of M. R. D. Foot and Colin Matthew on Gladstone's diaries, and a bestselling single-volume biography of Gladstone by Roy Jenkins, re-fashioned Gladstone as the progenitor of progressive Lib–Lab politics – the godfather of the SDP and the Liberal Democrats; a man whose ability to reach out to the political nation beyond Westminster gave him contemporary resonance. Gladstone's early Toryism was explained away as evidence of youthful folly on the path to Liberal redemption; in any case, was not Peel really a Liberal in disguise?

More recently, an alternative reading of Gladstone, paying full attention to his Peelite heritage, has been promoted by Richard Shannon. From the opposite political direction – and with less apparent contradiction than might at first appear – a more 'Conservative' reading of Peel has also challenged the idea, encouraged by Gladstone and his acolytes from the end of the nineteenth century, that Peel was the progenitor of Gladstonian Liberalism.[206]

Gladstone was undoubtedly a Peelite, and, like Peel, 'split' his party. However, unlike Peel, Gladstone managed to survive that split and retain sufficient sources of political support to sustain his executive power – however diminished – in his

---

205 Shannon, op. cit., 2007, pp. xi–xxv.

206 M. R. D. Foot, 'Morley's Gladstone: a reappraisal', *Bulletin of the John Rylands Library, Manchester*, Vol. 51, 1968–69, pp. 368–80; Roy Jenkins, *The British Liberal Tradition: From Gladstone to Young Churchill, Asquith and Lloyd George – Is Blair their Heir?*, Toronto, Toronto University Press, 2001; Richard Shannon, 'Matthew's Gladstone', *Parliamentary History*, Vol. 15, 1996, pp. 245–51; Richard A. Gaunt, *Sir Robert Peel. The Life and Legacy*, London, I. B. Tauris, 2010, Chapter 8.

final ministry (1892–94). This is a striking contrast with Peel's 'scorched earth' policy of breaking party ties asunder in his headlong determination to secure Corn Law repeal.

Privately, Gladstone subscribed to the view that he had been endowed by providence with a 'striking gift', which enabled him – 'at certain political junctures, in what may be termed appreciation of the general situation and its result' – to identify those subjects whose time had come for action. Gladstone identified these subjects as: the renewal of income tax in 1853; the disestablishment of the Church of Ireland in 1868; the proposal for home rule for Ireland in 1886; and the desire for a dissolution of Parliament and a campaign against the House of Lords, both in 1894.[207]

However, to read Gladstone's leadership of the Liberal Party and his four premierships merely through the interpretive prism provided by his own retrospective reading of this 'striking gift', or the increasing centrality of Irish affairs in his governments, is to neglect the comprehensive programme of legislative changes over which he presided – most especially in his first two governments. Gladstone's later obsession with the achievement of home rule, and his tenacious hold on the Liberal leadership, while undoubtedly central to any interpretation of Gladstone's overall career, can too readily be taken to suggest either an out-of-touch or over-idealistic view of his leadership. In fact, almost to the last, Gladstone retained a shrewd sense of his personal political capital and how to manage the different elements contained within the Liberal Party. Both were necessary to secure his executive authority in Parliament. He undoubtedly led the party from the front, taking personal responsibility for the most striking pieces of the legislative programme and leading the extra-parliamentary campaign to secure support for them in the country at large. Gladstone's use of mass meetings to gather support for a parliamentary programme marked an important stage in the transition from elite to mass politics, which his successors built upon. He left the party a major unresolved obstacle – in the shape of home rule – but also a mythology that was invaluable to future Liberal leaders. In the decades

---

207   Brooke and Sorensen, op. cit. [Gladstone], p. 136.

that followed Gladstone's death, Liberals across the country had good reason to miss the energy and enthusiasm with which he felt his causes and presented them to the country.

CHAPTER 9

EARL GRANVILLE
AND LORD HARTINGTON

TONY LITTLE

Neither Hartington nor Granville ever became Prime Minister, though both were asked. Both successfully filled major Cabinet posts for extended periods, exhibiting a high level of administrative competence, and – over the five years (1875–80) during which they led the Liberals – they turned a fractious, defeated remnant into an effective, election-winning party. The disappointment felt over the unexpectedly modest achievements of Gladstone's second adminis- tration was an – admittedly back-handed – tribute to the quality of the team bequeathed to him by Hartington and Granville in 1880.

- Spencer Compton Cavendish, Marquess of Hartington (1858–91), 8th Duke of Devonshire (1891–1908), born 23 July 1833, died 24 March 1908.

- Eldest son of 2nd Earl of Burlington (afterwards 7th Duke of Devonshire (1808–1891), and his wife, Lady Blanche Georgiana (1812–1840), daughter of 6th Earl of Carlisle.

- Schooled at home but attended Trinity College, Cambridge.

- Financially dependent on his father until he succeeded to the dukedom.

- Married Louisa, Dowager Duchess of Manchester 1892.

- MP North Lancashire 1857–68, Radnor 1869–80, North East Lancashire 1880–85, Rossendale 1885–91.

- Under-secretary, War Office 1863–66, Secretary for War (1866), Postmaster General 1868–70, Chief Secretary for Ireland 1870–74, Secretary for India 1880–82, Secretary for War 1882–85, Liberal Leader of the Commons 1875–80, leader of the Liberal Unionists 1886 onwards, Lord President of the Council 1895–1903.

- Granville George Leveson-Gower, Lord Leveson 1833–46, 2nd Earl Granville 1846–1891, born 11 May 1815, died 31 March 1891.
- Son of 1st Earl Granville (1773–1846) and Lady Henrietta Elizabeth Cavendish (1785–1862).
- Educated Eton and Christ Church, Oxford.
- Married: (1) Marie-Louise Pellina (c.1812–60), the widow of Sir Richard Acton and mother of Lord Acton, the historian, in 1840; (2) Castalia Rosalind Campbell (1847–1938), in 1865.
- Two sons, three daughters.
- MP for Morpeth 1837–40, Lichfield 1841–46.
- Master of Buckhounds 1846–48, vice-president of the board of trade 1848–51, Foreign Secretary 1851–52, Lord President of the Council 1855–58, 1859–66, Colonial Secretary 1868–70, Foreign Secretary 1870–74, 1880–85, Colonial Secretary 1886, Liberal Leader of the Lords 1855–91.

Both men were born into the heart of Whig aristocracy. This brought the connections useful to starting a political career early. As Granville explained when answering a charge of nepotism: 'I am obliged to admit that some of those who went before me had such quivers full of daughters who did not die old maids that I have relations upon this side of the House, relations upon the cross benches, relations upon the opposite side of the House.'[208] Both Granville and Hartington were MPs in their mid-twenties, both had achieved office by their early thirties, and both had been in the Cabinet before reaching forty. More importantly, they imbibed a common culture: a set of political values – dating back, however tenuously, to the Glorious Revolution – that valued Anglicanism, principally for its use to the state, and sympathised with Nonconformists, a reformist approach to executive government, and a devotion to the interests of the 'people' – those with a stake in the country, interpreted more broadly than just the landed classes.

Yet there were substantial differences between their personalities. Granville's father was an ambassador; indeed, he himself worked in the Parisian embassy in

---

208   Hansard, House of Lords, 14 May 1855, vol. 138, col. 506.

the 1830s, and brought to politics those diplomatic skills. He was urbane, genial and had a self-deprecating sense of humour, which, while sometimes leaving an impression of indolence, ensured he made few enemies. Lord Argyll described him as 'cool', 'judicial' and 'loyal'.[209]

Hartington's mother died when he was seven. He was educated at home by his father, leaving him reserved, with a bluff persona cultivated as a shield. Although not profound or original, he pondered on issues until he reached firm common-sense convictions, which he obstinately maintained. Hartington mis-spent his youth in a traditional aristocratic way, indulging a love of horseracing, entertaining Catherine Walters (a courtesan known as Skittles), and forming long-lasting friendships with the Prince of Wales and his 'fast' set. During the 1860s, Hartington began an affair with Louisa, Duchess of Manchester, which lasted until the death of her husband and their marriage in 1892. While an open secret in political circles, in public the proprieties were observed, adding another layer to Hartington's reserve. Louisa is reputed to have inclined him in a Con-servative direction. Lord Esher, one of Hartington's secretaries, alleged that his lifestyle created the 'mythical Hartington' – 'the man who loves pleasure to the exclusion of work, who is *altogether* without personal ambition, whose mind turns away from long and serious contemplation of dull subjects'. But he added: 'All this is fiction … Apart from politics, he has no *real* interest in life: and cut off from them, he would be, in reality, as bored as he appears to be by them.'[210]

Both men reached the Cabinet under Lord John Russell: Granville as Pay-master General in 1851; and Hartington at the War Office, in the short-lived 1865 ministry. More significantly, later in 1851, Granville replaced Palmerston at the Foreign Office, when Pam's independent foreign policy had exhausted the patience of Russell and the Queen. Granville's close relationship with Russell and natural skills were beneficially employed in the negotiations that brought the Peelites together with the Whigs and other Liberals to form the Aberdeen coali-tion. However, the coalition could not withstand the strains of the Crimean War,

209   *The Times*, 16 April 1891, p. 10.

210   Cited in Henry Vane, *Affair of State*, London, Peter Owen, 2004.

and Palmerston's more assertive leadership was required. Palmerston appointed Granville Leader of the House of Lords in 1855. The rivalry between Russell and Palmerston, which dominated Liberal politics throughout the 1850s, climaxed at the 1859 meeting in Willis's Rooms, taken as a defining moment in the formation of the Liberal Party. But Queen Victoria sought to avoid making the 'invidious' choice between them, by offering the premiership to Granville. Palmerston agreed to serve under Granville, but Russell made impossible conditions, and the monarch grudgingly bestowed the prize on Palmerston.

The leadership of the Lords was a position for which Granville was ideally qualified. Liberals did not enjoy a majority in the Lords, and had to secure the passage of any controversial legislation through tact, negotiation and judgement of what was possible. These were the skills Granville brought to the post. He led the Liberal peers for the rest of his life, except when Earl Russell was de facto leader in 1865–66. It is noteworthy that the relationship between the Commons and the Lords became much more confrontational at the end of the Victorian era, reflecting Granville's passing and the more aggressive style of his Tory opponent Lord Salisbury.

Hartington was first elected in 1857 as a supporter of Palmerston, and he maintained a Palmerstonian approach to foreign affairs, as well as a Palmerstonian scepticism of the benefits from domestic legislation. Russell's 1865 government was too short-lived for Hartington to achieve much, and it is in Gladstone's 1868 government that both men showed their strengths as administrators and legislators. At the Post Office, Hartington nationalised the telegraphs, and moved on to guiding the controversial secret-ballot legislation through the Commons.

Granville's principal contribution was navigating the Education Act, Irish land reform and Irish Church disestablishment through a hostile Conservative majority in the Lords – victories won, as his biographer explained, 'more by skilful manoeuvring and negotiation than any appeal to big battalions'.[211] As Colonial Secretary, Granville strengthened self-government in the white settler colonies

---

211   Lord Edmund Fitzmaurice, *The Life of Lord Granville 1815–1891*, London, Longmans & Co., 1905, Vol. 2, p. 5.

by making them responsible for their own defence, and facilitated a tentative expansion of empire in Africa. On Clarendon's death, Granville moved to the Foreign Office, where a shared belief in the 'concert of nations' strengthened his partnership with Gladstone. Arriving just as the Franco-Prussian War erupted, Granville preserved the neutrality of Belgium, but did not fully recognise the shift in the European balance of power towards Germany.

By 1873, the government – described by Disraeli, even in 1872, as 'a range of exhausted volcanoes' – had run out of steam. In trouble over reforms to the Irish universities, it tried to resign, but was obliged to stumble on until the election in 1874 – which was comprehensively lost. Gladstone was persuaded to remain as leader for the next year, but, in early 1875, wrote a formal letter of resignation to Granville.

The contest for the Commons leadership between Lord Hartington and W. E. Forster was to be decided during a meeting of opposition MPs at the Reform Club in February. Each man had his proponents – in Hartington's case, principally Harcourt – and each was representative of a substantial section of the party – Whig and radical – but each proclaimed his unworthiness for the role. Hartington wished to see the Whigs – with around 150 MPs (radicals and Irish with around seventy each) – have their own leader, but only the Irish took up this idea, forming a separate Home Rule Party. Forster is now acclaimed for his Education Act, but its passage had made him many enemies – not least among the party's Nonconformist supporters – and, recognising the numbers, radical elder statesman John Bright was deputed to advise Hartington of his victory.

The informally organised Victorian Liberal Party had no overall leader. Granville continued to lead in the Lords and a *Spectator* profile in January 1875 recognised his seniority:

> The fiercest partisans of candidates in the Commons begin their eulogies or
> their attacks by the preface, 'Lord Granville must of course be the chief ...
> Old Whigs, young Whigs, and priggish Whigs, dwellers in the cave and bit-
> ter radicals, aristocrats and reds, High Churchmen, broad churchmen, and

Nonconformists, trained ministers and new members are all as unanimous as Jonah in the whale in selecting for chief a middle-aged Peer, who has never been chief before.[212]

Lord Kilbracken, Granville's secretary, later recalled:

I believe that it is sometimes questioned whether he, rather than Lord Hartington, was the leader. All that I can say about it is that he certainly used, in private, to speak of himself as the leader, adding generally some modest words about Hartington's more conspicuous and more laborious duties, and that the meetings of ex-Cabinet ministers were summoned by him and almost always held in his house.[213]

The Queen would choose between them when she next appointed a Liberal premier. Meanwhile, the leaders faced greater difficulties.

The Liberal defeat of 1874 had given the Conservatives their first majority since 1841. Gladstone's achievements had come at the expense of compromise, which irritated supporters, and a heavy legislative programme, which exhausted ministers' and back-bench patience. The party needed to learn how to oppose Disraeli – a more populist, if not more popular, politician than Gladstone – to discover a new cause around which to unite, and to reorganise the constituencies. Most worryingly, Gladstone might have convinced himself that he had retired, but he remained an MP, and still engaged in public controversies.

The Granville/Hartington leadership style was very different from Gladstone's. More patient, more collegiate, more moderate and less driven by crusading enthusiasm, they gave Disraeli enough rope to entangle himself, and they gave the party time for reflection and recuperation. More in harmony with the imperial spirit, they did not automatically oppose Disraeli's expansionary approach, exemplified by the acquisition of shares in the Suez Canal Company, but they did

---

212 http://archive.spectator.co.uk/article/30th-january-1875/5/lord-granville.

213 Arthur Godley, *The Reminiscences of Lord Kilbracken*, London, Macmillan, 1931, p. 100–101.

oppose the flummery of the Royal Titles Act, which made the Queen Empress of India. They united the party behind a resolution to allow Nonconformist ceremonies in Anglican burial grounds, and in defence of school boards. By 1880, when the next election was due, Disraeli's posturing over the acquisition of Cyprus, unnecessary military expeditions against the Zulus and Afghans, and poor economic conditions had left his government deeply unpopular.

Hartington allowed W. P. Adam, the Chief Whip, the freedom to rebuild the party in the constituencies, but his traditional approach clashed against the innovations of Birmingham businessman Joseph Chamberlain, who, dissatisfied with the religious aspects of the Education Act, created the National Liberal Federation. This was a pioneering grass-roots body and a forerunner of the modern political party, but, knowing its purpose was to radicalise and control the Liberal Party, Hartington refused to address its first conference – souring his relations with Chamberlain, and giving an opportunity Gladstone quickly grasped.

Gladstone's retirement had proved short-lived. He grew irritated with Hartington and Granville's imperial and foreign policy, objecting strongly to the Suez purchase, and finally losing patience over their cautious reaction to the 1876 Ottoman massacre of Bulgarian Christians. Indignant about the atrocities, Gladstone also saw potential political advantage – 'As a party question this affords no despicable material.'[214] The official leaders, like Disraeli, were concerned more with great power rivalries – a Russian war of revenge on Turkey potentially posed dangers to the empire. Having visited Turkey, Hartington concluded that its Christian provinces were incapable of self-government. Despite warnings from Granville, Gladstone tabled resolutions critical of the government, behind which the party failed to unite. Foiled in Parliament, Gladstone appealed to the nation through the famous programme of speeches criticising Beaconsfieldism, known as the 1879 Midlothian campaign – perhaps the pinnacle of his popularity.

Following the Liberal victory in 1880, the Queen approached Hartington to

---

214   A. Ramm, *The Political Correspondence of Mr Gladstone and Lord Granville 1868–1876*, London, Royal Historical Society, (two volumes) 1952, Vol. 2, No. 1050.

form a new government. Against a background grass-roots campaign to bring him back, Gladstone refused to accept a subordinate position and would not guarantee loyalty to Granville or Hartington. Putting duty before ambition, the pair persuaded the reluctant Queen of Gladstone's inevitability, against her threat to 'abdicate' rather than have 'any *communication* with that *half-mad fire-brand* who w(oul)d soon ruin everything and be a *Dictator*'.[215]

Between 1880 and 1885, Granville served as Foreign Secretary and as unofficial deputy premier, acting as chief advisor, making routine Lords ministerial appointments, and chairing Cabinet meetings in Gladstone's absence. Hartington took the India Office, enabling a run-down in troop commitments to Afghanistan, but later he reverted to the War Office. He was universally regarded as Gladstone's heir apparent, but, increasingly, he was at odds with the Grand Old Man. Hartington was ultimately responsible for the appointment of Charles Gordon to evacuate the Sudan – a plan in which Gladstone persisted even though Gordon disobeyed instructions, becoming besieged in Khartoum. A Hartington-backed rescue mission under Lord Wolsey was obstructed by Gladstonian procrastination. Wolsey's arrival after Gordon's death disgraced the government and Hartington's shame was compounded when the government reneged on pledges to reclaim the Sudan. Hartington's disillusion was intensified by regular disagreements with Chamberlain, and completed by an Irish policy, vacillating between coercion and conciliation.

When the 1885 election left Irish nationalists holding the balance of power, Gladstone embraced home rule. In the ensuing crisis, Granville and Hartington enrolled on opposite sides. Hartington voted against the '3 acres and a cow' resolution[216] used to bring down Salisbury's short 1885 administration and refused to join Gladstone's Cabinet. The crisis intensified when the Queen questioned Granville's capability to run the Foreign Office. Gladstone's reliance on Granville was so intense that he suggested Granville become premier while he accepted a subordinate office, but it was Granville who compromised

---

215   Arthur Ponsonby in Henry Ponsonby, *Queen Victoria's Private Secretary*, London, Macmillan, 1942, p. 184.
216   A call for allotments for agricultural workers.

by returning to the Colonial Office. When the government's Home Rule Bill was defeated in June 1886 by Liberal rebels, Granville was still cajoling reluctant peers to accept appointments to the royal household. That was the end of his ministerial career and, when he died in 1891, Gladstone helped rescue his estate from financial embarrassment. It is hard to disagree with Kilbracken's assessment that Granville was:

> A very skilful and tactful party leader, and an extremely able man, very quick and clever, with an almost unequalled knowledge of men and things, who certainly did not seem to work hard, but nevertheless invariably did what he had to do, did it well, knew his brief, and, in the House of Lords and elsewhere, was exceedingly well able to take care of himself.[217]

However, his forte was that of the counsellor rather than the protagonist.

Unanimously, the Cabinet opted for another election, and the Liberal Unionist rebels – Hartington, Chamberlain and their allies – accepted an electoral pact with the Conservatives to save their seats and defeat the Gladstonians. Salisbury offered Hartington the opportunity to lead a government – an offer repeated early in 1887 after Salisbury's Chancellor Randolph Churchill resigned. Hartington refused because the Liberal Unionists were in a minority in the alliance, because it might drive Chamberlain back to the Gladstonians, and because he feared it would prevent Liberal re-union after Gladstone retired. Nevertheless, anticipating he might be outmanoeuvred, Hartington refused to join Chamberlain in round-table negotiations aimed at re-union under Gladstone, and, gradually, the antagonism between the two branches of Liberalism intensified to the extent that Hartington and Chamberlain joined a Unionist coalition government in 1895. The then Duke of Devonshire became Lord President of the Council, but, in practice, functioned largely as an elder statesman. Yet his liberalism was not entirely dead; the Duke sided with the free traders when Chamberlain began his campaign for Imperial Preference in 1903. He suffered a stroke in 1907 and died the following year.

217 Arthur Godley, op. cit., p. 104.

The counter-factual of a Hartington premiership, in Gladstone's absence, is easier to imagine than many such exercises. His government would have been less exciting than any of Gladstone's, led by – rather than seeking to create – public opinion, as demonstrated by the modest domestic priorities laid out in his 1880 election manifesto: continued extension of the franchise; reform of county and district government; and removal of 'the artificial and obsolete restrictions of law, which still hinder the natural distribution of the land, in the manner that will be most advantageous to the state'.[218] A Hartington government would have been more imperialist than Gladstone's, and obstinately opposed to Irish home rule. There would still have been tensions with radicals such as Dilke and Chamberlain, but later events proved that a modus vivendi between Hartington and Chamberlain was practicable. Hartington has sometimes been described as the last of the Whigs – he was not. But he was the last Whig plausibly considered for the premiership – a post he would have held with integrity, fearlessness and common sense. By the Third Reform Act of 1884, governing required the cultivation and inspiration of a mass electorate – skills he had never needed to acquire.

218   *The Times*, 11 March 1880.

CHAPTER 10

LORD ROSEBERY

IAIN SHARPE

Archibald Philip Primrose, 5th Earl of Rosebery, became leader of the Liberal Party in March 1894, when he succeeded William Gladstone as Prime Minister. His premiership lasted until June 1895, when the government resigned after losing a division in the Commons. Following the Liberals' landslide defeat in the following month's general election, he led the party in opposition until his sudden resignation in October 1896. Despite being a popular and charismatic figure in the country, Rosebery was a markedly unsuccessful party leader. Divisions within the Liberal Party, in particular, the disloyalty of his defeated rival for the leadership, Sir William Harcourt, who led the party in the House of Commons, undermined his position. Yet, his own shortcomings, including his lack of application to party management, a failure to set out his own political agenda, and his over-sensitive and highly strung personality, were the primary reasons for his failure to fulfil the hopes that many contemporaries had for him as party leader.

- Archibald Philip Primrose, 5th Earl of Rosebery (7 May 1847 – 12 May 1929), born in London.
- Educated at Eton and Christ Church, Oxford; sent down without taking a degree.
- Succeeded as Earl of Rosebery in 1868; inherited Dalmeny estate in Midlothian.
- Married (1878) Hannah de Rothschild (1851–90).
- Four children, of whom Harry and Neil served as Liberal MPs and Margaret married the Earl (Marquess after 1911) of Crewe, later a Liberal Cabinet minister.
- Organised Gladstone's Midlothian campaigns, 1879–80.

- Under-secretary, Home Office 1881–83, First Commissioner of Works and Lord Privy Seal, 1885, Foreign Secretary 1886, 1892–94, Prime Minister 1894–95, Liberal opposition leader 1895–96, president of the Imperial Federation League 1886–93, president of the Liberal League 1902–10.

A fter inheriting an earldom and seat in the House of Lords on the death of his grandfather in 1868, Rosebery declared his allegiance to the Liberal Party and made his maiden speech in the House of Lords in 1871. Over the next decade, he developed a reputation as an able platform orator, and became a leading light in the Liberal Party in Scotland. His reputation was enhanced by his organisation and financing of Gladstone's Midlothian campaigns in 1879–80. Following the Liberal victory in the 1880 general election, Gladstone offered him the post of under-secretary for India, but he declined – ostensibly because it would make his efforts in the election appear self-interested, but, at least in part, because he felt the position not senior enough. This marked the beginning of Rosebery's habit – frustrating to his colleagues – of refusing political office, or accepting only after much persuasion. He eventually accepted an under-secretaryship at the Home Office in August 1881, because the post seemed to provide an opportunity to create a separate government department for Scotland. He resigned in June 1883, ostensibly because he believed the government was neglecting Scottish matters, but also through frustration at not being promoted to the Cabinet, and because the Home Secretary, Sir William Harcourt, had failed to defend him when he was criticised in a House of Commons debate.

Rosebery's refusal of renewed offers of political office in 1883 and 1884 further highlighted his contrariness. Nevertheless, he demonstrated his value to the Liberal Party when, in July 1884, he made a widely admired speech in the House of Lords on the government's Reform Bill, which sought to extend the franchise. In February 1885, with the government in difficulty after the death of General Gordon in Khartoum, Rosebery accepted appointment to the Cabinet as First Commissioner of Works and Lord Privy Seal. This seems a surprising decision, given that he had been critical of the government's lack of resolve over

Egypt and the Sudan, but he wrote to Gladstone that, at a time of crisis, the government 'has a right to appeal to the public spirit, and place under requisition the energies of everybody'.[219] He remained in office until the government's resignation in June 1885.

Gladstone's offer of the Foreign Office in his third administration, formed in February 1886, represented a significant promotion for someone who had previously only served in the Cabinet for a few months. This rapid advancement was a result of Gladstone committing the party to the cause of Irish home rule: most of the Whig faction in the party, led by Lord Hartington, refused to serve in the new government, so Rosebery's presence as a representative of the moderate, aristocratic tradition in the party was essential. His position as a rising star of the Liberal Party was enhanced by his championing of the cause of empire, which became a more central question in British politics following the occupation of Egypt in 1882. For once, Rosebery accepted the offer without the need for cajolery. He had been critical of the indecisive diplomacy of Lord Granville during Gladstone's second administration, and now proclaimed his commitment to continuing the approach to foreign policy of his immediate predecessor, Lord Salisbury, thereby putting diplomacy outside party conflict. The Foreign Office was probably the government department to which he was best suited: the workings of diplomacy were sufficiently aristocratic and mandarin for his authority not to be challenged by colleagues, and it enabled him to demonstrate his instinctive understanding of the popular mood, arguing, as he did, that 'what is really peaceful is firmness. There is nothing so warlike as indecision.'[220] Although his first tenure lasted just six months, he could claim significant achievements, particularly in the Balkans, where he negotiated a European agreement, and in organising a naval blockade to deter Greece from attacking Turkey.

The Liberals suffered a heavy defeat at the general election of July 1886, which followed the failure of Gladstone's first Irish Home Rule Bill. Most of the Whig faction, and some radicals, led by Joseph Chamberlain, now seceded from the

219   Rosebery to Gladstone, 8 February 1885, quoted in Leo McKinstry, *Rosebery: Statesman In Turmoil*, London, John Murray, 2005, p. 133.

220   *The Times*, 10 February 1885.

party to form the Liberal Unionists, and entered into an alliance with the Conservatives. In opposition, Rosebery continued to act as the Liberal Party's expert on foreign policy (there was no formal shadow Cabinet). His prestige was further enhanced when, in 1889, he was elected to the newly created London county council and became its first chairman. This gave him a reputation, not wholly deserved, as a social reformer. He was unenthusiastic about the Liberal Party's 1891 Newcastle Programme, because he rightly believed it committed the party to minority causes that had little appeal to the wider electorate. His life was blighted by tragedy when his wife Hannah died of typhoid in 1890. Inconsolable, he withdrew from public life for eighteen months.

When Gladstone formed his fourth administration in 1892, after a narrow general election victory, Rosebery was expected to return to the Foreign Office, and his participation was deemed essential to the formation of a credible administration. Yet he had to be implored by colleagues, and even by the Prince of Wales, to accept the appointment. Once in post, Rosebery renewed his pursuit of continuity in foreign policy. He avoided committing Britain to any international alliances, but sought to shield Britain from French hostility over Egypt and Africa by cooperating informally with the Triple Alliance of Germany, Austria-Hungary and Italy. But such isolation meant that Germany could hold Britain to ransom in international disputes, and increased naval spending was required to counter the French threat in the Mediterranean. He also outmanoeuvred Little Englanders in the government to declare a protectorate over Uganda; although, in general, his policy was to consolidate, not expand, the empire.

In January 1894, when the First Lord of the Admiralty, Earl Spencer, proposed a dramatic increase in naval estimates, Gladstone found himself in a minority of one in the Cabinet, and indicated his intention to resign. He eventually did so, after some procrastination, when the Cabinet had rebuffed his suggestion that the government dissolve Parliament to fight an election over the House of Lords' rejection of the Irish Home Rule Bill and other Liberal measures. He held his last Cabinet on 1 March. Rosebery was probably the most popular Liberal figure in the country after Gladstone, and emerged as the front runner for the succession. His main rival was Sir William Harcourt,

Chancellor of the Exchequer. Two decades Rosebery's senior, and with considerably more Cabinet experience, Harcourt was an effective and popular figure in the House of Commons. Unfortunately, his bombastic and bullying personality meant that his Cabinet colleagues were unwilling to see him become Prime Minister. This did not deter his son Lewis (Loulou) Harcourt, who served as his private secretary, from scheming to secure the premiership for his father. It is unclear how far Rosebery actively sought the premiership. Despite his habitual displays of reluctance, he certainly discussed the succession with colleagues behind Harcourt's back. However, alone among the Cabinet, he appeared to believe a Harcourt ministry possible, on the grounds that: 'Harcourt will try to make his own government a success, but he will take care that no one else's is.'[221]

The most important factor in assuring the succession for Rosebery was that he was the only potential Liberal Prime Minister acceptable to Queen Victoria, who still had discretion over whom she asked to form a government. She broke with convention in not asking Gladstone for advice on who should succeed him (he would have recommended Lord Spencer – an experienced but lesser figure in the government). Had Rosebery declined, she might well have invited Lord Salisbury to form a Unionist administration. Rosebery believed that it would be humiliating for the party to admit that it could not carry on without Gladstone. Although he wrote a long letter to the Queen stressing his unfitness for the job, he allowed her to persuade him to accept, and he kissed hands on 5 March 1894. Rosebery's identification with imperialism, continuity in foreign policy, and apparently moderate opinions undoubtedly played a part in the monarch's choice. But ideology played little part in the thinking of Liberal Cabinet members in plumping for Rosebery over Harcourt. Indeed, John Morley, whose views were closer to Harcourt's on foreign and imperial policy, was among the most adamant supporters of a Rosebery premiership.

Rosebery's appointment was widely welcomed in the Liberal press, with the *Daily News* commenting that the 'accumulated evidence of Lord Rosebery's

---

221   Rosebery, 'Mr Gladstone's last Cabinet', *History Today*, 1 December 1951, p. 35.

popularity is emphatic and decisive'.[222] On 12 March, he addressed a meeting of Liberal parliamentarians in advance of the new parliamentary session, and assured the assembled company that the change in leadership did not presage a change in policy. He had inherited a difficult situation. Succeeding a leader of Gladstone's longevity and authority was inherently challenging. He complained of 'an inherited programme and inherited Cabinet'.[223] There remained some resentment among Liberal MPs about having a Prime Minister in the House of Lords. This might not have mattered if there had been a close working relationship with the Leader of the House of Commons, but Harcourt was resentful of being overlooked; he wanted to act as Prime Minister in all but name within the Lower House, and insisted on being consulted on foreign affairs. In addition, the Liberals were outnumbered by Unionists in the House of Commons, and were dependent for the government's survival on the support of Irish nationalists.

Rosebery made an inauspicious start as Prime Minister in his first parliamentary appearance in the role. Pressed by Lord Salisbury in the House of Lords over Irish home rule, he agreed that, before it could be enacted, 'England, as the predominant member of the partnership of the three kingdoms, will have to be convinced of its justice and equity'.[224] This was no more than a statement of political reality, but it appeared to indicate a requirement that, for home rule to pass, a majority of English MPs would have to vote for it, which, given the extent of the Liberals' reliance on Scottish, Welsh and Irish support, would be an impossibly high hurdle. His statement angered Irish nationalist MPs and his subsequent attempts to qualify it gave the appearance of weakness. It also led to the government being defeated by its own radical backbenchers on an amendment to the Queen's Speech calling for abolition of the Lords – a move clearly directed at Rosebery.

The first significant policy measure of the new administration was Harcourt's

---

222   *Daily News*, 5 March 1894.

223   Sir Edward Hamilton, 21 May 1894, in Dudley W. R. Bahlman ed., *The Diary of Sir Edward Walter Hamilton 1885–1906*, Hull, University of Hull Press, 1993, p. 265.

224   HL deb., 12 March 1894, vol. 22, col. 32.

1894 Budget. Government revenue was under pressure due to economic depression, and a further £3 million was needed to pay for increased naval estimates. Harcourt dealt with this by proposing consolidated and graduated death duties, an increase in the basic rate of income tax (coupled with allowances for those on lower incomes), and an increase in beer and spirit duties. This was one of the most important financial measures of the late nineteenth century, placing a greater burden of taxation on the wealthy, and triggering some fears of creeping socialism. Although this Budget was the one truly significant achievement of his administration, the Prime Minister was less than enthusiastic about it. He queried the level of the death duties, fearing they would alienate the Liberals' few remaining wealthy supporters. Harcourt responded with a sarcastic memorandum, Rosebery conspicuously failed to speak in favour of the Budget in the House of Lords, and the two men barely spoke for months afterwards. In many ways, it highlighted two different approaches to Liberalism: Harcourt's embracing the advent of class politics; and Rosebery wanting to keep the party in the centre ground. Their feud was further fuelled by a dispute over the Anglo-Congolese Treaty – an agreement to lease territory in Africa to the Congo Free State in exchange for land leased back to Britain that would allow the completion of the connection between South Africa and the Nile. Harcourt opposed the treaty, and complained about not having been consulted. To his delight, it foundered on both French and German opposition.

Thus far, Rosebery had failed to set out any distinctive agenda of his own, either for the party or the government. His early speeches as Prime Minister suggested that he wished to win back the Liberal Unionists and reunite the party as it had existed before Gladstone's conversion to home rule, but he then failed to take any practical steps to make this a reality. In the autumn of 1894, he attempted to take a new political initiative by championing the cause of House of Lords reform. As the Unionists consistently used their overwhelming majority in the upper chamber to block Liberal measures, there was an expectation that the Liberals should tackle the issue, but no consensus on how to do so. Many Liberals wanted to see the upper chamber abolished, or its powers of veto curbed. In contrast, Rosebery declared himself 'a second chamber man in principle',[225] called for a House of Commons resolution asserting the supremacy of the elected chamber, and proposed a joint sitting of both Houses in the event of a serious dispute. He failed to consult colleagues before speaking out, and they were reluctant to follow his lead, as the Lords had been relatively quiescent during 1894, so there was little sense of public hostility to the upper chamber. As a result, the key measures in the 1895 Queen's Speech were Welsh disestablishment and a temperance measure, known as 'local option'[226] – both leftovers from the Newcastle Programme. The latter was Harcourt's pet project. Neither enjoyed particular support from Rosebery, and they were essentially futile gestures that did not even come close to being enacted.

In the early months of 1895, Rosebery came close to mental breakdown, suffering from chronic insomnia. His anxiety may have been exacerbated by a fear of public scandal, after he was mentioned in the Oscar Wilde trial. The eldest son of Wilde's nemesis the Marquess of Queensberry had been Rosebery's private secretary, and had either committed suicide or shot himself by accident in September 1894. There were rumours that this was because he had been engaged in a homosexual affair with Rosebery. The mentally unbalanced Queensberry had formed a violent hatred of Rosebery, and denounced him as a 'snob queer'. Historians have disputed whether Rosebery was an active homosexual or merely the victim of malicious gossip, although it is likely that the decision to prosecute Wilde was influenced by fear of accusations of a cover-up.

Rosebery also felt undermined by his colleagues, not only Harcourt, but also those such as Morley, who had backed him for the premiership but failed to give him adequate support once in post. He threatened to resign after one House of Commons debate, when none of his Cabinet colleagues defended him after he was criticised by the radical backbenchers Sir Charles Dilke and Henry Labouchère. His standing with the radical Nonconformist wing of the party was further compromised by his association with horseracing – he owned the Derby winners in both 1894 and 1895. As the spring of 1895 wore on, by-election results, which

---

225 Speech at Bradford, reported in *The Times*, 29 October 1894.

226 'Local option' was a local prohibition measure, allowing plebiscites on pub closures.

had been encouraging in the early months of Rosebery's government, began to go against the Liberals, and there was an increasing sense that the government would not last long and that the Unionists would win the next election. On 21 June 1895, the government lost a vote on a shortage of cordite and small arms ammunition. Although it could have engineered a successful confidence vote to allow it to continue, Rosebery and Harcourt, in a rare moment of harmony, along with most other Cabinet members, agreed that the government should resign.

Lord Salisbury formed a coalition government with the Liberal Unionists, and denied the Liberals any opportunity to regroup in opposition by calling an election two weeks after taking office. It was the convention at the time that peers did not intervene in elections, so Rosebery was only able to make two major public speeches before the campaign started. He stressed reform of the House of Lords, but also warned against the party being too closely wedded to unwieldy programmes, commenting: 'You cannot present a dozen great questions in line.'[227] Neither Harcourt nor Morley followed his lead in their campaign speeches, the former stressing temperance reform, and the latter, home rule. There was a lack of campaigning energy from the Liberal front bench, and signs of organisational weakness as the party failed to contest 124 seats. The result was a catastrophic defeat for the Liberals – its worst result between the Great Reform Act and its post-1918 decline. Harcourt and Morley both lost their seats.

There were many reasons for the defeat. A survey by the *Westminster Gazette* showed that Liberal candidates primarily blamed Harcourt's Local Option Bill, which was seen as interference in the working man's freedom to enjoy a pint of beer – although home rule and a fear of socialism were also cited. The Welsh Disestablishment Bill had alienated Anglican voters, and an ongoing economic depression also undoubtedly harmed the Liberals. Without putting forward any alternative agenda for improving the economy, the Unionists argued, somewhat disingenuously, that Harcourt's 1894 Budget had driven capital out of the country and that the Liberals had prioritised marginal causes, such as Welsh

---

227   Speech at Eighty Club, 2 July 1895, quoted in Peter Stansky, *Ambitions and Strategies: The Struggle for the Leadership of the Liberal Party in the 1890s*, London, University of Arizona Press, 1964, p. 175.

disestablishment, rather than tackling real problems such as unemployment. Rosebery's friend Sir Edward Hamilton referred to 'three "b"s – beer, Bible and bad trade' – as the cause of defeat.[228]

Rosebery viewed defeat with indifference, even pleasure, having spent much of the campaign on a sea cruise. He saw the outcome not as a reflection on his leadership, but as a verdict on the chaotic condition of the Liberal Party he had inherited. He wrote to a friend that: 'The Liberal Party has become all legs and wings, a daddy-long-legs fluttering among 1000 flames; it had to be consumed in order that something more sane, more consistent, more coherent could take its place. It is purged as with fire.'[229]

There were fears among Liberal frontbenchers that he would retire from politics. Instead, he carried on, but informed ex-Cabinet colleagues of his intention to sever cooperation with Harcourt. This made co-ordination of policy between members of the former Cabinet virtually impossible, although the breach did not become public knowledge. Harcourt continued to lead the opposition in the House of Commons after winning a new seat. Although Rosebery made occasional public speeches trying to educate the party of the 'danger in too long a programme' (and, in one speech, stressed the independence of the Liberal Party from the Irish nationalists),[230] he made little effort to spell out an alternative Liberal agenda. Nonetheless, party fortunes began to revive in opposition, mainly due to Harcourt's success in forcing the government to abandon its proposed Education Bill, and there were favourable by-election results during 1896. Rosebery's resignation came suddenly in October 1896, after a speech by Gladstone on the question of Turkish atrocities, which differed from Rosebery's policy. With elements of the Liberal press contrasting Gladstone's moral authority with his own pragmatism, Rosebery felt his authority was being undermined, and, without consulting colleagues, announced his withdrawal from the party leadership in a speech at Edinburgh on 6 October 1896.

---

228   Hamilton's diary, 18 July 1895.

229   McKinstry op. cit., p. 382.

230   *The Times*, 19 October 1895.

Rosebery's resignation marked the end of his formal political career. Yet, as the party continued to lack strong leadership, many Liberals, especially those who shared his moderate, imperialist leanings, continued to wish for his return. Such hopes were fuelled by Rosebery's tantalising habit of making platform speeches, which appeared to signal a political comeback that did not materialise. He refused to recognise the destabilising effect this had on the party. His attitude to political activity was summed up by Asquith as being 'afraid to plunge, yet not resolute enough to hold to his determination to keep aloof'.[231] After Harcourt resigned as leader in 1898, he welcomed the accession of Campbell-Bannerman to the leadership. However, the outbreak of war in South Africa, in October 1899, caused renewed division in Liberal ranks. Along with other Liberal imperialists, Rosebery felt it was the Liberal Party's patriotic duty to support the war effort, while other Liberals opposed the war. In the summer of 1901, when Campbell-Bannerman angered the Liberal imperialists with his 'methods of barbarism' speech denouncing conditions in the concentration camps in South Africa, it appeared possible that the Liberal imperialists might secede from the party and join forces with Rosebery. When they failed to do so, Rosebery stated he would 'plough my furrow alone'.[232]

In December 1901, he made a famous speech in Chesterfield, which was again seen as heralding a political comeback. His comments on the war appeared to offer a basis for Liberal unity. He advised the party to adopt a 'clean slate' – unburdened by over-ambitious legislative programmes – and that it 'should not move very much faster than the great mass of the nation is prepared to move'.[233] Once again, however, he refused to return to Liberal politics, citing Irish home rule as the crucial obstacle. With Asquith, Grey, Haldane and others, he founded the Liberal League, which he may have intended as a putative breakaway party, but which ended up as a ginger group within the Liberal Party. Faced with

---

231   Asquith-Herbert Gladstone, 7 October 1900 (British Library Add. Ms. 45,989). This comment referred to
        Rosebery's peripheral contribution to the Liberal Party campaign in the 1900 general election, but applies
        equally to the rest of his career after resigning the party leadership.

232   *The Times*, 20 July 1901.

233   *The Times*, 17 December 1901.

Rosebery's failure to offer a decisive lead, the Liberal imperialist frontbenchers made peace with Campbell-Bannerman, with the need for Liberal unity having been heightened by the Unionist government's policies on education and tariff reform. Any possibility of Rosebery's return was finally dashed in November 1905, when he denounced the 'step-by-step' compromise on Irish home rule that Campbell-Bannerman had agreed with Asquith. He became increasingly hostile towards the Liberal government that took office in 1905, opposing what he saw as its drift towards socialism. Through an increasingly cantankerous old age, he continued to resist offers of public office, dying in 1929.

By any standard, Rosebery was one of the Liberal Party's least successful leaders. His accession to the leadership was less an endorsement of his own qualities, more a rejection of Harcourt by monarch and colleagues alike. He failed to develop an effective working relationship with his senior colleagues, or to put forward an electorally popular legislative agenda that the party could unite behind. He did not actively support the one truly significant measure of his administration. He took little interest in party organisation and management. Under his leadership, the party fell to a catastrophic electoral defeat, and remained out of power for over a decade afterwards. While in opposition, he began to spell out an alternative agenda for the party, but his decision to resign, rather than try to rally the party behind him, demonstrated his unsuitability for the rigours of political leadership.

Yet there is a case to be mounted in his defence. As others, from Arthur Balfour to Gordon Brown, have found, following a long-serving and successful leader is a difficult task, in which failure has become the norm. Despite the government's narrow majority and Harcourt's disloyalty, Rosebery showed that it was possible for the Liberals to continue in government without Gladstone. In a backhanded compliment, a Unionist journalist credited him with having 'kept a party without leaders, without a genuine majority, without a policy, without a programme, and without the confidence of the country, in office for some eighteen months'.[234] In addition, key elements of Rosebery's prescription for Liberal

234   Edward Dicey, 'The rout of the faddists', *Nineteenth Century*, August 1895, p. 192.

recovery had been adopted by the time the party took office again in 1905 – a fact little recognised because of his estrangement from the Liberals. The party did clean its slate, fighting the 1906 election unencumbered by a detailed legislative programme, and promising not to introduce an Irish Home Rule Bill in its first term. It also followed Rosebery's strategy of continuity in foreign policy.

Any plea in mitigation can only go so far. In the end, Rosebery was unsuited for party leadership. He was too sensitive and highly strung, and lacked the necessary determination, stamina and attention to detail in policymaking. Possibly, his repeated refusal to re-enter front-line politics after 1896 and have greatness thrust upon him shows that he knew this too.

CHAPTER 11

SIR WILLIAM HARCOURT

TONY LITTLE

Sir William Harcourt was an ebullient and combative personality well qualified to head a popular Liberal Party, a motivator of the rank and file who became an unexpectedly competent and conciliatory Leader of the House. His ministerial achievements at the Treasury and Home Office showed a first-rate administrator, but round the Cabinet table his irascible style proved too abrasive. Gladstone's longevity and the Queen's preference for Rosebery prevented him from reaching the leadership until 1896, when his ideas were too set to be adapted to the changing needs of the wider and more working-class electorate. He never had the opportunity to face an election as leader and made way for a younger man in 1898 after he failed to resolve the internal party disputes caused by Rosebery's imperial vision.

- Sir William George Granville Venables Vernon Harcourt (14 October 1827 – 1 October 1904), born to a patrician clerical family; educated privately and attended Trinity College, Cambridge.
- Called to the Bar in 1854.
- Married: (1) Marie Thérèse Lister (1835–1863) in 1859, two sons, one who died early and one who entered politics; (2) American-born Elizabeth (Lily) Cabot Ives (1846–1928) in 1876, one son.
- Elected Oxford City 1868, Derby 1880, West Monmouth 1895.
- Solicitor General 1873–74, Home Secretary 1880–85, Chancellor of the Exchequer 1886, 1892–95, Leader of the House 1894–95, Liberal leader 1896–98.

H arcourt was born into a renowned aristocratic Anglican clerical family. Like Gladstone, he had an older brother who became a Tory MP, and he maintained a friendship with Disraeli, who reputedly offered him a safe Tory seat. Like Gladstone, he disliked Palmerston's blustering foreign policy, and, in 1859, for his first foray into electioneering, he pitched himself against an official Liberal candidate. But, despite family expectations, Harcourt's political beliefs developed in a different direction. As a younger son, he was obliged to earn a living. Both at and after Cambridge, he acquired a reputation as a journalist and developed an admiration for Gladstone. He read for the Bar, and developed a lucrative practice in international trade and railways, which brought him into contact with senior ministers. His introduction into political society was managed by Lady Waldegrave – his aunt by marriage, and a renowned Whig hostess.

This background and the timing of his entry to politics influenced the causes Harcourt embraced throughout his career: a strong believer in the rule of law through the primacy of Parliament; a free trader; and a promoter of international harmony. He was antagonistic to imperial expansion, which he believed would arouse jealousies in other nations, and, as a corollary, he opposed expanding military expenditure. Though he argued for a shift in the tax burden towards the wealthier, he had no great faith in government intervention to solve general economic problems. In short, he espoused the classic liberal values of peace, retrenchment and reform.

In 1859, he married Marie Thérèse Lister – the stepdaughter of Whig Liberal Cabinet minister Sir George Cornewall Lewis, and the niece of Lord Clarendon. They had two sons. The older child died in infancy, and Harcourt developed a strong relationship with his second son Lewis (Loulou) following the death of his wife, shortly after Loulou's birth. Loulou became his father's secretary and principal political supporter, developing his own political career after his father's retirement.

Elected for Oxford City as a Liberal in 1868, Harcourt preferred the role of an independent backbencher to the early opportunity for office as Judge Advocate General, then a junior ministerial post. Despite his admiration for Gladstone, he used his independence to oppose aspects of religious teaching proposed in the 1870 Forster Education Act, methods used by Cardwell to abolish the purchase of military commissions, and the 1872 secret ballot legislation, preferring to retain a choice of open voting in public. He developed a reputation as a combative debater, and, in the final months of the first Gladstone government, he was offered – and he accepted – the more senior legal office of Solicitor General, though he was reluctant to accept the accompanying knighthood.

Opposition, between 1874 and 1880, suited his pugnacious temperament better; he happily attacked Disraeli's more grandiose policies. This period was valuable not only in building his reputation in the Commons, but in forging friendships with Hartington and Chamberlain – the leading personalities on the Whig and radical wings of the party. Nevertheless, he still had his difficulties with Gladstone, differing from him on the now arcane Public Worship Regulation Bill, with Harcourt taking the more 'Protestant' line in supporting the Tory government against the 'High Church' Gladstone. As a confirmed supporter of Lord Hartington's leadership of the Liberals in the Commons, he was uncomfortable with Gladstone remaining politically active after his formal resignation of the leadership in 1875, and he would have preferred Hartington rather than Gladstone as premier after the Liberal victory in 1880.

Nevertheless, Harcourt had no hesitation in accepting office under Gladstone as Home Secretary, and the gracious approach to his appointment began a lasting reconciliation between the two. Within the government, he was generally a positive force, urging the strengthening of its resources by the promotion of Rosebery and Dilke. The new Home Secretary was able to demonstrate his competence to run a major department, but also to exhibit both his leadership strengths and weaknesses. Gladstone's second government was an unhappy affair, with much less sense of direction, and beset by events, rather than controlling them. As a consequence, the Cabinet proved quarrelsome – its arguments intensified and personalised by Gladstone's frequent hints that he was on the verge of retirement. By 1885, they were more than happy to resign over a minor Budget defeat.

Harcourt's experience mirrored that of the government as a whole. Starting with the best of intentions, he enjoyed radical applause for the passage of a Ground Game Act, allowing tenants rather than just landlords the right to shoot hares and rabbits. But bills to improve the governance of Scotland – blocked by the Lords – and London – a victim of Cabinet disputes and crowding out – proved abortive. He exercised his administrative prerogatives to speed up justice, and, where possible, to commute death sentences, sometimes seeking to overbear the Queen's objections by the sheer length of his memos. Although he remained personally a convivial man of large appetite for food, drink and cigars, this period in the Home Office convinced him of the perils of drink.

Imperial policy and Ireland provided the most significant events that derailed the government. Of these, Ireland was the more immediately significant to the Home Secretary, though differences between Harcourt and some of his colleagues on empire had a greater long-term sway over his career.

The growth in the Irish Nationalist Party had been accompanied by an increasingly violent land reform campaign, exploited by revolutionaries seeking Irish independence. This climaxed in the assassination of a government minister, Lord Frederick Cavendish, in Dublin, and spilled over into bomb attacks in England. The Home Secretary naturally took charge of 'coercion' (anti-terrorist) legislation, and, like Churchill after him, rather enjoyed the opportunities given to the man responsible for the Metropolitan Police. Harcourt was naturally hostile to Parnell's obstructive tactics in the House, and to his association with rural violence, but he backed legislation to ameliorate the conditions of the Irish, in particular, the land reform passed in 1881.

Whether in the office or in Cabinet, Harcourt had a short fuse, though as one of his private secretaries recalled: 'His anger had much of the quality of summer lightning. It was fierce, but did not last long or do much damage.'[235] In a Cabinet debate over coercion, the Foreign Secretary Granville reported that Harcourt 'made one of his great speeches, riding a very high horse', alleging intrigues against him, while Chamberlain 'turned white with anger and struck the table violently'.[236] Though for Harcourt this outburst left no lasting resentment, for colleagues less sensitive than Chamberlain, such eruptions made

235   A. G. Gardiner, *The Life of Sir William Harcourt*, London, Constable, (two volumes) 1923, Vol. 1, p. 390.

236   Patrick Jackson, *Harcourt and Son*, London, Associated University Presses, 2004, p. 107. Quoting from the papers of the 5th Earl Spencer, as edited by Peter Gordon.

Harcourt almost intolerable. As Harcourt's official biographer acknowledged: 'He smote and passed on, unconscious of the sore heads he left behind him.'[237] However, while Harcourt's temper tantrums were a nuisance, in this period he was predominately an effective conciliator, or, as he called himself in a different context, the 'Great Pacificator'.

Gladstone's Midlothian campaign of 1879 had, in essence, been a heartfelt critique of Disraeli's acquisition of colonies for prestige rather than purpose – an analysis with which Harcourt sympathised. Yet, in government, Gladstone and his colleagues clumsily acquired responsibilities for Egypt and in the Sudan. Disagreements on Irish policy forced Forster's resignation and, from the other side, left Chamberlain deeply frustrated. Attacking Egypt caused Bright to leave, and dithering over the Sudan exhausted the patience of Hartington. With both Hartington and Chamberlain positioning themselves for the succession, Harcourt successfully used this rivalry to persuade Hartington and Chamberlain to remain in office.

The government's greatest achievement was the Third Reform Act, which ministers erroneously expected to generate an electoral advantage for the Liberals. When the 1885 election yielded a hung parliament, with Parnell holding the balance, Gladstone resumed control after pushing the party into the home rule crisis. In this short-lived government, Harcourt served as Chancellor of the Exchequer, annoying colleagues with demands for retrenchment, but with insufficient time for more than a 'steady-as-she-goes' Budget before the government's defeat. Harcourt's embrace of home rule, albeit as a marginally lesser evil than continued coercion, surprised observers of his antagonism to Parnell's party, and damaged his reputation for consistency. But, as a good lawyer and party man, once he had decided to stay with Gladstone, he argued the case vehemently.

The period 1886–92 established Harcourt's position as potential heir apparent to Gladstone. He took a leading role in speaking campaigns round the country, and relieved the ageing Gladstone of much of the burden of leading the opposition in the Commons. It was Harcourt who tried to bring about a re-union

---

237 Gardiner, op. cit., Vol. 2, p. 589.

with the Liberal Unionists, maintaining his friendship with Chamberlain, and enticing him to round-table talks held in his house early in 1887. Although unsuccessful, the talks reinforced Harcourt's reputation, and persuaded Trevelyan to re-join the Liberals. Harcourt built a close working relationship with John Morley – Gladstone's other principal lieutenant, and the man with the closest Irish contacts. He believed he had an agreement with Morley to prevent a peer succeeding Gladstone – the Malwood compact, named after Harcourt's New Forest country home. This period also saw the Liberal leaders accept, for the first time, a manifesto formulated by the National Liberal Federation conference – the 1891 Newcastle Programme. Harcourt happily endorsed the programme in his stump speeches, and mistakenly saw in the local veto of pub licences a campaign that would rally popular support for the party.

Harcourt revelled in the Unionist discomfort when letters implicating Parnell in nationalist violence proved to be forgeries, but the Parnell divorce scandal in turn undermined Gladstonian hopes of a runaway electoral victory, and Harcourt's advice to distance the Liberals from Parnell was reluctantly accepted. In Gladstone's final government, formed in 1892, Harcourt was again Chancellor. Despite his narrow majority, Gladstone insisted on piloting the Home Rule Bill through the Commons, only for it to be derisively dismissed by the Lords. Harcourt's half-hearted and tactlessly disobliging approach to the bill's financial provisions damaged his relations with Morley. His insufferable nagging of colleagues, particularly the army and navy ministers, to cut spending undermined his position among those from whom he would most need support. Yet it was insufficient to satisfy Gladstone, whose refusal to accept increased defence spending provided the real grounds for his 1894 resignation.

In choosing Gladstone's successor, the initiative lay with Queen Victoria. She sought a new premier who shared her own and Lord Salisbury's imperial vision. Gladstone was not consulted, and his candidate for the post, Lord Spencer, was ignored. Without hesitation, she sent for Lord Rosebery. Only if his Cabinet colleagues had collectively refused to serve under Rosebery could Harcourt have succeeded, and, even then, his ungeniality to the Queen would have been an obstacle. But Rosebery had courted his colleagues more assiduously than

Harcourt, and, indeed, retained the loyalty of some long after he resigned. Late efforts by Labouchère among the Liberal backbenchers proved abortive, as Loulou's conversations with Morley finally demonstrated to Harcourt the damage done by his intemperate style. Harcourt attempted to set conditions that would have significantly undermined Rosebery's power. He wanted a Commoner as Foreign Secretary, but Lord Kimberley was appointed and Harcourt secured no guaranteed separate access to the Foreign Office. He was also refused the flexibility to create policy independently in the Commons. Grudgingly he still accepted the Exchequer and leadership of the Commons.

Neither Rosebery nor Harcourt did much to reduce the tension within the government, and they were only intermittently on speaking terms. Rosebery continued a slyly expansionary imperial policy, and, to irritate Britain's leading colonial rival France, policies opposed by Morley and Harcourt. Rosebery further annoyed Morley by downgrading the priority of home rule, and Harcourt by opposing his fiscal policies. And yet, it was under Rosebery that Harcourt produced the 1894 Budget, which has subsequently been his chief claim to fame. When Gladstone resigned, the battle over naval expansion was lost, and Harcourt, faced with a deficit, seized the opportunity for a redistributive Budget. Initially, he planned a graduated income tax, but he settled for revising the death duty, raising the rate, and, more radically, extending it to landed property. Despite the objections of Rosebery and the Duke of Devonshire (previously Hartington), Harcourt tactfully managed the Finance Bill through Parliament, delivering the government its most substantial achievement. In the long term, this levy gradually undermined the wealth, and, hence, the power, of an aristocracy already under siege from the extension of democracy. Ironically, Harcourt's family were double victims of his tax, as he inherited his brother's estate shortly before his own death.

Harcourt's fourth Budget, in 1895, was a routine affair, but the principal businesses of government – a Welsh disestablishment bill, and Harcourt's second attempt to pass a local veto bill – were disrupted by a minor technical defeat on Campbell-Bannerman's salary. Glad to escape, Rosebery dissolved Parliament. The Unionists won a substantial victory in the subsequent election and Harcourt never held office again. Harcourt and Morley both lost their seats. Harcourt blamed unemployment in Derby and the intervention of brewery interests, but he had done little to conciliate organised labour interests. He was able to secure an alternative county constituency in Wales.

Defeat, however, did not bring reconciliation between the two leaders. Rosebery and Harcourt had each pursued his own line in the campaign, and each continued separately to lead the Liberals in their respective Houses afterwards. As Rosebery explained: 'No earthly power will induce me to take part in the dishonest hypocrisy of the last year or two.'[238] Resilient as always, Harcourt relished opposition and enjoyed the opportunity to criticise the uncomfortable coalition between Salisbury's Conservatives and the Liberal Unionists, forcing them to abandon their 1896 Education Bill in support of Church schools. When, later the same year, Rosebery used an intervention by Gladstone over the persecution of Armenians to resign the party leadership, Harcourt assumed the role. His position was never formally endorsed, but never formally disputed.

Sadly, Harcourt's leadership, although it continued until 1898, had come when he was too old and set in his ways. Superficially, it was successful. Harcourt, as always, put on a good show in the Commons, and, at least in the early part of his reign, continued to tour the country, boosting the morale of the party faithful. Between 1896 and 1898, Salisbury's government lost twelve by-elections and made only one gain. In two key areas, he failed to adjust to the spirit of the times – domestic and colonial policy. Harcourt's antagonism to colonial expansion was in tune with a substantial sector of his party, but the faction favouring imperialism included some of the most talented leaders of the next generation, such as Asquith, who hoped for the return of Rosebery. Inevitably, a colonial issue occasioned his greatest blunder. At the end of 1895, Rhodes inspired the Jameson raid into the Transvaal, expecting an uprising that would convert the Boer republic into a British colony. The raid was a fiasco, but a step on the way to the Boer War. Chamberlain, as Colonial Secretary, assured Harcourt of his ignorance of the plan – a denial Harcourt incorporated into the subsequent

---

238 Rhodes James, op. cit., p. 386.

parliamentary enquiry report, which was greeted with great scepticism and undermined confidence in Harcourt's leadership.

Shortly after Rosebery's resignation, Harcourt wrote to Morley:

> Of course the reasons given by Rosebery for bolting are not the true ones ...
> I believe he funked the future he saw before him – that he felt called upon to
> ... give a lead and that he did not know what to say, and so he took up his hat
> and departed.[239]

But the same is true of Harcourt. In this last period of his leadership, he proposed no new unifying domestic theme for Liberals, and was unsympathetic to the aspirations of the new working-class voters. It was another decade before the party embraced the New Liberalism of active government intervention.

In 1898, Harcourt resigned the leadership. The timing has not been fully explained. He was seventy-one and his son had recently married, removing his most significant prop, but there are suggestions, not least from Harcourt himself, that he was torpedoing an intrigue to restore Rosebery. If so, it was a great service, as he allowed the party, through a younger generation, to adapt to the challenges of the new century. He was succeeded by Campbell-Bannerman, but did not vacate the front bench, serving as CB's stand-in when required. He died in his sleep at the family home in 1904.

As a leader who never became premier, Harcourt cannot be judged primarily on his achievements. His record should include the whole period after 1886, when he provided much of the day-to-day leadership of the Liberals in the Commons. This he did with 'courage, obstinacy and determination', with 'fair, not extraordinary intellectual powers', and with 'a power of illustration rather than of imagination', but he was 'too careless of the feelings and too little respectful of the power of others'. Harcourt made this self-assessment in 1867.[240] Few would have dissented at the end of his life, nearly forty years later.

239 Jackson, op. cit., p. 281.
240 Ibid., p. 31.

CHAPTER 12

SIR HENRY
CAMPBELL-BANNERMAN

DAVID HOWARTH

Sir Henry Campbell-Bannerman – 'CB' to his contemporaries – led the Liberal Party from 1899 to 1908, and served as Prime Minister from 5 December 1905 to 3 April 1908, leaving office shortly before his death on 22 April. He was praised after his death for his courage, idealism, shrewdness and tenacity, and for his generosity and kindness; he was most frequently admired for his common sense. Above all, he was a great party manager. He healed the rifts in the Liberal Party left by his predecessors Rosebery and Harcourt, fully exploited the political opportunities offered by the Unionist government's mistakes and, in 1906, led his party to its greatest electoral triumph. He presided over a brilliant government, including three future prime ministers, which, despite a constant threat of defeat by the Tory-dominated House of Lords, enjoyed a string of legislative successes, including the protection of the right of trade unionists to organise strikes and the foundation of the probation service, and paved the way for the New Liberal agenda of its immediate successor.

- Sir Henry Campbell-Bannerman GCB (7 September 1836 – 22 April 1908), born Henry Campbell, youngest of six children of Sir James Campbell of Stracathro, owner of a successful textile, drapery and warehousing business, and his wife Janet Bannerman.
- Educated Glasgow High School, Glasgow University, Trinity College, Cambridge.
- Joined the family firm; made partner 1860.
- Married Sarah Charlotte Bruce 1860, no children.
- Added surname Bannerman in 1871 as a requirement of the will of his uncle.

- Fought (and lost) Stirling Burghs in 1868 by-election; elected in 1868 general election; held seat until death.
- Financial Secretary to the War Office 1871–74, 1880–82, parliamentary and financial secretary to the admiralty 1882–84, Chief Secretary for Ireland 1884–85, Secretary of State for War 1886, 1892–95, leader of the Liberal Party 1899–1908, Prime Minister 1905–08.

For all that achievement, Campbell-Bannerman is little lauded or even remembered. The three future prime ministers who served in his government – Asquith (his Chancellor of the Exchequer), Lloyd George (his president of the board of trade) and Churchill (who served as a junior minister at the Colonial Office) – all enjoy much greater posthumous fame. In the case of at least one of them, this amounts in some quarters to hero worship.

But, in terms of the history of the Liberal Party, Campbell-Bannerman stands on a par with, or even above, those men. He united the party's warring factions, whereas Asquith and Lloyd George's rivalry factionalised the party in the two decades after Campbell-Bannerman's death and Churchill opted to re-defect to the Tories. Campbell-Bannerman was the last Liberal to win a parliamentary majority for his party, whereas Asquith headed a minority government after 1910 and Lloyd George, in coalition, won a majority not for the Liberals but for the Conservatives. And Campbell-Bannerman had an instinctive sympathy with the trade unions (albeit not with socialism), which put him in a position to create the progressive alliance with Labour – an alliance that, had it survived, would have changed the course of twentieth-century British politics.

In contrast, Asquith, Lloyd George and Churchill, in their different ways, undermined any prospect of unifying the progressive forces in British politics. Churchill was never in sympathy with the unions or the left, as his actions as Home Secretary at Tonypandy came to symbolise. Asquith, though not unsympathetic, dealt the progressive alliance a fearsome blow by inviting the Conservatives into a coalition government in 1915. Lloyd George, albeit sharing Campbell-Bannerman's instincts, undermined any possibility of reviving a progressive alliance with the 'coupon election' of 1918 and his various fantasies in the early 1920s of creating a centre party between the Tories and the Coalition Liberals.

So, why is Campbell-Bannerman so rarely mentioned as a contender for the title of best Liberal Prime Minister, or even best Prime Minister, of the twentieth century? Three factors come to mind.

First, unlike Lloyd George and Churchill, he was not a great orator. Indeed, in his early days in the Commons, he was a poor speaker, holding his copious notes high in front of his face and failing to engage the House. His main virtues were those of the back room – an ability to unite people of different views into a common project, strategic clarity, and administrative efficiency. He was most frequently admired for his common sense. As Herbert Samuel put it: 'His premiership was common-sense enthroned ... He was the least flamboyant of men – apparently impervious to insult and wholly unaware of the need to ingratiate himself with press and public.'[241]

A second reason for lack of appreciation of Campbell-Bannerman is that he seems a transitional figure in Liberal history. He sits between the period of Gladstone – when the party stood for sound finance, opposition to the landed interest and expansion of the franchise – and the period of the New Liberals – characterised by the creation of the early institutions of the welfare state, and eventually Keynes's economics and Beveridge's system of social security. Indeed, even in the 1906 general election, when two-thirds of Liberal candidates referred in their election addresses to the need for social reform, Campbell-Bannerman proclaimed that the party's policy could still be summed up in the Gladstonian slogan of 'peace, retrenchment and reform', and he offered to reduce public expenditure too.

A third (and perhaps the most important) reason is that Campbell-Bannerman was what would now be called a 'low-ego' leader. He was naturally sociable and unpretentious, equally at ease with monarchs and working people. His style was not to seek the limelight or take the credit for others' achievements or overly

---

241 Roy Hattersley, *Campbell-Bannerman*, London, Haus Publishing, 2006, p. 141.

intervene in his ministers' work. He left departmental ministers largely to get on with their jobs. He seems to have seen his task as providing strategic direction and backing initiatives that needed his support.

Richard Haldane, an internal opponent of Campbell-Bannerman from the Liberal imperialist wing of the party (and, later, a defector to Labour), criticised Campbell-Bannerman for treating the Cabinet as 'a meeting of delegates', and leaving too much to individual ministerial initiative,[242] but even he appreciated the guidance and support Campbell-Bannerman gave to his military reforms. It would be wrong, however, to see Campbell-Bannerman as a sort of non-executive chairman, confining himself to arbitrating between colleagues and having no views of his own. He had firm principles and would act on them. It is just that, as Roy Hattersley put it: 'He was dangerously susceptible to rational argument.'[243] Those who rise to the heights of political fame are rarely the kind of people who are susceptible to rational argument.

Campbell-Bannerman's family background gave no hint of his career on the Liberal benches. His father was a Tory who served as Lord Provost of Glasgow, and twice stood unsuccessfully for Parliament. His older brother James did eventually serve as a Tory MP, as member for Glasgow and Aberdeen Universities from 1880 to 1906, stepping down at the general election of his brother's greatest triumph.

Campbell-Bannerman possibly converted to Liberalism at university, or possibly just after, in conversations with a radical employee of his father's; at least in 1860, two years after leaving Cambridge, he is recorded as having sent a friend in India a copy of John Stuart Mill's *On Liberty*. He was, by then, not just a Liberal, but a radical. It was in that same year he married Charlotte Bruce. By many accounts, he came to regard his marriage as the greatest preoccupation of his life, certainly more important than politics – although Charlotte's judgements of character, on which Campbell-Bannerman relied, were not without their own political significance. Their close and devoted relationship later

---

242   Richard Haldane, *Autobiography*, London, Hodder & Stoughton, 1929, p. 182.

243   Hattersley, op. cit., p. 5.

became a political issue in its own right, when Charlotte's poor health, and Campbell-Bannerman's determination to be by her side, were used against him by rivals for the leadership.

Campbell-Bannerman was elected to Parliament in 1868 at his second attempt, the first being a by-election in the same seat in the same year. The seat was Stirling Burghs, a scattered constituency including Stirling itself, Dunfermline, Inverkeithing, Queensferry and Culross. Both in the by-election and the general election, Campbell-Bannerman's sole opponent was the distiller John Ramsay, a moderate Liberal who had previously stood in Glasgow as a 'Liberal Conservative'. Ramsay had the support of the party establishment and was the official candidate. Campbell-Bannerman, however, launched an insurgent campaign on his own initiative, on the basis of an uncompromisingly radical programme. He favoured religious equality, disestablishment of the Scottish and Irish Churches, compulsory public education, extension of the franchise to all male householders, a secret ballot, county self-government, land reform and the simplification of land transfer, and a foreign policy based on free trade, not Palmerstonian adventures. The extension of the franchise before the general election helped to reverse his defeat in the by-election, and he was to hold the seat for the rest of his life. His grip on it was reinforced by his genial manner, his genuine pleasure in serving his constituents, and his relative industry (by nineteenth-century standards) as a constituency MP – he spent every June and July there for a series of meetings and speeches.

Apart from his extended travels around Europe (in the course of which he acquired a fluency in French not equalled by any subsequent British Prime Minister), after 1868, Campbell-Bannerman devoted himself entirely to politics, taking no further active part in the family business. Three of his first four recorded speeches in the House were on education, including supporting the University Tests Bill – designed to allow greater access to the universities of Cambridge, Durham and Oxford to religious minorities – and moving a private members' motion calling for compulsory primary education.

Two years later, he entered Gladstone's government. He had come to the notice of Edward Cardwell, the Secretary of State for War, who was in the middle of a remarkable series of reforms of the army: abolishing the purchase of commissions; creating territorially based regiments and a trained reserve; and cutting expenditure while increasing effectiveness and professionalism. One of Cardwell's aims was to establish civilian control of the army, which included bringing the army's finances fully within political control. For this purpose, he created the role of financial secretary to the War Office, and offered it to Campbell-Bannerman. Cardwell's clarity of purpose, financial prudence and administrative efficiency served as an example to Campbell-Bannerman for the rest of his career.

After Gladstone inadvisably called and lost the general election of 1874, Cardwell was raised to the peerage, and Campbell-Bannerman became a leading opposition spokesman on military matters. He defended the Cardwell reforms against Tory backsliding, and also took part in debates on Scottish affairs, proving himself to be a moderate on the question of temperance, but insisting that alcohol licensing should be a matter of local democratic control. At this point, his reputation was that of a genial, perhaps indolent party loyalist, who had certainly mastered his brief, but who did not seem particularly brilliant or even particularly ambitious. It was a reputation he suffered from in some quarters from that time forward, even into his premiership. He certainly enjoyed his creature comforts, including spending long holidays in Marienbad and reading French novels, but his apparent indolence was made possible by a level of efficiency gained by economy of effort.

Campbell-Bannerman again took up the post of financial secretary at the War Office after the Liberals returned to office in 1880, this time serving under Hugh Childers (fortunately a sound Cardwellian) as Secretary of State for War. In 1882, he moved to the admiralty as parliamentary and financial secretary – a promotion, and also a technical challenge. Since the First Lord was a peer, Campbell-Bannerman answered for the admiralty in the Commons. Despite his reputation for a somewhat relaxed attitude to his duties, he worked diligently to gain a sufficient understanding of the navy.

In 1884, he was promoted further into the notoriously difficult job of Chief Secretary for Ireland. His immediate predecessor but one, Lord Frederick Cavendish, had been murdered by Fenians in Phoenix Park in Dublin, and his immediate predecessor, G. O. Trevelyan, was so stressed by the constant threats of death and mutilation to which he and his family were subjected that his hair and the lashes of one of his eyes turned white. This was also the period of Irish obstruction in the Commons, in which nationalist members took every opportunity not only to frustrate government business, but also to hound and abuse ministers.

Campbell-Bannerman's first instinct, perhaps unsurprisingly, was to refuse the offer of the post, but – after consulting Charlotte, as ever a bolder spirit, and finding himself unable to compose a letter giving reasons to refuse, beyond his own self-interest – he accepted. It was a fateful moment – 'a turning point in CB's life'.[244] Gone was the somewhat diffident junior minister, who, though efficient, was, perhaps intentionally, a very low-profile figure. Instead, as Asquith later wrote: 'He became, during those months, for the first time, a distinctive figure in the House of Commons; and his keen humour and imperturbable temper made him an invaluable asset to his colleagues and his chief.'[245] In a pattern that was to repeat itself when he reached the premiership twenty years later, Campbell-Bannerman exceeded all expectations. Thought of as worthy and slightly dull, he turned out to be urbane, even witty, and, above all, fully in command of his brief. On the central question of home rule, he said little, but, in private, by April 1885, he was in favour of a 'Grattan's Parliament' – an Irish legislature within a union of crowns, and a separate Irish ministry.

Campbell-Bannerman served just over seven months as Chief Secretary. Gladstone's government fell on 8 June 1885, when the Irish leader Parnell changed sides and collaborated with the Tories unexpectedly to defeat the Budget. Campbell-Bannerman hoped that it might be possible to persuade the new Conservative government to resolve the Irish question by proposing a bill of its own, and to pass it with Liberal support. If that had happened, the whole history of the next 100 years might have been different. But his hopes were in vain: Salisbury, unlike Gladstone, was not prepared to risk the unity of his party for the sake of Ireland. Instead, Gladstone signalled his own conversion to home rule shortly after the election.

244 John Wilson, *CB: A Life of Sir Henry Campbell-Bannerman*, London, Constable, 1973, p. 78.
245 Ibid.

Contrary to Salisbury's hopes, the Liberals won the election in November/ December, albeit without a working majority if all the Irish nationalists voted with the Conservatives. In February 1886, Campbell-Bannerman entered the Cabinet for the first time, as Secretary of State for War. Oddly, his elevation seems to have owed something to Queen Victoria. Gladstone originally suggested that Childers return to the War Office, but the commander-in-chief, the Queen's cousin the Duke of Cambridge, strongly disliked Childers, and much preferred the more agreeable Campbell-Bannerman. The Queen adopted her cousin's view and objected so vehemently to Childers that Gladstone gave way and appointed instead her own suggestion – Campbell-Bannerman – whom she described in her journal as 'a good, honest Scotchman'.[246]

Gladstone's third government lasted only until June, when Joseph Chamberlain and Lord Hartington led ninety-three Liberal MPs to vote against their own government to defeat the second reading of the Home Rule Bill. The Liberal split was cemented at the election which followed in July; Gladstone's party was routed, and Salisbury returned to office, this time with support from what became the Liberal Unionist party. Campbell-Bannerman returned to opposition, from where he spoke on both military and Irish affairs, intervening very effectively on, for example, the Irish Land Bill of 1887. As the parliament went on, he increasingly returned to Scottish affairs, including Scottish education and local government. But there was also more time for his beloved Marienbad and French novels.

Gladstone returned to office for his fourth and last administration in 1892, heading a minority government dependent on the support of the Irish members. Campbell-Bannerman returned to the War Office as Secretary of State, and resumed both his previous style of work (he left for Marienbad within a week of being appointed) and his previous policy of Cardwellian reform and economy. His general support for retrenchment, however, did not extend to supporting Gladstone's demands for restraint in the naval estimates during the final crisis of Gladstone's career in 1894.

---

246 Ibid., p. 162.

Campbell-Bannerman's characteristic moderation and ability to get on with everyone helped him to survive the change of Prime Minister without incident. His quiet, genial and diplomatic style of politics also enabled him to engineer the removal of the Duke of Cambridge as commander-in-chief (then aged seventy-five, and no longer an intellectual asset to the army, if he ever had been). Although this eviction of the royal family from the upper reaches of the army's command structure was an inherently radical act, he managed it without offending the Queen or, indeed, the Duke, who blamed Rosebery.

On the same day that Campbell-Bannerman announced the retirement of the Duke to the Commons, the Conservative leadership engineered a parliamentary ambush on a vote on the army estimates vote, ostensibly complaining about a shortage of ammunition and censuring him, as the responsible minister, by moving to reduce his salary by £100. The Conservatives did not expect to win what became known as the 'cordite vote', only to cause embarrassment, but defeat followed from the complacency of the Liberal whips. The senior ranks of the army and the Liberal press supported Campbell-Bannerman, the *Manchester Guardian* describing him as 'the most popular War Minister of this generation'.[247] But Rosebery and the rest of the Cabinet, increasingly divided over the future direction of Liberalism after Gladstone, were in no mood to fight, and the government resigned. Campbell-Bannerman's personal position, however, was not adversely affected; the fact that many members of the Cabinet thought a Cabinet without him not worth having confirmed his standing as an indispensable figure in the party.

The 1895 election threw the Liberals out of power for the following ten years. Although Campbell-Bannerman had harboured ambitions of becoming Speaker of the House, he took over the leadership of the Liberal Party in 1899. He came to the post essentially by a process of elimination. Rosebery had resigned the leadership in 1896, his Imperialist tendencies completely at odds with the Gladstonian approach of Harcourt, the leader of the Liberals in the Commons. Harcourt in turn, battered by Liberal Imperialists such as Asquith and Grey, himself gave

247   Ibid., p. 207.

up the ghost in 1898. John Morley, perhaps accidentally, eliminated himself by associating with Harcourt's resignation. That left the only remaining options as Rosebery, whose return was unacceptable to the radicals; Asquith, difficult because he was unwilling to leave his lucrative practice at the Bar without compensation; and Campbell-Bannerman, who was popular and respected in most parts of the party and who on the matters that divided the Liberals followed a moderate line somewhere between the Gladstonians and the Liberal Imperialists. He was unanimously – if, on his part, somewhat reluctantly – elected leader of the party in the Commons at a meeting in the Smoking Room of the Reform Club on 6 February 1899.

Eight months later, the outbreak of the South African War reinforced the Liberal Party's divisions: in the Commons just over sixty Liberal Imperialists, led by Grey and Haldane, supported the war; just under seventy, led by Harcourt and Morley, opposed it; around thirty moderates, led by Campbell-Bannerman, opposed Joseph Chamberlain's jingoism but were not 'pro-Boer'; and about thirty others had no distinct position. The Conservatives, hoping to take advantage of those divisions, and of the fall of Pretoria in June 1900, called a 'khaki' election. In the end, however, Campbell-Bannerman's optimism and ability to rouse his troops around traditional Liberal themes, the failure of the Liberal Unionists to deliver on promises such as old-age pensions, and a general lack of enthusiasm for the election among the electorate produced a small increase in the Liberals' representation in the Commons.

The Boer War continued to dominate politics after the election, and the Liberals appeared to be as divided as before. By early 1901 the Boer armies had been defeated, but they resorted to highly effective forms of guerrilla warfare. The British response was systematically to destroy their bases of support, building networks of blockhouses and wire fences, burning the Boer farmsteads and imprisoning women and children in concentration camps. Campbell-Bannerman stepped up his criticisms of government policy, to the dismay of the Liberal Imperialists who tried, unsuccessfully, to tempt Rosebery back to the leadership.

On her return from a visit to South Africa on behalf of the South African Women and Children Distress Fund, Emily Hobhouse, sister of the Liberal intellectual L. T. Hobhouse, relayed to Campbell-Bannerman what she had seen. As she recalled later:

> Of all whom I saw at that time … he alone … seemed to have the leisure and
> the determination to hear and understand everything … As I dwelt upon
> the wholesale burning of farms and villages, the deportations, the desper-
> ate condition of a burnt-out population brought in by hundreds in convoys,
> the people deprived of clothes, bedding, utensils and necessities, the semi-
> starvation in the camps, the fever-stricken children lying … upon the bare
> earth … the appalling mortality … he was deeply moved – and now and
> again muttered sotto voce 'methods of barbarism, methods of barbarism'.
> He was right.[248]

Three weeks later, Campbell-Bannerman took his chance, at a dinner given to him and Harcourt by the National Reform Union at the Holborn Restaurant in London:

> What is that policy? That … we should punish them as severely as possible,
> devastate their country, burn their homes … I do not say for a moment that
> this is the deliberate and the intentional policy of His Majesty's Government,
> but … it is the thing which is being done at this moment in the name and by
> the authority of this most humane and Christian nation … A phrase often used
> is that 'war is war' but when one comes to ask about it one is told that no war
> is going on, that it is not war. When is a war not a war? When it is carried on
> by methods of barbarism in South Africa.[249]

Given Campbell-Bannerman's reputation as a weak orator it is ironic to note that his best-remembered utterance came in this brave and powerful speech. Just as 100 years later, when another leader of the party denounced an illegal

---

248 Ibid., p. 350.

249 The speech is reproduced in full in Duncan Brack and Tony Little eds, *Great Liberal Speeches*, London, Politico's, 2001, pp. 209–14.

invasion, the result was a torrent of abuse from the Tories and their supporters, who accused him of treachery and insulting the army.

The Liberal Imperialists regarded the speech as a virtual declaration of war and organised a congratulatory dinner for Asquith, who had publicly criticised Campbell-Bannerman (the successive dinners prompting the parliamentary sketchwriter Henry Lucy to write of 'war to the knife – and fork'). This time they over-reached themselves, as Campbell-Bannerman took the opportunity to call a meeting of all Liberal MPs to request a vote of confidence in his leadership. With Rosebery critical but declining to get involved, the Liberal Imperialists had no alternative leader and backed down. In December, Rosebery implicitly attacked Campbell-Bannerman's leadership in a speech in Chesterfield, calling for a 'clean slate' and a programme based on national 'efficiency', but although the speech was an oratorical triumph its central weakness played into Campbell-Bannerman's hands; as Campbell-Bannerman observed at the time, 'All that he said about the clean slate and efficiency was an affront to Liberalism and pure claptrap. Efficiency as a watchword! Who is against it?'[250]

On 31 May 1902, the war finally ended, helping greatly to heal the divisions within the party. Public opinion finally began to swing towards Campbell-Bannerman, as people realised he had been right about the war, and feared the legacy of bitterness on which the new South African federation was being built. Events then began to favour the Liberals. The Education Act of 1902 roused Nonconformist ire by subsidising Church schools out of the rates. In May 1903, Chamberlain launched his campaign for tariff reform, reuniting the Liberals under the banner of free trade and splitting the Unionists, several of whom (including Churchill) were to defect to the Liberals over the following two years. Asquith cemented his reputation within the party by supporting Campbell-Bannerman in arguing the free-trade case in a series of devastatingly effective speeches. And Alfred Milner, governor of the former Boer provinces, successfully promoted a scheme for using indentured Chinese labour in the gold mines of the Transvaal – 'Chinese slavery' – which, above all, reminded Liberals of the moral superiority of

250 Cited in J. A. Spender, *Life of Sir Henry Campbell-Bannerman*, London, Hodder & Stoughton, 1923, p. 14.

Liberalism over Toryism, and was to provide a potent symbol during the election campaign in 1906. Campbell-Bannerman did not engineer any of these events, but he exploited them successfully to create a united fighting force.

The Unionists nevertheless thought the Liberals too divided to govern. That is why, in December 1905 Balfour, his government fatally split, simply resigned instead of calling an election; he hoped to face Campbell-Bannerman with what he thought would be the impossible task of forming a Liberal minority government. But Balfour miscalculated. In September Asquith, Haldane and Grey had agreed during a fishing holiday at Relugas in Elginshire that each would refuse to serve under Campbell-Bannerman unless he agreed to go to the Lords, leaving the effective leadership of the party and the government with Asquith in the Commons. In the event, Campbell-Bannerman, yet again underestimated, stood firm and the plotters were unable to resist the lure of high office – the Home Office for Asquith, the Foreign Office for Grey and, rather disappointingly for him, the War Office for arch-plotter Haldane.

The Unionists' last throw of the dice had failed; Campbell-Bannerman took office on 5 December 1905. The subsequent election, in January/February 1906, was a Liberal triumph. Diners danced on the tables in the National Liberal Club as victory followed victory on the first nights of polling. In the end the party won 397 seats, Labour (the Liberals' allies in an electoral pact encouraged by Campbell-Bannerman) twenty-nine, and the Irish, also favourably disposed to the Liberals following an alignment around a common concept of 'step-by-step' home rule, eighty-two. The Unionists were reduced to just 156, their lowest total ever.

The government led by Campbell-Bannerman contained a glittering array of talent; three future prime ministers, Asquith, Lloyd George and Churchill, were joined, among others, by Haldane, Grey, Morley, Birrell and the first working man to become a Cabinet minister, John Burns. Over the following two years Campbell-Bannerman's government secured the freedom of trade unions to organise industrial action, funded the provision of free school meals, extended scholarships for working class pupils to grant-aided grammar schools (reserving 25 per cent of the places for them), extended compensation for injuries at work, provided for the medical examination of all schoolchildren, established the

National Trust, introduced the idea of probation for offenders, created a separate system of juvenile justice (and abolished the death penalty for juveniles), limited working hours in the coal mines to eight hours a day and prepared the way for the introduction of old-age pensions. Some of these apparently modest measures were forerunners of larger reforms later in the century. A generous settlement was reached with the former Boer republics, restoring South African autonomy on much better terms than could have been hoped for a few years earlier.

Yet it was also often a frustrating time. The Lords, dominated by the Conservatives, killed more radical Liberal proposals, including an Education Bill, a bill to end the situation in which some well-off voters had more than one vote and a Temperance Bill, and it weakened a programme of land reform. In response, Campbell-Bannerman proposed not to change the composition of the Lords but to replace its veto with a power only to delay (a 'suspensory veto'). Although he declined to press the matter further, judging that the time had not yet arrived to take on the Lords, his proposal was essentially adopted three years after his death, following the crisis caused by the Lords' rejection of Lloyd George's People's Budget. Campbell-Bannerman was also cautious about other constitutional issues, including women's suffrage, which he supported but was not prepared to divide the party over, and Irish home rule, though his personal credibility with the Irish nationalists stood him in good stead in that respect.

Campbell-Bannerman's time in Downing Street was from a personal point of view unhappy. Charlotte died in August 1906, in her beloved Marienbad. This was a devastating blow for her husband, and thereafter his own health began to decline severely. He suffered a series of heart attacks, to begin with fairly minor, allowing him to return to work quite quickly, but becoming increasingly debilitating during 1907 and 1908. In the end his prime ministerial tenure was short. He presided over his last Cabinet meeting and made his last speech to the Commons on 12 February 1908; the next day he suffered a serious heart attack. By early March, Asquith was effectively acting Prime Minister. On 3 April the King accepted Campbell-Bannerman's resignation. Too ill to move from Downing Street, he died there on 22 April 1908.

Campbell-Bannerman 'was an unusual person to emerge as the leader of a great political party in England, or indeed to be a politician at all', his biographer puts it, 'for he was easy-going, had little ambition and was inclined to let well alone'.[251] Yet he brought the Liberal Party back from one of the lowest points of its pre-1918 history, fought off constant sniping from his predecessor, Rosebery, and his supporters, constructed a political alliance stretching from the free-trade wing of the Conservative Party to the nascent Labour Representation Committee, and, in 1906 led his party to its greatest electoral success ever. He was a genuine radical, introducing reforms, as Roy Hattersley put it, 'with the apparent certainty that common sense commended each reform. And that is the mark of the true radical – the certainty that the changes he proposed in society were reasonable as well as right.'[252]

'Much historical comment has emphasised Campbell-Bannerman as a tactician, a shrewd (an oft-used word) reconciler of factions, a man who worked behind the scenes to deal with seemingly intractable problems.'[253] And perhaps this was his greatest achievement. Other Liberal leaders – Gladstone, Asquith, Lloyd George – left their party divided; others – Russell, Rosebery, Samuel – were unable to patch it up. Later Liberal leaders merely managed decline into marginal status. In contrast, Campbell-Bannerman produced a coherent Liberal government in circumstances when that was thought to be impossible, and did much to establish the character of what was to become, after his death, the most brilliant reforming administration of the century.

---

251   Wilson, op. cit., p. 15.

252   Hattersley, op. cit., p. 143.

253   Ewen Cameron, 'Maistly Scotch': Campbell-Bannerman and Liberal Leadership', *Journal of Liberal History*, Vol. 54, spring 2007, p. 33.

CHAPTER 13

HERBERT HENRY ASQUITH

TONY MORRIS

Herbert Henry Asquith is one of the giants of British Liberalism. He presided over the radical reforming government which put the New Liberalism into practice, laying the foundations of Britain's welfare state, establishing the Budget as an instrument of social policy and breaking the power of the House of Lords. His widely admired administrative skills, however, failed the unprecedented challenge of the First World War, and the resulting split with his colleague Lloyd George almost destroyed the party he led for eighteen years.

- Herbert Henry Asquith (12 September 1852 – 15 February 1928), born at Morley in Yorkshire to Joseph Dixon Asquith (c.1825–60) and Emily (née Willans).
- Educated at City of London School and Balliol College, Oxford.
- Balliol College fellowship (1874–82); called to the Bar (1876); took silk (1890).
- Married: (1) Helen Melland (c.1855–91) in 1877, five children; (2) Margot Tennant (1864–1945) in 1894, five children, only two survived infancy.
- MP East Fife 1886–1918, Paisley 1920–24.
- Home Secretary 1892–95, Chancellor of the Exchequer 1905–08, Secretary of State for War March to August 1914, Prime Minister 1908–16, leader of the Liberal Party 1908–26.
- Created First Earl of Oxford and Asquith in February 1925.

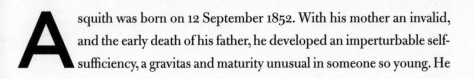

Asquith was born on 12 September 1852. With his mother an invalid, and the early death of his father, he developed an imperturbable self-sufficiency, a gravitas and maturity unusual in someone so young. He pursued his studies conscientiously, at Oxford falling under the influence of Balliol College's most famous master, Benjamin Jowett, and the leading idealist philosopher T. H. Green. Without unduly exerting himself he secured a first in Greats, and left Balliol with a distinguished reputation and a coterie of friends who, like him, shared 'the effortless superiority of Balliol men'.[254] The assured serenity with which he was seen to have attained academic distinction prompted more confidence in his judgement than was perhaps merited.

Asquith was called to the Bar in June 1876. He did not enjoy immediate success and had to supplement his meagre earnings with his Balliol fellowship and his wife's small annual allowance; he married Helen Melland, the daughter of a Manchester physician, in August 1877. They settled in Hampstead where their five gifted children, four sons and a daughter, were born. Helen, a gentle and kindly woman, had little interest beyond her home and family. In 1891, she contracted typhus and died, leaving Asquith emotionally drained but free to move into the wider social circles to which he aspired. He left Hampstead, settled his children in Dorking in the care of a housekeeper and nanny and began an earnest courtship of Margot Tennant, the sixth daughter of Sir Charles Tennant, a Scottish industrialist and entrepreneur. When Asquith married Margot in 1894 some of his friends were puzzled that he should be attracted to such a notoriously tactless and egotistical socialite, so very different from Helen; but he loved her passionately and admired her social confidence, fearlessness and éclat – and also her glittering social world, to which he was now introduced. As passionate in her loyalties as in her animosities, highly ambitious for her husband's success, the dramatic change she effected in his life was bathetically, if significantly, marked by her insistence in future that his family should address him as Henry and not, as formerly, Herbert or Bert.

Asquith's work on the parliamentary oath and the 1883 Corrupt Practices Act brought him to the attention of senior Liberals. His friend Richard Haldane was elected to the House in 1885 and encouraged Asquith to seek a seat of his own. Adopted for East Fife, where he proclaimed himself to be an 'advanced Liberal', Asquith won a narrow victory in the 1886 general election. He impressed

---

254 Asquith, quoted in J. Jones, *Balliol College: A History*, Oxford, Oxford University Press, 1997, p. 226.

with his maiden speech, in which he 'assumed the manner of a frontbencher',[255] but he was an infrequent speaker, concentrating on his legal career. A fastidious reluctance to play the parliamentary drudge – 'He will never do a day's work for us', Sir William Harcourt once complained to John Morley[256] – did him no long-term harm. He spoke rather more frequently in the country, but the occasions were carefully chosen to create the maximum impact.

Asquith was appointed Home Secretary in Gladstone's final government, formed in 1892. His time in office was marked by constructive if cautious reforms, including a significant strengthening of the factory inspectorate and a considerable improvement in the working conditions of certain dangerous trades. But the Lords' defeat of his carefully drafted Employers Liability Bill confirmed him in his belief that opportunities for constructive measures had been needlessly lost because of Gladstone's obsession with Ireland. Gladstone's successor Rosebery kept Asquith at the Home Office, where Welsh disestablishment fully absorbed his energies. Out of office after the 1895 defeat, Asquith condemned Rosebery's resignation as party leader in 1896 as selfishly motivated and made without thought for party interests. His criticism of Rosebery did not imply any enthusiasm for his successor Harcourt, however; he thought him 'undignified, entirely lacking in the least sense of public duty' and in 1898, he in turn condemned Harcourt's resignation as 'cowardly, egotistical and entirely unjustified'.[257]

Asquith was seen as a potential successor to Harcourt but backed the more experienced Henry Campbell-Bannerman, partly because he needed his barrister's income; he returned to his legal work, attending Parliament infrequently. Along with other Liberal Imperialists, he broadly supported the Conservative government's policy during the Boer War, but managed to maintain a cordial relationship with Campbell-Bannerman, assuring him that he would never be associated with any aggressive movement against fellow Liberals or any attempt to weaken the party. From 1902, the ending of the war, and Unionist measures on education and licensing

255   J. A. Spender and C. Asquith, *Life of Lord Oxford & Asquith*, London, Hutchinson, 1932, Vol. 1, p. 56.

256   A. G. Gardiner, *The Life of Harcourt*, London, Constable, 1923, Vol. 2, p. 152.

257   Asquith memorandum, quoted, Spender and Asquith, op. cit., Vol. 1, p. 122.

reform and tariffs, helped to reunite the Liberals, and Asquith's campaigning on these issues established him as a leading spokesman for the whole party. Newly enthused for the political fray, Asquith exposed the fallacies and contradictions in Chamberlain's arguments for tariff reform in a series of brilliant, forensic speeches.

Such was the change in the political climate that a Liberal victory at the next election now appeared probable. Asquith and his closest colleagues, Haldane and Edward Grey, agreed between themselves that when the Liberals came to power they would insist on Campbell-Bannerman going to the Lords, Asquith taking the Exchequer and leading the party in the Commons, Grey being given either the Foreign or Colonial Office and Haldane being appointed Lord Chancellor. This scheme, known as the Relugas compact, came to nothing when Campbell-Bannerman refused to budge and offered Asquith the Treasury; abandoning his fellow plotters, Asquith accepted immediately.

In the 1906 election the Liberals won an overall majority in the House of 132, and in any straight clash with the Tories, they could count on the support of their usual allies, giving them a huge majority of 356. Liberals eagerly anticipated a series of radical reforms. Inevitably there were tensions within Campbell-Bannerman's Cabinet, representing as it did the different Liberal groups, but the Prime Minister relied on Asquith to mediate between discordant opinions. In debates in the chamber he was his party's most forceful and incisive front-bench performer, eloquent, succinct, lucid and decisive. As Chancellor he held a politically prestigious post, but what made him a commanding figure in the government was the power vested in him to range over all fields of policy, and the universal recognition that he was the Prime Minister's successor.

A more technically competent Chancellor than many of his predecessors, Asquith enjoyed his time at the Treasury and would remember it as his most gratifying ministerial experience. He introduced his first budget on 30 April 1906, speaking with such ease and fluency that his permanent secretary declared it was as though he had been introducing budgets all his life. Despite his reputation as 'a respectable, more or less conservative type of financier',[258] he introduced

---

258   Quoted in Stephen Koss, *Asquith*, London, Viking, 1976, p. 79.

highly significant reforms. His second budget, in 1907, overturned Gladstone's, and the Treasury's, belief that it was impracticable to distinguish between taxation for earned and unearned income, reducing the tax on earned incomes of less than £2,000 a year from a shilling (5p) to ninepence in the pound, and increasing death duties. Significantly, his assertion that Chancellors should not treat each financial year as self-contained and budget not for one but for several years clearly allowed for innovatory financial planning.

He set aside part of a surplus achieved by Haldane's military reforms for a scheme of non-contributory old-age pensions to be introduced in 1908. This reallocation of revenue from expenditure on the army to the promotion of social welfare was seized upon by angry Tories, who accused him of deliberately endangering Britain's security to secure doles for the idle and bribes to silence feckless socialists; Rosebery thought it prodigal and likely to undermine the empire. Asquith believed, however, that the provision of pensions was a duty the state owed to its citizens. Seventy-year-olds whose income did not exceed 10 shillings (50p) a week who were not otherwise disqualified would receive 5 shillings (25p) weekly, and married couples 8 shillings and 9 pence (44p). The scheme was estimated to cost £13 million a year and be achievable without significant extra taxation, though in fact the cost turned out to be an underestimate. Nonetheless, Asquith can take the credit for 'preparing the way for Lloyd George's development of the Treasury as a positive rather than negative force in British government'.

In April 1908 Campbell-Bannerman, his emotional and physical energy long eroded, resigned as Prime Minister. Asquith's succession was certain; throughout Sir Henry's ministry he had been his trusted lieutenant and had effectively held the reins of power since Campbell-Bannerman's heart attack in November 1907. He became Prime Minister on 8 April 1908. The great radical editor of the *Daily News*, A. G. Gardiner, provides a prescient contemporary portrait:

> If not the finest, subtlest, most attractive, he was incomparably the most effective and most powerful intellect in the Commons ... The sentences of his orderly speech march into action like disciplined units marshalled and drilled.

Detachment from the pettiness and meanness of controversy is largely the source of the growing authority he has established over the House ... His power of work is unequalled, his strength of mind backed by a physique equal to any burden ... A ready and powerful debater.

Gardiner also recorded Asquith's 'reticence, his dislike of display that would probably prevent him gaining more than a small hold upon the affections of the public'. Not an intellectual in the Balfourian style, he 'neither constantly reflected upon received ideas, nor possessed Lloyd George's aptitude as a man of action'. He also 'lacked John Simon's persuasiveness as an advocate'.[259]

The Cabinet he assembled balanced experience with youth, the bold and energetic with the sage and cautious, the tough with the emollient. Of the new appointments, the combination of Lloyd George at the Exchequer and Winston Churchill at the board of trade, 'the radical twins', gave the administration a sharp, progressive profile. As importantly, Crewe's appointment as Colonial Secretary and Liberal leader in the Lords acknowledged the party's small but significant Whig element. Asquith's preferred modus operandi as premier was to act as co-ordinator of the legislation promoted by ministers; but the intransigence of the Lords with its permanent Unionist majority caused him to adopt a more direct and active role. The Upper House rejected or mutilated proposed legislation on licensing, education, housing and town planning, and two Scottish bills concerning land values and smallholders. Asquith, anticipating troubles over the Budget and the forthcoming Finance Bill, warned that a crisis could not long be delayed. 'The Budget of next year will stand at the very centre of our work by which we will stand or fall and by which we shall certainly be judged in the estimation of the present and of posterity.'[260]

There were opponents of Lloyd George's 'People's Budget' proposals even within the Cabinet but Asquith backed his Chancellor 'through thick and thin

---

259   A. G. Gardiner, *Prophets, Priests and Kings*, London, Alston Rivers, 1908, pp. 54–60. See also: M. and E. Brock eds, *Margot Asquith's Great War Diary 1914–1916*, Oxford, Oxford University Press, 2014, pp. v–vi.

260   Speech to Liberal MPs at National Liberal Club, December 1908.

with splendid loyalty'.[261] While not revolutionary, the Budget's intent was certainly radical; it provoked the decisive conflict with the Lords, although that had not been its primary intention. In the country Asquith impressed audiences with his forceful speeches emphasising the budget's financial and constitutional importance. Nevertheless, in November 1909 the Lords ignored convention and rejected the Finance Bill on its second reading. Asquith responded with a motion declaring that the Lords' action had been a constitutional breach, a usurpation of the rights of the Commons. Next day, in a magisterial speech, he condemned 'this new form of Cæsarism' that would convert the Lords into 'a kind of plebiscitary organ'. But the King's secretary, in response to Asquith's inquiry, advised him that the creation of sufficient peers to overcome the Unionist majority in the Upper House was impossible; it would embarrass and prove difficult for the King. Parliament was therefore prorogued.

Asquith opened the election campaign of January 1910 with a deliberately circumspect address. A throwaway remark that he would not resume office unless safeguards were secured was generally understood to mean that he already possessed the King's agreement for the creation of peers. In the end the two main parties ended up almost equal, 274 Liberals to 272 Unionists. The overall Liberal majority remained, however, guaranteed by the votes of Irish and Labour MPs. Asquith was tired and thoroughly dispirited by the prospect of not only having to face a protracted struggle with the Lords but a painful re-examination of Liberal intentions concerning home rule; the Liberals could no longer ignore the interests of the Irish party upon whose favours they now relied for their majority. When he met the new parliament, to the disappointment of his followers he announced that he had not asked the King for a guarantee; Murray, the Chief Whip, thought it the worst speech he had ever heard Asquith make. During the prolonged debates in Cabinet over the Parliament Bill designed to curb the power of the Lords, however, Asquith recovered his impetus. Now he assured the House that he would not seek dissolution without gaining the

---

261   Lloyd George in conversation with D. R. Daniel, quoted in John Grigg, *Lloyd George: The People's Champion 1902–1911*, London, Faber & Faber, 1978, p. 178.

guarantees he had previously failed to secure. Murray reversed his earlier criticism and praised Asquith's 'grand parliamentary triumph'. Within a fortnight, the Finance Bill was reintroduced. The Lords approved it without a division.

King Edward's death in May transformed the political situation by throwing into confusion what so recently had seemed settled. The agreed solution, to call a constitutional conference, pleased only the party mandarins. In the face of irreconcilable differences the conference inevitably collapsed. Asquith no longer procrastinated and sought an immediate dissolution. A secret agreement had been secured from a reluctant King George that, if necessary, sufficient peers would be created to ensure the powers of the elected House should not be usurped by the hereditary. Asquith played a dominant part in 1910's second election campaign, concentrating on the constitutional issue of 'peers versus the people'. The result of the election in December confirmed the Liberals in power, with almost no change from the outcome in January.

Feelings over the Parliament Bill ran extraordinarily high in both Houses. Asquith's speeches, cool and restrained though powerful and eloquent, contrasted with the wild belligerence of other speakers. On 24 July 1911 Asquith was howled down by a mob of Unionist MPs, described by Churchill as 'a squalid, organised attempt to insult the Prime Minister'. He was accused of being a traitor, of hounding King Edward to a premature grave and acting as the lackey of the Irish leader Redmond in an unholy alliance with Irish separatists financed by American dollars. But despite the behaviour of 'Die-hards' and 'Ditchers', it was the 'Hedgers' among the Unionist peers who, acknowledging political reality, narrowly won the day. The passage into law of the Parliament Act in August effected significant constitutional change, yet in the best Liberal tradition, Asquith had sought to make the existing constitution work, and the Lords retained significant powers. By patching rather than reformulating he achieved a radical purpose within a conservative framework. He now stood at the zenith of his prime ministerial career.

Now in his late fifties, he wrote to Viola Tree, 'through another birthday but I feel no older, on the contrary, younger than I did this time last year'. His strong physical constitution had allowed him for years to abuse his body, but too little exercise, unrelenting work, constant emotional demands both professionally and domestically and excessive dining and wining inevitably left their mark. Despite his declared pretensions he had become jowly and corpulent. In October 1911 Constance Battersea told her sister that she had been shocked by the change in his appearance: 'Red and bloated, quite different from what he used to be.'[262]

Asquith's administration was now pressed on all sides. As his parliamentary majority was, in part, sustained by Labour votes, it would have been wiser had he handled industrial and trade union disputes with particular care. This he never found easy. Trade unionists in their turn were disconcerted; to them Asquith always sounded too much the lawyer. He knew they were unhappy and uneasy about the Osborne Judgment of 1909, forbidding trade unions to collect a levy for political purposes, but he was unnecessarily dilatory in reversing its consequences. He was unsuccessful in attempting to stop a railway strike because although he believed the men's grievances were real he obdurately refused to go beyond the offer of a royal commission. The men were finally persuaded to return to work by the emollient cajolery of Lloyd George.

When the coal miners threatened action in the spring of 1912, Asquith swallowed the principle of a minimum wage but not their specific demands for its level. The strike went ahead, and after attempts to negotiate a compromise settlement failed, emergency legislation was pushed through the Commons. Emotionally exhausted, a tearful Asquith told the House, 'We have done our best in the public interest.' Within months, London's dock workers struck. When a Cabinet committee Asquith had previously set up failed in its attempt to mediate, he made a further effort on his own. That too failed. The strike eventually foundered on the intransigence of the employers, who refused to settle for anything less than complete victory.

The Liberal government's authority to deal with the problems experienced in 1912–13 was diminished by the Marconi scandal, alleged insider trading involving Lloyd George, Murray, Herbert Samuel and Rufus Isaacs. Margot was much

---

262 Both quotations – the letter to Viola Tree and by Constance Battersea – from Colin Clifford, *The Asquiths*, London, John Murray, 2002, pp. 185–6.

concerned that Lloyd George and Isaacs, the two main culprits, would take advantage of Asquith's generosity, for he had told her he intended to stand by both of them. Political convenience would have suggested they be dismissed. Asquith defended both men stoutly and the House exonerated them. This result owed more to the restraint of the Unionist leaders, discomforted by the blatant anti-Semitism shown by their supporters, than to Asquith's loyal defence of the two men.

It seems somewhat paradoxical that Asquith, who rated the capacity and intelligence of women so highly and who chose women as his intimate confidants, should have been actively opposed to their enfranchisement. J. A. Spender argued he did so 'for frankly sentimental reasons': he believed that women looked upon the right to vote 'with a languid and imperturbable indifference'. He also feared that the Unionists, not the Liberals, would be the likely beneficiaries from an extension of the franchise. The suffragettes made him the subject of their special attention, but the more they verbally and physically threatened him, the more determined became his opposition. Until 1911 he used the excuse of Cabinet differences to avoid proposing a measure that he knew a majority of Liberal MPs favoured. In 1911, he was reluctantly obliged to admit that a majority in the Cabinet now supported female enfranchisement, but when, in 1912 a measure was introduced, it fell at its second reading. In January 1913 a fourth Reform Bill was dropped after a ruling by the Speaker. Asquith was not displeased by this unexpected decision, describing it in a letter to Venetia Stanley as 'a coup d'état that bowled the Women over for this Session'. For him it came as a 'great relief'. With imprisoned suffragettes refusing to eat, a Prisoners' Temporary Discharge for Ill-Health Act – the so-called Cat & Mouse Act – was passed; it was a desperate and unsatisfactory measure permitting the repeated release and re-arrest of prisoners who otherwise would have died. Asquith's unspoken fear was that the militants might take to the warpath. Keir Hardie suggested the obvious solution: to give the women the vote. This Asquith would not do, although he assured the Commons in 1913 that his opposition was neither dogmatic nor final. He finally changed his mind in 1918 and supported the Representation of the People Act which gave the vote to most women aged over thirty.

As Asquith admitted to Venetia Stanley, he always had 'a slight weakness for the companionship of clever and attractive women'. His fondness for his 'little harem', as Margot called them, was a 'weakness' she, just as Helen before her, learned to accept. In his sixties, his children's social circle, the 'coterie', kept him in contact with a great many attractive, clever young women. He was particularly close at different times to Viola Tree, then Venetia Stanley and later Venetia's married sister Sylvia Henley. He would write to the Stanley girls in particular, twice, sometimes three times in one day. There were also walks and carriage drives. Thus, he insisted, he was saved from 'sterility, impotence, despair', enabled by his 'love' for them to 'still see visions and dream dreams' despite 'the daily stress of almost intolerable burdens and anxieties'.[263] Though his written and undoubtedly spoken declarations of love were unrestrained in their ardour it is most unlikely he ever had sexual intercourse with any of his 'harem'. He was, however, an inveterate groper.

Welsh disestablishment remained unfinished business. Though rejected by the Lords in 1913, a bill was reintroduced the following year and finally approved by the Lords in September 1914, though its immediate operation was suspended. Welsh disestablishment spoke to the heart of the Liberal Party, but home rule, whose introduction the Parliament Act now made possible, was a much more ambiguous issue. Asquith was not part of the Cabinet committee that drew up the Home Rule Bill and had always thought that the price for home rule would almost certainly involve a bargain concerning the Protestant majority population of Ulster. The bill was introduced in April 1912 and defeated in the Lords the following year. The same thing happened in 1913 and 1914, giving the Unionists time to whip up opposition. Bonar Law, who had succeeded Balfour as Tory leader, had warned Asquith that he intended to be 'very vicious', but the Prime Minister did not appreciate the extent to which Bonar Law was prepared to play the Orange card and encourage the people of Ulster to resist any attempt to force them into a self-governing Ireland. When the Tories in their desperation attempted to play the royal card, Asquith warned the King off this

---

263 See Asquith to Venetia Stanley, in Brock, op. cit., pp. 431, 467.

dangerous constitutional ground. Behind the scenes there were secret talks to see if an agreement could be found, but to no avail; stubbornly Asquith, even on the edge of civil war, maintained his belief that the political process would eventually find a compromise solution.

Against a background of both unionist and nationalist volunteer forces recruiting and arming, in March 1914, Brigadier Gough and more than sixty other officers at the Curragh army base in Ireland declared their refusal to coerce Ulster should it resist home rule by force. General Paget, their commander-in-chief, confused by Secretary of State for War Seely's instructions and Churchill's bullying, had unnecessarily raised the issue that prompted the so-called mutiny at the Curragh. After issuing statements and redrafts without Cabinet approval, Seely was forced to resign; a justifiably angry Asquith, to the surprise then delight of almost everyone, took his place at the War Office. Once there, characteristically he did nothing, but in itself his presence at the War Office was sufficient to reassure the public.

Discussions on Ireland's and Ulster's future continued; in July, an all-party conference proved inconclusive. The threat of civil war in Ireland remained real until the outbreak of European war in August absorbed all political energy. When the Home Rule Bill passed into law in September 1914, like Welsh disestablishment, its operation was suspended. The Tories claimed the party truce had implied its indefinite shelving; Asquith denied ever making such a pledge, at which Bonar Law likened the Prime Minister's behaviour to the Kaiser's treacherous invasion of Belgium. Asquith took Bonar Law's absurd comparison in good part; it is doubtful that he realised Bonar Law was in deadly earnest. Asquith's attitude towards the Irish question, despite much provocation, remained balanced, honourable and equable. However, it is doubtful whether a policy that brought Ireland to the brink of civil war and was halted only by an international disaster of unprecedented magnitude can be counted as either wise or efficacious.

Defence and foreign policy issues often posed difficulties for the Liberals; opinions were frequently sharply divided, and often Asquith's best practical solution was, as far as possible, to keep contentious issues away from Cabinet attention. Since Anglo-French military staff conversations initiated in 1906, the army had planned for military involvement in continental Europe. Asquith first learned about this in 1911. He publicly maintained that he deprecated such secret arrangements and insisted that such *pour parlers* should be non-committal and be approved by the Cabinet; but the existence of the staff conversations effectively made the 1904 Anglo-French entente an alliance. Asquith subsequently observed that this process constituted 'a concurrence of untoward events working towards a conclusion no one intended and no one could defend'.[264] Yet as Prime Minister, if he was to keep Britain's foreign policy options open for as long as possible he was obliged to employ just such means.

Asquith's patience and determination never to rush his colleagues ensured that by 1914 the Cabinet was more united on foreign policy than for many years previously. This unity, however, depended on a degree of ambivalence: it was not certain to what policy exactly the British government was committed. After the Austrian ultimatum to Serbia Asquith did not, like Churchill at the Admiralty, attempt in any way to influence events, or, like Grey at the Foreign Office, try to secure peace by reviving the congress system with a conference of the powers. Members were confused and for the most part reluctant to become embroiled in any war.

On 2 August, it was Grey who sought a firm response to the French request that the British Navy secure their northern coast. Next day in the Commons it was Grey who made the speech that effectively announced war. Asquith's contributions were to approve the King's direct appeal to the Tsar and Churchill's mobilisation of the Fleet; on 2 August he refused to despatch the army's Expeditionary Force to France, but reversed his decision the next day. On 4 August he briefly informed the House that the British ambassador in Berlin would ask for his passport at midnight if Germany ignored Britain's ultimatum and refused assurances of Belgium's neutrality. Finally, on 7 August, he told the House that Britain's interest in Belgian neutrality, as declared in the 1839 Treaty of London, for him had been 'the crucial, almost governing position'. He left it to Grey to talk of 'honour' and of international obligations owed to entente partners. He

264 See Koss, op. cit., p. 143.

was content to play the appropriate part: as Liberal leader keeping his party and Cabinet together, scarcely losing any save a few irreconcilable dissentients, and as a national leader, to support the ultimatum deciding upon war with Germany.

Asquith's appointment of Field Marshal Kitchener as War Minister helped to quash any doubts about the ability of a Liberal administration successfully to wage war. In the first months of the war, Cabinet colleagues thought that Asquith's qualities of temper, tact and courage had never been more noticeable, though some thought him too considerate towards the opposition. He set out the case for war with Germany to the British people with dignity and without bombast. He never believed, as did so many others, that the war would be over by Christmas; he emphasised the likelihood of a protracted struggle. As chairman of the Defence Committee, however, he had made no plans in advance to streamline decision-making. The efficiency and effectiveness of the War Council, set up in November with a membership of eight, was undermined by existing cheek by jowl with various informal ad hoc arrangements as well as the Cabinet, still the supreme decision-making body.

Before the end of 1914, as it became clear that the troops entrenched along the Western Front were engaged in a long-term slogging match with the German Army, politicians began to search for a quicker way to victory. Asquith supported Churchill's proposal that the navy force the Dardanelles, knocking out the Ottoman Empire and opening a safe supply route to Russia. The eventual outcome of an impossible enterprise entered into without adequate planning was not victory but bloody stalemate, then retreat. Meanwhile, Field Marshal French blamed his inability to break through the German lines in the west upon insufficient supplies of ammunition. Whipped up by his allies in the press and the opposition, the so-called 'shells campaign' was in full flood by mid-May 1915 when Admiral Fisher, who had regularly threatened to resign, finally did so, even ignoring Asquith's order to return at once to his post. Fisher avowed that Churchill was impossible to work with and that he had been against the Dardanelles campaign from the beginning.

Bonar Law insisted that Fisher's resignation created 'an impossible situation', and Lloyd George concurred. The answer, he told Asquith, was coalition.

Asquith, 'in an incredibly short time', was persuaded of this opinion. Similarly swiftly, the procedure to replace the Liberal government with a coalition was agreed. A week of intense negotiations followed. Asquith remained as Prime Minister but to satisfy Tory prejudices Churchill had to quit the Admiralty and he sacrificed his friend Haldane. The Tories had demanded parity of representation but Asquith successfully ensured Liberal dominance.

Asquith found it almost impossible to hide his contempt for most of his new Tory partners and this, combined with his unbending, awkward manner, did not make for comfortable leadership. The public image of a resilient leader which he had achieved in the war's early months rapidly faded. Continued military failures induced worries that, together with excessive work, undermined Asquith's health; in October, a concerned Margot described her husband as 'absolutely done'.[265] His executive failings, particularly his reluctance to get rid of Kitchener, who was proving increasingly difficult to work with, prompted increasing restlessness among Cabinet members, not ameliorated by his establishment of a small War Committee intended to have a very small membership and the replacement of French with Haig as army commander. In early 1916, however, the introduction of conscription for single men with the loss of only John Simon from the Cabinet may be counted a success. During those last months in 1915, while the Tory press scorned Asquith's abilities as a war leader, in the Cabinet, although there was undoubted discontent there was no overt opposition to his leadership. Ministers understood that Asquith was needed to keep the coalition's disparate strands together.

In the face of continued recruitment problems, in May 1916, Asquith introduced a further measure of general conscription, extending the obligation to married men. He could not have enjoyed the task for he knew only too well that those who advocated conscription did not want him as Prime Minister while his supporters hated conscription as an affront to Liberal values. And yet his measure succeeded. Little wonder Margot thought him a magician: 'Everyone was

---

265   See Brock, op. cit., entries for 17 and 19 October 1915, pp. 200–204.

stunned. The betting was 100–1 against ever adopting conscription.'[266] In the middle of one crisis came another, the Easter Rising in Dublin. Birrell resigned as Irish Secretary and once more Asquith temporarily took charge of a department. Whether his plan to rescue constitutionalism in Ireland from Sinn Fein would have succeeded was always doubtful, but the unreasonable behaviour of the Unionists made the task impossible.

Continued failure to break through on the Western Front, including the huge losses of the Somme offensive, further undermined the government's position. In June, however, Kitchener's death at sea provided an unexpected political boon. Asquith knew that he should have removed the troublesome war minister long before yet even now procrastinated over his replacement. He should have offered the vacancy to Bonar Law, thus binding the Tory leader politically closer, but hesitated and in the end was obliged to accept Lloyd George. The Tory press hailed Lloyd George as Jehovah – a sure sign of the way in which the political wind was blowing.

The war was now in its third year and yet there was still no sign of victory even on the horizon. Margot supposed that if anything were to happen to Asquith, 'every serious person in England would find it impossible to name his successor'. She made no mention of Lloyd George's name. In September the death of Asquith's eldest son, Raymond, killed fighting on the Somme, was a staggering personal blow and undoubtedly impaired Asquith's effectiveness. He did not speak of his grief but it left him dull and listless. He found it difficult to concentrate and failed to attend several meetings of the Cabinet. The accumulated disappointments of 1915 and 1916 concentrated upon Asquith, who was unscrupulously attacked in the Tory press as 'pro-Hun' and a 'traitor'. Their avowed intent was to drive him out of office. Instead the squalid campaign temporarily inspired him to assert his authority; he demanded departmental plans for 1917 before attending a conference in Paris. But his conference companion, Lloyd George, returned to England convinced if the war were to be won there had to be fundamental changes in the structure of command and the direction of policy.

---

266   Ibid., 4 May 1916, p. 257.

He wanted the day-to-day conduct of the war handled by a small, independent War Committee with full powers; it would keep in close touch with the Prime Minister but he would not be a member. Amazingly, Asquith agreed to a version of this plan. Two days later, after Carson leaked it to the press, *The Times* asserted that Asquith had been 'disqualified on the grounds of temperament', a blow deliberately aimed below the belt at Squiff's known fondness for strong liquor. Asquith attempted to reverse out of the obvious political cul-de-sac by repudiating the plan, but his attempt to reconstruct his government failed and on the next day, 5 December, he resigned. He had tried, he told the King, but he had been advised by his Liberal and Unionist colleagues that his resignation was the only solution to a difficult problem. Where Asquith had failed, Lloyd George succeeded and became Prime Minister at the head of the second coalition government.

Asquith's resignation was not, as some have argued, a technical manoeuvre designed to see him rapidly returned to power, but a reluctant recognition that it was time for him to abandon a position where he no longer had a base on which to maintain a government. He commanded neither sufficient votes in the House nor colleagues in the Cabinet. Colonel Hankey, Secretary of the War Council, absolved Asquith of all blame for the fall of the coalition government, asserting that it failed not because of inadequate leadership but 'from inherent political weakness'. Asquith 'never wavered in his unswerving determination to see the war through to final victory', yet was unsuited temperamentally to be a war leader. He lacked dynamism and was more disposed to conciliate and compromise than to direct. His caution risked compromising military victory and he failed to reconcile national sentiment with wartime necessity. Despite these shortcomings he could take pride in his administration's conduct of the war's initial phase and the building-up of a military machine which Lloyd George in his turn developed. Asquith's achievements make him worthy to be considered as 'one of the outstanding figures of the Great War'.[267] The accepted family explanation for the collapse of the coalition was betrayal: 'It was impossible

---

267   See concluding chapter of G. H. Cassar, *Asquith as War Leader*, London, Hambledon, 1994.

for him to go on when his closest, most trusted colleague [Lloyd George] was working all the time against him in closest cooperation with [the press baron] Northcliffe, his deadliest assailant.'[268]

Asquith declined the King's offer of a peerage and remained in the Commons, his leadership of the Liberal Party confirmed at a party meeting on 8 December. In May 1917, he turned down Lloyd George's offer of the Lord Chancellorship. He should have accepted but was unwilling to play the elder statesman. This left him in the impossible position of knowing too much yet unable to say much; consequently, even his mildest criticism was dismissed as the vituperation of a disappointed man, but if he chose to say nothing this only angered and irritated his supporters. His wife expressed serious doubts whether Asquith was 'a born fighter; perhaps he is too great a gentleman ... The Liberal Party would be dead forever if we hold our tongues now.'[269]

Disappointment reached new heights at his abject performance in the Maurice Debate of May 1918. Hopelessly mishandled, Asquith's censure motion based on Major General Sir Frederick Maurice's allegation that the War Cabinet had deliberately held soldiers back from the Western Front, and had lied to Parliament about it, was lost by 108 votes to 295. It was not ignored that Lloyd George had risen to the occasion with a magnificent parliamentary performance. Six months later Lloyd George employed the voting list for the Maurice division as a test of loyalty in the 1918 'coupon' election. The coalition's demand for 'Revenge and Reparation' trumped Asquith's appeal for 'Reconciliation and Reconstruction', a greatly enlarged electorate returning 338 Unionists while the Liberals were reduced to 165 – but 136 were Lloyd George's Coalition Liberals, leaving a rump of only twenty-nine loyal to Asquith. East Fife, the constituency Asquith had represented since 1886, rejected him by 8,996 votes to 6,994.

Displaying amazing equanimity, he comforted a tearful Margot with assurances that he not only did not mind, but that it was 'a great relief'. And yet he

---

268   Violet Bonham Carter to Mary Herbert, 26 December 1916, in Mark Pottle ed., *Champion Redoubtable, Diaries and Letters of Violet Bonham Carter, 1914–45*, London, Weidenfeld & Nicolson, 1998, p. 98.

269   See Clifford, op. cit., p. 450. This study, usefully revealing the man behind the politician, places Asquith in the context of his family.

chose to cling to political life. He missed the House and disapproved of the coa-
litionists' methods and policies. Although the hazards of a contested election
did not appeal, his certainty that Lloyd George had selfishly injured both Liberalism and the party irresistibly drew him into the electoral lists. Standing at a
by-election in Paisley in February 1920, he handsomely won the three-cornered
contest. He resumed the leadership of the party but it was a tiny rump, going
nowhere; and as Grey put it, Asquith was by now merely 'using the machine of
a great political brain to rearrange old ideas'.[270]

In October 1922, the coalition dissolved and the ensuing general election
showed that Liberalism had ceased to be a central force in British politics; only 117
MPs were elected, of which sixty were Asquith's adherents. With effective parity
between the two groups, Asquith could scarcely claim to be the only guardian of
true Liberalism. Though he gave little active encouragement to it, there was an
undoubted feeling for Liberal reunion. This remained hesitant, however, until
Baldwin, who had that spring succeeded Bonar Law as Tory leader, announced
he would seek a mandate for protection. This provided the necessary catalyst
for Liberal reunion. Parliament was dissolved in November and a Liberal free-
trade manifesto was issued, signed by both Asquith and Lloyd George. Asquith
had hoped that the Liberals might achieve 200 seats but they secured only 158,
in third place behind Labour, with 191, and the Conservatives with 285. Given
that the Conservatives had lost their majority, Asquith was prepared to put
Labour in power. He never doubted that the experiment of permitting Labour
form its first administration as a minority government was right any more than
he regretted, eight months later, that it was his amendment that brought them
down – but in practice the experience was disastrous, confirming the view that
future elections would be a straight choice between Conservatives and Labour.
In the October 1924 election, the Liberals lost three-quarters of their seats to
end with just forty; in a straight fight with Labour, Asquith lost his fourth and
last parliamentary election at Paisley.

In 1925, Asquith was appointed Earl of Oxford and Asquith. He retained the

---

270   Cited in T. Wilson, *The Downfall of the Liberal Party 1914–35*, London, Collins, 1966.

leadership of his party for another eighteen months, only resigning in October 1926 after a protracted and bitter dispute with Lloyd George who clearly out-manoeuvred him over the party's response to the general strike. Temporarily incapacitated by a stroke, Asquith was robbed of his last real opportunity at the annual party conference to regain control. He was left, in his own words, with resignation as 'the only wise and honourable course'. The alternatives, he told Margot, were 'to lead a squalid faction fight against LG in which he would have all the sinews of war; or to accept his money and patch up a hollow and humiliating silence. (He was) quite resolved to do neither.'[271]

Asquith died on 15 February 1928. Recalling his political career, friends spoke of him as 'the last of the Romans'. The intended compliment was justified. In his public life he disliked self-advertisement, possessed a high sense of honour, respected institutions and believed in the seemly conduct of public affairs. He was not a great tribune of the people but he was undoubtedly a great servant of the state. He was possessed of high integrity, iron nerve and commanding intellectual ability. These qualities of character and intellect enabled him to sustain high political office for many years in times of national struggle and crisis in foreign and domestic affairs.

It was only towards the end of his long political life that he lacked the necessary resilience to resist and to defend himself from those attacks that eventually overbore him. His favoured apophthegm – 'Wait and see' – was neither deployed as frequently as opponents insisted, nor did it indicate that he was lethargic. What he never understood was why it was important, as Bonar Law told him, that he should always seem to be busily engaged about the nation's affairs. This was especially true in wartime when the public required dramatic, immediate, decisive actions. His disposition was to be cognisant of and balance every probability before reaching a decision. To his critics, this often seemed more akin to procrastination than wisdom.

He was not a charismatic leader, but rather a judicious chairman of Cabinet,

---

271   Quoted R. Jenkins, *Asquith*, London, Collins, 1964, p. 517. See also, for his daughter's view, Pottle, op. cit., pp.160–72.

an enabler, content to trust the leading ministers he had chosen to initiate legislation. They, in their turn, could count upon his loyal support. In Cabinet, it
suited his disposition even as it fulfilled his proper constitutional role to be *pri-
mus inter pares*. This was an effective, fruitful and successful working formula for
the progressive Liberal administration that he led in peacetime – well illustrated
by the combination of Asquith and Lloyd George as premier and Chancellor.
The real tragedy, as R. B. McCallum observed, was that 'the alliance of the two
finest minds of modern Liberalism' should ever have been broken.[272]

---

272   R. B. McCallum, *The Liberal Party from Earl Grey to Asquith*, London, Victor Gollancz Ltd., 1963, p. 186.

CHAPTER 14

DAVID LLOYD GEORGE

KENNETH O. MORGAN

David Lloyd George is one of the greatest and, at the same time, one of the most controversial politicians in the history of the Liberal Party. He played a central role in the great reformist administrations of 1905-16. As party leader between 1926 and 1931, he introduced Keynesian economics to the Liberal programme and to British politics. But his period as war leader and Prime Minister, from 1916-22, split the Liberal Party into rival factions, presaging its catastrophic post-war decline, and his political wizardry could also be seen as duplicity; as Baldwin put it, he had a 'morally disintegrating effect' on all who dealt with him.

- David Lloyd George (17 January 1863 – 26 March 1945), born in Manchester to Welsh parents; father died in 1864, leaving him to be raised by his uncle, Richard Lloyd, in Llanystumdwy, Caernarfonshire.

- Educated locally, trained as a solicitor.

- Married: (1) Margaret Owen (1866–1941) in 1888, five children, of whom two, Gwilym and Megan, also entered politics; (2) his secretary and long-term mistress Frances Stevenson (1888–1972) in 1943.

- Elected for Caernarfon Boroughs in 1890 by-election; held the seat until stepping down in 1945.

- President of the board of trade 1905–08, Chancellor of Exchequer 1908–15, Minister of Munitions 1915–16, Secretary of State for War 1916, Prime Minister 1916–22, leader of the Liberal Party 1926–31.

D avid Lloyd George and the idea of leadership went closely together. His heroes were strong men like Caesar, Cromwell, Napoleon, Theodore Roosevelt – and, alas! on one fateful occasion in 1936 Adolf Hitler, whom he christened the 'George Washington of Germany'. He was a lifelong admirer of the executive style and the presidential mode. After an early visit to the Commons in 1880, aged seventeen, he spoke approvingly of the leadership approach of a Norman invader. 'I will not say but that I eyed the assembly in a spirit similar to that in which William the Conqueror eyed England on his visit to Edward the Confessor, the region of his future domain'.[273]

As a young MP he was naturally impressed by Gladstone, his party's 'Grand Old Man'. He was 'head and shoulders above anybody else I have ever seen in the House of Commons'.[274] But the two were far too removed in age and, even more in philosophy, especially in their attitudes towards government and property, to be mutually sympathetic. Gladstone had an Anglican's hostility towards Nonconformists, and had 'no real sympathy with either the poor or the working class'. As Liberal leader, he was closest to old Whigs like Lord Granville and filled up too many posts in his last government of 1892–94 with 'mangy old hacks'.[275] Within the Liberal ranks, Lloyd George felt far more affinity with Joseph Chamberlain, the provincial voice of Nonconformist radicalism, and of social and municipal reform.

Lloyd George's greatest hero as political leader was not a British public figure at all, but Abraham Lincoln. Lincoln's defence of the Union had given him an immense stature among Liberals, especially in Wales, where Lloyd George's venerable 'Uncle Lloyd' was a passionate admirer. His brutal death on the eve of victory in the Civil War led to the rapid emergence of a cult of Lincoln as hero and martyr, and Lloyd George subscribed to it in full. Lincoln had many qualities which appealed to the young Welsh MP. He came from a humble background, the log cabin of legend, much like Lloyd George's childhood in the

---

273   William George, *The Making of Lloyd George*, London, Faber, 1970, p. 101.

274   Lord Riddell, *Lord Riddell's War Diary*, London, Nicholson & Watson, 1933, p. 33 (17 March 1915).

275   George, op. cit., p. 100.

shoe-maker's house in Llanystumdwy. He was another country lawyer. He was a natural democrat and the instrument of populism. As a leader he was both idealist and realist; the man who freed the black slaves but who also saw how liberal principles had to be trimmed to ensure victory. Above all, Lincoln was a great war leader, a civilian unafraid to take key strategic decisions in wartime.

Lincoln's example foreshadowed Lloyd George's astonishing achievements in peace and in war in seventeen years in government. But for the other side of his career, his casual approach towards his own party and the distrust he too often inspired among his colleagues, we must look not to Lincoln's example, but to the deeply complex personality of Lloyd George himself.

In his first decade and a half in Parliament, Lloyd George showed remark-able talents as an emerging opposition leader. Only twenty-seven when elected for Caernarfon Boroughs in April 1890 (a Liberal gain), he had self-belief and self-confidence. He was also intensely ambitious. Before his marriage to the long-suffering Margaret, he chided her for not understanding sufficiently his urge 'to get on' and wrote ominously of 'the wheels of my Juggernaut'.[276] In his early years as an MP, perhaps down to 1899, he showed considerable oratorical talents and a command of the Commons which inspired much admiration. But there was also a restless rebelliousness which aroused much anxiety. He showed little concern for the political difficulties of his party which scarcely enjoyed a major-ity in the Commons in 1892–95: his Welsh colleague Tom Ellis, who became Liberal whip, knew this all too well. He led a 'revolt' of four Welsh back-bench MPs against the party leadership in 1894 because of the failure to give priority in the government's legislative programme to Welsh disestablishment. In June 1895 he tried to graft on to the Disestablishment Bill, grinding its way through its committee stage, a proposal all his own for a national council to handle the disendowment of Church funds. The government majority sank to only two at one stage and it fell on a different issue a few days later. The episode reinforced the doubts felt about him by the Liberal high command, especially the Home

---

276   Lloyd George to Margaret Owen, 1885: printed in Kenneth O. Morgan ed., *Lloyd George Family Letters, c.1885–1936*, Cardiff, University of Wales Press, 1973, p. 14.

Secretary of the time, Herbert Asquith, who suspected Lloyd George's reliability and loyalty from that time on. He chided Ellis for whitewashing his Welsh colleague 'after the underhand and disloyal way in wh[ich] he undoubtedly acted'.[277]

Rebelliousness in Westminster was shortly followed by similar manoeuvres in Wales itself: Lloyd George in many ways was as much an outsider in Welsh politics as in English. In the winter of 1895–96 he tried to hijack Liberalism in Wales for his *Cymru Fydd* movement, an attempt to make it a vehicle for a version of Welsh home rule. This led to a huge row at the Welsh Liberal conference in January 1896, where many bitter feelings about Lloyd George and his campaign surfaced; he complained to his wife how he was howled down by 'the Cardiff Englishmen' and their supporters from mainly anglicised South Wales.[278] *Cymru Fydd* collapsed. Lloyd George would never sacrifice energy and prestige on behalf of a lost cause, and he moved away from more parochial Welsh issues to wider British themes.

His style as opposition leader, however, emerged to its greatest advantage in his opposition to the war in South Africa in 1899–1902. He was not a pacifist and was not without sympathy for imperialism – witness his early support for Joseph Chamberlain. But he saw this as an unjust war inflicted on a small rural people (rather like the Welsh) by pro-consular bullies like Milner and by an alliance of political and industrial interests in Britain symbolised by Chamberlain. He attacked government policy with great passion and his letters are full of admiration for the pluck shown by the Boer farmers. He mobilised Liberal opposition to the war with much skill, drawing on the support of English anti-war figures like the cocoa manufacturer George Cadbury, whom he persuaded to put money in to buy up the *Daily News* as an anti-war newspaper. It was Lloyd George who introduced his party leader, Sir Henry Campbell-Bannerman, to Emily Hobhouse, the courageous woman who had exposed the virtual genocide of Boer mothers and young children in the concentration camps on the Rand. From her Campbell-Bannerman derived the immortal phase about 'methods

---

277   Kenneth O. Morgan, *Wales in British Politics 1868–1922*, Cardiff, University of Wales Press, 1963, pp. 152–8, quoting Asquith to Ellis, 30 November 1895 (Nat. Library of Wales, Ellis Papers, 74).

278   Lloyd George to Margaret Lloyd George, 16 January 1896.

of barbarism' being practised in South Africa. At the same time, Lloyd George was anxious to try to build bridges across the party. In his own distinctive way he became a voice for party unity. It was ironic that the meeting in Birmingham Town Hall in December 1901 at which he was shouted down by a jingo mob, and might even have been killed, prevented him delivering a speech of internal party conciliation directed to the leading Liberal Imperialist, Lord Rosebery.

The Liberal revolt against the 1902 Education Act added to his stature. His tactics were an adroit combination, endorsing Liberal antagonism towards a bill that put Church and other denominational schools on the rates, paid for by ratepayers of all religious persuasions and of none, but also giving his opposition to the act a distinctive flavour by turning back to the Liberal grass-roots in Wales. He sensed that more effective than passive resistance by individual Liberals refusing to pay their rates would be co-ordinated resistance by the Welsh county councils. It was they who had to administer the Education Act, and in the local elections of 1904 the Liberals achieved virtually a clean sweep. This led to virtual blanket resistance to implementing the act or devoting ratepayers' funding to denominational schools, and several cases came before the high court. Lloyd George, a trained solicitor, showed a remarkably cavalier approach to councils breaking the law. In the end, it produced a messy legal stalemate and after 1906 the crisis died away. Still, Lloyd George had shown leadership powers in galvanising the Liberal democracy against perceived vested interests in church and state. Allied to his other political activities, notably in joining other leading Liberals in defending free trade against the threat posed by Chamberlain's campaign for tariff reform and imperial preference, it reinforced his standing in the party, on a whole range of issues, the Old Liberalism as well as the New. When the Unionist government resigned in December 1905, and the Liberals scored a landslide victory of huge dimensions, it was clear that the youthful Welsh radical would be one of their commanding figures.

The next nine years of Liberal government were a searching test for Lloyd George's leadership qualities. He passed it triumphantly, emerging as a dynamic minister first at the board of trade and then as a dominant Chancellor of the Exchequer. By the outbreak of war in August 1914, he was clearly the most influential and

powerful member of the Cabinet. At the board of trade, doubts about his ministerial capacity, such as his casual way with statistics, were dispelled. More significant,
he was a leading influence in many of the government's new progressive initiatives. The product of a traditional rural, chapel-bred society in Wales was also the
audacious voice of the so-called New Liberalism. Under his leadership, his party
left the cautious imperatives of Gladstonian Liberalism substantially behind, and
championed the ideology of humanitarian welfare and social reform.

At the board of trade, he immediately showed a wider range of leadership
qualities than hitherto. He was now the head of a key department, appointed to
stimulate trade, manufacturing and financial services and charged with producing a free-trade response to the Unionists' cry for tariff reform. With no previous
background, he showed a remarkable ability to master industrial and other statistics with great rapidity, which impressed the civil servants. He was unusually
open-minded and pragmatic in his handling of trade issues, and drew on a wide
range of policy advice. In particular, he seemed highly flexible in his attitude
towards both free trade and protection, an outlook unique in the Liberal Cabinet.
One private advisor of importance was W. H. Dawson, a strong enthusiast for
German protectionism and social welfare, who helped to steer Lloyd George's
interests towards this 'untrodden field of politics'.[279]

A particular talent was his ability to handle deputations. He could sense their
divisions, their weak points and personal tensions, and turn them to advantage.
He described how he had met 'the commercial people of Cardiff' who thought
him 'the best president of the board of trade ever' and spoke of him as 'the next
Liberal Prime Minister'.[280] Thus, he got broad industrial backing for his Merchant Shipping Bill, directed largely against foreign shipping competitors to
British vessels. He also proved adept at handling trade union deputations, an
unfamiliar audience but one always open to ministerial concern and flattery.
From that time onwards, he was regarded as the government's master industrial conciliator.

---

279   Kenneth O. Morgan, *Ages of Reform*, London, I. B. Tauris, 2011, p. 80.
280   Lloyd George to Margaret Lloyd George, 31 July 1907.

He was also a great success at the board of trade partly because he was thought to be successful, through his own capacity for self-promotion and his links with prominent journalists like A. G. Gardiner of the *Daily News*. His success with the Merchant Shipping Act was lauded to the skies. His averting of a national railway strike in 1907 gave him further acclaim, even King Edward VII expressing approval – despite reservations from the railwaymen's trade unions, who sacked their leader Richard Bell MP in consequence.

His record spoke for itself as a time of creative legislation. The Merchant Shipping Act was a breakthrough in policy; the Patent Act was a similar valuable service for manufacturers and inventors; the Port of London Authority brought together a variety of diverse groups to create a single directing body; the Census of Production was a valuable technical reform. It brought acclaim not only from his own backbenchers but also to a degree from across the House; Bonar Law and Austen Chamberlain became new friends of future importance. At the same time, his sympathetic, unstuffy attitude towards the unions, settling disputes both on the railways and among the cotton spinners, made him regarded as a kind of patron of labour.

A far more important field lay ahead, when he went to the Treasury in April 1908 after Asquith succeeded Campbell-Bannerman as Prime Minister. Lloyd George's first task was the agreeable one of carrying through Asquith's proposal for old-age pensions, which he did very adroitly, making the new scheme somewhat more generous (or expensive, according to taste) with provisions for married couples. But his ambitions went far beyond the traditional role of the Chancellor in matching income with expenditure and balancing the budget. In revolutionising the role of the Treasury to make it a launch-pad for long-term social reform, he came to be seen as the supreme instrument of the New Liberalism. He also provided a boost to the flagging fortunes of the Liberal Party, a progressive answer to Chamberlainite tariff reform and the new challenge of the Labour Party.

He consulted at length with a small team of private advisors, notably the Quaker social reformer Seebohm Rowntree and his colleague, Charles Masterman, while Winston Churchill, who succeeded him at the board of trade, became

a powerful ally. But the main strategy was very much his own. He began with a
private tour of Germany in the summer of 1908, using one of the new motor cars
loaned him by him by Sir Charles Henry, a wealthy Liberal MP. Here he studied
in depth national and local social insurance schemes in Germany, a foundation
for a new comprehensive welfare system. He also, perhaps unwisely, dabbled
in foreign policy, with private talks with the German Foreign Minister, Bülow.
When he returned he spent the winter, often in private conclave with Churchill
and Masterman, working out the financial base for a new programme of social
reform. He had to deal with immediate budgetary problems, meeting the cost of
old-age pensions and the new Dreadnought battleships, and solving problems
in the financing of local government. But his objectives ranged far wider. The
result, the hugely ambitious 'People's Budget', the Finance Bill of 1909, transformed the pattern of social policy. It also revolutionised the constitution, with
long-term consequences.

The Budget was progressive and redistributive, with an increase in the rates
of income tax, a 'super-tax' on the rich, a rise in death duties on estates, and
taxes on petrol and licensing the new motor cars. But these were broadly within
traditional lines of taxation. Far more sensational were the new land taxes –
emphatically Lloyd George's work and a consequence of his growing role as
party leader. There were three new land taxes, of which the most controversial
was a 20 per cent tax on the 'unearned increment', the rise in land values through
general community development. They were resisted by some senior Liberal
ministers, Haldane loftily claiming that Lloyd George did not understand his
own Finance Bill – a view which debates in committee soon demolished. But
with the support of Churchill and crucially, the Prime Minister, Asquith, Lloyd
George got it through Cabinet. It was a frank, open challenge to conventional
fiscal orthodoxy, to views of property and the class system – and, if necessary,
to the House of Lords. Lloyd George did not presume that the Lords would
reject the budget, a thing unknown since the reign of Charles II. But when that
extreme policy was pursued by the Upper House, he carried the fight to them
with belligerent speeches up and down the land. The sharply personal tone of
his assaults on the Lords, and individual peers such as the Duke of Marlborough,

alarmed polite society and Edward VII. But it excited radicals and younger voters, and spurred his party on to narrow victory at the polls.

In the subsequent struggle with the Lords that led to the passage of the Parliament Act in 1911, it was Asquith, not Lloyd George, who was the main figure. The success in negotiations with the crown that led to the two general elections of 1910 – both of which saw the government scrape home with Irish and Labour support, and the defeat of the 'die-hard' Tory peers in August 1911 – was due largely to Asquith's calm grasp of legal and constitutional realities. But he and Lloyd George, the diplomat and the demagogue, were an immense partnership. There is no evidence at all at this stage of any fundamental tension between them. As a party man, Lloyd George at this period was at his most committed, standing up boldly to everything the Unionists chose to throw at him – 'St Sebastian of Limehouse' in a famous *Punch* cartoon. He stimulated constituency parties, he interacted closely with the Liberal press, he communicated with mass audiences. Asquith recognised his indispensability for his party. When in 1912, Lloyd George might reasonably have been asked to resign after his implication in some murky dealings over the purchase of shares in the American Marconi company, Asquith defended his Welsh colleague in all the debates and the committee of inquiry.

Lloyd George's unique personal qualities of leadership came out most strongly in the major legislative consequence of the 1909 Budget, his National Insurance Act of 1911. This followed on from his tour of Germany in 1908 and his enthusiastic survey of its social security schemes. The outcome was a comprehensive system of health insurance (under which citizens would have 'to lick stamps for Lloyd George') along with a limited scheme for unemployment insurance. The foundation was laid down, thirty years before the Beveridge Report, for an enduring welfare state. It was an extraordinary display of energy, imagination and enterprise. For weeks on end, starting with private conclaves in an elegant hotel on the French Riviera, he was furiously engaged, with Seebohm Rowntree, Sir John Bradbury of the Treasury, and, most importantly, Sir John Braithwaite of the Inland Revenue, in meetings on the details of his scheme. When back in London he saw deputations galore, most crucially the industrial assurance companies whom he persuaded to take on the running of his health insurance scheme. Another diplomatic victory was persuading the trade unions also to run the system for working people, which effectively took labour on board behind a contributory scheme which many workers saw as simply a poll tax.

The National Insurance Act, with the huge bureaucracy it necessarily created, was the work of many hands. But it was clearly Lloyd George who took the key decisions at every stage. Chief among them was his eventual commitment to 'be virtuous' over a national insurance fund, creating a fund of undistributed reserves rather than distribute it to individual contributors and let it 'fructify in the pockets of the people' on traditional Gladstonian lines. He was determined that his new social venture should appear financially sound, while the familiar principle of insurance provision gave it a broad popular credibility. It was fiercely attacked by the British Medical Association on self-interested professional grounds (as was the National Health Service in 1948). There were popular campaigns against having to buy stamps, and the Unionist opposition made political capital. Lloyd George fought back passionately – but his eventual triumph lay less in partisanship than in building up a broad consensus on the social equity of this massive initiative. He won support even from opponents like Austen Chamberlain. Even now, there was visible Lloyd George the consensus man and national statesman.

This succession of triumphs – old-age pensions, the People's Budget, the Parliament Act and national insurance – made Lloyd George clearly the dominant figure in the Liberal government down to 1914. Among his Cabinet colleagues, he was far from universally liked or trusted, partly on class grounds. He tended to commune with a small group of radical advisors in government – Masterman, Rufus Isaacs and Christopher Addison, a doctor of growing political weight. Asquith now used his Chancellor far beyond the confines of the Treasury. In 1912, he successfully negotiated with the trade unions to end a national miners' strike over a national wage. In 1914, he was asked by Asquith to try to broker a settlement of the Irish impasse, trying to find a viable settlement for Protestant Ulster as the prospect of Irish home rule loomed. He was also regarded as a bridge to the angry suffragettes. At the same time, in 1914 he re-emerged as a Liberal crusader, with a new nationwide campaign for land reform, including

such novelties as the rating of site values. In his native Wales he was a fierce participant in debates on the Welsh Church Disestablishment Bill.

Yet at this key time there was detectable a quite different form of leadership,
not quite as an anti-Liberal, but at least of someone following his own maverick course in party terms. At the height of the party conflict over the House
of Lords in 1910, he approached leading Unionists to raise the prospect of a
bipartisan coalition. Significantly, Asquith and other leading Liberals were not
consulted (though Churchill showed clear sympathy). Lloyd George argued
that the parties should come together to pursue higher national purposes –
primarily a comprehensive programme of social reform and national defence,
rather on the lines of the New Nationalism programme of Theodore Roosevelt
in the United States 1912 presidential election. Party issues like free trade, Welsh
disestablishment, the House of Lords, even Irish home rule, he deemed to be
'non-controversial' and capable of separate settlement. It got nowhere in the
end, as the Unionists backed down. Asquith, when he eventually got to hear
about it all, pronounced that the 'non-controversial questions' were indeed
highly controversial, and formed the very substance of political dialogue. By
the time of the second general election of 1910 in December, the entire edifice
of proposed coalition had collapsed, as the chimera it undoubtedly was. But
it was a highly significant indication of Lloyd George's view of Liberalism and
of leadership. Several times before, he had attempted an approach to political
opponents – in Wales in 1895 over disestablishment, in 1904 over education
– in an attempt to move the political debate on to more relevant and contemporary subjects. It left something of a mixed legacy in his career now. Some
leading Unionists, notably Balfour and Bonar Law, developed a more sympathetic relationship with him which would yield results in 1916. On the other
hand, Asquith, Grey and other prominent Liberals were reinforced in their
distrust of their maverick colleague.

The outbreak of war in August 1914 gave his qualities of leadership a totally
new character. The tensions between his politics and his party became ever
more pronounced. He advanced relentlessly to the heights of supreme power.
As wartime Prime Minister from December 1916 he was to display a personal

ascendancy never previously known. But in the process he left the grand old Edwardian Liberal Party weakened and beyond recovery.

He had genuinely been uncertain about his attitude to war in the last days of July but the invasion of Belgium gave him a major reason for backing entry into war which his pre-war membership of the Committee of Imperial Defence had foreshadowed. Thereby he risked losing key elements of his old radical, anti-war Nonconformist constituency. At first as Chancellor, he had to confront a huge financial crisis, to rescue the markets, preserve the gold standard, and shore up the banks and the City. There was a mood of panic in the City, the 'flapping penguins' as Lloyd George contemptuously called them; the Stock Exchange closed down and the Bank of England found its reserves close to exhaustion. His resolution and intellectual brilliance now brought him high praise from John Maynard Keynes among other future critics. In a week of resolute action, in conjunction with Cunliffe, the governor of the Bank of England, Lloyd George restored confidence. New Treasury notes were issued. Bank rate went up to 10 per cent. After a week, the capitalists' panic was over. It was another extraordinary demonstration of Lloyd George's capacity to act, and to absorb arcane technical data, this time relating to the money markets.

But in a wider sphere he was drifting away from Liberal shibboleths and looking to a reorganisation of government on the basis of national unity. The war itself encouraged this process with the electoral truce and the loosening of conventional party ties, but Lloyd George was pre-eminent among those who responded. By the end of 1914, he was engaged in discussions to try to find a more peripheral strategy to turn the fortunes of war around after early disasters on the Western Front. In the spring of 1915, he joined many Unionists and the Northcliffe press in voicing alarm at the perceived shortage of shells and other munitions of war. His political support was broadening. The labour movement now looked on him with favour after he negotiated the 'Treasury agreement' with the trade unions in March 1915 in which the latter agreed to the 'dilution' of the workforce by unskilled workers (including women). But in his own party, he was an increasingly lonely figure, attacked by colleagues like McKenna and Runciman, and quarrelling violently with his old comrade Masterman. When political manoeuvres at the centre led to Asquith forming a new coalition government in May 1915, including Unionists and also Labour, Lloyd George did indeed act like a staunch Liberal. He helped Asquith to stay on as premier, and ensured that the coalition would have Liberals like Grey, McKenna and Simon in the key offices of state (though not Churchill or Haldane, who were sacrificed). His apparent selflessness won the rare commendation of Asquith's waspish wife, Margot – 'Lloyd George has come grandly out of all this ... he has the sweetest nature in the world.'[281] But he himself went to the new apolitical Department of Munitions, where his work testified more to the creed of 'national efficiency' in full statist mode rather than anything resembling traditional Liberal individualism. He stood as an isolated figure, with his Liberal ally Addison close beside him, keeping a watchful eye.

The political manoeuvres of wartime impelled him increasingly towards working with the Unionists. This was especially notable in the furious Cabinet battle for military conscription, which most Liberals resisted on grounds of principle, but which Lloyd George strongly supported, seeing it as a yardstick of the national commitment to total war. Asquith was compelled to give way or resign; through severe pressure, Lloyd George won the day, with key Unionist allies like Curzon, Long, Lansdowne and the Irish Unionist Edward Carson. Lord Riddell noted how the Tories were now his intimates: 'It looks as if he is going the same road as Chamberlain'.[282] As important in the longer term was the formation of a kind of Lloyd George support group on the back benches, the 'Liberal War Committee', including men like Sir Alfred Mond, Freddie Guest and the notorious 'Bronco Bill' Sutherland. But his backing among Liberals was limited; the majority remained loyal to their old leader, Asquith.

Lloyd George's status was elevated further in June 1916 when he was made Secretary of State for War in succession to Kitchener, who had drowned at sea. But this office had already been weakened, and the war news, particularly the horrors of the Somme, and failures in the Balkans which saw Romania collapse,

---

281 Cameron Hazlehurst, *Politicians at War*, London, Cape, 1971, p. 249.

282 Riddell, op. cit., pp. 136 (9 November 1915).

remained depressing. Asquith's mismanagement of the aftermath of the Easter Rising in Dublin seemed further proof of his lack of urgency or leadership. Sir Maurice Hankey on 12 November 1916 described Lloyd George's views, as given to Asquith, as 'most pessimistic and lugubrious' and he spoke of resignation.[283]

The outcome was the dramatic first week of December 1916, resulting in a *putsch* in which Lloyd George supplanted Asquith as Prime Minister. He did so as an individual, not as a Liberal leader. His allies in the pressure for Asquith to recast the government and set up a Supreme War Council were the Unionists, Bonar Law and Carson, with the mercurial press baron Max Aitken as a kind of go-between, and the background endorsement of Northcliffe, owner of *The Times*. It was a desperate initiative by Lloyd George, but it succeeded because he managed to win over first the official leaders of the Unionist Party, then by one vote the Labour Party after he promised them to give a Labour man (Henderson) a seat in the War Cabinet. But Liberal support was also crucial, though acquired in a way that was ultimately damaging for the party. A group of Liberal backbenchers, headed by Addison, David Davies and F. G. Kellaway, declared their support for him as he became premier on 7 December. Addison had shown him a list of over 150 Liberal MPs who, in a crisis, would back Lloyd George rather than Asquith. But they would back him as a man, not as a party colleague. His detachment from the party was all too stark.

The pattern of Lloyd George's wartime premiership confirmed this leadership style. He governed more as a president than a regular politician, and visited Westminster infrequently – far less so than Churchill in the Second World War. He built up his personal machine as Prime Minister in a unique way that underlined his authority. He set up a War Cabinet of five members in which he was the only Liberal. Ministers were brought into the government, including businessmen like Lord Rhondda, Lord Devonport and Sir Eric Geddes, and later the South African General Smuts. The Prime Minister bolstered his authority with a new Cabinet Office, headed by Maurice Hankey and his fellow countryman, Thomas Jones, to draw up minutes and impose a discipline – and also

283   Stephen Roskill ed., *Hankey: Man of Secrets*, London, Collins, 1970, p. 318.

prime ministerial control – unknown in Asquith's time. He appointed a range of officials in Downing Street, many of them Welsh. The 'garden suburb' of special advisors working in huts in the garden of No. 10 was less influential than legend made out but it suggested Cabinet government turning into prime ministerial government.

So far as he was politically able, it was Lloyd George who called all the shots. He involved himself directly in wartime strategy, as Lincoln, that other civilian war leader, had done, in negotiations with the French and the Americans, and in resisting the power challenge from the military commanders Haig and Robertson; the removal of Robertson in February 1918 was a personal triumph. The Prime Minister also negotiated directly with the trade unions, not always successfully, and promoted an attempted settlement with the Irish in 1917, a disastrous failure since it led to the Irish Nationalist Party being pushed aside by the republican Sinn Féin. On the PR side, he communicated with the public directly: his major speech on a post-war settlement in February 1918 was made not in the Commons but to a mass audience of trade unionists. He kept up close links too with the press, including the French and American papers, and beat down critical Liberal journalists at home. He was the most media-conscious of political leaders, the most articulate, the most visible, the most charismatic.

As his mind gravitated to ideas for post-war politics, he realised that he had to have a base for what he saw as the probable scenario of 'a fight between him and Henderson' as head of government – 'national unity' and the brute force of capitalism ranged against the challenge of Labour. He had to create a party machine, something he lacked since the Liberals had remained utterly divided in the Commons since December 1916, with Asquith serving as a kind of leader of the opposition. He did manage to shore up the Liberal elements in his government in July 1917 by co-opting two powerful party colleagues, Winston Churchill and Ivor Montagu, into it. But he remained politically adrift, a Prime Minister without a party. The solution came in May 1918 with the Maurice debate. General Maurice, former head of military intelligence, had alleged in the press that Lloyd George and Bonar Law had lied in telling the Commons that British military strength at the front was higher in 1918 than it had been a year earlier.

Asquith moved a somewhat feeble vote of confidence; Lloyd George defended himself brilliantly and demolished the opposition. It was a fine, if factually questionable, defence of civilian as against military war leadership. But the outcome was calamitous for the Liberal Party. Out of 106 votes against the government, ninety-eight were Liberals.

This provided the basis for a post-war distinction between pro- and anti-Lloyd George Liberals. Two months later, Lloyd George's Liberal whip, Freddie Guest, negotiated a secret pact with the Unionists ('the coupon', as it was derisively called) to divide up the seats at the next election. On a very rough and ready basis, about 130 seats were allocated to the Liberals, or Coalition Liberals as they came to be called. The unexpectedly rapid ending of the war that autumn speeded things up enormously. Liberal ministers gathered in the Commons in November to approve the very Liberal-sounding coalition manifesto, written up by the famous Liberal historian, H. A. L. Fisher, which they would present to the electors in alliance with the Unionists.

The coalition triumphed, winning a huge majority with 473 seats (the Sinn Féin members declined to attend the House). Independent anti-government Liberals numbered barely thirty; Asquith himself was among the fallen. The deep split in the party's ranks, institutionalised by the 'coupon', was traumatic and seemed unbridgeable. So this was a new role for Lloyd George, not party leader but head of perhaps half a party, a loose, opportunist Liberal group with no nationwide organisation, uncertain funding, little press backing, torn between hopes of reunion with old comrades and the prospects of power offered by the coalition. Their future depended on the whims of the Unionists and Lloyd George's prestige, retained after his wartime ascendancy. It was a recipe for disaster, and so it proved.

Lloyd George was to remain as peace-time premier for almost four more years. In that period the presidential mode of the war years was reinforced. His political isolation was rapidly seen as a profound sign of vulnerability. He still claimed to be a Liberal in spirit, and some of his government's early policies well illustrated this claim. There was a final impressive burst of the pre-war New Liberalism, with Liberal ministers largely involved with domestic policy.

Addison, the new Minister of Health, embodied it. His 1919 Housing Act began the totally new principle of a subsidised local authority housing programme; the state would cover the differential between the capital cost of a house and the amount it earned in the rent that working-class tenants could afford. It soon ran into financial trouble and was a major target for the Anti-Waste movement in the country. In time, from subsidising local authorities the government turned to the highly speculative idea of subsidising private builders. By mid-1921 the inflated cost of the programme was proving highly expensive; Addison was sacked by Lloyd George after an angry public argument. At the same time, the programme did provide over 200,000 new council houses; it touched upon an area of policy the pre-war New Liberalism had ignored. There were other progressive social measures. Old-age pensions were significantly raised. Most importantly, unemployment insurance was much extended beyond the narrow confines of Lloyd George's scheme of 1911, a godsend when unemployment rapidly mounted from mid-1920. A dramatic new initiative during the war, Fisher's Education Act of 1918, created a new structure of free state education, improved conditions for teachers and promoted post-school education. All these suffered under the Geddes Committee's 'axe' in 1922. But they served as a reminder that the social impetus of Lloyd George's Liberalism was still alive.

There were other policy initiatives to please Liberals. After a distinctly mixed role in the Paris peace conference, Lloyd George became a voice for a more equitable financial settlement in Europe. He withdrew British troops serving with the White forces in Russia, and achieved both a trade pact and de facto recognition of the new Bolshevik regime. Nearer home, Ireland, where a post-war programme of retaliation and repression directed against Sinn Féin and the Irish Republican Army had alienated old Liberal home rulers (some of whom moved over to the Labour Party), quite suddenly became a focus for Lloyd George's diplomatic talents at their most impressive, with close attention to detail this time. He negotiated an Irish Free State treaty, bringing peace to Ireland (albeit on the basis of partition) and succeeding where Pitt, Peel, Gladstone and Asquith had all failed. In India, there was considerable reform with the Chelmsford–Montagu proposals for provincial self-government, while General Dyer was dismissed after the catastrophic atrocity at Amritsar. In January 1922, just after the Irish negotiations, Lloyd George contemplated a general election called on a programme of peace and economic stability. His record, he believed, was one which large numbers of Liberals, as well as most Conservatives, could endorse.

But Liberal initiatives in policy would not make him an acceptable Liberal leader. The way in which his government had been formed, the bitter relations between him and his erstwhile Asquithian colleagues, made him quite unacceptable. There was already Liberal anger at his huge private fund, accumulated from donations from rich capitalists and destined for obscure purposes of his own. He had shown scant leadership in handling his old party anyway. Local party machinery was run down and suffering from low morale; as a result there were many by-election losses to Labour in such areas as Yorkshire and south Wales. The Coalition Liberals lacked coherence both in ideas and in organisation. Hopes of building a wider political base were equally unrealistic. Despite his version of 'beer and sandwiches at No. 10', contacts with Labour had been fatally severed by his handling of disputes with the miners and other workers. The failure to honour a promise to nationalise the mines, and anger caused by his out-manoeuvring of the major unions in preventing a general strike on 'Black Friday' in April 1921, soured his relations with the working class from that time on. Lloyd George's government of national unity had turned into an anti-labour front.

As for the Conservatives, Lloyd George's unorthodox methods of government repelled them. A symbol of this came in 1921 when he summoned a meeting of Cabinet not to anywhere in England but to Inverness Town Hall. His remote presidential methods, his long absences from Parliament, his private links with the press and with wealthy possible donors to his Fund made his regime look like a constitutional perversion. This meant that an apparently minor issue – his creation of peers and knights *en masse* in return for political donations – gained political significance. Cronies of little talent or integrity found their way into the Upper House. Lloyd George seemed to preside over a corrupt style of government reminiscent of the days of Walpole. The stench of bribery and dishonour surrounded this coalition, and indeed the very idea of coalition, for decades to come.

If Lloyd George was to have any future as a political leader, it could clearly not be as the head of a reunited Liberal Party. The alternative route to further power was a union or 'fusion' of the two wings of the coalition. The chances of the coalition Unionists ever agreeing, however, were remote, with widespread pressure in the constituencies for a break with Lloyd George, and the Unionist Chief Whip, George Younger, an open and avowed political opponent. In any case, in private meetings with his Liberal ministerial colleagues in the spring of 1920 it became clear that almost all rejected the idea of a merger with the Unionists outright. Apart from Addison (on grounds of social reform) and Churchill (on grounds of anti-Bolshevism), they all insisted that they were still Liberals, committed to time-honoured principles and priorities. Fusion was thus a total non-starter.

From that time on, the political future and very purpose of the coalition seemed quite obscure. Formed in special circumstances at the time of victory in late 1918, it now faced a very different world, in which economic depression was mounting. There was growing class conflict between capital and labour, and the international situation was marked by failure in almost every sphere of operations, culminating in the possibility of a needless war with Turkey in its clash with the Greeks in the late summer of 1922. What could Lloyd George offer as a party leader? In his coalition scheme of 1910 he had at least suggested setting aside party conflict for the sake of powerful national objectives, above all long-term social reform. Even in 1918, there were promises of a thriving brave new world for heroes. In 1922, there was nothing, other than keeping Lloyd George in office. On 19 October, the Unionist backbenchers turned against their leaders. They had had more than enough of Lloyd George's adventures and misadventures. By a large majority of 187 to eighty-seven they voted the coalition down and Lloyd George out of office. His years of leadership were over.

The final phase of Lloyd George's career can be dealt with briefly – ironically, since he did finally become Liberal leader in October 1926, after the ageing Asquith finally bowed out following the general strike, and served in that position until the political and financial crisis of August 1931. But by this time, his position was of marginal importance at best. His party was deep in a process of continuous decline.

After the 1922 election, he headed a rump of fifty-five Lloyd George Liberals, shedding supporters to the Conservatives by the week. His own great weapon, the notorious Fund, was deeply damaging rather than a source of strength. His only credible route back was reunion with his angry former Asquithian brethren. In fact, they did come together in the 1923 election when the outgoing Conservative Prime Minister, Stanley Baldwin, a key figure in the party revolt against Lloyd George in 1922, called for protection of the home market. For a brief moment, in a singularly fluid election, the Liberals saw a rise in their parliamentary strength, winning 158 seats. But the minority Labour government that followed was more damaging to the Liberals than to Labour, with its massive trade union base. The 1924 general election saw the Liberal tally of seats slump from 158 to only forty.

Where he did make a positive impact, however, was in the realm of policy. As Masterman declared, 'I've fought him as hard as anyone else, but I have to confess, when LG came back to the party, ideas came back to the party.'[284] After he became leader he launched a series of major policy initiatives, stemming from an annual summer school which attracted a series of brilliant economists like Hubert Henderson, Walter Layton and even his old adversary Keynes, who observed that: 'I oppose Mr Lloyd George when he is wrong and I support him when he is right.'[285] The old statesman's scheme for combating unemployment and industrial decline with a bold policy of national development and financial pump-priming anticipated Keynes's own *General Theory* published in 1936. Lloyd George sponsored a series of major policy documents: *The Land and the Nation* (the 'Green Book'), *Britain's Industrial Future* (the 'Yellow Book') and, most cogent of all, *We Can Conquer Unemployment* (the 'Orange Book'). They were radical documents reminiscent of Lloyd George's younger days. The 'Green Book' proposed 'cultivating tenure' for land, a form of land nationalisation. The 'Yellow Book' advocated in part a planned economy based on public-private partnership. The 'Orange Book' advocated a bold use of state financing to stimulate

284   See Lucy Masterman, *C. F. G. Masterman*, London, Cass, 1968, p. 346.

285   Robert Skidelsky, *John Maynard Keynes: The Economist as Saviour, 1920–1937*, London, Macmillan, 1992, p. 249.

employment, purchasing power and economic activity generally. As always, Lloyd George was not a man in thrall to convention. Rather than propose a depressing policy of cuts and mass deflation, he aimed to seize the initiative to promote national development. It is not surprising that, at a time of party fluidity, his ideas appealed to independent-minded younger men like Oswald Mosley on the left and Harold Macmillan and Robert Boothby on the right. His programmes were by far the most challenging of those offered to the electors in 1929. Since the main alternative was Baldwin's 'Safety First', they could hardly fail to be so.

Lloyd George, therefore, even in his mid-sixties, was still a political and intellectual leader of rare charisma. In the years 1927–29 he showed astonishing energy in by-election campaigns and policy initiatives. Alone of the three party leaders he looked like a figure with genuine solutions to the nation's economic problems. But his party was a frail and deceptive instrument. Serious figures in it like Sir John Simon refused to campaign with him. The grievances associated with his wilful handling of his massive fund aroused huge resentment. The Liberals faced the fundamental problem of deciding whether their allegiance lay with the right or the left, as they still do. Lloyd George, with his kaleidoscopic background, was not the man to resolve it. Nor was his dramatic style of self-projection what was needed by a weary nation desperate for a return to 'normalcy'.

The Liberal tally of seats in 1929 was a mere fifty-nine. The next phase of minority Labour government in 1929–31 was another damaging period. Lloyd George himself contemplated a possible alliance with Labour if they offered the alternative vote. In early 1931, Addison (now a member of MacDonald's Cabinet) acted as a kind of mediator and was offered a position as trustee of the Lloyd George Fund as a reward. But, as Lloyd George explored possibilities of allying with Labour, some of his party were going the other way. Simon and Sir Robert Hutchison formed a kind of breakaway group which looked to work with the Conservatives; Simon even uttered the supreme heresy and murmured sympathy for the idea of tariffs. Here was the origin of the National Liberals, the 'Vichy Liberals' in Dingle Foot's angry phrase, Tories in all but name. By 1931, the Liberal Party was a shambles, a series of splinter groups. Lloyd George's proposals were savagely criticised within the party even by

Lord Reading, formerly Sir Rufus Isaacs, his old comrade-in-arms at the time of the 1911 National Insurance Act.

In the economic crisis of August 1931, Lloyd George, perhaps fortunately, was in hospital for an operation and unable to participate in the deals which saw the official Liberals, now led by Herbert Samuel, join the newly formed National Government under MacDonald, and then reluctantly stay on in office for the 1931 'doctor's mandate' election. Lloyd George's great party ended up split – not into two as in 1918 but into three: thirty-three official Liberals, thirty-five 'National Liberals' under Simon and a Lloyd George family group of four Independent Liberal members. It was a humiliating outcome.

Lloyd George had no role henceforth as any kind of Liberal leader. While he devoted time to writing his *War Memoirs* and his account of the Peace Treaties, he remained personally a figure of great stature both at home and internationally. He could still provide unique inspiration as a crusader – witness his 'New Deal' election programme in 1935, another political disappointment. He could still thrill the House of Commons, as no one else, not even Churchill, could do, as in an extraordinary speech in June 1936 flaying Baldwin's government for its 'cowardly surrender' in not supporting the League of Nations over Abyssinia. But he could also give reminders of how irresponsible his initiatives could be when he paid a disastrous visit to Hitler at Berchtesgaden in 1936. His passion for strong leaders responded to the glamour of the *Führerprinzip* amid the Wagnerian backdrop of the Bavarian Alps. Perhaps his response was just an old man's vanity, glorying in the recognition that he was still a world figure.

His last gift to his country was a powerful speech denouncing Neville Chamberlain after the Norway fiasco in May 1940, paving the way for Churchill to take over as the inspirational saviour of the nation in this war. His last vote in the Commons was in early 1943, appropriately cast on behalf of the Beveridge Report. But he was now a defeatist, declining figure, talking of peace talks with the Germans. Churchill angrily attacked him for one Commons speech, comparing him with the aged Marshal Pétain in Reynaud's Cabinet of 1940. He last emerged in public life in the 1945 New Year's honours list, in which he received an earldom – though he never took his seat in the Lords, dying at his Welsh home in March 1945. Wales's Great Commoner had surrendered finally to titles and honours, unlike Churchill, who was buried in Blaydon churchyard in a small Oxfordshire village as a free-born English citizen.

The bewildering upheavals of Lloyd George's career naturally suggest a variety of interpretations of his role as a Liberal leader. Of his powers of vision and imagination, his astonishing achievements in passing major legislation and effecting political and social change, his ability to inspire and revitalise the nation at times of crisis, there can be no doubt. But as a Liberal leader he was, almost simultaneously, the best and the worst of them all. He transformed his party's timeworn domestic policies with the message of the New Liberalism of social welfare. He laid low the overweening power of the unelected House of Lords. He voiced the new democracy as no one else could or did. He brought into existence a new Ireland which would never again torment British public life, at least not in the way that it had before 1914. In international affairs after the war, despite the many weaknesses of the Versailles settlement, he alone of the victorious leaders tried to promote reconciliation and economic recovery. In the '20s, he was a Keynesian before Keynes.

But as party leader it all turned to dust. He did not really believe in traditional parties; he pursued long-term goals, not immediate loyalties. Ironically he was to criticise his heroes for precisely this failure. Of Teddy Roosevelt, who left the Republicans in 1912 to form his own Progressive Party, he commented that 'he should never have quarrelled with the machine'.[286] Too often he assumed that political power could be won without a basis of trust or loyalty. Perhaps he was too much the Welsh Baptist outsider, unable to appreciate the residual solidarity that gave cohesion to British public life, lacking a sure feel for its history. He ignored Burke's vision of political leadership: 'It begins in respect for the social order ... It is therefore rooted in a sense of history, rather than one of science.'[287] The conquering hero thus turned into the amoral adventurer, adored by the masses but deeply suspect at close quarters. The centenary of the

---

286 For Lloyd George on Roosevelt, see *The Truth about the Peace Treaties*, London, Gollancz, 1938, Vol. 1, pp. 231–2.

287 Jesse Norman, *Edmund Burke*, London, William Collins, 2013, p. 286.

First World War seems most unlikely to redeem him in this sense, or re-install him as the architect of victory in 1918, as an adoring public conventionally sees Churchill and 1945. The most creative genius in our political history suffers for misinterpreting and misusing the supreme quality in which he believed, that of leadership. The apostle of Abraham Lincoln forgot his hero's greatest precept, that a house divided cannot stand.

CHAPTER 15

SIR HERBERT SAMUEL

JAIME REYNOLDS

Herbert Samuel was a leading figure in the Liberal Party for over fifty years from its zenith before the First World War to the nadir of its fortunes in the mid-1950s. With Archibald Sinclair, he was the last independent Liberal to serve in the Cabinet before the 2010–15 coalition and remains the last Liberal to hold one of the four great offices of state, as Home Secretary until 1932. His career was built on his formidable competence as an administrator, organiser and mediator and his record as a progressive thinker and legislator. Nevertheless, his period as Liberal leader from November 1931 to November 1935 was one of calamitous decline for the party.

- Herbert Louis Samuel (6 November 1870 – 5 February 1963), born in Liverpool into a wealthy Jewish family.
- Educated at University College School, Hampstead and Balliol College, Oxford.
- Married his first cousin Beatrice Franklin (1871–1959) in 1897; they had four children.
- MP for Cleveland, Yorkshire 1902–18 and Darwen, Lancashire 1929–35.
- Chancellor of Duchy of Lancaster 1909–10, 1915–16, Postmaster General 1910–14, 1915–16, president of the local government board 1914–15, Home Secretary 1916; 1931–32, First High Commissioner for Palestine 1920–25, leader of the Liberal Party 1931–35, leader of the Liberal Party in the Lords 1944–55.
- Ennobled as Viscount Samuel in 1937.

amuel was born into an Ashkenazi Jewish family that had emigrated to England from what is today western Poland in the late eighteenth century. The family made money in Liverpool commerce and rose into the wealthy upper middle class. It became even wealthier in the international financial boom of the 1850s and 1860s when his uncle founded Samuel Montagu & Co., the merchant bank, which was second only to the Rothschilds in the wealth league of Jewish banking houses. When Herbert's father died in 1877 Montagu became his guardian. Samuel was thus born into the Victorian patrician elite and was able later to devote himself to politics, philosophy and travel, untroubled by the need to establish a career and earn a living.

He was educated at a progressive school and Balliol where he obtained a First. While at university Samuel rejected his family's Orthodox Judaism and adopted an agnostic outlook for the rest of his life. Though he maintained his links with the Jewish faith and community, and in later life became one of its respected figures, his ideas on religion were shaped by a rationalist, scientific humanism.

His commitment to Liberal politics and social reform began early, inspired by the campaigns in Whitechapel for his uncle who was the local radical MP, and of his brother Stuart, the local London county council member and later MP. While at Balliol he was selected as candidate for South Oxfordshire, the district around Henley, which he contested and narrowly lost at both the 1895 and 1900 general elections. During this period he was also closely involved in building up the Liberal Party organisation in the Home Counties and nationally.

Samuel was firmly on the progressive wing of the party, immersing himself in the problems of urban and rural poverty, actively supporting the 1889 dock strike and associating closely with the Fabians, particularly the Webbs and Graham Wallas. He was active, with Ramsay MacDonald, in the 'Rainbow Circle' of Liberals and Socialists. Samuel rejected *laissez-faire* liberalism and took advanced positions on the social issues of the day. He described himself as a 'meliorist'– 'one who believes the present is on the whole better than the past, but that effort is needed to make it so'.[288] In his early election campaigns, he ran as a

---

288   Bernard Wasserstein, *Herbert Samuel: A Political Life*, Oxford, Clarendon Press, 1992, p. 1.

'Labour radical' or 'Liberal and Labour' candidate and although not a socialist, his politics were never shaped by the anti-socialism that gripped some sections of the Liberal Party in the interwar period. Nonetheless, his thinking remained anchored within the framework of Liberalism and his attachment to the Liberal Party and free trade never wavered. The clarity and comprehensiveness of Samuel's ideas can be seen in his *Liberalism. An Attempt to State the Principles and Proposals of Contemporary Liberalism in England* (1902), one of the seminal works of the New Liberalism of the early 1900s. As the title indicated, with the author's typical dry detachment, the book aimed to present the mainstream Liberal view on the key social and political issues of the day, rather than promoting Samuel's own personal viewpoint.

Samuel became an MP for the Cleveland division at a by-election in November 1902 and was aligned with the Asquithian, Liberal Imperialist wing of the party, much concerned with improving social and economic conditions to raise 'national efficiency'. As under-secretary at the Home Office from December 1905 he was in the thick of the social reform programme of the Liberal government piloting through legislation on working hours, the probation service and child welfare. In fact, the entire constructive legislative work of his career was packed into these two or three years and his Commons skills and mastery of detail were highly rated by Asquith and others. He entered the Cabinet just after his rivals Churchill and Runciman, as Chancellor of the Duchy of Lancaster (from June 1909), serving later as Postmaster General (from February 1910), where he modernised the Post Office, then one of the largest businesses in the world employing over 200,000 people. He was president of the local government board from February 1914 to May 1915.

As Postmaster General, the responsible minister for the contracts to establish an empire-wide network of wireless communication, he was mired in the Marconi scandal of 1912–13, even though, unlike Lloyd George and Rufus Isaacs, his own conduct in the affair had been entirely above reproach. Depicted by Hilaire Belloc and Cecil Chesterton as the lynchpin of a corrupt Jewish conspiracy, Samuel defended himself with his usual composure and clarity. Despite coming out of the ordeal with clean hands, his very innocence and the 'prim, proper and precise' way that he conducted himself seems to have increased his unpopularity with some of his Liberal colleagues. In particular, Lloyd George may have resented the contrast between Samuel's irreproachability and his own ambiguous behaviour, the seed perhaps of his later detestation of Samuel.[289]

At the local government board, Samuel's ambitious plans for slum-clearance and urban planning, announced in a speech delivered in Sheffield in May 1914 were frustrated by the outbreak of war. He did however launch a major expansion of maternity and child welfare centres. His social radicalism did not extend to women's suffrage on which – in line with the Liberal leadership – he took a cautious position, motivated in large part by concerns over the electoral impact of enfranchising middle-class and predominantly Conservative women. Nevertheless, it was on Samuel's motion that women were given the right to stand for election to Parliament in 1918.

Despite being on the 'peace' wing of the party, he helped Asquith to rally the Cabinet for war when Germany infringed Belgian neutrality. He was initially outside the Cabinet when the coalition government was formed in May 1915 but re-entered it in November. In January 1916 he replaced Simon as Home Secretary when the latter resigned in protest at the introduction of compulsory military service, and was responsible for handling the aftermath of the Easter Uprising in Ireland.

Samuel stood by Asquith in the December 1916 crisis despite Lloyd George's efforts to persuade him to stay on at the Home Office. He had little in common temperamentally with Lloyd George and did not expect his government to last. In the massacre of the Asquithians at the 1918 general election, Samuel lost Cleveland and withdrew from party politics for nearly a decade.

After a few months as Special Commissioner for Belgium, he served from July 1920 to July 1925 as High Commissioner for the Palestine Mandate. For Samuel Zionism was 'the one political passion of a singularly passionless career'.[290] From before 1914 he worked tirelessly for the establishment of a Jewish national home in a multi-national Palestine, but as High Commissioner he failed in his

289 Ibid., p. 143.
290 Ibid., p. 204.

objective to win Arab agreement for such a constitution. Instead his period of office began the separate development of the two communities within their own divided institutions.

Retiring to Italy to study philosophy, he was persuaded by Baldwin to return to serve as chairman of the 1925–26 commission of inquiry into the coal industry, part of the deal to head off a miners' strike. During the 1926 general strike his uninvited and unofficial mediation was pivotal in enabling the TUC to abandon the strike. When Lloyd George replaced Asquith as leader, Samuel re-entered party politics in February 1927 as head of the Liberal Party Organisation. As a skilled organiser and mediator, acceptable to all the factions, he played a major part in the Liberal revival that was dashed by the 1929 general election, in which he made one of the few Liberal gains – by a narrow majority – in the usually Tory textile town of Darwen, Lancashire.

Samuel was Lloyd George's deputy in the 1929–31 parliament. He was propelled into the acting leadership on 27 July 1931 when Lloyd George was suddenly incapacitated by prostate problems that demanded an emergency operation. This was precisely the time when the 1931 financial crisis broke and rocked British politics to its foundations, splitting both the ruling Labour Party and the Liberals and leading to the formation of the National Government. The crisis was a pivotal moment in twentieth-century British politics. It was the point at which the three-party system, revived by Lloyd George in the late 1920s, gave way to the bipolar system that survived intact for the next half century and, indeed, in many of its essentials, to the present day. It proved to be the nemesis of the old Liberal Party. Not until the twenty-first century did British Liberalism re-occupy the ground it lost in those events. Samuel struggled vainly to do the right thing for the country and to save his party and the cause of free trade for which it stood, but he could do little against the forces that were unleashed, and it is a matter of speculation if any other leader could have done better.[291]

---

291 Lloyd George certainly thought he could have done so, and brutally criticised Samuel. For an account of the crisis, and speculation on whether Lloyd George might have achieved more, see my 'What if Lloyd George had done a deal with the Tories in 1931?', in D. Brack and I. Dale eds, *Prime Minister Boris and Other Things That Never Happened*, London, Biteback Publishing, 2012.

The first phase of the crisis in August centred on Prime Minister Ramsay MacDonald's efforts to force spending cuts on a reluctant Labour Cabinet in order to stem a run on the pound that threatened to tip sterling off the gold standard. In parallel, MacDonald was negotiating with Samuel for the Liberals and Neville Chamberlain for the Tories to win their backing for any proposals the minority Labour government could agree on. On 24 August MacDonald abandoned efforts to win over his Cabinet opponents and accepted the King's invitation, encouraged by Chamberlain and Samuel, to form a temporary caretaker government with the task of pushing through an emergency package of cuts within six weeks or so. As the overwhelming majority of the Labour Party went into opposition, MacDonald was dependent on Tory and Liberal support.

Initially it seemed that this outcome was favourable for the Liberals. It was widely welcomed by the party, including dissidents grouping around Sir John Simon who had been close to secession. Lloyd George, whom Samuel regularly consulted during the negotiations, did not demur at this stage. Samuel returned to the Home Office and Lord Reading became Foreign Secretary. The deal also appeared to scupper the Tories' desire for an immediate election as MacDonald and Samuel both favoured giving the National Government more time to stabilise the economy, thereby reducing the pressure to abandon free trade, before submitting itself to an election to be deferred until 1932.

However, it soon became clear that Samuel had walked into a deadly trap. The Conservatives, aided and abetted by the Liberal dissidents, pressed MacDonald for an early election.[292] To Samuel's dismay, MacDonald's resistance soon crumbled. On 5 October the Cabinet agreed to an election, with each party fighting on its own programme under a general statement issued by MacDonald seeking a 'doctor's mandate' to carry through whatever steps were necessary to restore the economy – not excluding protectionist measures. Samuel extracted

---

292   The election uncertainty triggered renewed pressure on the pound, and, on 21 September, Britain came off the gold standard. The collapse of gold removed much of the original economic case for the National Government, but it had none of the catastrophic effects that were feared in August and led to a revival of the economy in 1932.

an empty promise that an inquiry would be held before any proposal could be made to introduce a general system of tariffs.

Samuel insisted that the Liberals fight on their own free-trade platform, but the election left the government and Commons dominated by an overwhelming Tory protectionist majority. The Liberals were hopelessly split between the Samuelites, the dissident Liberal Nationals led by Simon, and Lloyd George, who vehemently opposed the election and the continued Liberal support for the government.

The election was a massive landslide for the National Government or more accurately for the Conservatives (470), flanked by thirty-five Simonite 'Liberal Nationals' and only thirty-two Samuelites, facing an opposition comprising fifty-two Labour MPs and Lloyd George's family group of four MPs. Despite Tory opposition, Samuel had a personal triumph in Darwen where he retained his seat with an increased majority.

The final stage of the crisis for the Liberals came in 1932 with the ending of the free-trade system under which the British economy had functioned since the mid-nineteenth century. After a perfunctory inquiry, the Conservatives forced through a general tariff in early 1932 against the impotent opposition of the Samuelites who remained in the Cabinet which 'agreed to differ' over the introduction of the import duties. But when in September 1932 the Cabinet decided to go ahead with the protectionist Ottawa agreements, Samuel and his fellow Liberal ministers, under pressure from the party rank and file, resigned from the government while continuing to support it from the back benches. In November 1933, again under activist pressure, Samuel finally abandoned this strange compromise and took the party into opposition.

This political lack of direction was matched by a calamitous decline in Liberal Party organisation, morale and electoral fortunes, even more so after the party left the government. Samuel's balanced intellectual approach to politics, sense of duty and rather dry, uncharismatic personality did not inspire the voters. Lacking Lloyd George's funds, the party fielded only 161 candidates in the 1935 general election and won only twenty-one. Samuel lost his own seat at Darwen and resigned the leadership. The Liberals had slid to the status of a minor party in apparently terminal decline.

After his peerage in 1937 Samuel acted as deputy Liberal Leader of the House of Lords, taking increasing responsibility from the (more) elderly Lord Crewe. Samuel was one of the few leading Liberals to support Chamberlain's appeasement policy and the Munich agreement, and even after the war he continued to believe that this was the correct course. In 1939, Chamberlain offered him a place in the Cabinet, but having consulting party colleagues Samuel declined. He was Liberal leader in the Lords from 1944 to June 1955. He remained one of the Liberals' main campaigners, especially in the 1945 and 1950 general elections and was the first British politician to deliver a party political broadcast on television.

After 1935, Samuel pursued his long-held ambition to write about philosophy and science and was president of the Royal Institute of Philosophy from 1931–59. He also achieved popularity as a broadcaster on *The Brains Trust* in the mid-1940s. Samuel died on 5 February 1963, by which time the Liberals' revival was in full swing.

Herbert Samuel's rise to the leadership was unsought and accidental though in terms of Commons skill, organisational energy and capacity, and progressive political outlook and achievement he was in certain respects highly qualified. However, as a dry patrician Jewish agnostic intellectual his popular appeal was limited especially in the interwar period when MacDonald and Baldwin were perfecting the art of engagement with the new mass electorate. He was never liked at Westminster, not only because of racial prejudice, but because of his imperturbable self-assurance, efficiency and lack of passion. Simply he was regarded by some as cold and priggish.

His ideas were shaped by the New Liberalism of the two decades before the First World War and especially a deep interest in improving the conditions of the poor which he had experienced at first hand in the East End, his first campaigns in Oxfordshire and later as member for the slump-hit mill-town of Darwen. A certain Gladstonian rectitude and Fabian/New Liberal authoritarianism were evident in his puritanical approach to social questions, such as his defence of theatre censorship and prudish view of sexual matters. He was a social engineer and no libertarian.

He certainly lacked the popular touch and partisan guile that was required of a Liberal leader in the precarious electoral circumstances of the interwar years. It is evident that the party's fortunes sank disastrously under his watch compared with Lloyd George's leadership until 1931, and it was left to his successor Archibald Sinclair to stabilise the party's position. Even if much of this decline was due to forces and circumstances beyond his control, this upright, conciliatory and stalwart establishment figure was not the man to reverse the trend. Nevertheless, his unwavering loyalty to Liberalism undoubtedly helped to avoid its complete collapse in the most difficult phase of its interwar decline and to sustain it in the long years in the political wilderness that followed.

CHAPTER 16

SIR ARCHIBALD SINCLAIR

DAVID DUTTON

Archibald Sinclair led the Liberal Party through ten difficult years (1935-45),
but only one general election (1945). The party he inherited from his predeces-
sor, Herbert Samuel, comprised only twenty-one MPs; that which he bequeathed
to Clement Davies a decade later had been further reduced to just twelve. Yet
during his career Sinclair twice held posts of Cabinet rank. Leading a party
that was in evident decline posed its own distinctive problems, different from
those associated with a party of government or principal opposition. Sinclair's
leadership divides naturally into two halves, before and after the outbreak of
the Second World War. Until 1939 his priorities were to hold his party together
and work out the best strategy to ensure its survival as a significant factor in the
nation's politics. In this he had some success, despite an unfavourable political
climate. With the coming of war, however, Sinclair willingly subordinated the
interests of his party to those of the country and, after 1940, became almost totally
absorbed in running the Air Ministry within Churchill's coalition government.
Assessments of his leadership must necessarily be both balanced and nuanced.

- Archibald Henry Macdonald Sinclair (22 October 1890 – 15 June 1970), only son of Clarence
  Granville Sinclair (d. 1895) and his wife Mabel Sands (d. 1890).
- Educated Eton and Sandhurst.
- Inherited baronetcy of Ulbster from his paternal grandfather in 1912.
- Married (1917) Marigold Forbes, by whom he had two sons and two daughters.
- Entered Parliament in 1922 as Liberal MP for Caithness and Sutherland, a seat he held until
  defeated in the general election of 1945 (stood, unsuccessfully, for the same seat in 1950).

- Secretary of State for Scotland 1931–32, Secretary of State for Air 1940–45, leader of the Liberal Party 1935–45.
- Created Viscount Thurso, 1952.

A rchie Sinclair's leadership of the Liberal Party can be summed up by the circumstances in which he attained the position in 1935 and then, a decade later, surrendered it. The 1935 general election was a catastrophe for the Liberals. The party was reduced to a parliamentary strength of just twenty-one MPs. With the exception of Sinclair, the entire front bench including the existing leader, Herbert Samuel, lost their seats. The former's elevation to the leadership was thus less an achievement than a 'foregone conclusion'.[293] Because of the Second World War, no further general election was held until 1945. This time it was Sinclair's turn to lose his seat. The Liberals' overall performance was even worse than ten years earlier. The toll of the top brass was again severe. Sinclair's own defeat was by the narrowest of margins, but it was a defeat nonetheless. As in 1935, a change of leadership was inevitable, rather than a matter of choice.

It was therefore Sinclair's lot to lead the party through a decade of serious decline. His primary concerns were inevitably different from those illustrious predecessors who had formed cabinets, led governments and passed legislation into law. Sinclair's task was to maximise Liberal influence in a hostile political climate, hold a disputatious party together and prepare for the day when Liberalism's fortunes would finally turn the corner. Historical circumstances also ensured that he was the last Liberal leader to hold a post of Cabinet rank before the formation of the 2010 coalition.

Born in 1890, Sinclair was an orphan by the age of five. His unsettled childhood was spent moving between the homes of members of his extended family. From Eton he progressed to Sandhurst and thence an army career. In 1912, on

293 *Manchester Guardian*, 27 November 1935, cited in J. Rasmussen, *The Liberal Party*, London, Constable, 1965, p. 39.

his grandfather's death, Sinclair became a baronet with a 100,000-acre estate in north-east Scotland. He served with distinction in the Great War, becoming second-in-command to Winston Churchill in the Royal Scots Fusiliers. The two men developed a close friendship, perhaps the most significant political association of Sinclair's career. But age, personality, public standing, as well as military rank, contrived to prevent a true partnership of equals. Indeed, some believed that, throughout his life, Sinclair would, metaphorically at least, stand to attention in Churchill's presence.

Encouraged by Churchill to pursue a political career, Sinclair was chosen to stand as a Lloyd Georgeite Liberal for Caithness and Sutherland in the 1922 general election. He was widely advised that his chances of success would be greater under Asquithian colours, but sought support from both camps and comfortably defeated his Asquithian opponent.[294] Unopposed in the elections of 1923 and 1924, Sinclair gradually made his mark in Parliament. Meanwhile, Churchill returned to the Tory fold. Interestingly, Sinclair gave enthusiastic approval to a speech in September 1924 in which Churchill claimed that no gulf of principle now separated Liberals and Conservatives.[295] Keen to relax 'the grip of the old gang', Sinclair supported Lloyd George's attempts in the late 1920s to modernise Liberal Party policy.[296] But the Liberals' performance in the 1929 election convinced him of the need for electoral reform. It was, he noted, ironic that the first contest fought under a universal franchise should leave the 5,500,000 Liberal voters essentially disfranchised.[297]

The Liberals held the balance of power during the minority Labour government of 1929–31, but an increasingly divided party failed to take advantage of its opportunities. It was a difficult moment for Sinclair to take on the role of Chief Whip. Instilling a sense of discipline into the parliamentary party bore an uncanny resemblance to herding cats. Even so, Sinclair played a leading role in

---

294 Sinclair to Churchill 15 April 1922, cited in I. Hunter ed., *Winston and Archie*, London, Politico's, 2005, p. 162; G. De Groot, *Liberal Crusader*, London, Hurst & Co., 1993, p. 51.

295 Sinclair to Churchill, 29 September 1924, cited in Hunter, op. cit., p. 181.

296 De Groot, op. cit., p. 70.

297 Sinclair to Churchill, 4 June 1929, cited in Hunter, op. cit., p. 193.

negotiations that might have produced a formal Lib–Lab coalition.[298] As it was, the failure of MacDonald's Cabinet to agree on a package of economy measures led to the sudden creation of the all-party National Government, in which Sinclair took office as Scottish Secretary without, to begin with, a seat in the Cabinet. The Liberal leadership passed to Herbert Samuel, with Sinclair recognised as his right-hand man and likely eventual successor. But around half the parliamentary party, led by Sir John Simon, began to coalesce into a separate grouping. In practice, Sinclair's ministerial tenure was dominated by the economic agenda, particularly the possible introduction of tariffs. For Liberals it became largely a question of tactics – balancing the national interest against longstanding Liberal principles, and determining whether free trade could best be defended inside the government or in opposition – and Sinclair emerged as the party's principal tactician.

A general election in October 1931 left the Conservatives in overwhelming control of the government and made tariffs an inevitability. Sinclair and his free-trade colleagues were now dangerously exposed – 'wilderness bound' as Churchill warned.[299] The introduction of the Import Duties Bill early in 1932 almost prompted their departure, but nominal government coherence was maintained by the celebrated 'Agreement to Differ'. Matters came to a head later that year following the Ottawa Agreements that created a scheme of Imperial Preference. This was a step too far for most free-trade Liberals and the Samuelite members (though not the Simonite Liberal Nationals) resigned on 28 September, while continuing to sit on the government benches. But this indeterminate position was clearly unsatisfactory. Liberals, including Sinclair, took refuge in generalisations and platitudes, fearful that clear policy pronouncements might worsen internal party differences. There was a commitment to maintain independence, but little indication of what this stance was designed to achieve. By 1933, Sinclair agreed with the party rank and file that it was time to go into outright opposition, and the decisive step was taken on 16 November.

298   A. J. P. Taylor ed., *My Darling Pussy*, London, Weidenfeld & Nicolson, 1975, pp. 135–7.
299   Hunter, op. cit., pp. 196–7.

But it was not obvious that moving into formal opposition significantly improved the party's fortunes. Most by-elections went uncontested; where a candidate was fielded, results were usually unimpressive. The party's image remained one of 'hopeless disunity'.[300] Liberals had no reason to face the 1935 general election with anything but apprehension, not least because lack of finance and crumbling organisation precluded more than 161 candidates being fielded. After the predictable disaster, Sinclair was elected 'chairman of the party', but the designation 'leader' was adopted within a matter of months.[301] Whatever his title, he confronted an unpromising inheritance.

Heading a now tiny parliamentary party, Sinclair himself inclined towards caution, doubting whether the Liberals could sustain their credentials as a nationwide organisation much longer.[302] Others contemplated Liberals joining one or other of the two main parties to try to liberalise them from within.[303] But the government itself offered Liberals the chance to project a distinctive identity for perhaps the first time since leaving office in 1932. The turning-point came with the Hoare–Laval crisis of December 1935. Having recently proclaimed their firm commitment to the principles of the League of Nations, ministers now seemed ready to buy off Mussolini's aggression at the territorial expense of Abyssinia. If 'the Hoare–Laval Plan did not save Abyssinia … it did … save the Liberal Party for a further lease of life'.[304] In a telling indictment of 'appeasement', Sinclair warned Anthony Eden, Hoare's successor as Foreign Secretary, that 'aggression is an appetite that grows by what it feeds on'.[305] It was the start of a process whereby Sinclair established his party as the champion of the League, collective security, international cooperation and the importance of morality in foreign policy. 'The Liberals had

---

300 Sinclair to Samuel, 4 May 1935, cited in R. Grayson, *Liberals, International Relations and Appeasement*, London, Cass, 2001, p. 8.

301 *Liberal Magazine*, November–December 1935 and April 1936.

302 Sinclair to Scott 19 November 1935 (Thurso MSS, II, 71/2).

303 De Groot, op. cit., p. 114.

304 D. Johnson, *Bars and Barricades*, London, Christopher Johnson, 1952, pp. 73-4.

305 De Groot, op. cit., p. 117.

finally found a distinctive political territory to call their own.'[306] But getting the Liberal message across was not easy. No more than half the parliamentary party of twenty-one MPs were regular Commons attenders. Much responsibility devolved on Sinclair himself. His oratorical style was not to everyone's taste. Thomas Jones wrote of 'an orator in the Victorian tradition, rolling periods, rotund phrases ... quite out of fashion today', while 'Chips' Channon waspishly suggested that the Liberal leader 'provides a pleasant interval during which one can go out for a drink or a cup of tea'.[307]

For all that, Sinclair mounted a constructive and coherent critique of British foreign and defence policy over the remainder of the decade. Unlike Labour, he accepted the need for rearmament, initially to make the League an effective instrument for maintaining peace. Later, his emphasis shifted to the importance of Britain forging bilateral agreements to underpin the League's collective security, appealing during 1937 to Prime Minister Neville Chamberlain to do everything to bring the United States into a defensive alignment. Following the Anschluss in March 1938, Sinclair called upon Britain to organise a 'system of collective security against aggression'. His vision resembled Churchill's 'Grand Alliance'.[308] As the Czechoslovak crisis intensified, he joined with Lord Crewe, Liberal leader in the Lords, to press Chamberlain to make it clear that an unprovoked attack on Czechoslovakia would not be regarded with indifference by Britain, which would support France if she became involved in armed conflict on this issue.[309] Speaking in the subsequent Munich debate, Sinclair insisted that the agreement reached by Chamberlain could not be regarded as a victory for negotiation. The Prime Minister, he suggested, should read *Mein Kampf* to discover Hitler's true intentions.[310]

Sinclair maintained his trenchant critique through the first months of 1939. He

---

306   Ibid., p. 120.

307   T. Jones, *A Diary with Letters*, London, Oxford University Press, 1954, p. 487; R. R. James ed., *Chips*, London, Weidenfeld & Nicolson, 1967, p. 181.

308   A. Stedman, *Alternatives to Appeasement*, London, I. B. Tauris, 2011, pp. 94, 130.

309   Viscount Samuel, *Memoirs*, London, Cresset, 1945, p. 277.

310   A. Wyburn-Powell, *Clement Davies*, London, Politico's, 2003, p. 73; Grayson, op. cit., p. 127.

welcomed the Polish guarantee in March, but understood the need to rally Russia to the cause if the new policy were to have substance. He clearly succeeded in getting under Chamberlain's skin. 'Archie infuriates me with his hypocritical cant,' complained the premier. 'He takes every opportunity of saying that we shall never do any good till we get rid of the PM.'[311] Only on the eve of war did Sinclair concede that now 'criticism must be set aside'.[312]

Yet it had not been easy to keep the party united behind him. Fourteen Liberals voted against the government over Munich, but four voted in support and two failed to vote. Over the introduction of conscription early in 1939, disunity was even more obvious. Some found the leader's support for rearmament hard to reconcile with the traditional Liberal commitment to reduced government expenditure. In such circumstances it might have seemed logical for Sinclair to seek common ground with critics of government policy in other parties. But his initial attitude towards inter-party cooperation was inherently cautious. He worried that too overt a courtship of non-Liberals would alienate some of his own followers, telling one correspondent: 'My job must be to talk about things which unite and strengthen the party rather than those which arouse suspicion and disunity.'[313] By 1938, he was prepared to take greater risks, supporting Popular Front candidates in the Oxford and Bridgwater by-elections.[314] Always, though, he preferred cooperation with like-minded individuals rather than a formal arrangement with Labour.

Revamping party policy afforded an insufficient basis for a Liberal revival. Sinclair set up the Meston Committee to examine party organisation. Its central recommendation led to the replacement of the National Liberal Federation by the Liberal Party Organisation. But the position in the constituencies showed no end to a long-term spiral of decline, with local parties struggling to survive. Remaining pockets of strength depended more on personalities than any residual

---

311   N. Chamberlain to Hilda Chamberlain, 5 March 1939, and to Ida Chamberlain, 8 July 1939, R. Self ed., *The Neville Chamberlain Diary Letters*, Ashgate, Aldershot, 2005), Vol. 4, pp. 390, 427.

312   House of Commons debates, vol. 351, col. 16.

313   Sinclair to A. W. Ward, 23 November 1936, cited in Grayson, op. cit., p. 123.

314   M. Pugh, 'The Liberal Party and the Popular Front', *English Historical Review*, cxxi, pp. 1343–4.

organisational structure. Liberal performance in local elections continued to weaken and the party's financial footing remained fragile. Nor was the Liberal family re-united. The Liberal Nationals were left largely unchallenged in their constituencies with long-term consequences for Sinclair's party. Liberals may have been in better heart at the end of the 1930s than at the beginning, but any suggestion of a 'recovery' must be carefully circumscribed.

With the outbreak of hostilities in September 1939, Chamberlain offered Sinclair a post in his government, though without a seat in the War Cabinet. A meeting of Liberal leaders confirmed that this exclusion from the body decid-ing and controlling policy was an insuperable barrier and the offer was declined (although Samuel offered his services in a purely personal capacity). Instead, Lib-erals could 'best support the vigorous prosecution of the war from an independent basis'.[315] But Sinclair became a more trenchant critic of the war government than these words seemed to imply. Chamberlain, however, resisted Churchill's renewed suggestion that Sinclair should be brought into the government. The inside information revealed in the latter's criticisms suggested that he was being briefed by Churchill and led to an angry spat between the Liberal leader and the Prime Minister.[316]

A Commons debate on 7 and 8 May 1940 on the failure of Britain's military expedition to Norway quickly changed into a general indictment of the govern-ment's handling of the war thus far. Sinclair called upon Parliament to speak out – 'Let us insist upon ... a policy of the most vigorous conduct of the war' – but he stopped short of encouraging resignations from the government.[317] Nonetheless, sufficient Conservatives either abstained or voted against the administration in the resulting division to make Chamberlain's position untenable, and by 10 May Churchill had replaced him as Prime Minister. Sinclair was immediately offered the Air Ministry in the new government, though still without a War Cabinet seat. But when Churchill conceded that Sinclair could attend that body whenever

---

315   J. Vincent, 'Chamberlain, the Liberals and the Outbreak of War, 1939', *English Historical Review*, cxiii, pp. 374-9.

316   James, op. cit., p. 242.

317   Hunter, op. cit., p. 217.

matters of major political importance, including possible peace terms, were being discussed, it was difficult for him to refuse his friend's invitation.

Yet Sinclair's return to government never quite held the significance that the headship of a wartime service ministry might seem to suggest. In general, Churchill was looking for a competent administrator at the War Office, not an architect of high strategic policy. 'The appointment of Archie to Air and Anthony [Eden] to War', noted Baffy Dugdale, 'is taken to mean that Winston intends to run the War himself.'[318] As Air Minister for the duration of the German war, Sinclair was 'thoroughly competent, completely devoted and highly respected … a great gentleman'.[319] He stood up for his department and sometimes prevailed against Churchill's opposition, but he suffered from a poor grasp of technical issues. The appointment of Lord Beaverbrook to the new Ministry of Aircraft Production complicated matters and led to many disputes in which Beaverbrook was always likely to prevail, especially once he entered the War Cabinet in August 1940. Churchill admired Sinclair's personal qualities, but was more impressed by Beaverbrook's executive skills in the supply and repair of aircraft.[320] In turn, Beaverbrook was highly critical of Sinclair, claiming that the Air Ministry was 'thoroughly rotten' and Sinclair a 'thoroughly bad minister … hoodwinked by his subordinates'.[321] The appointment of the congenial Charles Portal as chief of the air staff in October 1940 and Beaverbrook's replacement by Moore-Brabazon the following May eased matters for Sinclair.

It fell to him to wind up an important Commons debate on 20 August 1940 at the height of the Battle of Britain in a speech which, while generally applauded, seemed to 'Chips' Channon to make the 'magnificent exploits of our airmen seem dull and trite'.[322] On another occasion he insisted that Britain would never use her air power as an instrument of terror. Yet he increasingly championed the controversial tactics of bomber command. The arguments in favour of 'area' over

318   N. Rose ed., *Baffy*, London, Vallentine, Mitchell, 1973, p. 170.

319   M. Dean, *The Royal Air Force and Two World Wars*, London, Cassell, 1979, pp. 100–101.

320   K. Young, *Churchill and Beaverbrook*, London, Eyre & Spottiswoode, 1966, p. 144.

321   J. Colville, *The Fringes of Power*, London, Hodder & Stoughton, 1985, p. 165.

322   James, op. cit., p. 264.

'precision' bombing, he told Churchill, were 'simple, clear and convincing'.[323] In public, however, Sinclair failed to admit that 'the RAF did not have the capacity to bomb accurately and that in consequence it had settled for second best … wanton killing'.[324]

A Liberal governmental presence was, in one sense, an isolated beacon in the party's long history of decline. Yet it would be difficult to argue that it derived any lasting advantages from its occupation of office. Overall, the Liberal presence was too small to exert any obvious impact on the tone of Churchill's administration. For example, no Liberal sat on the key Reconstruction Priorities Committee, looking at the implementation of the Beveridge Report.[325] There was no distinctively 'Liberal' area of government to match Labour's impact on domestic policy and post-war planning. Moreover, in his devotion to the war effort, Sinclair effectively abandoned his role as party leader. Consequently, it was almost as if two Liberal parties emerged – one accepting Sinclair's line that party differences must be shelved in wartime; the other striving to sustain an independent Liberal identity. In practice, then, the war years posed 'more a threat than an opportunity to the Liberals'.[326]

While the Liberal Party never moved into formal opposition, it sometimes appeared to want to do so and Churchill had to write to Sinclair, criticising his party's performance in parliamentary divisions.[327] Discontent focused on the wartime electoral truce. On the surface, the leadership's line prevailed. Official Liberals never contested wartime by-elections. But several candidates of Liberal inclination did stand as independents. Donald Johnson (Chippenham), Honor Balfour (Darwen) and Margery Corbett-Ashby (Bury St Edmunds) all came surprisingly close to success.[328]

Much party frustration was inevitably directed against the leader. The group

---

323   Hunter, op. cit., p. 220.

324   De Groot, op. cit., p. 192.

325   P. Addison, *The Road to 1945*, London, Jonathan Cape, 1975, p. 221.

326   M. Baines, 'The Survival of the British Liberal Party 1932–1959', Oxford University DPhil thesis, 1991, p. 66.

327   Churchill to Sinclair, 31 January 1942, cited in Hunter, op. cit., p. 338.

328   M. Baines, 'The Liberal Party and the 1945 general election', *Contemporary Record*, 9(1), 1995, p. 50.

Radical Action, formed in 1941, had the objective of keeping the party firmly to the left of the political spectrum. But it was also a protest against Sinclair's seemingly ineffectual leadership.[329] In 1943, the local party in Paddington tried to organise a protest against Sinclair's practice of signing letters of support for governmental (but non-Liberal) by-election candidates and Johnson later attributed his own narrow defeat at Chippenham to the leader's endorsement of his Conservative opponent.[330] Overall, there was a fear that Sinclair was so enveloped in Churchill's web that he would seek to extend the coalition into the post-war era or even go the way of the Liberal Nationals before him.[331] This was probably unfair, but critics sensed an increasing dilution of true Liberalism in Sinclair's make-up and he was unsuccessful in persuading the party that his own tactics were sound. The declaration of March 1944 that Liberals would fight the next election 'as an independent party ... on an advanced Liberal programme' lessened anxiety, but underlying fears persisted about Sinclair's true intentions.[332]

The Churchill coalition was dissolved after the defeat of Germany and a general election called for 5 July 1945. The party faced the contest with some optimism, but it was misplaced. Liberals rejoiced in claiming the new popular hero, William Beveridge, as one of their own, but the latter's ideas were not a Liberal monopoly and the electorate was clear that Labour was the most likely party to translate Beveridge's vision into reality. Liberal Party organisation had suffered most during the war years and the majority of its candidates were inexperienced, sometimes embarrassingly so. The Liberal campaign was unexceptionable, but unexciting. Sinclair had almost totally neglected his constituency during the war and his 'personal vote' was now a waning asset. Nonetheless, he privately predicted his own victory and a hung parliament nationally.[333] In the event, Sinclair came third in a desperately close contest, just sixty-two votes short of victory. Across the country the picture was bleak. Liberalism's pre-dissolution strength

---

329   Baines, op. cit., 1991, p. 56.

330   A. Thorpe, *Parties at War*, Oxford, Oxford University Press, 2009, p. 233; Johnson, op. cit., p. 247.

331   M. Pottle ed., *Champion Redoubtable*, London, Weidenfeld & Nicolson, 1998, pp. 275–6.

332   Thorpe, op. cit., pp. 52, 234.

333   Sinclair to Samuel, 6 July 1945, cited Baines, op. cit., 1995, p. 54.

of eighteen MPs was reduced to twelve. Just 8.8 per cent of Liberal candidates even secured second place. Only the most tortuous argument could conclude that the party whose stewardship Sinclair now handed over to Clement Davies was stronger than the one he had inherited in 1935.

For some time Sinclair, still only fifty-four years of age, remained something of a leader over the water, or more accurately in his Highland estate beyond the Great Glen, not least because his victorious Conservative opponent had oddly promised to resign and fight a by-election once the Japanese war ended. Significantly, Davies's title was only 'chairman of the Liberal Parliamentary Party'. The by-election never took place, but it was not until Sinclair was again defeated at Caithness and Sutherland in the 1950 general election that the issue was fully resolved. In December 1951 the Liberal Council effectively closed matters with a resolution expressing continued confidence in Davies's leadership.[334] Sinclair had gradually reconciled himself to Davies's position, especially once the latter's initial enthusiasm for left-leaning policies had cooled. Sinclair himself concluded after the party's disastrous performance in 1950 that the time had come to negotiate with the Conservatives.[335] This was not a total abandonment of the doctrine of Liberal independence, but it did show the limitations of a strategy to which Sinclair had been wedded since the early 1930s.

Sinclair now accepted a seat in the Lords as Viscount Thurso in the expectation of succeeding the elderly Samuel as the party's leader in the Upper House. Reconciled to the end of his Commons career, he was 'greatly pleased by the prospect of leaving his cold hermitage in Caithness for the rhetorical delights of Westminster'.[336] But a severe stroke early in 1952 thwarted his hopes, while a second stroke in 1959 left him permanently incapacitated. He died on 15 June 1970, four months short of his eightieth birthday.

·   ·   ·

334   Rasmussen, op. cit., p. 43.

335   Davies MSS, J/3/23, Sinclair to Davies 3 May 1950.

336   R. Cockett ed., *My Dear Max*, London, The Historians' Press, 1990, p. 128.

Archibald Sinclair's leadership of the Liberal Party divides naturally into two halves. Writing to him in late 1944, the MP Wilfrid Roberts warned that the 'memory' of Sinclair's pre-war leadership would 'fade' if he failed to 'give more of a lead in future'.[337] History runs the same risk. Sinclair certainly began with some basic advantages. Somewhat like Jo Grimond, he cut an impressive figure, having what a later generation would call 'charisma'. 'He was a romantic figure', recalled Violet Bonham Carter, 'gay, gallant and good looking.'[338] The journalist, Colin Coote, wrote of 'a person of irresistible charm, allied to the face and figure of an Adonis'.[339] More substantially, by 1939 Sinclair had restored a sense of purpose to his party after the confusion and divisions that characterised his predecessor's leadership. In a decade that destroyed the reputations of so many contemporaries, Sinclair deserves credit for his stance on issues of foreign policy and principled opposition to appeasement. Liberalism reaffirmed its separate identity after coming near to losing it. If, by contrast, Sinclair was a poor party leader in wartime, such a statement should be qualified by recognition of his determination to put country before party. His stewardship of the Air Ministry was painstaking and meticulous. Disinclined to delegate, he visibly over-worked to the detriment of his health. In a government of 'tired and jaded men', Sinclair 'lived completely at his office, was burnt out and had "a face like parchment"'.[340] Meanwhile, the party's rank and file 'wandered erratically in various directions'.[341] Liberals failed to reach a consensus on the extent to which the post-war world would require a regulated economy. They needed the sort of direction only Sinclair had the stature to provide; but he was otherwise engaged. In the last months of the war, Beveridge became 'effectively the joint leader of the Liberal Party'.[342] His rapid elevation spoke eloquently of the extent to which Sinclair, absorbed at the Air Ministry, was no longer the public

---

337   De Groot, op. cit., p. 216.

338   V. Bonham Carter, *Winston Churchill as I Knew Him*, London, Eyre & Spottiswoode, 1965, p. 443.

339   C. Coote, *Editorial*, London, Eyre & Spottiswoode, 1965, p. 159.

340   A. J. P. Taylor ed., *Off the Record*, London, Hutchinson, 1973, p. 376.

341   De Groot, op. cit., p. 206.

342   Thorpe, op. cit., p. 56.

face of Liberalism. Among the working classes, only 3 per cent had even heard of him.[343] So Liberalism lost the sense of purpose that Sinclair had valiantly struggled to re-establish only a few years earlier. In wartime, 'the disintegration of his party was a measure of his loyalty to the country'.[344]

343   M. Baines, 'The Survival of the British Liberal Party', in A. Gorst, L. Johnman and W. S. Lucas eds, *Contemporary British History 1931–61*, London, Pinter, 1991, p. 17.

344   De Groot, op. cit., p. 217.

CHAPTER 17

CLEMENT DAVIES

ALUN WYBURN-POWELL

Clement Davies is probably the least known of all the Liberal leaders. He described his own leadership as one of 'almost supine weakness'.[345] *He was only intended to be an interim leader, but he ended up leading the party for eleven years and holding it together during its darkest time, from 1945 to 1956. By turning down Winston Churchill's offer of coalition in 1951, he preserved the independence of the Liberal Party and saved it from probable extinction.*

- Clement Edward Davies (19 February 1884 – 23 March 1962), born in Llanfyllin, Montgomeryshire.

- Youngest of seven children of Moses and Elizabeth Davies, owners of a small business.

- Took a first-class honours degree in law at Trinity Hall, Cambridge.

- Became a barrister and King's Counsel; also pursued a business career, becoming managing director of Unilever.

- Married Jano Elizabeth in 1913.

- Four children, three of whom died at the age of twenty-four in unrelated incidents.

- Elected Liberal MP for Montgomeryshire in 1929, and held seat until his death in 1962, as a Liberal 1929–31, Liberal National 1931–39, independent 1939–42 and Liberal again from 1942.

- Leader of the Liberal Party, 1945–56.

---

345   Letter, Davies to Gilbert Murray, 11 May 1950, J/3/26, Clement Davies Papers, National Library of Wales.

Davies did not achieve this by some supreme optimism, in fact he constantly worried that he was to be the party's 'omega'. With hindsight, Davies can be seen to have saved the Liberal Party mainly because of things he did not do. He did not lose his own seat – as Asquith, Samuel and Sinclair had done. He did not see the party split under his leadership – as Gladstone, Asquith and Lloyd George had. He did not profess strong policy attachments and thus managed to avoid a civil war between the polarised wings of the parliamentary party. He did not become embroiled in a scandal as Thorpe was to do, nor was he involved in dubious financial dealings as Lloyd George had been. He did not accept the offer from Churchill of a coalition and a Cabinet seat for himself, which could have seen the Liberal Party subsumed into the Conservatives.

Former colleagues of Davies's insisted long after he had died that he was not an alcoholic and that this was a smear put about by his opponents. But his own family were not in denial about it. He managed to avoid alcohol, sometimes for years at a stretch, but at times of severe stress he indulged in binge-drinking, disappeared completely from public view and was unable to continue his work for several weeks. Inconveniently, the times of greatest stress were general elections.

Davies was not even primarily a politician. His greatest achievements arguably came in his other careers as a lawyer and as managing director of Unilever. In 1925, he won the largest legal settlement in British corporate history up to that point in a dispute over the price of chemicals. In his first year as party leader, Davies still earned over £15,000 from his business interests, dwarfing his £600 annual salary as an MP.[346]

However, Davies was not born into a wealthy family. His parents were seed merchants, auctioneers and estate agents, with fluctuating financial fortunes. They were bilingual English and Welsh-speaking Nonconformists. Clem, born on 19 February 1884, was the last by nearly eight years of seven children. Both girls and all except one of the five boys went on to achieve degree-level education. Davies went to Trinity Hall, Cambridge and read law, but only after he had spent four years working in auctions and on the land. He therefore had a

---

346   Alun Wyburn-Powell, *Clement Davies – Liberal Leader*, London, Politico's, 2003, p. 150.

stable, hard-working upbringing which put him in touch with most sections of his community and often with those in financial distress who had been forced to sell their property.

At Cambridge, Davies joined the Union but did not take part in any of the debates. It was not that he had little to say: he was renowned for his endless gushing rhetoric, but he was too nervous to participate. Davies graduated with a first, became a law lecturer and then a barrister and eventually a King's Counsel. Lloyd George tried to persuade Davies to stand as a Liberal candidate in the 1910 elections, but he decided to concentrate on his legal career. In 1913, Davies married Jano, a language teacher with Welsh ancestry. They had four children, three of whom were to die at the age of twenty-four, in unrelated incidents. The eldest son, David, died from an epileptic fit after a drinking bout. Their daughter, Mary, committed suicide by electrocuting herself, although her parents refused to accept the inquest verdict. The third child, Geraint, died in an accident on Salisbury Plain during the Second World War. The youngest, Stanley, survived into his eighties, burdened by the fears and expectations piled onto him by the fate of his siblings.

In 1929, Davies was elected at his first attempt as the Liberal candidate in Montgomeryshire. He was a supporter of Lloyd George, although with reservations about the potential impact of his proposed land reforms. Had he entered politics in 1910, Davies might have reached the position of a senior law officer in the government, but his election in 1929 offered little prospect of ministerial office. In the turmoil of 1931, following the collapse of Ramsay MacDonald's second Labour government, Davies allied himself to the Liberal National faction. In the early days the division between Liberals and Liberal Nationals was quite fluid and several MPs swapped back and forth. Davies considered himself at the time to be a follower of Robert Hutchison, rather than of John Simon who came to be regarded as the official leader of the Liberal Nationals. In 1933, when Samuel's Liberals crossed the floor of the House of Commons, Davies remained on the government benches. He stayed with the Liberal National faction until December 1939, when he withdrew his support from Neville Chamberlain's administration, citing 'so many instances of failure ... to take the measures necessary for the vigorous prosecution of the war' and an absence of 'the reso-lution, policy or energy ... to meet the crisis'.[347]

In May 1940, Davies was instrumental in Churchill's accession to the pre-miership, persuading Lloyd George to make his 'last decisive intervention' in the House of Commons during the Norway Debate, which led to the resigna-tion of Chamberlain. When one of Beaverbrook's employees commented to him 'Thank God!' on being told of the new premier, Beaverbrook replied, 'Don't thank God, thank Clem Davies.' Churchill offered Davies a viscountcy, which he declined; he was still a commoner at his death. Davies was also offered junior ministerial office working under Arthur Greenwood, Minister without Portfo-lio, which he also declined, considering that it would be demeaning for him to work as a subordinate to someone he regarded as his equal. For the rest of the war, Davies took the position of a candid friend of Churchill, being willing to challenge the Prime Minister from the back benches. From 1939 to 1942, Davies remained an independent MP. He allied himself with some of the other independ-ents, particularly Eleanor Rathbone, Vernon Bartlett, A. P. Herbert and Denis Kendall. Davies also became close to Liberal MP Tom Horabin and in August 1942 Davies re-joined the Liberal Party. The two became leading members of Radical Action, a left-wing pressure group within the Liberal Party.

In the 1945 election, the Liberal Party lost its leader Archie Sinclair, its Chief Whip Percy Harris, and its leading thinker William Beveridge. Davies survived the election and was chosen as interim leader, pending the expected return to Parliament of Sinclair. There was little competition among the twelve Liberal MPs for the party leadership in 1945. Four were newly elected and most of the others had drifted too far to the left or right to be credible candidates.[348] The only serious contenders for the party leadership were Davies and Wilfrid Rob-erts, Liberal MP for North Cumberland since 1935. The fact that seven of the twelve Liberal MPs sat for constituencies in Wales was probably the deciding factor in Davies's favour. Davies's Liberal National past led to some suspicions

347   Ibid., p. 95.
348   Jaime Reynolds and Ian Hunter, 'Liberal Class Warrior', *Journal of Liberal Democrat History*, Vol. 28, autumn 2000, p. 17.

about the strength of his adherence to liberalism. The split between the followers of Lloyd George and Asquith was still detectable in the party and policy positions were polarised, with much of the weight on the left and right wings and little in the centre. This made for a party very difficult for Davies to steer.

Davies commissioned a thorough review of the Liberal Party, the outcome of which appeared in 1946 as *Coats off for the Future!* The report made grim reading for the party: 'Unlike our predecessors ... we have been unable to conclude that Liberalism has passed through its worst trials and survived them ... On the contrary, we have been forced to realise that the world is faced with the possible eclipse of British Liberalism.'[349] There was little political space for a third party in the prevailing political consensus and the Liberals had to fight even for a monopoly on this limited turf.

Early in his leadership Davies was involved in a partially successful initiative to reunite the Liberals with the Liberal Nationals. The Liberal National Party had begun to disintegrate during the war. Parts of the Liberal Nationals broke away and reintegrated with the Liberals, including the London Liberal Nationals in 1946, although neither the Liberals nor the Liberal Nationals had MPs in any of the eighty-three constituencies covered by the merger. The independence of the rump of the Liberal Nationals was curtailed in 1947 by the Woolton–Teviot Agreement and eventually it was subsumed into the Conservative Party.

Davies's track record in Parliament leading up to 1945 placed him on the radical left of British politics, advocating major land reforms and nationalisations. He had been elected without Labour opposition in Montgomeryshire in 1945 and even with the local endorsement of the Transport and General Workers Union. Sinclair worried that Davies would try to outflank Labour on the left.[350] However, after 1945 Davies's stance appeared to moderate again. He supported all the early nationalisations of the Attlee government and the formation of the National Health Service, arguing that 'it would be ignoble to hinder that work

---

349 *Coats off for the Future!*, Liberal Party Organisation, 1946, 08139.c.98, British Library.
350 Wyburn-Powell, op. cit., p. 171.

merely because it happens to be in the hands of other people'.[351] However, he disagreed with the Labour Party when it came to the debate on the steel industry in 1949. Observers (and detractors within the party) saw this as a 'drift to the right'. Davies's position had certainly moderated from his strident left-wing stance of 1945, but one consistent theme of Davies's outlook was his commitment to Britain's role in Europe. He was alone among the British party leaders in welcoming Jean Monnet's wish to see Britain as the nucleus of a European political and economic union. Davies favoured Britain's membership of the European Coal and Steel Community and the country's full participation in the moves which led to the formation of the EEC.

At the 1950 general election the Liberal Party faced a strategic choice over whether to fight on a broad or narrow front. To have any credibility that it was fighting to win the election, the Liberals had to field candidates in at least 313 constituencies – half the seats in the Commons. In the event the party managed to find 475 candidates, a significant increase on the 306 in 1945. The increased number of candidates meant that the party's share of the vote went up from 9 per cent in 1945 to 9.1 per cent, but the average vote per candidate fell and 319 lost their deposits. Nine MPs were returned – a net loss of three. Jo Grimond was newly elected as the Liberal MP for Orkney and Shetland, taking the seat from the Conservatives.

After Sinclair's failure to return at Caithness and Sutherland, Davies was re-elected unanimously as leader, but his position became increasingly difficult as the party was more polarised than before. Megan Lloyd George, Edgar Granville and Emrys Roberts were firmly on the left wing, but Donald Wade had been newly elected as Liberal MP for Huddersfield West as result of a pact with the local Conservatives. There were calls from some within the parliamentary party for a pact with the Conservatives and from others for a pact with the Labour Party. Davies's inclinations were put to the test after the 1951 election. The Liberal Party was forced by lack of candidates and finance to fight on a narrow front, fielding only 109 candidates. Of these only six were successful. The

---

351 *Liberal Magazine*, July 1946, p. 309.

overall result of the general election, a narrow victory for the Conservative Party, led to Churchill's invitation to the Liberals to form a coalition with a seat in the Cabinet for Davies. However, tempting as this last chance for ministerial office was, Davies was willing to abide by his party's view. He consulted the party's executive, who voted by eleven votes to one to reject the offer of the coalition. Only Violet Bonham Carter was in favour of acceptance. Davies thus declined Churchill's offer. This reassertion of independence helped to prevent the further erosion of the Liberal Party's identity. In addition, Davies's most outspoken critics in the parliamentary party had lost their seats in the 1951 election and so the party became more coherent and easier to lead.

Davies managed to put a brave face on the avoidance of electoral annihilation or takeover and was able to claim defiantly that although 'our beachhead is not enlarged ... it remains ... we refuse to be stamped out'.[352] Davies's age and health took their toll on his limited leadership abilities, but the party limped on to the 1955 election with Davies still in charge. Davies appeared unready to hand over, but in the face of a groundswell of opinion calling for a reinvigoration of the party leadership, he hastily re-wrote his leader's speech for the Liberal Party assembly in Folkestone in September 1956, and announced his resignation.[353] He was replaced as leader by the obvious successor, Jo Grimond.

Numerically, the Liberal Party in Parliament was in a worse state at the end of Davies's leadership than at the start. He had inherited a party with twelve MPs and handed it on with six, but there had been a turning point in the party's fortunes. During Davies's leadership the party pulled out of its nosedive and stabilised itself on a bumpy, but stable, path. The party's lowest share of the vote at only 2.6 per cent occurred at the 1951 general election. At the 1955 election there was a minuscule improvement to 2.7 per cent. The low point in party membership was around 1953, with a slight recovery taking place before Davies left office. The early signs of recovery showed up most clearly in terms of by-election performance. In December 1954 (four years before the

352   David Dutton, *A History of the Liberal Party*, Basingstoke, Palgrave, 2004, p. 177.

353   Handwritten draft resignation statement, B/5/2, Clement Davies Papers, National Library of Wales.

Torrington by-election victory), the party nearly snatched the seat of Inverness from the Conservatives. It was the Liberals' highest share of the vote in a three-way by-election since 1932 and the improvement was sustained. In the nineteen by-elections fought by all three major parties since the war leading up to Inverness, the Liberals had averaged only a 9.3 per cent share of the vote, but in the nineteen by-elections from Inverness onwards the Liberals averaged 25.2 per cent. There was clearly a step change in party performance well before Davies left office in 1956. He may not have been the direct cause of the improvement, but it had undoubtedly started under his leadership.

Tenacity was Clem Davies's greatest virtue – grim, miserable tenacity – tenacity accompanied by a sense of importance for himself and his party, which was not really justified by any numerical measure. Davies maintained a Liberal shadow Cabinet. As a privy counsellor, he insisted on taking his place as one of the three major party leaders at ceremonial events and so maintained the façade of a more significant party.

Davies did not keep to a steady political position over his thirty-three years in Parliament; he went from being a radical Lloyd George-supporting Liberal in 1929 to a compromising Liberal National in the 1930s, to a radical left-wing independent during the war, then back to a middle-of-the-road pragmatic politician in the 1950s. Davies, the pessimistic, inconsistent and weak leader dogged by alcoholism and personal tragedy, managed, against all the odds, to ensure the continued existence of the near-extinct Liberal Party at a time when the country was generally satisfied with a two-party consensus and did not really need to listen to a third moderate voice. He helped the Liberal Party survive the corporatist post-war era, inhospitable to liberalism, so that it could benefit from the more congenial and individualistic circumstances of the 1960s.

CHAPTER 18

JO GRIMOND

PETER BARBERIS

Jo Grimond was widely regarded as one of the heroic Liberal Party figures of the second half of the twentieth century. He was described by Paddy Ashdown as a 'lion of the liberal cause'.[354] *In some ways, he was a mercurial character. Born into wealth (if not social 'position'), he nevertheless associated himself with meritocracy; he remained faithful to the Liberal Party while doing more than most to engineer its alliance with other political forces; he received much praise for having revived his party's fortunes, though it enjoyed its greatest post-war electoral successes when he was no longer leader; and, both before and during his leadership, he established a reputation for a radical, left-leaning modernism that later gave way to stronger strains of anti-statism.*

- Joseph (Jo) Grimond (29 July 1913 – 24 October 1993), born in St Andrews.
- Educated at Eton and Balliol College, Oxford.
- Called to the Bar (Middle Temple) in 1937.
- Married Laura Bonham Carter in 1938.
- Unsuccessfully contested Orkney and Shetland 1945, MP for Orkney and Shetland 1950–83, relinquished seat in 1983.
- Leader of the Liberal Party 1956–67, caretaker leader May to July 1976, Privy Counsellor from 1961.
- Raised to the peerage as Lord Grimond of Firth, 1983.

J o (Joseph) Grimond was the youngest of three children and the only son born to Joseph and Lydia. Joseph senior owned a jute factory in Dundee. Although sold during the 1920s upon the decline of the industry, the business brought wealth enough for the family to live in comfort. Thus, Jo attended preparatory boarding schools before being admitted to Eton as an Oppidan (fee-paying pupil). The young Grimond reflected something of the Greek harmony of body and mind, being both an accomplished sportsman and an outstanding intellect. From Eton he went up to Balliol College, Oxford, having won a highly competitive Brackenbury history scholarship. He took a first in PPE. Coming up from Oxford in 1935, he was admitted to Middle Temple and was duly called to the Bar. For a short time he went into chambers and served briefly as a marshal to a circuit judge.

While at Oxford, Grimond made what was to be a lifelong resolution. As he later remarked: 'I decided to be a politician and a Liberal politician at that.'[355] His father had an allegiance to the Liberals, though the family was not politically active. That was to change when he met and married Laura, daughter of Sir Maurice and Violet Bonham Carter and granddaughter of former premier H. H. Asquith. Throughout their marriage, Laura remained a source of active encouragement; she was in some ways the keeper of her husband's radical conscience. Family connections may have played a part in his adoption as the prospective Liberal parliamentary candidate for Central Aberdeenshire. But war put paid to any such ambitions for the moment and he enlisted with the 2nd Fife and Forfar Yeomanry. Most of his war was spent stationed in the UK, though in the later stages he found himself in Belgium and Normandy. When the war in Europe ended and party political conflict resumed, he contested the seat of Orkney and Shetland in the ensuing general election of July 1945. He did so as Major Grimond. Unable to dislodge the sitting Conservative MP, he fell short by only 329 votes, beating the Labour candidate into third place. His return to civilian life was marked by successive spells first as director of personnel in the European headquarters of the United Nations Relief and Rehabilitation

---

355 Jo Grimond, *Memoirs*, London, Heinemann, 1979, p. 64.

Administration, then as secretary of the National Trust for Scotland. When Parliament was dissolved in February 1950, Grimond again contested Orkney and Shetland, this time successfully. He continued to represent the constituency, successfully defending his seat on nine occasions until he relinquished it in 1983.

As an MP, Grimond remained faithful to the liberal tradition of 'pavement politics'. He never neglected his constituents. Both the remoteness and the unusual characteristics of Orkney and Shetland gave him rein to make his mark. In the House of Commons and elsewhere he championed the special needs of those who inhabited the sparsely populated small islands as well as of those in the respective mainlands of Orkney and Shetland. And while distance precluded weekly return journeys from Westminster, he made a point of going back every other weekend when Parliament was in session and of holding regular surgeries, at that time something of a novelty among MPs. He bought a house in Firth, near Kirkwall (Orkney) that remained his main home base.

As one of nine Liberals in the parliament of 1950–51, Grimond now became Chief Whip. Though small in number, they were a potentially mutinous crew. Grimond's appointment failed initially either to bring greater unity within the parliamentary party or to stem the haemorrhage of high-profile members to each of the other main parties, including three who had lost their seats as Liberals. In truth, it was not Grimond's fault; but he was not equipped with any great aptitude for the job he had been given. Certainly he had little stomach for sustained immersion in minutiae or the heavy hand of discipline. The task may have been beyond anyone at that time. For during the early 1950s the very future of the party remained in doubt. That it retained its integrity owed more to the skill of party leader Clement Davies than to the efforts of the newly elected Chief Whip. Grimond publicly acknowledged that Davies 'refused all temptation to till the easy fields where ... sweet things were to flower'.[356] Increasingly, though, Grimond was becoming the public face of the party. He championed 'conscience' causes such as the abolition of the death penalty and reform of the law against homosexuality, at the same time campaigning vigorously and

356 Liberal Party conference, Llandudno, 16 April 1956.

successfully for the creation of a press council. He was vice-chair of the Council for the Defence of Seretse Khama.[357] He was also an active member of the Movement for Colonial Freedom, as well as of other groups such as the Commonwealth Parliamentary Union, the Commonwealth Parliamentary Association and of the Inter-Parliamentary Union. In his maiden speech he had called for devolution – or home rule as he preferred to call it, at that time very much a minority interest, even north of the border. Like most mainstream politicians of the 1950s, Grimond acknowledged both the virtues and the realities of the so-called 'Keynesian consensus', though he feared that too much was being promised in its name. The latter foreshadowed the more strident anti-statism that was to mark his later years, along with the championing of small business and disaggregated pay bargaining.

When Clement Davies stepped down from the party leadership, Grimond was the only viable successor. Rhys Hopkin Morris was deputy chairman of the Commons' Ways and Means Committee, Roderic Bowen was inured to his legal work, while the other two Liberal MPs (Arthur Holt and Donald Wade) held their seats by virtue of local pacts with the Conservatives that could not be relied upon indefinitely. Moreover, two months earlier Grimond had, in the words of the *Manchester Guardian*, 'left the (annual) assembly as crown prince'.[358] Thus, he was duly chosen, taking the reins on 5 November 1956 – the day on which British and French troops took Port Said in the Suez Canal zone and on which Soviet tanks were rolling into Hungary. In Parliament, the Liberals, including Grimond, had at first been sympathetic to the Eden government over Suez, but then swung against. This shift of allegiance precipitated further resignations from the party. And in February 1957, following the death of Rhys Hopkin Morris and despite the absence of a Conservative candidate, the Liberals lost the seat of Carmarthen. Ironically, the victorious by-election

---

357 The heir to a chieftainship in the British Protectorate of Bechuanaland (now Botswana), Seretse Khama had married an English woman. The British government was worried about the implications in neighbouring South Africa, now entering its apartheid phase. Liberals were outraged both at the decision that Khama be exiled and at the failure to publish a report that had been commissioned.

358 *Manchester Guardian*, 29 September 1956.

candidate was Megan Lloyd George, daughter of the illustrious Liberal premier and a defeated former Liberal MP who now carried the Labour colours. The Liberals were left with five MPs, the party's lowest ever presence in the House of Commons. Moreover, Grimond was forced to vacillate in his support for the Liberal contestant Morgan Davies, who had been dubbed as the 'Suez candidate'. It was an inauspicious start to his leadership.

Under Grimond's stewardship better days were to come. From the late 1950s until the mid-'60s, there was a general upturn in the party's electoral fortunes. It began slowly to look like a serious political party – more so than at any time since the 1920s, albeit falling short of the decisive breakthrough that would allow it to return to government. Strong by-election performances during the early months of 1958 in Rochdale and then in Torrington lent credibility to rising hopes. At Torrington, Grimond's brother-in-law Mark Bonham Carter triumphed, the first Liberal gain in a contested by-election since 1929. But it was the Liberal victory at Orpington in March 1962 that seemed for a time to presage a seismic shift in the political landscape. The Liberal candidate Eric Lubbock (now Lord Avebury) transformed a Conservative majority of 15,000 into a Liberal one of nearly 8,000 – and on a turnout of 80 per cent. In the general election of October 1959, the Liberal 'rebirth' had been consolidated with a modest upturn in the popular vote and, having contested barely half the constituencies, the return of six MPs. After Orpington much better was now expected. An opinion poll published by the *Daily Mirror* in March 1962 recorded the Liberals with a slender lead over both the other main parties.

Grimond was undoubtedly at the apex of the Liberal revival. To many people beyond the ranks of party supporters and activists he *was* the Liberal Party. And for most within the party he was quite simply an inspirational leader. Only the hardest-bitten critic such as the *Daily Herald* (in September 1962) could see him as more of a figurehead than a leader. He was an engaging platform speaker, a gifted communicator with a wealth of ideas to impart. Above all, he was entirely comfortable in front of the television cameras. As the critic Bernard Levin once said, he came over as 'miraculously free, frank, honest and upright'.[359] On top

---

359   'Taper' (Bernard Levin), *The Spectator*, 28 August 1959.

of that, he maintained a steady output of regular journalistic contributions from the early 1950s onwards, to say nothing of six full-length volumes, together with numerous pamphlets and other ephemera.

Under Grimond's leadership, the Liberal Party grew – in membership, in the number of active constituencies sending representatives to the annual assembly and in its outreach. Grimond's youth and vigour undoubtedly helped to give the party new wind. At forty-three, he struck a contrast with his predecessor who was seventy-two upon retirement. And he remained the youngest leader of any of the main parties until Harold Wilson (only three years Grimond's junior) took the helm at the Labour Party in February 1963. This may have helped the Liberals, the Young Liberals no less, to attract new members. In the past the party had given grist to its critics who, however unfairly, wanted to portray Liberals as somewhat anachronistic, off-beat, cranky or self-indulgent. But under Grimond such caricature had far less resonance. Certainly, the Liberals drew from the disaffected among the ranks of the Labour and, perhaps especially, the Conservative parties. He also fired the imagination of 'political virgins' – people who had never engaged in politics or felt moved to join any political party but who now saw in Grimond a freshness and honesty that they had seen in no other leading politician. And without his applying any direct powers of persuasion, Grimond's persona encouraged a number of public personalities to stand as Liberal parliamentary candidates, for example the broadcasters Ludovic Kennedy and Robin Day. Future party leaders David Steel and Paddy Ashdown, together with leadership contender John Pardoe, are among the many party luminaries to have cited Grimond as the inspiration that attracted them to become active members. Indeed, it is remarkable how, for many members at all levels in the party, Grimond provided and in some cases still provides the point of reference, a kind of political 'gold standard'.

As party leader what type of message did he impart; what was his stock-in-trade of ideas? His tone during those years was that of the no-nonsense, progressive reformer – vision tempered by realism. That is to say that he was a moderniser, while cognisant of some of the downsides of modernity, such as the threat to communities. He cautioned that reason and intellectual conviction, laudable qualities, must be allied to 'vision'; that without vision, social engineering (in which he believed) would be futile and possibly harmful. His message was nevertheless one of confidence in the future and the promise of a better tomorrow, while eschewing Whiggish notions about the linear march of progress. These characteristics are perhaps best illustrated in his internationalism, a defining dimension of liberalism from the nineteenth century onwards. Grimond believed in self-determination and was dedicated to the cause of decolonisation. He was a strong supporter of the United Nations and a critic of successive summit meetings which he considered to be inimical to the underlying UN principle of collective security. He was also a vigorous supporter of NATO; indeed he remained very much a cold warrior. Yet he questioned the need for Britain to possess an independent nuclear arsenal, a view which, while having many adherents in his own party, did not receive universal acclaim. Indeed, on this issue perhaps more than any other, Grimond took matters into his own hands. Some within the party felt that they had been bounced, not least in the way that their leader had introduced the idea in a *Liberal News* article. That said, he maintained his position while rejecting outright unilateralism, a delicate balance that was one of his most skilful policy manoeuvres. At the moral level, Grimond was worried about the proliferation of nuclear weaponry; tactically and politically, he thought that it should suffice for Britain to enjoy protection under the United States' umbrella. While by no means uncritical of the Americans, he was and remained an enthusiastic Atlanticist. And, as for most Liberals, he actively campaigned for Britain's membership of the European Community. From the late 1940s Liberals had established themselves as the most unequivocal supporters of greater European integration, spurred on by federalist proclivities. It was under Grimond's leadership that the Liberals became the first of the mainstream parties formally to adopt the policy of EEC membership, as it did in 1962. Grimond set the scene, though the key speech was made to the party assembly by Mark Bonham Carter. Not all Liberals were enamoured with the EEC. Some, such as Oliver Smedley, considered its implications as a customs union to be incompatible with the principle of international free trade. But the Liberals' centre of gravity rested with the EEC, not least the party leadership. Indeed, the Liberals and, later, the Liberal Democrats were to remain the most avowed champions of a more integrated Europe and of Britain's membership. What was distinctive about Grimond's contribution to the debate during these years was the fearless welcome he gave to the consequent prospect of diminishing national sovereignty.

In these and other ways Grimond maintained during this period a well earned reputation as a radical. He continued to uphold the cause of home rule; he called for the reform of Parliament and of the electoral system; he staked his faith in the virtues of employee share ownership. The latter, in particular, was a policy that Grimond championed throughout his career. It gave expression to the perceived virtues of individualism, a counterweight to excessive corporate power along with the creation and wider distribution of wealth. Closely allied to the idea of share ownership is that of participation, itself a vehicle for the education and uplift of the individual, thus facilitating (if not always guaranteeing) the progress of humankind. Of course Grimond was hardly original in his espousal of these ideas and principles; they were long-established Liberal touchstones. But he articulated them at greater length and in finer detail than almost any of his contemporaries, certainly among the party leadership. They featured strongly in two books that he published while party leader – *The Liberal Future* and *The Liberal Challenge*, published in 1959 and 1963 respectively.[360] These books remain a monument to 'radical Jo' and served to define Grimond and his party. They captured the imagination of many among the purveyors of informed opinion; how far these two works penetrated the popular consciousness is more difficult to assess. More immediate popular engagement emanated from some of his platform speeches. In a speech at Carlisle in June 1964 he enunciated the charter for 'new man' – a plea for a more meritocratic, technology-friendly flowering of talent, facilitated by the lifting of tax, restrictive practices and other burdens. And in another speech, remarkable in that it was delivered with a general election campaign already underway, he waxed lyrical in identifying the longing that each citizen had for a beauty in everyday life that 'bears the stamp of individual greatness and is not just a symbol of material

---

360   *The Liberal Future*, London, Faber & Faber, 1959; *The Liberal Challenge: Democracy Through Participation*, London, Hollis & Carter, 1963.

success or a maimed travesty born of months of human pettiness in committees and councils'.[361] That was in September 1964. Yet it is the speech that he
had given to the Liberal assembly twelve months earlier for which he remains
perhaps best remembered. He told his rapt audience of the 'shoddiness, the
lick of paint on rotten boards, the lack of candour, the lack of quality in those
that lead us, which makes people contract out of their responsibilities'.[362] He
complained about a 'twentieth-century Ruritania' in which background still
counted for more than ability and from which young people felt alienated. It
was the conclusion to his seventy-minute oration that captured the headlines:

> War has always been a confused affair. In bygone days commanders were
> taught that when in doubt they should march their troops towards the sound
> of gunfire. I intend to march my troops to the sound of gunfire ... There are
> enemies, difficulties to be faced, decisions to be made, and passions to be gen-
> erated. The enemies are complacency and wrong values and inertia in the face
> of incompetence and injustice. It is against this enemy we march.

The gunfire speech, as it came to be known, was stirring stuff, perhaps Grimond's finest moment on the platform, though by no means untypical of the
inspiration that he had often induced among the party faithful. In some ways
he was able to feed off the 'mood of progressivism' that prevailed during the
early to mid-1960s and that had already found expression across the Atlantic
in John F. Kennedy's 'new frontier'. Given the radicalism of his message and
the inflection that he imparted, Grimond's leadership struck many as liberalism with 'a left-hand drive'.[363]

In the late 1950s and more seriously from the early 1960s, Grimond had
begun to develop his ideas for a radical, centre-left realignment in British politics. There had been loose talk of a Lib–Lab pact, fuelled partly by dissension

361   Speech at Paisley Town Hall, 23 September 1964.
362   Speech to the Liberal Party assembly, Brighton, 14 September 1963.
363   James Margach, *Sunday Times*, 15 September 1963.

within Labour ranks. But ranks closed as the 1964 general election approached. The election saw further consolidation of the Liberals' position – more candidates and more votes than at any election since 1950 and now nine MPs. It was not the critical breakthrough, though with Labour and the Conservatives closely matched, the Liberals were left tantalisingly short of holding the balance in the Commons. With such a narrow overall Labour majority, the new parliament was unlikely to run its course. And nor did it. But when the country again went to the polls in March 1966 the verdict was clear – a 99-seat Labour majority. Although the Liberals now had a presence of twelve in the House of Commons, any prospect of holding the balance disappeared – and, with it, any possibility for the moment of Grimond's hopes for realignment. In fact, not all Liberals had been enamoured by their leader's overtures to other forces. As party president Nancy Seear famously told delegates: 'We have not spent these years isolated but undefiled in the wilderness to choose this moment of all moments to go, in the biblical phrase, a'whoring after foreign women.'[364]

Immediately after if not before the 1966 general election, Grimond had begun to ponder his future as leader. The suicide of his eldest son at the height of the campaign had been a bitter personal blow. It was no surprise when in January 1967 he announced his resignation as party leader. In the ensuing leadership campaign, Grimond gave his support to Jeremy Thorpe, his successor as it turned out.

Grimond had led from the front in galvanising the party faithful, not only within Parliament but in the country at large. He had become a household name – more so than any Liberal leader since Lloyd George. And if he failed to fashion to everyone's satisfaction an answer to the eternal question – 'What do the Liberals stand for?' – he nevertheless left much more than a vapour trail of policies and visionary ideas. Organisationally and financially, the party was in better shape than when he assumed the leadership. Here, though, credit was largely due to others.

Matters of organisation and the detail of party management had never been

---

364   *The Guardian*, 23 September 1965.

Grimond's forte. Yet he was assisted by a small number of extremely able lieutenants in whom he trusted and to whom he had the good sense to delegate.
Among them was his brother-in-law and sometime MP Mark Bonham Carter,
one of his speechwriters and a confidant throughout the leadership years. In
matters of parliamentary management Grimond was served by three successive
chief whips – Donald Wade (1956–62), Arthur Holt (1962–63) and Eric Lubbock (Lord Avebury) (from 1963). At the party headquarters, he maintained a
close association with Pratap (Lord) Chitnis who was prompted to join the party
after hearing Grimond speak at a rally in the Royal Albert Hall. Chitnis went on
to head the party's Local Government Department and, later, the Liberal Party
Organisation itself. He was an accomplished grass-roots organiser and another
of Grimond's speechwriters. Other headquarters staff who played a significant
role included chief agent Edward Wheeler and Harry Cowie, director of research.

The efforts of these and other individuals belied the shoestring organisation that was the Liberal Party throughout Grimond's tenure as leader. Finance
remained a perennial problem, though the rejuvenation of the party as a political force did bring some expansion to the coffers. Compared with, say, Jeremy
Thorpe, Grimond was not an accomplished fundraiser. Nor was he attuned to
the schedule of meetings and routine party functions, especially during the later
years of his leadership. Only occasionally did he attend meetings of the Executive
Committee. But it was he who proposed the creation of a standing committee
that became the Organising Committee and which assumed responsibility for
key tasks such as the drafting of manifestos and other policy documents. It was
at Grimond's behest that the Political Research Unit was created in 1957, among
other things to conduct opinion polling.

For the most part Grimond worked with the grain of the party bureaucracy.
Yet he was never in any sense its prisoner. Indeed, he was not averse to working
alongside or beyond the framework of the party organisation when he saw fit. He
set up various policy committees and was partly responsible for the launching
of pamphlets and other occasional publications, including the *New Directions*
series, supervised by a committee led by Grimond. He was instrumental in the
setting up in the early 1960s of a number of panels, including those on consumer

protection; transport policy; housing; and local government reform. For the latter he helped to enlist the services of Professor Bryan Keith Lucas, a Liberal sympathiser if not a party activist. Indeed, he consciously drew upon people from outside the party, often academics such as Ralph (Lord) Dahrendorf, Alan Peacock and Michael Zander. And to the consternation of party managers, he was inclined on occasion to go 'off message', usually by way of introducing a new idea or proposal before it had been properly ironed out through the regular policymaking channels. Yet despite this, when Grimond announced his decision to stand down as leader there was genuine sadness in the party at all levels and an acknowledgement that they had been privileged to serve under one who would leave a lasting legacy for Liberal politics and British politics more generally.

Grimond would take back the reins of leadership a decade later, though only briefly, as caretaker. In 1976, his successor Jeremy Thorpe was forced to resign as Liberal leader, following allegations that were famously to land him in court. The party was in crisis and in need of a leader. Responding to the call from colleagues, Grimond was duly elected. One critic denounced the move as 'marching backwards to the sound of gunfire'.[365] But Grimond insisted that he be made 'caretaker leader', resisting suggestions for a longer term arrangement. He held the fort for two months (May–July) until the election of David Steel.

If no longer the party leader, Grimond remained an active force in British politics. He supported the Heath government's efforts to take the UK into the EEC. He did so despite the extreme difficulties encountered in obtaining satisfactory agreement over fisheries policy, a matter of great importance to the people of Orkney and (especially) Shetland. He campaigned for a yes vote in the Scottish referendum of March 1979, though not before having secured what amounted to an opt-out for the people of his constituency, who remained strongly opposed. He had ridiculed the proposals of the Callaghan government, warning that 'simply transferring the Scottish Grand Committee to Edinburgh will not set the bagpipes playing'.[366]

Grimond continued to play his part in Liberal Party politics. Following the

---

365   James Fenton, 'A temporary Fortinbras', *New Statesman* 14 May 1976, p. 632.

366   *The Times*, 9 February 1976.

general election of February 1974, Jeremy Thorpe might have yielded to the lure of office, so keeping Edward Heath in 10 Downing Street. But senior figures within the Liberal Party effectively vetoed the idea. Among them was Jo Grimond, though he was less implacably opposed than some of his colleagues. When newly elected leader David Steel became engaged in talks that would yield the Lib–Lab pact of 1977–78 that sustained the Callaghan government, Grimond was equivocal. He certainly thought that his young successor could and should have struck a harder bargain. He was slow to see in Roy Jenkins's 1979 Dimbleby lecture the possibilities for furthering his own crusade for a realignment of centre-left politics, yet he became one of the strongest adherents to the idea of an alliance between the Liberals and the newly formed SDP. Jenkins generously called him the 'father of the Alliance'.[367] Grimond gave his support to the subsequent merger of the two parties, putting his imprimatur upon the proposal presented to the party assembly at Blackpool in January 1988. He said that it was better to preserve liberalism in practice and, hopefully, in government than to have it 'preserved in some glass case'.[368]

Free from the responsibility of leadership, Grimond had proceeded from the late 1960s to enjoy licence in expressing his opinions. To some he had become something of a loose cannon, described by fellow Liberal MP Russell Johnston as a 'dilettante revolutionary'.[369] In a heightened output of journalism and other written offerings, he was occasionally drawn adrift by the wayward pen. But he was scarcely revolutionary. Rather, he was an increasingly disillusioned radical expressing frustration at what he saw as an encrusted establishment – the tight grip of the two main parties, the bureaucracy, big business and trade unions. These had long been among his bêtes noirs, now only more so.

In 1979, Grimond published his memoirs, a ruminative collage of names and events. Either side of the memoirs, he produced two treatises, *The Common Welfare* (1978) and *A Personal Manifesto* (1983), together reflecting something

---

367   Jeremy Josephs, *Inside the Alliance*, London, John Martin, 1983, p. 57.

368   *The Times*, 24 January 1988.

369   *The Times*, 12 September 1968.

of the 'synoptic later Grimond'.[370] The central themes included the distinction between a welfare society, of which Grimond approved, and the welfare state which he believed to have become distended and distorted such that it had betrayed its original, Beveridge-inspired principles. But he still thought that there must be limits to the dominion of the market; that they should yield to the 'common good'; that everyone should have an equal start in life. In matters of foreign policy he maintained a more expansive vista. He insisted that Britain's interests lay in the success of the EEC which should be upheld despite its 'petty tribulations'; that talk about British sovereignty was 'pedantry'.

In 1983, Grimond was elevated to the peerage, becoming Lord Grimond of Firth. Having long called for a fully elected second chamber, it was by no means certain that he would accept the honour. In typically irreverent fashion, he later referred to it as 'a well-run old folks' home'.[371] As a peer he remained active in public life, not only in speeches made from the red benches but also in other forums, not least in his journalistic output. He died at home in Orkney after a short illness.

Following Grimond's death, there were tributes in abundance – predictably so from among former colleagues and liberal standard bearers. From political opponents there were also generous notices, exceeding the polite routines that are customary on such occasions. Over many years, Grimond had struck a chord as a man of integrity; as Labour peer Lord Richard put it, he was 'a man who gave politics a good name'.[372] In the light of more recent events, that is no mean accolade. What, though, did Grimond achieve during his career? How did he accomplish those feats? And where does he stand in the pantheon of liberalism?

When Grimond assumed the leadership, the Liberal Party was at low ebb. As noted above, its survival initially owed as much to his predecessor Clement Davies. Nevertheless, under Grimond's leadership there was a distinct upturn in morale at all levels; and there was a consolidation and strengthening of party

---

370   *The Common Welfare*, London, Maurice Temple Smith, 1978; *A Personal Manifesto*, Oxford, Martin Robertson, 1983.

371   *Daily Telegraph*, 20 August 1984.

372   HL Debs 25 October 1993, Col. 708. 5th series (1992–93) Vol. 549.

organisation. Slowly but surely, electoral fortunes improved. In the general election of 1964, the Liberal Party came close to holding the balance, but not close enough. Even under Grimond's leadership, the Liberals were unable to make the decisive breakthrough. By the time he laid down the leadership, Britain remained, at best, a two-and-a-half-party system. As Grimond had built upon the work of his predecessor, so Thorpe and Steel were able to stand on his shoulders. To Grimond must be accorded some of the credit for electoral advances made during the 1970s and even the 1980s. In particular, his earlier efforts to develop a radical centre-left realignment were the seed bed for the Alliance and, by extension, the subsequent Liberal/SDP merger. That, again, was a considerable achievement. Grimond had always understood the importance of good party organisation, even though in practical terms it was never his abiding strength. He was never a hands-on party manager; nor was he a great fundraiser. But Grimond's achievement went wider and deeper than that or than the realignment of party structures. When a third (or fourth) force challenges two main parties that have long enjoyed domination, it is tempting to dismiss any advance as simply the passing phase of 'protest'. But Grimond gave the Liberal Party and liberalism as a creed something far more substantial – a sense of identity and credibility. How did he do it?

Grimond's achievements rest in part upon his personal qualities. He was not only an inspirational leader of the Liberal Party but also a standard bearer for liberalism. He had charm and charisma, allied to a great gift for communication. Yet he was no demigod. Ideas were his stock in trade – expressed fearlessly, sometimes controversially, always with clarity and incisiveness. Throughout his career and especially during his years as leader the party faithful rallied to his call. When he was no longer party leader he continued to prompt others to reflect upon wider issues, even when he took positions that left some observers a mite bemused. Such was the nature of the man that those who did not share his inclinations were nevertheless prepared, in the true spirit of Voltaire, to respect his claim to free expression.

Where, then, does Grimond stand in the liberal 'hall of fame'? He never held any office of state or other governmental position. That was hardly his failing, though it inevitably limited his achievements – at any rate in terms of service to the country. It is difficult to compare him with the likes of Gladstone, Asquith, Lloyd George or even a Herbert Samuel or Nick Clegg, all of whom held high office. What Grimond might have achieved in office must remain a topic for idle speculation. On the other hand, his reputation may have gained from the fact that he was never obliged to soil his hands in the often grubby business of government, so allowing him to maintain a reputation for integrity and vision. He was a figure of real substance who left a lasting legacy, perhaps more so than many who did hold office. At a gathering of the Liberal History Group held around the turn of the millennium, he was voted the best Liberal leader of the twentieth century.

Grimond's brand of liberalism was a complex one, subject to changing inflections. He claimed to read J. S. Mill's *On Liberty* every year and he certainly drew from Mill. He has also been seen as heir to the legacy of T. H. Green, though there is barely a mention of Green in any of Grimond's writings. Certainly Grimond had little time for the paraphernalia of metaphysics. But he consistently proclaimed the need for 'values' and for 'quality' in life as a touchstone for liberalism, not just the utilitarian calculus of 'quantity'. In part it was his belief that politics – especially progressive politics – had begun to neglect this dimension that explains the shift in emphasis from the growth-orientated bearings of the early and mid-1960s. In part, too, he began to see the state as having overreached itself. Thus, he had more to say about its potential threat to the liberty of the citizen than about its role as an enabler. But he never became a Conservative of any stripe. On the contrary, his liberal radicalism remained undiminished as reflected in his sustained internationalism, regard for the rule of law, the upholding of minority rights and the need for greater individual autonomy, yielding an enhanced quality of life more widely shared. These are among the principles for which Grimond stood and by which, along with his personal qualities, he is fondly remembered.

CHAPTER 19

JEREMY THORPE

ROBERT INGHAM

During his nine years as Liberal leader, Thorpe presided over some of the party's brightest post-war moments and some of its most dismal periods. He failed to stop the Liberals' late-'60s slide, and the result of the 1970 election was one of the party's worst ever. Yet he was the outstanding media performer of the political class of 1974, and led the Liberal Party to what looked like the edge of a major breakthrough in that year's February election. However, he was unable to maintain the momentum, and the party slipped back in the October 1974 election. His departure from the leadership amid a swirl of rumour and gossip about his possible involvement in an attempted murder cast a long shadow over his entire career. Disentangling these elements to reach an objective assessment of Thorpe's capabilities as a political leader is challenging.

- John Jeremy Thorpe, born 29 April 1929, died 4 December 2014.
- Third child and eldest son of John Henry Thorpe, Conservative MP for Manchester Rusholme 1919–23, and Ursula Norton-Griffiths, daughter of Sir John Norton-Griffiths, Conservative MP for Wednesbury 1910–18 and Wandsworth Central 1918–24.
- Barrister and television presenter.
- Married: (1) Caroline Allpass in 1968 (she died in 1970), one son; (2) Marion Stein in 1973, a concert pianist formerly married to a cousin of the Queen (she died a few months before Thorpe in 2014).
- Liberal MP for North Devon 1959–79; finished second in 1955 and 1979.
- Liberal leader 1967–76.

Born into upper-middle-class comfort, Thorpe was subject to a number of strong but sometimes unsettling influences in his early years. These included a domineering mother, a father whom he loved but who at times suffered financial and health problems, Eton, and the United States, where he lived during the war. However, his most significant political influence was Megan Lloyd George, Liberal MP for Anglesey, who was a close friend of Thorpe's mother. Thorpe's instinctive Liberalism matured as a result of his contact with Lloyd George and the Liberals in her circle and throughout his career he had a special interest in racial equality and internationalism.

At university Thorpe gained a reputation as a showman and superb mimic who put immense energy into politicking, becoming president of the Oxford Union Society and the university Liberal Club and Law Society. His academic studies were almost entirely neglected and he scraped a third-class degree, at times relying on friends to write his essays and on last-minute cramming for exams. After graduation, he was briefly and unsuccessfully a barrister. Working for television proved a better use of his talents and later helped him make use of what was still a new medium for political communication.

However, Thorpe was single-minded in his determination to reach the House of Commons, lead his party and achieve high office. He was interviewed as a potential Liberal candidate when he turned twenty-one in 1950 and made such a good impression that he was considered as a possible successor to Clement Davies in Montgomeryshire, when the party leader retired. Thorpe did not want to wait and decided to look for a seat in the south-west with a good Liberal tradition and was adopted for North Devon in 1952. He became more widely known within the party at the Liberal assembly the following year by declaring that if a motion on phasing out agricultural subsidies was passed he, and other south-west candidates, would repudiate the party line. Thorpe's pragmatism, combined with a touch of drama, carried the day.

North Devon was one of the bright spots for the Liberals in the 1955 election as he added 4,000 to the Liberal poll. He did the same again in 1959, narrowly winning the seat from the Conservatives. Victory was celebrated with a torch-light procession, an Edwardian tradition which Thorpe revived and which critics nicknamed 'Jeremy's Nurembergs'. Thorpe's success was based on his charismatic campaigning and sheer hard work over a number of years. He was particularly adept at remembering the names and personal details of people he met. Stories abound of Thorpe meeting voters and recalling a previous conversation years earlier and asking them about their families, their jobs or their livestock.

Being elected at such a young age, and, unlike most of his colleagues, without the assistance of a local pact or 'understanding' with another party, Thorpe was immediately feted as a rising star in the Liberal Party. He loved the gothic surroundings and procedures of the House of Commons and was a good speaker. His main contributions were on international affairs, particularly in relation to the Commonwealth. He was a strong supporter of African self-determination and came to know many of the men who led African countries after independence. As early as 1950 he had called for South Africa to be expelled from the Commonwealth because of its policy of apartheid. He was prominent in anti-apartheid protests in the 1960s and organised an international petition against Nelson Mandela's death sentence. He opposed the 1962 Commonwealth Immigrants Act, which restricted immigration from Commonwealth nations for the first time.

One of Thorpe's most well-known political interventions related to Rhodesia, whose white leadership resisted majority rule and issued a unilateral declaration of independence in 1965. Thorpe had long taken an interest in this part of Africa and from the start of the crisis mooted the possibility of the UK using force to bring the Rhodesians into line. At the Liberal assembly in 1966 he spoke of how 'high-flying planes' could be used to ensure that a railway line bringing oil into Rhodesia from Mozambique could be 'nipped'. Thorpe was widely attacked for proposing that the dispute with Rhodesia should be escalated in this way and was thereafter nicknamed 'Bomber Thorpe' by right-wing opponents. Party leader Jo Grimond distanced himself from Thorpe's remarks, damaging Thorpe's credibility.

Thorpe was an advocate of British membership of the common market, on the grounds that it would deepen the political ties between European nations, 'lifting the curse of war from relations between nations'.[373] As party leader he helped ensure that the European Communities Bill, which provided for the UK to join the common market, received a second reading in the Commons despite opposition from Labour and numerous Conservative rebels, amid stormy scenes during which he was assaulted by a Labour MP. He was later an effective campaigner for a yes vote in the 1975 referendum. He was also a vocal supporter of Tony Benn in his campaign to be able to disclaim his peerage and remain a member of the House of Commons. However, it was outside Parliament that Thorpe made his most significant contribution when, in 1961, he helped found Appeal for Amnesty, which sought to support political prisoners and was the forerunner of Amnesty International.

Within the Liberal Party, Thorpe had two linked interests: organisation and finance. He made his own arrangements for targeting resources at promising constituencies, known as the Winnable Seats scheme. Winnable Seats was every inch a Thorpe initiative. It was secretive, kept from the gaze of formal party committees for as long as possible, and the source of the money used by Thorpe was opaque. Comparisons were made with Lloyd George's personal fund. Thorpe was ruthless in insisting that recipient Liberal associations met activity targets and that candidates came up to scratch, a complete departure from previous practice. He demanded that candidates be changed when he thought it necessary. Whether Winnable Seats made a difference to the Liberals' performance in the 1964 and 1966 elections is open to question but targeting resources in this way was later to become central to the campaigning ethos of the Liberal Democrats.

Thorpe was also active in seeking new sources of finance for his habitually cash-strapped party. He was a consummate fundraiser, unafraid to ask brazenly for a large cheque. In 1965, he caused something of a stir within the party by contesting and winning the position of party treasurer, which he used to enhance his reputation for organisational dynamism. However, critics suggested that some

---

373   Jeremy Thorpe, 'European Democracy', in *Europe: the case for going in*, published for the European Movement, London, British Council, 1971, p. 96.

of his financial dealings lacked transparency and that he placed unreasonable demands on party staff. Later, in 1970, he secured what was then the party's largest ever donation, £150,000, from Jack Hayward, a businessman who did not even support the Liberals politically.

When Jo Grimond indicated his wish to step down from the party leadership in 1967 Thorpe was the likeliest candidate to replace him and the one with most support in the party at large. The election, in which only the twelve sitting MPs could vote, was organised swiftly. Thorpe won six votes, to three votes each for Emlyn Hooson and Eric Lubbock. A second ballot, to determine which candidate could win a majority of the votes, was averted when Thorpe's opponents withdrew.

The leadership election was an illustration of Thorpe's difficulties in uniting his parliamentary party, some of whom were never convinced that he was a capable leader or were concerned about aspects of his private life. Grimond was always likely to be a hard act to follow, not least because of the affection he inspired from his followers, but Thorpe often made things worse for himself. While Grimond was an ideas man, who encouraged policy debate, Thorpe seemed uninterested in policy. He had a barrister's knack of being able to crib information quickly for a debate but did not seem to have ideas of his own. He had a poor grasp of economics and was unable to formulate a response to the Labour government's economic difficulties in the late 1960s, for which he was criticised by the party's executive committee.

On assuming the leadership Thorpe announced a major fundraising campaign, to generate £1 million in time for the election due in 1970 or 1971. The campaign was a flop, not least because some of the grandiose fundraising events Thorpe planned lost money. As the party's financial position deteriorated, there were disagreements with party staff, leading to the departure of the respected head of the party organisation, Pratap Chitnis, in 1969. There were also mutterings within the party about how Thorpe appeared to enjoy the trappings of leadership, the garden parties, official functions and royal receptions, more than was seemly for a Liberal.

The Conservatives were the primary beneficiaries of the Labour Party's problems in the late 1960s, the only relief from the gloom for the Liberals being the party's victory in the Birmingham Ladywood by-election in 1969, in which Thorpe played little part. The 1970 election was a disaster, with only six of the thirteen Liberal MPs returned, most with tiny majorities. Thorpe's majority in North Devon was slashed to just 369. Shortly afterwards Thorpe's wife, Caroline, was killed in a car crash. As he mourned, and planned a monument to commemorate her life, the Liberal Party drifted.

During this period, Thorpe struggled to manage the party's youth wing. The Young Liberals spanned a broad range of radical viewpoints, including community campaigners, proponents of direct action, opponents of the state of Israel and extreme left-wingers. They were vibrant and energetic but also had the capacity to embarrass the party leadership. Generally supportive of Thorpe at first, they quickly became disillusioned. Thorpe tended to alternate between patronising the Young Liberal leaders and angering them with crass attempts to influence their elections. However, the Young Liberals played a significant role in the revival of the party's local government base, employing innovative community politics techniques, which also delivered an unlikely by-election gain at Sutton and Cheam in December 1972. This result, and victories at Rochdale, Ripon, Berwick and the Isle of Ely in 1972–73 suddenly transformed the party and Thorpe. The Liberals once again seemed like a fresh, modern alternative to the jaded major parties. Thorpe's energy and his emphasis on national unity in response to economic crisis struck a chord with the electorate and helped the Liberals to their best result since 1929, winning 6 million votes but just fourteen seats in the February 1974 election.

Labour won the most seats, 301 to the Conservatives' 297, resulting in a hung parliament. Tory Prime Minister Edward Heath invited the Liberals to form a coalition, in which Thorpe would become a Cabinet minister. Thorpe demanded electoral reform in return and agreed to take soundings from party colleagues. Although naturally tempted by the offer, there seemed little chance that the Conservatives would make meaningful concessions on electoral reform and a Conservative–Liberal coalition would not command a majority in the Commons. There was also a question of legitimacy given that the Conservatives had lost nearly forty seats and there was little enthusiasm within the Liberal Party for a deal. With a coalition ruled out, Harold Wilson became Prime Minister and called a second election in the autumn in an attempt to win an outright majority.

With his majority in North Devon increased to 11,000, Thorpe threw himself into campaigning around the country in order to achieve the breakthrough for which his party yearned. His most striking gimmicks were hovercraft tours of the south-west and the north-west coasts, which attracted some criticism for their cost and for attracting humorous headlines when they were disrupted by bad weather. Thorpe's message to the electorate was essentially the same as in February – Britain needed a government of national unity to deal with the economic crisis. However, the party's economic prescription, based on a statutory prices and incomes policy, was not distinctive. The Liberals slipped back in terms of votes cast and seats won as Labour won a narrow majority, a bitter disappointment to Thorpe and the party.

Assessments of Jeremy Thorpe's contribution to Liberal politics are inevitably influenced by the events surrounding his resignation as Liberal leader in May 1976 and his subsequent prosecution, and acquittal, for conspiring to murder his former lover, Norman Scott. Rumours of Thorpe's relationship with Scott had been known to some since the mid-1960s but came out of the blue for many senior Liberals and the party's rank and file when the *Sunday Times* published love letters between the pair. Thorpe's trial, which related to a botched attempt to murder Scott in November 1975, brought out more lurid stories about the misappropriation of funds given to Thorpe for political purposes and some of the people with whom Thorpe was connected. Thorpe always maintained that he was innocent but failed to acknowledge that these disclosures and the charges had brought an end to his political career. In seeking to maintain his political profile he served only to damage the party. He defended North Devon in 1979 but lost his seat, days before his trial began. Later in 1979, he was diagnosed as suffering from Parkinson's disease and thereafter slipped from public view.

Thorpe's great strengths as a political leader were his charisma, which enabled him to connect with the public, on television and in person, and his energetic campaigning. Both were necessary to ensure that the Liberal Party was noticed at a time when its fortunes were at a low ebb and it could seem irrelevant to the nation's political debate. In addition he was an instinctive Liberal, naturally on the side of the underdog, who was unafraid of championing unfashionable causes. In supporting decolonisation, UK membership of the common market, abolition of the death penalty and gay rights he risked alienating many of his constituents but was never held back by such considerations.

However, Thorpe was hampered by significant weaknesses. He was a tactician rather than a strategist, at his best dreaming up a new way of raising money but unable to develop and articulate a long-term strategy for his party. This was compounded by his lack of interest in policy, which led to the party offering little that was new to the debate about how to end the UK's economic decline during his period in charge. Thorpe was a poor party manager and, as a result, he failed to take advantage of the opportunities provided by the activism of the Young Liberals and the development of community politics. As Peter Hain put it, the party leadership did not understand community politics and would not have liked it had they done so. Thorpe did not see the connection between the Liberals' burgeoning strength in local government in certain areas of the country and the possibility of winning parliamentary seats in those places. In his view, all that was required to win a seat at Westminster was a media-friendly candidate, money and a 'Liberal tradition' in the local area. When he did campaign in places like Sutton and Cheam, where Liberal strength was based on community campaigning, he provided the 'cream on top of the cake' rather than the key ingredient for success.[374]

The February 1974 election was Thorpe's finest hour. He captured the mood of the nation in arguing that a government of national unity was needed to replace the sterile battle between left and right and helped the Liberals capture a welter of protest votes. However, much of the Liberals' advance was built on sand and could not be sustained into the autumn and beyond. The manner of Thorpe's

374   Susan Barnes, *Behind the Image*, London, Jonathan Cape, 1974, p. 283 – quote provided by Trevor Jones.

departure from the leadership and his subsequent trial damaged the Liberals, adding to the perception in some quarters that the party was a home to all manner of cranks and oddities. All in all, Thorpe can hardly be considered a successful party leader.

CHAPTER 20

DAVID STEEL

DAVID TORRANCE

Leader of the Liberal Party from 1976 to 1988, David Steel was the public face of the party during a particularly eventful phase in its post-war history. He assisted in the birth of the Social Democratic Party and led his party, in alliance with the SDP in 1983 and 1987, to the highest number of votes (though not seats) for a third party in British electoral history. He was also unusually popular for a third-party leader, and utilised that rare (for a politician) commodity, together with a sharp tactical and strategic sense, to nudge a minority party into a position of greater influence. In that respect, Steel, the party's longest-serving leader after H. H. Asquith, provided an important bridge between the Liberals' post-war decline and their rise to become a serious contender for (coalition) government, even though that bridge often appeared in danger of collapsing amid internal discontent and external events beyond Steel's control.

- David Martin Scott Steel (b. 31 March 1938), born in Kirkcaldy to a Church of Scotland minister, David, and his wife Sheila.
- Educated in Edinburgh and Nairobi, Steel then worked as a television presenter and for the Scottish Liberal Party.
- Married Judith (Judy) Mary MacGregor in 1962.
- Three children, of whom one, Catriona Bhatia, also entered politics.
- Elected for Roxburgh, Selkirk and Peebles in 1965 by-election; held the seat (which became Tweeddale, Ettrick and Lauderdale in 1983) until stepping down in 1997.
- Leader of the Liberal Party 1976–88, knighted in 1990 and ennobled as Baron Steel of Aikwood in 1997. Presiding Officer of the Scottish Parliament 1999–2003.

David Martin Scott Steel was born on 31 March 1938 in Kirkcaldy, Scotland, a 'son of the Manse' (the late Jeremy Thorpe considered this the key to Steel's character), his father – also David – being a minister with the Church of Scotland (and later moderator of its general assembly). His childhood was spent moving from place to place, school to school, and even country to country. Indeed, probably the most important part of Steel's early life was a four-years stint in Nairobi.

His father had been posted there by the Kirk and, in the twilight years of British rule, had became embroiled in domestic politics dominated by the Mau Mau uprising. Although Steel junior knew little of this at the time, he imbibed both his father's Presbyterian radicalism and witnessed colonial racism at first hand; the attitudes of his contemporaries towards coloured children left him with a lifelong abhorrence of racial prejudice.

A bright if unremarkable student, Steel completed his schooling at George Watson's College back in Edinburgh, where his political ambitions were honed in the school's Literary Society. At the University of Edinburgh Steel engrossed himself in more formal political activity, joining the Liberal club (later becoming its president) and Students' Representative Council while falling under the spell of the then Liberal leader Jo Grimond.

After running a successful campaign to have Grimond installed as university Rector, Steel's political path was set. Towards the end of his degree he was selected to fight the Edinburgh Pentlands constituency and, upon graduation, began working for the Scottish Liberal Party in Edinburgh. He also married a fellow law graduate, Judy MacGregor, who would become an important part of Steel's political life as well as mother to his three children.

Steel later observed himself that luck was the single, and perhaps most important, element of his early political career. There was a degree of luck in a vacancy arising for the relatively winnable constituency of Roxburgh, Selkirk and Peebles (it had been Liberal briefly between 1950–51), which he fought at the 1964 general election, and further luck in it falling vacant just months later when the incumbent Conservative MP died.

Following an energetic by-election campaign, Steel was elected Parliament's youngest MP with a significant majority. As 'baby of the House' another piece of luck helped establish him as a backbencher of note and potential future leader of his party, when he secured a place in the ballot for private members' bills. After some reflection, Steel settled upon reform of Britain's abortion laws.

The subsequent legislative battle honed many of Steel's political skills: a capacity for hard work (if not particular attention to detail), tactics (the bill faced bitter opposition in Parliament), flair for forging cross-party alliances (the avuncular support of Labour Home Secretary Roy Jenkins was crucial) and media manipulation (a brief television career meant he was relaxed on camera and pithy in print). Against expectations, the bill passed and Steel's liberal credentials were established.

Importantly, Steel espoused Liberal radicalism while dressing, and indeed looking, like a Young Conservative; he certainly did not appear like a stereotypical beard-and-sandal-wearing Young Liberal. Thus, on the basis of the Abortion Act he became established in the public mind as a conservative radical, more likely to pursue his ideals via Parliament than at the barricades. Although not an original thinker, Steel made otherwise fringe political issues appear important and mainstream.

Ideologically, he was liberal both socially and economically, but more than anything else racial prejudice was guaranteed to fire him up, producing his best arguments and oratory. Indeed, when it came to African issues Steel consistently stuck his neck out: campaigning against a Springboks tour in his rugby-mad constituency, and getting himself banned from visiting the Rhodesia of Ian Smith.

Steel consolidated his parliamentary success with the Abortion Act with similarly high-profile work on both national issues (Commonwealth affairs and immigration) and those closer to home (Scottish home rule and borders affairs). There were also disappointments. Steel sometimes found Jeremy Thorpe, Jo Grimond's successor as leader, frustrating, while the 1970 general election – in which he narrowly held on as one of a depleted band of six Liberal MPs – looked like a serious check on Liberal advances made since the 1962 Orpington by-election.

It was at this point Steel, who soon became Liberal Chief Whip, started to map out his preferred vision for the party. For the next six years, culminating in his election as leader, he continually lectured, cajoled and occasionally bounced the party into taking coalition politics more seriously. In short, Steel believed the Liberal Party had to adapt to the reality of its political status or die. As Chief Whip, he was, according to *The Times*'s Geoffrey Smith, 'no more than a partial success',[375] neither consulting widely enough nor particularly good at maintaining relations with the wider party. Steel had little time for party committees, although with only five MPs to shepherd, it was not in any case a particularly demanding job, nor one whose status meant much to the general public. A high-profile role in the 1975 referendum on the UK's membership of the European common market reinforced this conviction, as well as cementing important relationships with figures like Roy Jenkins. When Jeremy Thorpe finally resigned following months of destabilising speculation about his private life, Steel competed with John Pardoe for the Liberal leadership. Although there was little between the two candidates in terms of policy, important differences in temperament emerged during the campaign. Steel appeared the cooler, safer pair of hands and secured a handsome victory – the first mainstream party leader with a mandate from the party members (rather than just parliamentary colleagues).

At this point the Liberal Party remained strong on principle but weak when it came to putting that principle into practice. At the February 1974 general election the party had secured 19.3 per cent of the vote and even had discussions about a formal coalition with Edward Heath's beleaguered Conservatives, but Jeremy Thorpe's leadership was not strategically equipped to keep hold of those new voters and capitalise on a historic post-war high. Having spent the last few years trying to force his party to face up to this weakness, Steel's decade plus as leader would be characterised by attempts to make the Liberals more relevant and influential.

Steel's prescient maiden leader's speech, in which he spoke of the 'rocky road' ahead, set out his aim of political realignment in terms that made many Liberals uncomfortable. There was more discomfort when, just a few months later, their

---

375   David Torrance, *David Steel: Rising Hope to Elder Statesman*, London, Biteback Publishing, 2012, p. 63.

still youthful leader negotiated the 'Lib–Lab pact' with the much older James Callaghan's minority Labour Party. Steel's calculation was that by appearing to have influence, however slight, in the corridors of power, Liberal prestige – and therefore the party's electoral prospects – would rise accordingly. To that end, Steel was much more interested in the mechanics of his very personal 'agreement' with Prime Minister Callaghan than any specific policy it might deliver.

The pact was the defining period of Steel's first two years as party leader. History, however, has not been kind to what he has called 'a parliamentary but not government coalition – a unique experiment'. Writing in 1996, Don MacIver said it was 'seen by some as a missed opportunity, by others as simply a misjudgement, but by few as a triumph'.[376] Similarly, the Liberal Party's most perceptive historian, David Dutton, concluded that its 'achievements were limited and its impact upon the Liberal Party of questionable value'.[377]

Contemporary assessments were more charitable, *The Times* calling it 'a brave attempt to establish the conditions in which minority government can be made to work'.[378] Matt Cole identified three phases in the development of the pact: the first was one of relative harmony within and between the partners; the second one of crisis which broke the trust underpinning the pact; and the latter period was one in which the spirit of the pact had gone, though it lived on in practice. In all three phases Liberals secured achievements, but they were of diminishing significance and came at increasing cost.

For Steel, the pact brought almost exactly what he wanted: a taste of power for the Liberal Party and the invaluable experience of being locked into the mechanism of government, something denied to Liberals since the end of the last war. In *A House Divided*, Steel's excessively detailed account of the pact, he listed four achievements: fulfilling the 'main short-term objective of controlling inflation', providing 'much-needed parliamentary stability', demonstrating 'that bi-party government' could keep the 'extreme dogmas of the larger party

---

376   Don MacIver ed., *The Liberal Democrats*, London, Prentice Hall/Harvester Wheatsheaf, 1996, p. 180.

377   Dutton, op. cit., p. 230.

378   Alistair Michie and Simon Hoggart, *The Pact: The inside story of the Lib–Lab government, 1977–78*, London, Quartet Books, 1978, p. 178.

... under control' and, finally, presenting 'the country with the first taste of a distinctive Liberal policy'.[379]

All four were accurate, but only up to a point – for example, John Pardoe managed to get profit-sharing schemes included in the 1978 Budget (although the coveted prize of proportional representation for direct elections to the European Parliament, was not secured). To be fair to Steel, he had been consistent in what he expected to get out of the pact, constantly imploring his colleagues not to harbour unrealistic expectations. Its relative success also hinged upon Steel's capacity for forging political relationships, in this case with the Prime Minister. Therefore the agreement was a product of the two men; as Steel later said, 'it's fair to describe it as a Steel–Callaghan pact'.[380] The Liberal leader had simply operated within his means, realising his party's relative weakness in the Commons could not compel hundreds of Labour MPs to vote contrary to their own beliefs.

The journalist John Cole reckoned Steel's performance during the Lib–Lab pact 'had been a virtuoso one',[381] with the young Liberal leader more than holding his own in the company of older, more experienced political figures. Even David Owen later praised Steel for 'courageously exert[ing] some influence on a Labour government'.[382] Even so, Steel would consistently overstate some of what the pact had apparently achieved, chiefly that during the eighteen months of the agreement, the UK's monthly rate of inflation had fallen from 20 to less than 9 per cent, accompanied by only a modest 0.5 per cent increase in unemployment. This was true, but the extent to which Liberal support helped achieve this is a moot point. As Michie and Hoggart concluded in 1978, 'the Liberals cannot fairly claim that their support *in itself* helped to rescue the economy'.[383]

---

379   David Steel, *A House Divided: The Lib–Lab Pact and the Future of British Politics*, London, Weidenfeld & Nicolson, 1980, pp. 152–53.

380   Mark Oaten, *Coalition: The politics and personalities of coalition government from 1850*, Petersfield, Harriman House, 2007, p. 193.

381   John Cole, *As It Seemed To Me*, London, Phoenix, 1996, p. 39.

382   David Owen, *A United Kingdom*, Harmondsworth, Penguin, 1986, p. 38.

383   Michie and Hoggart, op. cit., p. 179.

The pact did, however, mean the Labour government could continue without constant threat of collapse, thus enabling ministers to get inflation under control. But this also brought problems, as Steel himself concluded; the pact's 'most obvious defect' was that the 'failure and unpopularity of the Labour government' rubbed off on the Liberals. 'We were lambasted for simply keeping in office a government which had outstayed its welcome.'[384] Steel also missed an opportunity to refashion Liberal philosophy as traditional ideological boundaries broke down, his attempts being more rhetorical ('I want our party to become the militants for the reasonable man')[385] than real. He lacked, in the words of Alistair Michie and Simon Hoggart, a 'revolutionary vision of a new Liberal society'; rather, Steel's ideal Britain was simply to be a more 'agreeable version of the present one'.[386]

Michie and Hoggart concluded their history of the Lib–Lab pact with the following qualified – but broadly accurate – assessment:

> In 1976, just before Steel took over, the Liberal Party was going nowhere at all. It lacked ambition, it lacked a lot of drive, and it lacked a leader who had any concept of what might be done with the votes and the support that the party had accumulated through the early '70s. What Steel offered was a direction, a purpose and an ambition. Within months of becoming leader he had placed the party absolutely at the centre of British political life, and had made it too important to be ignored by anybody.[387]

'Many Liberals at the time believed that the pact would either bring the party to the pinnacle of power, or else destroy it altogether,' wrote Jeremy Josephs several years later. 'But the truth was far less dramatic. It did neither.'[388] It certainly helped the Liberals move away from the fringes of British politics, proving the

---

384   Steel, op. cit., p. 153.

385   Torrance, op. cit., p. 123.

386   Michie and Hoggart, op. cit., p. 66.

387   Ibid., p. 183.

388   Jeremy Josephs, *Inside the Alliance*, London, John Martin Publishing, 1983, p. 6.

party could exercise influence – however modestly – upon one of the main parties. Callaghan's government, however, was on its last legs and, already months from a general election, it fell on a vote of no confidence in March 1979, that failure of the earlier devolution referendum in Scotland having lost it crucial support.

Widely anticipated wipe-out for the Liberals at the 1979 general election (the party had shed votes and council seats during the eighteen-month pact) did not transpire, with Steel snatching victory from the jaws of defeat with a spirited campaign that returned all but a few of the party's incumbent MPs. And when the Labour Party began to tack to the left as the Thatcher era began, Steel moved deftly (if heavy-handedly at times) to orchestrate the second phase of his 'realignment' strategy.

Rather than recruiting Roy Jenkins, then out of Parliament but nevertheless de facto leader of the Labour right, to the Liberal Party, Steel encouraged him to launch what became the SDP in 1981. For a while, everything appeared to go to plan: an 'alliance' was forged between the two parties and, fuelled by political novelty and growing discontent with a Conservative/Labour duopoly, it polled so well that Steel famously exhorted delegates to 'go back to your constituencies and prepare for government' at the 1981 Liberal assembly.[389]

Although in the context of coalition government that was not a wild prediction, it appeared less credible in the aftermath of the Falklands conflict and a once-again-popular Conservative Party led by Margaret Thatcher (relations between the Iron Lady and Steel had been cool since the Lib–Lab pact). The resulting general election was to be make or break for the Alliance, and although Steel proved more attractive to voters than the curiously dated Jenkins, a troubled campaign culminated in the traumatic Ettrick Bridge Summit (thus named after the Steels' Borders home). Steel allowed himself to be coaxed into an ill-fated coup attempt, which temporarily strained relations between him and the SDP leader.

During this period the areas in which Steel was weak, policy development and party management, became even more pronounced, particularly in the wake of the 1983 general election when the high hopes of the Alliance were dashed by a

---

389   Torrance, op. cit., p. 149.

combination of bad luck (the Falklands), hubris (unrealistic expectations) and a deeply unfair electoral system (first-past-the-post). Steel even tried to resign, arguing in a parting shot (later withdrawn) that 'having spent seven years largely on Liberal strategy', he wanted to 'devote more time to writing and speaking on Liberal philosophy and policy'.[390]

In fact, he ended up spending yet more time on Liberal (and Alliance) strategy (after, that is, a short sabbatical), making the best of a bad situation via a dual leadership – inevitably dubbed 'the two Davids' – with David Owen for the duration of the 1983–87 parliament. Although relations between the two were never as bad as the media claimed, nor were they as close as the more temperamentally similar Steel and Jenkins. More to the point, there was strategic tension throughout: while Steel was impatient for a full merger (which he attempted by stealth), Owen was determined to maintain the SDP as a distinct party in (largely) his own image.

For a while by-election successes (and substantial local election gains) enabled the two Davids to keep the show on the road, a tribute to Owen's intellectual energy and Steel's media prowess, although, beneath this impressive façade, the Alliance was barely progressing at all. Steel's obvious integrity and considerable stamina, not to forget his stirring platform oratory, equipped him with wide popular appeal. Even after his political peak in 1983, polling revealed consistently high approval ratings.

And whatever the faults of the Liberal Party, poor discipline and a tendency to dance on the head of a pin, they were mirrored by faults in the SDP, unquestioning loyalty to Owen's leadership coupled with unimaginative policymaking. If the Liberals often resembled little more than a 'debating society' (as Steel had once put it), Social Democrats, in the words of Simon Hoggart, were 'London intellectuals surveying a declining Britain from the comfort of Holland Park'.[391] The political scientist Ralf Dahrendorf memorably described them as a 'party in search of a better yesterday'.

390 Ibid., p. 177.
391 Ibid., p. 308.

The terminal phase came after the 1986 Eastbourne (Liberal) assembly, during which Steel took his eye off the ball; expecting his party to support a joint defence policy with the SDP (which included provision for nuclear weapons), instead the assembly backed the general idea but with the crucial caveat that it had to be non-nuclear. Having been humiliatingly rebuffed, Steel turned bitterly on his party, betraying an impatience with internal democracy and ideological purity that had long characterised his relations with the party. By that point he had been leader for more than ten years – longer than Thorpe and Grimond – and it showed. If Eastbourne was the inevitable consequence of Steel's weak party management, then the joint policy declaration of 1988 (which was probably issued to the press without Steel even reading it) was the inevitable consequence of his lack of policy engagement. With some exceptions, such as 'industrial partnership' and African affairs, Steel's interest was not in the policies themselves but the overall mood he was trying to generate. He always had more sympathy than feel for big domestic issues, particularly on economics, where he cheerfully confessed to not really understanding the technicalities.

Yet what Steel lacked in grasp of detail he made up for in terms of leadership. He could be ruthless – ruthless in his fight against John Pardoe in 1976, ruthless in despatching David Owen in 1987 and, above all, ruthless in dealings with his own party. Such steeliness was necessary for any leader, particular that of a small third party, but some felt Steel could have done more to address his weaknesses. Jo Grimond thought he could have appointed someone to 'explore and co-ordinate the many new ideas sprouting all over the place and weld them into a structure which people would instantly recognise as the core of Liberalism',[392] while Des Wilson believed he could easily have maintained a closer relationship with his party. Steel was a good and effective Liberal leader, but had he engaged a little more with party and policy, he might have been a formidable one.

That said, Steel did turn out to be a very good *former* leader. As, at first, foreign affairs spokesman and, later, deputy Liberal Democrat leader in the House of Lords (he swapped the Commons for the Upper House in 1997), Steel did his

392 *The Scotsman*, 13 May 1988.

best not to make life difficult for Paddy Ashdown, although there was occasional tension behind the scenes. Also, as the first Presiding Officer of the Scottish Parliament, between 1999–2003, Lord Steel guided a fledgling institution through numerous growing pains, not least its choice of an expensive new home at Holyrood. After standing down as a Member of the Scottish Parliament in 2003 Steel devoted more attention to the House of Lords, doggedly campaigning for piecemeal reform rather than a radical overhaul.

It typified the Steel approach: gradual, ecumenical and establishment-friendly rather than a more ambitious, ideologically purist, big-bang pitch. Throughout his long and eventful political career, this had yielded modest results, usually in conjunction with others (sustained pressure over Scottish devolution and apartheid were good examples). Having been what Michael Foot called a 'rising hope' between the 1960s and 1980s; Steel was, by the early twenty-first century, content to be an elder Liberal statesman.

Although he never held ministerial office, Steel's career was one of political impact out of all proportion to his status as the leader of a small (later larger) third party. As a young backbencher in the 1960s he affected a lasting and important reform to Britain's abortion laws; during the Lib–Lab pact of 1977–78 he wielded influence if not power; while in the 1980s he was a central figure in a political realignment that came close to breaking the mould of UK politics. And, later in life, Steel played a prominent role in a new, devolved Scottish Parliament. Not a bad balance sheet for someone outside the political mainstream.

Steel's political career can also be seen as a proxy for significant changes in post-war British politics: the relative decline of two-party dominance, the growing influence of modern campaigning and media techniques and, less positively, the steady drift from ideology towards less dogmatic, and arguably more opportunistic, politics. All were features in Steel's life and times. Indeed, his has also been a remarkably consistent biography, with little change in his character and central political beliefs between his undergraduate career and his semi-retirement in the House of Lords.

But while undoubtedly talented, Steel ended up playing some aspects of the game better than others. With Steel having never actually implemented any policy, his carelessness with detail – although not evident at first – became well known. Aware that his agile mind would usually extract him from the tightest intellectual spot, he made little attempt to remedy the weakness. His closer acquaintance with the Scottish Liberal Party, meanwhile, left him largely ignorant of the English party, which he never really made any effort to win over. Steel instinctively preferred the intimacy and camaraderie of the Scottish Liberal scene.

Steel was at his best during his early years as an MP, as Des Wilson put it, 'a genuinely liberal and humane campaigner, combining courage with charm and intelligence'.[393] Radical in his views on race relations and abortion, he nevertheless sought to affect change by orthodox political means. Politics to Steel was the art of the possible, ideological purity held no interest for him; realism combined with dogged persistence did.

He often found his own party frustrating. During the 1970s Steel was rarely in sympathy with the growing 'community politics' section of the Liberal Party. While they worked hard to build Liberal support from the bottom up, Steel appeared to favour a top-down approach which stressed strategy over policy and, as those at the bottom saw it, a distressing tendency to see potential allies in other parties. To them Steel could be a little *too* realistic, casually admitting that Liberals did not have to fight *every* constituency for the Liberals were never likely, in their own right, to actually *form* a government.

Steel correctly stated that the Liberals could not survive with such a small base of consistent supporters, but nor was he particularly interested in identifying a solution by mending cracked pavements and establishing local government bases, even when such techniques produced tangible results in 1972–73, and again in 1979. Instead, he continued to rely upon protest votes, which remained the case even under the Alliance from 1981–87. Nevertheless, it could be argued that Steel helped salvage the Liberal Party from the debilitating Jeremy Thorpe scandal that dominated the first half of 1976.

Steel, to be fair, was acutely aware of his political weaknesses and strengths.

393   Torrance, op. cit., p. 304.

'I do not think I will ever be awarded full marks for either party management or pioneering policies,' he reflected in his memoirs. 'Where I believe I made a contribution was in articulating our values and attitudes in a way which brought a huge public response.'[394] This was a fair assessment, and indeed Steel later recognised a little of himself in Charles Kennedy, the Liberal Democrat leader from 1999–2006. 'There is an apparent diversity between the broad appeal to the electorate,' Steel told Kennedy's biographer Greg Hurst, 'mainly on television and at public meetings, and the detailed management of the team in Parliament … Ideally you want someone who combines both.'[395]

Steel's relationship with his party was indeed remote and often pained. As Geoffrey Smith wrote, in exercising his leadership Steel had not always paid 'sufficient regard to the sensitivities of his party'. In this regard he anticipated the Blairite style of leadership, promoting an ideology-lite agenda while bouncing his troops into strategic positions many did not much like, then trying to make it all better with a barnstorming speech. And like Blair, Steel was not unusual in not liking the party he led. Its obsessions irritated him, and worse, its internal structures sent him to sleep. 'He wanted order, his kind of order,' judged *The Economist*. 'They preferred, or behaved as though they preferred, an aimless anarchy – politics as street theatre.'[396]

Des Wilson's critique, that Steel's radical instincts were dulled by his absorption 'with the machinations of politics rather than its purpose' also contained an element of truth. It was easier, in some ways, to be radical while unencumbered by leadership or government office, while as political trends waxed and waned Steel showed little sign of revising the view of the world he had first imbibed as a young man in Africa and Edinburgh. While Owen (to be fair) and the 'dead parrot' acknowledged the impact of Thatcherism, Steel stuck to his script about PR, devolution and workers' councils. Although sincere and consistent, by the late 1980s it had become a rather limited political vision. As Hugo Young judged

---

394   David Steel, *Against Goliath: David Steel's Story*, London, Weidenfeld & Nicolson, 1989.

395   Greg Hurst, *Charles Kennedy: A Tragic Flaw*, London, Politico's, 2006, p. 246.

396   Torrance, op. cit., p. 309.

in 1988, Steel had 'failed to produce any compelling vision of a Liberal or any other kind of non-Thatcherite Britain'.[397]

Nevertheless, as Liberal leader Steel possessed a number of thoroughly admirable qualities, not least an anti-authoritarian instinct – he consistently stood up for underdogs at home or abroad – while displaying remarkable steadiness under fire. Much of this could be traced to his background as a 'son of the manse', a spiritual provenance that also gave Steel a natural reserve seemingly at odds with his public persona. As James Naughtie put it, 'his appearance is that of the outsider, but his instincts drive him to try to be the insider'.[398]

His contribution remained significant: having completed an odyssey comprising the Lib–Lab pact, the Alliance and finally the 1988 merger, Steel forced his party to shape up and confront the prospect of holding power in a way none of his immediate predecessors had. And while the new party (with its developing name) had a difficult birth, the result was a tighter organisation with a more coherent political philosophy. By 1997, the Liberal Democrats were making gains that would have been unthinkable in the 1970s and 1980s.

While the 2010 Conservative–Liberal Democrat coalition might have cast a shadow over Steel's 'realignment' strategy, at the same time the 'mould' of two-party politics had finally been broken and all the hopes and aspirations of 1983 and 1987 fulfilled – at least in theory. As Hugo Young concluded, Steel was 'a manoeuverer not a dreamer, a brilliant maximiser of small positions rather than a field marshal who might transform the course of war'.

And, furthermore, he was always realistic. As John Pardoe put it, 'David Steel achieved a significant amount of what he was *trying* to achieve',[399] and that was not a bad political legacy. In 1981, Steel had implored his party to 'prepare for government' and while he did not personally strike the penalty, he got his party into the arena – where they have remained ever since.

---

397   Ibid., pp 310–11.

398   Ibid., p 311.

399   Ibid., p. 314.

CHAPTER 21

ROY JENKINS

JOHN CAMPBELL

Roy Jenkins was leader of the Social Democratic Party for less than a year, from July 1982 to June 1983. But he was, with Shirley Williams, David Owen and Bill Rodgers, one of the four founding co-leaders of the party in 1981-82, and much the most senior and experienced of the four: the one without whose vision and political weight the party would never have come into being. Jenkins always, however, envisaged the SDP as a catalyst rather than an end in itself, created to work in close alliance with the Liberals in the short term, leading naturally to an eventual merger in the longer term, meaning he was also the midwife, or godfather, of the Liberal Democrats.

- Roy Harris Jenkins (11 November 1920 – 5 January 2003), born in Abersychan, Monmouthshire, son of Arthur Jenkins (Labour MP for Pontypool, 1935-46) and Hattie Jenkins.
- Educated at Abersychan County School, University College, Cardiff, and Balliol College, Oxford.
- Served in Royal Artillery and at Bletchley, 1941-45.
- Married Jennifer Morris (b. 1921) in 1945, three children.
- MP (Labour) for Southwark Central 1948-50 and for Birmingham, Stechford 1950-76.
- Minister of Aviation 1964-65, Home Secretary 1965-67, 1974-76, Chancellor of the Exchequer 1967-70, deputy leader of the Labour Party 1970-72, president of the European Commission 1977-81, co-founder of the Social Democratic Party 1981.
- MP (SDP) for Glasgow Hillhead 1982-87, leader of the SDP 1982-83, ennobled as Baron Jenkins of Hillhead 1987, chancellor of Oxford University 1987-2003, leader of the Liberal Democrats in the House of Lords 1989-98.

- Author of twenty-three books, including *Mr Balfour's Poodle* (1954), *Asquith* (1964), *Gladstone* (1995) and *Churchill* (2001), as well as his memoirs, *A Life at the Centre* (1991).

J enkins was born, ironically, into the heart of the Labour Party; but he was always instinctively a liberal and for most of his career saw no contradiction between the two traditions. His father, Arthur Jenkins, had started life as a coal miner; but after winning a miners' scholarship to Ruskin College, Oxford, he rose rapidly through the South Wales Miners' Federation to become a town councillor, county councillor and eventually – by the time Roy was fifteen – MP for Pontypool. He served as parliamentary private secretary to Clement Attlee throughout the war, so that Roy grew up knowing all the leading figures of the 1945 Labour government as family friends. As an Oxford undergraduate in 1940 he led – with his friend and future Cabinet colleague Tony Crosland – a Social Democratic breakaway from the Communist-dominated Labour Club: an uncanny precursor of the SDP breakaway forty years later. After war service, first in the Royal Artillery and latterly as a code breaker at Bletchley, he failed to win the safe Tory seat of Solihull in the Labour landslide of 1945, but won Southwark Central at a by-election in 1948, becoming the youngest member of the House at the age of twenty-seven, before transferring in 1950 to the suburban Birmingham seat of Stechford, which he represented until 1976.

As a young MP Jenkins flirted briefly with left-wing ideas of wholesale nationalisation and punitive taxation; but as a strong supporter and close friend of Hugh Gaitskell, he quickly mellowed to a revisionist position that retained little trace of old-style socialism. He had no time for the doctrinaire opposition-mindedness of the Bevanite left, but argued in a personal manifesto *Pursuit of Progress* (1953) that Labour should mature into a moderate, inclusive party of social and constitutional reform that would aim to represent the whole left-leaning half of the country, alternating in office with the Conservatives as the natural successor of the nineteenth-century Liberal Party of Gladstone and Asquith. After writing a short loyal campaign biography of Attlee in 1948 he developed a highly successful second career as a historian specialising in the late-Victorian/Edwardian period: significantly his first book in this vein, *Mr Balfour's Poodle* (1954), an account of the 1911 House of Lords crisis, contained an appendix illustrating the close overlap between the seats won by the Liberals in 1906 with those won by Labour in 1945. He followed this with biographies of the Victorian radical Sir Charles Dilke (1958) and his political hero, the Liberal Prime Minister H. H. Asquith (1964), on whom he seemed almost consciously to model himself. His publisher Mark Bonham Carter (Asquith's grandson) and the Liberal leader Jo Grimond were among his closest friends. Jenkins did not at this stage take the Liberals seriously as an independent political force, but he always felt a sentimental attraction to them and both before and after the 1964 election he was keen to promote possible cooperation with them in the event of a close result.

As a self-confessed 'semi-detached' backbencher in the late 1950s he was a leading campaigner for liberal reforms – the abolition of the death penalty, the decriminalisation of homosexuality and abortion, easier divorce, longer licensing hours, the abolition of theatrical censorship – all designed to reduce the intrusive power of the state and increase personal freedom. In 1958, following a long campaign by the Society of Authors, he successfully carried a private members' bill to relax the law on obscene publications, which made possible the publication of *Lady Chatterley's Lover*, *Lolita* and other previously unpublishable titles. The next year, when invited to write a Penguin Special putting the Labour case for the 1959 election, he included a whole final chapter ('Is Britain civilised?') setting out the liberalising agenda which he hoped a Labour government would implement – even though it was far from being official Labour policy and was anathema to many Labour voters.

When Hugh Gaitskell died suddenly in 1963 Jenkins thought he was unlikely to win advancement from Harold Wilson, and very nearly left politics to become editor of *The Economist*. But Wilson persuaded him to stay and when Labour returned to office the next year rewarded him with a succession of senior jobs. As Minister of Aviation (outside the Cabinet) he quickly proved himself an exceptionally clear-sighted and decisive minister, leading to rapid promotion in 1965 to be the youngest Home Secretary since Churchill in 1910. His first period at the Home Office was a classic instance of the right man in the right job at the right time: in less than two years Jenkins was able to deliver not only the legalisation of homosexuality (between consenting adults) and abortion (with appropriate safeguards) – both achieved not directly by government legislation but by means of private members' bills to which he skilfully persuaded a doubtful Cabinet to give government time – and the abolition of theatre censorship by the Lord Chamberlain, but also the first effective legislation to outlaw racial discrimination. The death penalty had already been abolished under his predecessor in 1965; divorce reform was the responsibility of the Lord Chancellor; and Jenkins did not have time to act on licensing, drugs or Sunday trading. Nevertheless, Mary Whitehouse and the Tory press dubbed him the godfather of the permissive society – which he preferred to call the 'civilised society' – and ever afterwards tried to lay all the ills of modern society – crime, drugs, immigration, pornography and family breakdown – at his door.

In 1967, following the devaluation of sterling which represented the humiliating failure of the government's central economic policy dictated by Wilson and his first Chancellor, James Callaghan, Wilson moved Jenkins to the Treasury where he was again extraordinarily successful. After two more years of nerve-racking sterling crises Jenkins managed by means of swingeing spending cuts and higher taxation – targeted particularly on the wealthy while protecting benefits – to shift resources from consumption into exports, avert a second devaluation and restore the balance of payments to credit by the end of 1969. His success encouraged Wilson to call an early general election in June 1970, by which time Jenkins was widely seen as Wilson's heir and natural successor.

When Labour unexpectedly lost the election he was easily elected deputy leader in place of George Brown; but within eighteen months he had destroyed any possibility of inheriting the leadership by his refusal to reverse his long-standing support for Britain joining the European common market. A decade earlier he had supported Macmillan's application when most of the Labour Party, from Gaitskell downwards, had still been opposed. In office, Wilson had made a second unsuccessful application – vetoed again by General de Gaulle – but was committed to making another try. Had Labour been returned in 1970 Jenkins would have been Foreign Secretary leading the negotiations. Out of office, however, most of the Labour Party opportunistically swung around to oppose the Heath government's application; in the face of huge pressure to toe the new line Jenkins led a substantial rebellion of sixty-nine Labour pro-Europeans against a three-line whip which was decisive in securing a comfortable Commons majority in favour, as a result of which Britain finally joined the European Economic Community on 1 January 1973. Despite this he was re-elected to the deputy leadership; but a few months later he resigned in protest at the shadow Cabinet's decision to support a referendum to keep open the question of British membership. He retired to the back benches where he attempted – somewhat half-heartedly – to restore his leadership credentials by making a series of policy speeches published as a slim paperback entitled *What Matters Now*. By now, however, Labour under the influence of Tony Benn and the left wing-dominated trade unions had swung sharply left and adopted an aggressively class-based socialist programme – not only anti-European but committed to unilateral nuclear disarmament and wholesale nationalisation of the economy – viscerally opposed to everything Jenkins stood for.

When Labour narrowly won the February 1974 election he reluctantly went back to the Home Office. But he was out of sympathy with the leftward trend of the Labour Party and increasingly disillusioned with the tribal nature of two-party politics perpetuated by the first-past-the-post electoral system which no longer reflected the views of the voting public. The experience of leading, with Ted Heath, Jeremy Thorpe and others, the successful 'Yes' campaign to keep Britain in Europe in the 1975 referendum opened his eyes to the possibility of cross-party cooperation and the case for proportional representation; but he found no support from his Cabinet colleagues who accused him of secretly hankering for coalition. His second term as Home Secretary nevertheless enabled him to build on the achievements of his first by strengthening his earlier race relations legislation – outlawing discrimination in private clubs as well as housing and employment – and introducing the first Sex Discrimination Bill setting up the Equal Opportunities Commission: taken together these still form the legislative foundation of the diverse multicultural society we have today. He made no headway, however, in arguing for the relaxation of the Official Secrets Act nor for the incorporation of the Universal Declaration on Human Rights into British law. Jenkins's liberalism no longer had any place in the Labour Party of the 1970s. Following the IRA bombing of Guildford and Birmingham, however, he was compelled by public outrage to introduce the 1976 Prevention of Terrorism Act. Designed as a temporary measure, it was renewed annually until replaced by the Blair government's still more repressive measures after 2001. This was an ironic legacy for an avowed liberal.

When Wilson resigned in 1976 Jenkins felt bound to stand for the Labour leadership; but he was never going to win and gained just fifty-six votes. He hoped that Jim Callaghan might offer him the Foreign Office, the one great office he had never held; but he was too ardently pro-European for a party that, despite the referendum result, was still deeply suspicious of positive engagement with Europe. So rather than struggle on in an uncongenial Labour Cabinet he accepted the offer, originating from President Giscard d'Estaing and Chancellor Schmidt, to become the first British president of the European Commission, based in Brussels. This involved giving up his seat in Parliament. Most commentators assumed that he was leaving British politics for good; but he was careful to leave open the possibility that he might return if the political situation evolved in such a way as to create an opportunity – as it did.

Jenkins's four years in Brussels were generally a frustrating time: his one important achievement was to put the issue of monetary union back on the agenda, leading to the creation of the European Monetary System and paving the way for the eventual adoption (by most members, but not Britain) of the euro. But the opportunity to look at British politics from outside led him to see more clearly the opening for a new party to break the stale and distorting two-party duopoly of Labour and Conservative: between the Tories, returned to office under Margaret Thatcher in May 1979 on a doctrinaire free-market platform, and a Labour Party more than ever dominated by the sectarian and anti-democratic left, there was a gaping vacancy in the centre which the Liberals by themselves were too lightweight to fill. Invited by the BBC to deliver the annual televised Dimbleby Lecture in November 1979, Jenkins seized the opportunity to call for a revival of what he called the 'radical centre'. It immediately attracted a huge response from disillusioned moderates who felt themselves unrepresented by either of the two main parties. During 1980 – his last year in Brussels – Jenkins had to decide how best to channel this public hunger which he had correctly discerned. He quickly concluded, with the agreement of the Liberal leader, David Steel, that he should not simply join the Liberals, but try to encourage a substantial defection of moderate Labour MPs to establish a new party distinct from but complementary to the Liberals. After much agonising, three former Cabinet ministers – David Owen (Foreign Secretary for the last three years of the Callaghan government), Shirley Williams and Bill Rodgers (both of whom had lost their seats in 1979) – plus another dozen Labour MPs who despaired of Labour under the newly elected leadership of Michael Foot took the plunge and joined with Jenkins to form the SDP, launched with an immense media fanfare in March 1981.

For a time the new party, with its four co-leaders, looked as if it really might 'break the mould' of British politics. With unemployment touching three million, riots in a dozen cities that summer and Mrs Thatcher the most unpopular Prime Minister in living memory, the hastily cobbled-together Liberal–SDP Alliance scored a series of sensational by-election victories and by the end of the year was registering 50 per cent in the polls. Jenkins himself surprised observers who had thought him an ageing fat cat with his career behind him (though he was still only sixty) by very nearly capturing the formerly safe Labour seat of Warrington in July and then boldly fighting and narrowly winning the formerly Tory-held seat of Glasgow Hillhead in March 1982. This turned out, however, to be the high-water mark of Alliance success. Just a week after Hillhead, Argentina invaded the Falkland Islands. Mrs Thatcher's risky but successful expedition to recapture them released a wave of patriotic emotion which transformed the political landscape, making her triumphant re-election all but certain and leaving the Alliance scrapping with Labour for a distant second place. Jenkins's return to the Commons enabled him to see off the challenge of David Owen to secure the sole leadership of the SDP in July. In an outwardly polite but tense campaign Owen contrasted his youth, energy and self-proclaimed 'radicalism' with Jenkins's age and alleged conservatism. He made a strong showing and even looked as if he might win; but a sufficient majority of party members – 26,000 to 21,000 – judged that Jenkins's central role in the formation of the SDP and good relations with the Liberals still gave him the better claim. Crucially, however, the prospect of his becoming Prime Minister, which had seemed a realistic possibility just a few months earlier, had evaporated. Almost from the moment he won, Jenkins did suddenly seem old, tired and ponderous, while the Alliance, no longer sustained by the heady scent of power, began to come apart at the seams.

Jenkins's eleven months as leader of the SDP were a huge disappointment. The main reason was the transformation of the political scene following the Falklands War. But the fading of the hope of instant success also exposed serious strains both within the SDP and within the Alliance; while Jenkins himself performed poorly in the role of leader. So long as it was winning by-elections in the first heady months after its launch the SDP had attracted wide support both from disillusioned members of the older parties and from so-called 'political virgins' with no previous allegiance; while at Westminster a continuing trickle of Labour MPs – eventually twenty-seven, plus one Tory – defected to swell its parliamentary strength. But it was never clear exactly what sort of party it was supposed to be: a party of the left or of the centre. The four co-leaders represented three possible answers. On the one hand, Jenkins's idea, from the Dimbleby Lecture onwards, had been to create a wholly new party of the centre, closely allied to the Liberals, to attract middle-of-the-road moderates and progressives alienated by the extremes of Thatcherism and socialism. Shirley Williams and Bill Rodgers, however, had left Labour only very reluctantly and initially saw the new party as a reformed Labour Party embodying old Labour values which they felt had been betrayed by the left-wing militants; while David Owen had his own vision of a dynamic young party modelled on his own impatient but rootless radicalism. In particular, he wanted to carve out a distinct identity for the SDP as a fourth party with the minimum possible cooperation with the Liberals, whom he frankly despised.

The Williams/Rodgers conception failed simply because the new party failed to secure a big enough defection from Labour: the loss of just twenty-seven MPs damaged Labour and split the anti-Conservative vote but never seriously threatened Labour's position as the principal party of the left. Too many major figures on the Labour right – Denis Healey, Roy Hattersley, John Smith and others – whose politics were not essentially different from the SDP's (including a good many of those who had been Jenkins's supporters in 1971–76) chose to stay with Labour and fight to regain control of the party from within. The trade unions, one or two maverick individuals excepted, showed no interest in abandoning Labour. The SDP was thus too easily portrayed as an elitist middle-class party of Roy Jenkins's friends – an impression Jenkins himself made very little effort to counter. Owen's fourth-party idea, however, flew in the face of political reality. The Liberals had built up since the early 1970s strong local organisations on the ground, and were not going to disappear. In a polarised political system it was already hard enough for a third party to win enough seats to make a breakthrough: there was never a chance for two parties fighting each other in the centre. So Jenkins's centrist strategy of Alliance with the Liberals – which those early by-election victories showed to have a considerable positive attraction – was the only viable way forward, as Williams and Rodgers quickly came to see. Owen, however, having persuaded himself that Jenkins's closeness to the Liberals was a betrayal of the SDP's independent potential, never reconciled himself to Jenkins's leadership and remained sourly disaffected up to the 1983 election.

But the Alliance itself quickly ran into difficulties after the initial euphoria, mainly over the allocation of seats. (There were few serious differences over policy). In theory the two parties complemented each other neatly; the Liberals had organisation on the ground but no leaders with experience of government, while the SDP brought to the partnership four former Cabinet ministers and several more ex-ministers, as well as a freshening influx of talented recruits from other walks of life. These needed to be found winnable constituencies. But established Liberal candidates who had often been nursing hopeless seats for years were unwilling, since the sudden upturn in their prospects, to step aside for SDP carpetbaggers. At Jenkins's level of lofty agreement with David Steel the broad principle of the two parties working amicably together to fight a roughly equal number of seats seemed natural and easy. The detailed negotiations on the ground, however, were painfully difficult, and led to some bitter rows which damaged the image of the Alliance.

All these problems might have been overcome by more dynamic leadership. Unfortunately, once he had secured the position to which he thought his seniority entitled him, Jenkins proved seriously unsuited to the job. For one thing, he was tired: the two by-elections he had fought, plus the leadership election against David Owen, had taken a lot out of him. He had made his career by bursts of concentrated energy, with time to recover in between: he had never been strong on the sort of sustained stamina that leadership in the media age demands. (In addition he was beginning to suffer the effects of an underactive thyroid, not yet diagnosed.) Secondly he had never, even when deputy leader of the Labour Party, been bothered with the detail of party management; he took little interest in organisation and only reluctantly got involved in the problem of seat allocation. He could make an inspiring conference speech, but he was not good at motivating and mobilising supporters in committee rooms and village halls around the country: he was shy with people he did not know well and came across as aloof or arrogant. Third, he was unexpectedly ineffective in the House of Commons. Fifteen years earlier, as Home Secretary and Chancellor, speaking at the despatch box cheered on by the ranks of government supporters behind him, he had dominated the House by superb debating skill and style. Coming back after his exile in Brussels, however, as the leader of a small party with just a handful of MPs below the gangway, with no despatch box to lean on and heckled mercilessly by the likes of Dennis Skinner, he seemed clumsy and long-winded: at Prime Minister's questions Mrs Thatcher brushed him aside with patronising ease. This failure in the arena where he had previously excelled seriously damaged his confidence. More important, he was equally uncomfortable on television, where he had never shone but where his long-winded answers and lofty patrician drawl now seemed almost laughably old-fashioned. He simply did not look or sound like the leader of a radical alternative government.

Moreover, his lack of interest in party organisation extended to policy development. Here too he had shown the same lack of interest in his Labour Party days. The SDP had set up numerous policy committees devising policies for every area of national life; but Jenkins's broad-brush sense of history was more

stirred by the once-in-a-generation opportunity to break the mould of politics and recreate the Gladstonian/Asquithian Liberal Party of 'conscience and
reform', while seeing Britain belatedly play a positive role in Europe. Detailed
policy, particularly in electorally critical areas like health, education and welfare, did not excite him to anything like the same extent. The one policy he
did take seriously, as a former Chancellor, was formulating a detailed plan
for cutting unemployment, which, as a result of Mrs Thatcher's crude mon-
etarist assault on manufacturing industry, was still around three million and
rising. He first expounded this plan – designed to take a million claimants off
the register in two years by a mixture of public works, incentives to employers and wage control – during his two by-elections in 1981–82; and with some
elaboration it remained his central policy proposal in the run-up to the 1983
general election, presented as the sensible middle way between the Tories'
callous indifference and Labour's reckless extravagance. It was a thoroughly
sound Keynesian policy, with clear echoes of Lloyd George's 'We Can Conquer Unemployment' campaign in 1929; but in 1983 it seemed old-fashioned,
worthy but irrelevant at a time when Mrs Thatcher was successfully projecting the message that only free enterprise could restore prosperity in the long
term and some transitional unemployment was a necessary price to pay in the
meantime. Jenkins's plan accordingly made little impact. Likewise his call for
a truce in the 'frontier war' between privatisation and further nationalisation
seemed merely to defend the status quo.

In an age increasingly obsessed by youth, Jenkins's principal selling point –
his experience as a successful former Chancellor and Home Secretary – actually
cast him as a throwback to the age of Wilson and Heath, if not of Asquith. In
the Thatcher decade politics had moved on and at sixty-two Jenkins seemed
almost as elderly as the 69-year-old Michael Foot. As the general election
approached David Steel agreed that Jenkins should be put forward as 'Prime
Minister designate' in the event that the Alliance was in a position to form a
government. The trouble was that Steel – eighteen years younger, better on
television and much quicker on his feet – was far more popular: polls showed
that the Alliance would do better if he was leader, and Steel came under huge

pressure from his own party to ditch Jenkins and head the campaign himself. At the so-called 'Ettrick Bridge summit', held at Steel's house in the Scottish borders ten days before polling, the pugnacious Liberal ex-MP John Pardoe demanded that Jenkins's role be downgraded; Shirley Williams and Bill Rodgers would not hear of it, however – though David Owen remained conspicuously silent – and the attempted coup was foiled. In fact, Jenkins raised his game in the last week of the campaign and the Alliance's poll ratings improved: its final share of the vote (25.4 per cent) was just 2 per cent behind Labour (27.6 per cent). But this gained them only twenty-three MPs (seventeen Liberal, six SDP) compared to Labour's 209; while the Conservatives (with 42.4 per cent) piled up a massive overall majority of 144. Jenkins managed narrowly to hold Hillhead but most of those, including Williams and Rodgers, who had defected to found the new party in 1981 lost their seats. By the standards of the Liberal Party over the past sixty years it was actually an impressive result – better than Jeremy Thorpe had achieved in 1974, better even than Lloyd George in 1929; but measured against the high hopes of two years earlier it was a cruel disappointment.

Jenkins immediately resigned the SDP leadership. Many of his friends would have liked him to stay on, but Owen effectively forced his hand and he had lost the will to resist. Owen, one of the six surviving MPs, was elected unopposed and lost no time in putting his own stamp on his tiny party. After the unsatisfactory experience of the double-headed campaign not only Jenkins, but Williams and Rodgers too, now wanted to press on with deepening the links between the two Alliance parties, with a view to eventual merger. But Owen, though forced to accept the inevitability of some co-ordination, was determined to maintain the separate identity of the SDP and set his face firmly against merger. Over the next four years, while unwilling to force an open breach, Jenkins became increasingly concerned that Owen was leading the SDP away from his broad and inclusive vision to something much more narrow and exclusive, embracing neo-Thatcherite ideas such as the internal market in the NHS and exaggerating minor differences over renewing Trident in order to paint the Liberals as irresponsible unilateralist disarmers. After the

1987 election, at which the Alliance vote fell to 22.6 per cent, Jenkins (who had lost his seat) backed David Steel in moving for an immediate merger. Owen still refused to countenance it; but by a clear though not massive majority of 57–43 per cent the SDP membership voted against him. The Liberals in a separate ballot overwhelmingly agreed, and in March 1988 the new merged party known – after a slight hiccup over the name – as the Liberal Democrats came into existence. Jenkins, now in the House of Lords, continued to play an active role as the party's leader in the Upper House and a strong supporter of the new leader, Paddy Ashdown.

When Tony Blair became Labour leader in 1994 and completed the process of turning 'New Labour' into something very close in policy and ethos to the original SDP, Jenkins – now writing a biography of Gladstone – saw a new opportunity to heal the historic split between the Liberal and Labour parties and recreate the sort of broadly liberal, left-of-centre party he had always hankered for. He managed to persuade Blair and Ashdown, in the run-up to the 1997 election, to explore the possibility of forming a Labour–Lib Dem coalition to deliver proportional representation and thereby, it was hoped, make the twenty-first century a Liberal century, as the twentieth had been predominantly Conservative. 'The project', as it was codenamed, failed principally because 'New Labour' won such a landslide majority that it did not need the Lib Dems; but in reality neither Blair nor Ashdown could have sold the idea to their respective parties. As Prime Minister, Blair appointed Jenkins to head a commission on electoral reform which duly recommended a slightly over-complicated scheme of proportional representation; but again he faced too much opposition in his own Cabinet to push it through, and Jenkins's report was stillborn. In his last years Jenkins became disillusioned with Blair on other fronts as well – by his failure to take Britain into the euro, by the tabloid-driven illiberalism of his successive Home Secretaries and by his enthusiasm for foreign wars: his last speech in the House of Lords before his death in 2003 was a prescient warning against joining the American invasion of Iraq.

Jenkins's leadership of the SDP was thus a very brief unsuccessful episode in an exceptionally long and generally distinguished career. By most of the criteria by which political leadership is judged he was a failure. He was ineffective in Parliament, poor on television, uninterested in party management and policy development, and he lost the only election he fought as leader. But in one respect he did display outstanding leadership. By raising, in his Dimbleby Lecture in 1979, the banner that led to the formation of the SDP he showed vision and considerable courage. He was then the principal figure in bringing together the various strands of disaffected Labour and unattached middle opinion to create a new party which very nearly broke the two-party mould of British politics. Without the unforeseeable accident of the Falklands War it might very well have done so. Arguably the only effect of the SDP in the short term was to split the anti-Conservative vote in 1983 and 1987 and keep Mrs Thatcher in power with hugely distorted majorities for the whole decade. This was a danger Jenkins was aware of at the outset, but he thought it a risk worth taking. Though it fell short of its most ambitious objective the SDP still changed the face of British politics. Over the next dozen years it led first to the formation of the Liberal Democrats – a stronger and more disciplined third party than the old Liberal Party which grew steadily in strength over the next twenty years – and then to the emergence of 'New Labour' which embodied, at least initially, exactly the sort of 'big tent', progressive party the SDP had been designed to be.

Above all, Jenkins left in several areas a remarkable legacy which entitles him to be judged a great liberal, if not a great leader. His social reforms as Labour Home Secretary in the 1960s and 1970s – homosexuality, abortion, censorship, race relations and gender equality – swept away outdated Victorian restrictions and made Britain a freer, more equal (in some respects) and more diverse society. His early and determined advocacy of Britain joining the European Community played a decisive role in achieving a longstanding Liberal objective. And he was one of the first to see, back in the 1970s, that the old Labour/Conservative class-based duopoly entrenched by the first-past-the-post electoral system no longer represented the views of a more fluid and unattached electorate. It has taken another forty years for that reality to become widely accepted; but Jenkins – historian as he was – saw how politics had to change.

As leader of the SDP in 1982–83 he was a disappointment. But as a prophet of liberalism into the future, his message will continue to resonate.

CHAPTER 22

DAVID OWEN

TUDOR JONES

Dr David Owen was leader of the Social Democratic Party between 1983 and 1987. He led the party assertively and effectively during that period, imbuing it with a distinctive strategic and ideological vision. In spite of the SDP's electoral alliance with the Liberal Party, Owen was opposed to a gradual movement towards a merger between the two parties. Following the 1987 general election he opposed Liberal leader David Steel's call for a 'democratic fusion' of the parties. In the light of an internal SDP members' ballot which narrowly endorsed merger negotiations, Owen resigned as SDP leader in August 1987. He became leader, however, of a breakaway party, the 'continuing' SDP, formally established in March 1988, which was eventually wound up in June 1990.

- David Anthony Llewellyn Owen (b. 2 July 1938), born in Plympton, near Plymouth.
- Educated at Bradfield College and at Sidney Sussex College, University of Cambridge, where he read medicine.
- After training at St Thomas' Hospital medical school, he became a neurological and psychiatric registrar at that hospital.
- Becoming involved in Labour Party politics after the 1959 general election, he was elected in 1966 as Labour MP for Plymouth Sutton (Plymouth Devonport from 1974).
- Married Deborah Schabert in 1968; three children.
- Navy Minister 1968–70 in 1966–70 Labour government, Health Minister 1974–76 and Foreign Secretary 1977–79 in 1974–79 Labour governments.
- Co-founder of the Social Democratic Party 1981, leader of SDP 1983–87, led 'continuing' SDP 1988–90.

- Retired as Plymouth's longest-serving MP in 1992; subsequently ennobled as Lord Owen of the City of Plymouth.
- Appointed co-chairman of the Steering Committee of the International Conference on the Former Yugoslavia (August 1992 – June 1995).
- Made a Companion of Honour, 1994.

O wen became leader of the Social Democratic Party in late June 1983, succeeding Roy Jenkins, its first leader, unopposed. Owen, Jenkins, Bill Rodgers and Shirley Williams had originally been the new party's co-founders in March 1981. It had been established in the face of important developments within the Labour Party since 1979. These included major constitutional changes in 1980–81 involving an electoral college for choosing party leaders and mandatory reselection of all sitting Labour MPs between general elections. In addition, policy commitments were endorsed in 1980 to a unilateralist nuclear defence policy, to unconditional withdrawal from the European Community, and to a substantial extension of state ownership and control of industry. Finally, in November 1980, under the party's existing procedural rules, Michael Foot, veteran tribune of the Labour left, was elected as the new party leader, narrowly defeating Denis Healey.

The SDP was thus launched against the background of what its co-founders perceived to be a major shift of power towards the left within the Labour Party. During the period of the SDP's infancy twenty-seven former Labour MPs and one former Conservative MP were to join its ranks. Six months after its launch, in September 1981, an electoral alliance was formally endorsed and ratified between the SDP and the Liberal Party.

In assuming the leadership of the SDP in 1983, David Owen was able to draw upon his own previous ministerial experience in the 1966–70 and 1974–79 Labour governments. The culmination of that had been his appointment at the age of thirty-eight as Foreign Secretary, following the death of Anthony Crosland. At the Foreign Office, Owen had established good relations with the Prime Minister, James Callaghan. His initial focus was upon Israel–Egypt relations, Rhodesia and negotiations with the European Community over Britain's contributions to the EC budget. His later concerns involved Iran and the issue of strategic nuclear weapons. Owen later candidly admitted that his own style as Foreign Secretary was 'not beyond reproach' since he had been 'too brash and abrasive'. He set himself a 'taxing' pace, but his 'impatience was too often on display and a little more time should have been spent on mollifying bruised egos'.[400]

David Owen became the second leader of the SDP following the 1983 general election, held on 9 June, when the Liberal–SDP Alliance won a massive vote of just over 7,780,000, fewer than three-quarters of a million votes behind Labour, with a national vote share of 25.4 per cent, only 2.2 per cent less than Labour's. But owing to the workings of the first-past-the-post electoral system, the Alliance won only twenty-three seats, as opposed to 209 for Labour, with the Liberals winning seventeen seats and the SDP six. Although the Conservatives under Margaret Thatcher's leadership won a commanding majority of 144, this was still the best third-party result, in terms of national vote share, since 1923.

Of the original 'Gang of Four', Bill Rodgers and Shirley Williams, the latter of whom had dramatically won the Crosby by-election in November 1981, had both lost their seats at the 1983 general election, as had all but five of the other twenty-six sitting SDP MPs who fought that election.

Owen and Roy Jenkins, a high-profile by-election victor in March 1982, had both held on in Plymouth Devonport and Glasgow Hillhead respectively. In these bleak circumstances David Owen, heading a parliamentary team of only six MPs, was thus in a strong position to shape the character, direction and strategy of his own party. As the political scientists Ivor Crewe and Anthony King have observed: 'For the ensuing four years, between the 1983 and 1987 general elections, David Owen *was* the SDP and the SDP *was* Owen ... He was the party's leader in fact as well as in form. Few challenged his authority.'[401]

In the aftermath of the 1983 general election David Owen's central strategic aim as the new leader was to secure the SDP's independence as a fourth

400 David Owen, *Time to Declare*, London, Michael Joseph, 1991, p. 265.

401 Ivor Crewe and Anthony King, *SDP: The Birth, Life and Death of the Social Democratic Party*, Oxford, Oxford University Press, 1995, p. 303.

national political party and to seek to achieve, in cooperation with the Liberals, the ultimate goal of electoral reform and consequently a change in Britain's party political structure. He was, however, strongly opposed to the SDP's gradual movement towards a merger with the Liberal Party. Indeed, he later stated that he considered that the arrangements for parliamentary seat allocation between the two Alliance parties for the 1983 general election, which were finalised by September 1982 and widely regarded within the SDP as tilted towards the Liberals, to have been a decisive turning-point in the direction of merger.[402] Moreover, in September 1982 Owen recorded in his diary that he was opposed, on both ideological and pragmatic grounds, to what he feared was the relentless advance towards a merged party. First, he stated that he was 'temperamentally and philosophically a believer in the tradition of social democracy', considering 'that it exists as a separate strand of political thought capable of being mobilised into a political party', and hence, he implied, as one distinct from British Liberalism. Second, he opposed a merged party on the basis of a hard analysis of 'the electoral consequences of such a merger', believing that it would produce 'insufficient votes to challenge the two-party monopoly of Conservatives and Labour...'[403]

In addition, in his various pronouncements as SDP leader after 1983 Owen deployed other arguments in favour of his party's independence. The joint 1983 Alliance manifesto had benefited, he maintained, from a diversity of views – for example, the SDP's on defence policy and the Liberals' on industrial partnership. He claimed, too, that the Alliance campaign had benefited from the popular appeal of two separate parties working together. Above all, the Alliance's declared aim was to achieve electoral reform through a voting system based on proportional representation. That would lead in practice, Owen argued, to a new style of politics involving both competition and cooperation between independent parties, together with the probability of coalition governments. Owen's underlying electoral aim and strategy, for the SDP and the Alliance, thus appeared to be the cautious but arguably realistic one of breaking the mould of not only

---

402   See Owen, op. cit., 1991, p. 559. For a contrasting view of the 1982 seats deal, see Crewe and King, op. cit., pp. 189–90.

403   Owen, op. cit., 1991, p. 560.

the existing party system but also the established British system of single-party government. That aim and strategy seemed, therefore, in his view entirely compatible with the SDP's continued independence.

As well as promoting as SDP leader that central strategic aim, David Owen was also concerned to reposition his party ideologically in a distinctive manner. Instead of pursuing what Jo Grimond had called 'that old political nirvana of the middle ground', Owen favoured a more radical and unorthodox approach. 'If we could simultaneously break right on the market and left on social policy', he later wrote, then the SDP, he believed, 'could find an electorally attractive mix'.[404] Such a combination of market realism and social concern, of competitiveness and compassion, would also differentiate the SDP, and the Alliance, both from the state collectivism of the Labour Party and from the often unfettered economic liberalism of the Conservative Party under Margaret Thatcher's leadership.

This concept of a social market economy, which Owen had first developed in a 1981 lecture, was further elaborated in his writings, including in his *A Future That Will Work* (1984), and his speeches from October 1983 onwards. By 1984, the concept had become closely identified with Owen's leadership and was officially adopted as a central SDP policy position at the party conference of that year. Within the Alliance, however, and sections of the Liberal Party in particular, this ideological stance proved controversial. Within the original Gang of Four, too, Bill Rodgers warned at the time of the danger of the SDP, and Owen, emphasising 'toughness' as the dominant mood at the expense of 'tenderness' in the social market approach, while Roy Jenkins referred in a coded manner 'to some ludicrous suggestions ... that the SDP is on its way to becoming a junior Thatcherite party'.[405] Owen himself, however, was indifferent to such strictures, later stating that 'the label of "sub-Thatcherite" ... did not worry me ... It was a small price to pay to rid the SDP of being stuck in the 1970s, promising a better yesterday.'[406]

---

404   Ibid., p. 599.

405   William Rodgers, 'My Party – Wet or Dry?', Tawney Society Lecture, 16 May 1985; Roy Jenkins, Tawney Society Lecture, July 1984.

406   Owen, op. cit., 1991, p. 599.

More broadly, Owen's critics argued that Owen's concept of a social market economy lacked a clear or precise meaning. It was unclear, they maintained, whether the main emphasis lay on the 'social' or the 'market' factor of the formula. It was consequently unclear what the economic and social policy implications of the idea were for the SDP's, and the Alliance's, programme and strategy. Nonetheless, through Owen's assiduous advocacy, the social market economy was one of the few distinctive ideas to emerge from SDP thinking between 1983 and 1987. In its broad commitment to combine market realism with social concern, it thereby anticipated, too, later ideological developments on the centre-left during the 1990s and thereafter.[407]

· · ·

In the manner in which David Owen as SDP leader promoted his own conception of his party's strategic and ideological aims he clearly displayed a number of impressive leadership qualities. These included devotion to the SDP itself, effective party management, energy, determination, courage, industriousness, keen intelligence, a firm grasp of a wide range of policy issues, and political vision. In addition, Owen was a highly effective communicator of the SDP's principles, policies and purpose, maintaining for himself and his party a high media profile. A thoughtful platform speaker, he was also very impressive both in the House of Commons and on television. In his frequent media appearances he came over to the general public as direct, intellectually honest, and on policy issues both knowledgeable and refreshingly unpredictable in conventional left/right ideological terms.

On the debit side, however, some of Owen's senior colleagues often found him irascible, moody and lacking in the quality of collegiality. One of these, David Marquand, a former Labour MP and leading social-democratic thinker, later referred to Owen's 'singular inability to establish relations of trust with associates

---

407 For a detailed analysis of the debate within the Alliance over Owen's concept of a social market economy, see Tudor Jones, *The Revival of British Liberalism: From Grimond to Clegg*, Basingstoke, Palgrave, 2011, pp. 118–30.

who have independent political weight of their own'.[408] As a consequence, relations between Owen and the remainder of the Gang of Four were often strained. Shirley Williams, for example, later observed, with regard to what was widely perceived as Owen's autocratic style of leadership, that: 'David was a formidable leader but he was not a team player.'[409] Bill Rodgers, too, later wrote that, while Owen's 'bravura performance' as party leader 'did much for the reputation and morale of the SDP', the party itself had to be one that was 'made in his own image, following wherever he chose to lead'.[410]

Nevertheless, Owen, as a leader of a party with only six seats in the House of Commons, established himself after 1983, through both his outstanding parliamentary performances and his impressive media profile, as one of the leading figures in British politics. This was reflected in his high poll ratings. In national opinion polls between 1983 and 1987 the proportion of people who approved of Owen's leadership of the SDP never fell below 45 per cent, and the ratio of those who approved to those who disapproved was usually two-to-one or more. Within the SDP itself he was widely regarded as an inspirational leader of substance.

In 1986, however, a dispute over defence policy, the one area in which substantial differences of opinion existed between, and to some extent within, the two Alliance parties, appeared to raise questions about Owen's tactical judgement. This arose from a report, due to be published in June 1986, of an Alliance joint commission on defence and disarmament, which had been set up in 1984. The commission's report concluded its proposals for an agreed Alliance defence policy in favour of Britain's continued membership of NATO, of a continued American military presence in Europe, and of the continued presence of US bases, including nuclear bases, on British soil. But on the contentious issue of the future of Britain's independent nuclear deterrent, the report deferred the question of 'whether, and if so how' the British Polaris missile system should be replaced when it became obsolete in the late 1990s.

408 David Marquand, 'Good and bad fairies,' review of 'David Owen Personally Speaking to Kenneth Harris', *The Observer*, 30 August 1987.

409 Shirley Williams, *Climbing the Bookshelves*, London, Virago, 2009, p. 311.

410 Bill Rodgers, *Fourth Among Equals*, London, Politico's, 2000, p. 253.

On the eve of the Council for Social Democracy's spring meeting in Southport, in May 1986, Owen reacted angrily to a story in the *Scotsman* newspaper
which claimed misleadingly, after a lunch meeting between its lobby correspondent and David Steel, that the Alliance commission's report would not commit
the Alliance to replacing the Polaris system. The headline of *The Scotsman*'s lead
story read: 'Alliance report rejects UK deterrent: Owen's nuclear hopes dashed.'
Owen responded by reaffirming his conviction, in his speech at Southport, that
Britain should remain a nuclear weapons state, and that if the Alliance intended
at the next general election to advocate the cancellation of the Thatcher government's Trident missile programme, then it should also stress the need for a
viable replacement.

A subsequent Alliance defence statement in mid-December 1986, presented
by Owen and Steel, attempted to defuse what had become a very public row
between, and within, the two Alliance parties. It declared that the Alliance was
committed to a minimum British nuclear deterrent until it could be safely negotiated away in a global multilateral disarmament agreement. The statement was
thus an endorsement of Owen's, and the SDP's, well-established position on
the issue of a British nuclear deterrent. But where arguably he had shown questionable tactical judgement was in overreacting to the original *Scotsman* story
when in reality he was in a strong position on the issue, with an effective veto
over the form of an agreed Alliance defence policy for the next general election.
In spite of his characteristic directness and intellectual honesty on a vital issue of
national security, it appeared to be the case that in the circumstances, as Crewe
and King have maintained: 'It cannot be said that the SDP leader miscalculated
– because he did not calculate.'[411]

The outcome, however, in the short term was highly damaging in terms of
conspicuous divisions caused by the dispute within the SDP and the Liberal
Party, together with a fall in an Alliance poll rating of 35 per cent in January 1986
down to 23.5 per cent by the year's end. But a sustained Alliance advance in by-
elections during 1986 was followed by a strong performance in the May 1987

411   Crewe and King, op. cit., p. 355.

local elections, in which the equivalent of a national vote share of 27 per cent provided the highest base of support from which any third party had launched itself into a general election since the 1920s.

The 1987 general election, however, held on 11 June, revealed some of the shortcomings of the Alliance itself. In the first place, its election manifesto was a negotiated document which reflected the process of compromise entailed in its long period of preparation by members of the two Alliance parties. As Richard Holme, one of the Liberal members of the manifesto team, later observed: 'Negotiated manifestos are not a good idea, whether intra-party, or, as this was, between parties. They tend towards the lowest common denominator rather than the highest common factor.'[412]

As a consequence, it seemed to David Owen, as he later pointed out, that from his perspective:

> We could not openly endorse the social market for Liberals felt that positioned us too close to the Conservatives; we could not wholeheartedly support the British nuclear deterrent, for the Liberals were still deeply divided on this issue.[413]

As for the campaign itself, John Pardoe, former Liberal MP who chaired the Alliance campaign committee (appointed, as he later wryly observed, 'because I was the only Liberal acceptable to David Owen whom David Steel was prepared to countenance'), found it 'the most dispiriting experience of my political life'. Apart from 'a tedious manifesto' on which to campaign, he faced the problem that, in his view, the two Alliance parties 'had much less in common than they believed and far less than they claimed'.[414]

In spite of those difficulties, as well as uncertainties that arose from the dual leadership with regard to how the Alliance would react if it held the balance of power after the election, the Liberal–SDP Alliance at the 1987 general election

---

412 Richard Holme, 'Alliance Days,' *Journal of Liberal History*, 18, spring 1988, p. 12.

413 Owen, op. cit., 1991, p. 682.

414 John Pardoe, 'The Alliance Campaign', in Ivor Crewe and Martin Harrop eds, *Political Communications: The General Election Campaign of 1987*, Cambridge, Cambridge University Press, 1989, p. 55.

won twenty-two seats, seventeen to the Liberals and five to the SDP. The two parties secured 23.1 per cent of the total British vote, with 7,300,000 votes. In the face of another comfortable Conservative majority of 102, the Liberals and SDP had clearly failed to hold the balance of power, or to replace Labour as the main opposition to the Tories, or even to secure a significant bridgehead in the House of Commons. Furthermore, among the individual casualties three of the original Gang of Four, Jenkins, Rodgers and Williams failed to be elected. The SDP and Liberals had nonetheless, through their alliance, achieved in the 1980s the best third-party results in two successive elections since the 1920s. Yet the overall result, in effective political terms, for the Alliance, and for the SDP in particular, was one of bitter disappointment.

In the weekend in June following the general election, David Steel responded to a statement made in Plymouth by David Owen just hours after the final election results were declared, which indicated the SDP leader's opposition to a merger between his party and the Liberals. In response, in a drafted memorandum, Steel called for a 'democratic fusion' of the two parties. This was a goal he had already declared in July 1986, on the occasion of the tenth anniversary of his accession to the Liberal leadership, to be both inevitable and desirable.

Owen, however, remained firmly opposed to Steel's advocacy of a 'democratic fusion,' and called for an internal ballot of SDP members on the question of whether to begin merger negotiations with the Liberal Party. That proposal was eventually endorsed in August 1987 by 57.4 per cent of those members who voted, with 42.6 per cent supporting the continuing independence of the SDP. Since, however, the turnout was 77.7 per cent, this meant that, in effect, less than half the total SDP membership (that is, 44.6 per cent) had actually voted for advancing towards a merger.

In the wake of the result of the ballot, David Owen resigned as SDP leader on 6 August 1987. In a letter to rank-and-file Social Democrats written in late June 1987 he had argued, in defence of the need to maintain the SDP as a separate party, that:

> Without the SDP, the Alliance would never have been able to maintain the policy stance that we did over the Falklands, over the miners' dispute, over

the Right to Buy council house legislation, over the market economy, over the
Prevention of Terrorism Act, over deployment of cruise missiles ... and over
the minimum nuclear deterrent. There are a host of other policy areas where
the SDP voice has been crucial.[415]

Owen's emphasis on such significant policy differences separating the SDP
from its Liberal allies over the previous six years thus, as Crewe and King later
observed, conveyed 'the clear impression that the Alliance with the Liberals
had never been a partnership of principle but only a not-very-happy marriage
of convenience'.[416] Two other British political scientists made a similar judgement, with which David Steel concurred, that for Owen:

> The Alliance ought never have been a 'partnership of principle', but a plain
> and simple electoral pact ... If the relationship was only to be an electoral
> pact, his dislike of joint spokesmen, joint policymaking and joint selection, his
> rejection of a single leader, and his veto over clear organisational links, all can
> be seen as a perfectly coherent political position. Most Liberals never under-
> stood that that was David Owen's basic attitude to the Alliance.[417]

Owen's decision to resign as SDP leader, and to decline to join a merged party,
was thus clearly compatible with his longstanding reluctance to surrender the
political independence of his party. But more questionable democratically in
the eyes of those in both Alliance parties who favoured merger, including the
remainder of the Gang of Four, was the fact that very soon after the outcome of the
ballot Owen and his followers were starting the process of setting up a breakaway
party, the 'continuing' SDP, that would in practice compete with, and hence act
in opposition to, the new merged party. Those in favour of merger had tended
to overlook the future possibility of that development and had underestimated,

415 Quoted in Owen, op. cit., 1991, p. 722.
416 Crewe and King, op. cit. p. 396.
417 David Butler and Denis Kavanagh, *The British General Election of 1987*, London, Macmillan, 1988, p. 76;
     quoted in David Steel, op. cit., 1989, p. 283.

too, the residual loyalty of many SDP members to their party and their deep respect for Owen as its leader.

In the meantime, the 1987 Liberal assembly in September voted overwhelmingly for merger negotiations, which began tentatively at the end of the month and concluded, after nearly four months, in mid-January 1988. The new merged party, initially named the Social & Liberal Democrats, was formally launched on 3 March 1988, with David Steel and Robert Maclennan as its joint interim leaders.

In view of the disputes and tensions underlying the formation of the new party, and the oversights that have been noted of those who advocated it at its inception, it had thus been, in Chris Cook's phrase, a 'merger most foul'.[418] Nevertheless, the sustained case for merger on the pragmatic ground of the need to use scarce resources – human, organisational and financial – more efficiently had remained a strong one.

In contrast, the problems facing Owen's 'continuing' SDP – in terms of building up a mass membership; of competing electorally with the new merged party; and of the nature and extent of its own electoral appeal – appeared formidable. Above all, it would face the difficulty of surviving within an electoral system which, in the absence of proportional representation, would provide little if any room for a fourth national party. Indeed, Owen himself later maintained that at its inception he had been one of the 'continuing' SDP's 'most reluctant recruits' and 'had not accepted it would be viable'.[419] It was, however, formally established in March 1988. Just over two years later, Owen's initial doubts were ultimately confirmed by his re-launched party's disastrous by-election performance in Bootle in May 1990. In its aftermath the 'continuing' SDP was finally wound up the following month.

It had nonetheless clearly been the case that in the years before the merger David Owen, through his leadership qualities and political stature, had raised the reputation, morale and national and media profile of his party. Indeed, he had helped to keep the SDP alive between 1983 and 1987. In spite of their reservations

---

418   Chris Cook, *A Short History of the Liberal Party, 1900–2001*, Basingstoke, Palgrave, 2002, p. 188.

419   David Owen, op. cit., 1991, p. 732.

about his autocratic style of leadership, within the original Gang of Four Shirley Williams, as we have seen, considered him 'a formidable leader', while Bill Rodgers acknowledged that he was 'outstanding in the House of Commons, impressive on television and commanding in the councils of the party'.[420] To many other observers of British politics in 1987–1988 it seemed, too, that a new merged party of the centre from which Owen would be absent might well, in view of his national standing and parliamentary presence, be, at least initially, all the weaker for that. The tensions underlying Owen's absence were certainly one significant factor contributing to the new merged party's painful infancy, from which, under the leadership of Paddy Ashdown, and subsequently renamed the Liberal Democrats, it gradually and tentatively recovered.

420 Rodgers, op. cit., p. 253.

CHAPTER 23

ROBERT MACLENNAN

MATT COLE

The injunction 'Do not underestimate the determination of a quiet man' became the object of understandable mockery when used by Iain Duncan Smith as the beleaguered Tory leader in 2002. Yet it makes a fitting tribute to the former SDP and Liberal Democrat leader Robert Maclennan. Though he was regarded as reserved and even ponderous, and as leader was criticised for weakness, Maclennan had an impressive record of electoral success and legislative achievement based upon liberal principles; and it is no exaggeration to say that the Liberal Democrats owe their establishment partly to Maclennan's readiness to absorb the anguish of hysterical internal conflict at the party's most vulnerable moment.

- Rt Hon. Robert (Bob) Adam Ross MacLennan, born 26 June 1936 in Glasgow to doctors Isabel and Sir Hector Maclennan.
- Educated at Glasgow Academy, Oxford, Cambridge and Columbia Universities.
- Barrister 1962–66.
- Married Helen Cutter (1968) with whom he has two children and a stepson.
- MP for Caithness and Sutherland 1966–97, Caithness, Sutherland and Easter Ross 1997–2001 – Labour 1966–81, SDP 1981–88, Liberal Democrat 1988–2001.
- Minister for Prices and Consumer Protection 1974–79, leader of the SDP 1987–88, joint leader of Social & Liberal Democrats 1988, president of Liberal Democrats 1994–98.
- Ennobled as Baron MacLennan of Rogart in Sutherland, 2001.

I n 1966, Maclennan became the first Labour MP for Caithness and Sutherland, the former stronghold of Liberal leader Archibald Sinclair. The defeat by only sixty-four votes of the Liberal MP George Mackie (who was later to sit on the Liberal Democrat benches in the Lords alongside Maclennan) was unexpected, reflecting not only the national swing to Labour but Maclennan's efforts 'beavering away in the constituency during the short '64–66 parliament'.[421]

Maclennan developed a close relationship with his constituents, familiarising himself with the complexities of the nuclear energy business at the Dounreay power plant (the largest local employer), while encouraging artists and actors to make the area a Highlands arts centre, and helping fellow farmers market their beef and sheep (Maclennan and his wife still maintain a farm in Caithness). On his journey through three party labels and a change in constituency boundaries, Maclennan was able to build his majority up to over 8,000 (36 per cent) and in 2001 handed the seat over to his Liberal Democrat successor John Thurso, Sinclair's grandson.

Though his first fifteen years in Parliament were spent as a Labour MP, Maclennan was from the outset closely associated with what were to be the ideas and personnel of the future Liberal Democrats. In his first year, he was chosen to present to the Commons the proposals of the Latey Committee to lower the age of majority to eighteen, implemented in 1969. He also became parliamentary private secretary to George Thomson, a Labour Cabinet minister who was to join the SDP alongside him.

After Labour's defeat in 1970 Maclennan joined the Public Accounts Committee (on which he sat for the remainder of his time in the Commons) and became a front-bench spokesman on Scottish affairs and defence. He firmly took the side of Labour's pro-Europeans, joining the rebellion led by Roy Jenkins in 1972 in favour of EEC membership; he was the only one of Jenkins's acknowledged 'intimates' to urge the future SDP founder to challenge Harold Wilson's leadership. Nonetheless, in a characteristic show of patience, he remained loyal to Labour in

---

421   Liberal Democrat Voice, tributes to Lord Mackie, 18 February 2015, accessed 7 April 2015 (http://www.libdemvoice.org/scottish-liberal-lord-mackie-of-benshie-dies-at-95-44721.html).

the hope that it would 'return to sanity', as he said in urging (without success) MP Dick Taverne not to leave in 1973.[422] When Labour returned to power the following year Maclennan piloted through the Consumer Credit Act as a junior minister to Shirley Williams, Secretary of State for Prices and Consumer Protection.

After Labour's defeat in 1979 Maclennan was one of the first to support Jenkins in the formation of the SDP – the only MP at that stage who later became a Liberal Democrat MP – and even 'toyed seriously' with the idea of joining the Liberal Party directly.[423] He was the SDP's only Scottish MP until Jenkins won Glasgow Hillhead in 1982, and took policy portfolios ranging from agriculture to home and legal affairs; but perhaps his longest-lasting contribution was as chief architect of the SDP's constitution, many features of which were imported into the Liberal Democrats' structure seven years later. Given the constitutional controversies in the Labour Party which had given birth to the SDP, this was no dry legal exercise, as Maclennan recognised:

> The constitution of a political party defines the processes whereby it reaches
> its decisions. It also reflects the attitude of that party to the workings of democ-
> racy itself ... [The SDP's constitution] seeks to ensure that those who lead
> the party will not dictate to the party but equally that they are not shackled
> by other institutions of the party.[424]

It was in the wake of the 1987 election, and during the dark days of the merger between the Liberals and Social Democrats, that Maclennan suffered the severest criticism and yet gave his most valuable service to his party. He was accused by both sides in the controversy of simultaneous manipulation and feebleness, and certainly he made some major public errors; and yet it was partly by his willingness to bear this criticism that any agreement was forged at all.

---

422 Ian Bradley, *Breaking the Mould: the Birth and Prospects of the Social Democratic Party*, Oxford, Martin Robertson, 1981, p. 56.

423 Hugh Stephenson, *Claret and Chips: The Rise of the SDP*, London, Michael Joseph, 1982, p. 29.

424 *SDP Newsletter* No. 3, 1981.

David Steel's proposal for merger, made immediately after the Alliance's failure to break the mould at the 1987 election, divided the Social Democrats. The SDP leader David Owen immediately declared that he would not join a merged party, while his predecessor Roy Jenkins enthusiastically backed merger. Maclennan initially sided with Owen, but accepted the verdict of a ballot of SDP members, which supported the opening of merger talks. Owen promptly resigned the SDP leadership, leaving only Maclennan and his friend and constituency neighbour Charles Kennedy in support of the merger process. Maclennan, as the senior of the two, took over as the party's third and final leader at the end of August 1987. He had already earned the contempt of the Owenites for his 'betrayal' of their party; he was now about to embark on a strategy which would infuriate Liberals by trying to bring as many of the Social Democrats – perhaps even Owen himself – with him into a merged party by maximising its likeness to the SDP. As one Liberal critic put it, 'he seemed determined to out-Owen Owen'.[425]

Maclennan promised his party that he would 'drive a hard bargain',[426] pressing for commitments to NATO membership and nuclear defence in the new party's initial policy statements, and to SDP-style postal ballots in its constitution. Most controversial was his insistence that the name of the party be the Social & Liberal Democrats, with the shortened title being 'Democrats'. He objected to 'Liberal Democrats' on the grounds that Owen, like a wedding usher, would urge SDP members to divide at the aisle: 'Social Democrats this way, Liberal Democrats that way'.

In protracted and tense negotiations, he often became visibly upset, banging his fist on the table and on one occasion walking out and giving the Liberals five minutes to agree to his terms. These episodes, and his publication with David Steel of a proposed policy statement including VAT on children's clothes and the restriction of child benefit (the press conference for which was cancelled before the document was hastily withdrawn), earned Maclennan the sarcastic nickname 'Big Mac' at Westminster, reflecting his reputation as a man promoted

---

425   Crewe and King, op. cit., p. 417.

426   'Maclennan Takes Over', *The Social Democrat*, 28 August 1987, p. 1.

beyond his talents, 'a difficult and strangely emotional negotiator, not an obvious leader' in Alan Beith's view.[427]

The offence given to Liberals by these attempts at railroading was only exacerbated when he and Kennedy took their prizes from the negotiations to Owen's home in full view of the press. Owen dismissed this as a 'disgraceful' stunt which 'reeked of insincerity' and drew the conclusion that 'the most charitable explanation of Bob Maclennan's conduct over those few days is that he was close to having a nervous breakdown'.[428] Maclennan's position was widely regarded as symbolic of the SDP's vulnerable condition, and a critical history of the party assesses him as 'altogether too fragile and lacking in confidence'.[429] Even close, longstanding colleagues such as Shirley Williams describe him as 'thin-skinned, sensitive to criticism' and 'not cut out for the sour and savage politics of the 1980s'.[430]

These criticisms were understandable, at least at the time, from those closest to Maclennan's more uncharacteristic outbursts, to the misconceived 'dead-parrot' policy document and from those already suspicious about the merger process. In retrospect, however, it can be argued that Maclennan's role had to be taken by any leader who hoped to bring the Social Democrats – or a sizeable proportion of them – into the new party in the face of the appeal of Owen. His apparent madness was in reality a sort of martyrdom, albeit not always a dignified one.

With Steel, Maclennan assumed the joint interim leadership of the new Social & Liberal Democrats for the brief interregnum between March and July 1988 while its leadership election took place. Its new leader, Paddy Ashdown, came to draw on Maclennan's expertise and experience in support of his leadership during the early difficult period of the Liberal Democrats' existence, taking

427   Alan Beith, *A View from the North: Life, politics and faith seen from England's northernmost constituency*, Newcastle-upon-Tyne, Northumbria University Press, 2008, p. 114.

428   Owen, op. cit., 1991, p. 738.

429   Crewe and King op. cit., p. 421.

430   Williams, op. cit., p. 316.

his advice, for example, on the best approach to hung parliament scenarios.[431] Maclennan's relationship with the party members was reflected and consolidated by his election as party president in 1994. During his term, party membership rose to over 100,000 and Liberal Democrat presence in local government grew every year; he served a second two-year term unopposed.

He was also the Liberal Democrat spokesman on the arts and home and constitutional affairs, surprising Tony Blair by upstaging him at the 1993 Police Federation conference with a speech the future Prime Minister called 'one of the most electrifying I've ever heard'.[432] However, it was in the area of constitutional reform that Maclennan achieved perhaps the most enduring part of Ashdown's partnership with New Labour, working with Labour front-bench spokesman Robin Cook to agree proposals, launched in March 1997, for the incorporation of the European Convention on Human Rights into UK law, freedom of information legislation, devolution to Scotland and Wales (and elections by proportional representation to their parliaments), an elected authority for London, removal of the hereditary peers from the House of Lords, proportional representation for the European elections, and a referendum on voting reform for Westminster elections. Most were introduced by Labour after their 1997 victory, and Maclennan joined the Joint Cabinet Committee of Labour ministers and Liberal Democrats reviewing a range of policy topics including the constitution and relations with the EU.

That the bulk of the Cook–Maclennan agreement came into effect testifies to the patience and strategic sensitivity of both its authors. While most of it had been Liberal Democrat policy for years (or was a watered-down version of it), much was new for Labour, but dovetailed with Tony Blair's moves to modernise his party. The overwhelming size of Labour's majority after 1997, however, meant that there was a limit to what could be achieved; in particular, the promised referendum on electoral reform was never held. Maclennan was criticised by some Liberal Democrats for continuing on the Cabinet Committee afterwards,

---

431   See, for example, Paddy Ashdown, *The Ashdown Diaries Volume One 1988–1997*, London, Allen Lane, 2000, p. 110, a reference to discussions in February 1991.

432   Tony Blair, *A Journey*, London, Hutchinson, 2010, p. 121.

but his determination to pursue the relationship while any hope remained was characteristic of his approach. He nonetheless gave expression to the same frustrations as his critical colleagues in a retrospective review of the Cook–Maclennan proposals.[433]

In 2001, after thirty-five years in the Commons, Robert Maclennan became Lord Maclennan of Rogart and joined the Liberal Democrat peers. He spoke for the party on European Affairs and was chosen as a member of the Convention on the Future of Europe under Valery Giscard d'Estaing which forged the ill-fated EU treaty of 2004.

Maclennan's service to his party has not always been recognised, and was not always evident to the fast-moving media or impatient colleagues. Helen Bailey was right to describe Maclennan as 'more successful than visible';[434] it was his low profile that sometimes made the success possible. Shirley Williams called him 'a serious man and an extraordinarily conscientious one',[435] and even amid criticism Alan Beith acknowledged that Maclennan always proved 'a natural Liberal'.[436] This rare combination of qualities made Maclennan a vital leader of the Liberal Democrat cause at some of its times of greatest need.

433   Robin Cook and Robert Maclennan, *Looking Back, Looking Forward: The Cook–Maclennan Agreement on Constitutional Reform, Eight Years On*, London, New Politics Network, 2005.

434   Helen Bailey, 'Robert Maclennan MP', in Duncan Brack et al. eds, *Dictionary of Liberal Biography*, London, Politico's, 1998, p. 246.

435   Williams, op. cit.

436   Beith, op. cit.

CHAPTER 24

PADDY ASHDOWN

DUNCAN BRACK

Paddy Ashdown, leader of the Liberal Democrats from 1988 to 1999, ranks as one of the most effective and successful Liberal leaders since the collapse of the Liberal Party in the 1920s. Although the Liberal Democrats won more seats under Charles Kennedy and entered government under Nick Clegg, Ashdown inherited the party in much worse shape than Kennedy and left it in better shape than he found it, unlike Clegg. He created, out of the wreckage of the Liberal–SDP Alliance, a professional, modernised and effective political force. He took it through the wrangles over its name and collapsing support in the opinion polls to a new respectability, stunning local election and by-election victories and a higher number of Commons seats than at any time since 1929. And yet, his grand strategy of working together with the Labour Party, based on a common progressive agenda, to change the face of British politics forever – 'the project' – ultimately ended in failure.

- Jeremy John Durham Ashdown (b. 27 February 1941), born in India to a family of soldiers and colonial administrators.
- Grew up in Northern Ireland (hence his schoolboy nickname 'Paddy'); educated at Bedford School.
- Served in the Royal Marines (including Special Boat Section), 1959–72; diplomat and spy, 1972–76.
- Married Jane Courtenay in 1962; one son, one daughter.
- Fought Yeovil in 1979; elected in 1983, held seat until stood down in 2001.
- Leader of the Liberal Democrats 1988–99, high representative and EU special representative for Bosnia & Herzegovina 2002–06.
- Awarded KBE 2000, GCMG 2006, CH 2015.

- Ennobled as Baron Ashdown of Norton-sub-Hamdon, 2001.
- Chair of Liberal Democrat 2015 election campaign.

A shdown came into the Liberal Party as an outsider, with no long record of political activism. Nevertheless, his upbringing and early experiences clearly helped to generate strong political views. His father, ex-Indian Army, argumentative, politically radical and never afraid to hold a minority opinion, was a key figure, and his upbringing in Northern Ireland left him with a dislike of sectarianism (reinforced by a period of soldiering in the province in 1970–71). His years at boarding school in Bedford gave him self-confidence and self-discipline, together with an enquiring mind and a drive to learn and to compete; also self-sufficiency and a dislike of clubbishness. His years in the army, and the social structure behind its officer class, reinforced his progressive beliefs.

Initially a Labour supporter, Ashdown lost his sympathies for the party at the time of Barbara Castle's abortive attempt to reform industrial relations law in the late 1960s and Britain's drift towards industrial conflict under the Wilson and Callaghan governments. He only joined the Liberal Party by a lucky chance. In January 1974, while digging in the garden of his cottage in Yeovil, he was interrupted by a Liberal canvasser, who 'wore an orange anorak, looked rather unprepossessing and had a squeaky voice to match'.[437] Despite Ashdown's scepticism, he invited him in, and 'two hours later, having discussed liberalism at length in our front room, I discovered that this was what I had really always been. That Liberalism was an old coat that had been hanging in my cupboard, overlooked all these years, just waiting to be taken down and put on.'[438]

Two years later he gave up his diplomatic career and set about contesting the apparently hopeless constituency of Yeovil – a decision he described as 'naive to

---

437 Paddy Ashdown, *A Fortunate Life: The Autobiography of Paddy Ashdown*, London, Aurum Press, 2009, p. 156.
438 Ibid.

the point of irresponsibility. It just happens also to be the best decision I have made in my life.'[439] Displaying characteristic energy and drive, he built up his local electoral base, recruiting a formidable team of campaigners and applying the community politics approach promoted by the Association of Liberal Councillors. In 1979, he achieved his immediate objective of taking second place from Labour, and the party also won all the council seats it contested the same day. Although his plan had been to win the seat at the third election, he actually succeeded at the second attempt, in 1983.

His campaigning background helped him to build a reputation among the grass roots of the party and he proved an effective spokesman, first on trade and industry and then on education, during the 1983–87 parliament. He once observed that he never felt happy in the chamber of the House of Commons unless both the other two parties were attacking him. Having largely stayed clear of the bitter arguments over merger in the winter of 1987–88, he stood for the leadership of the new Social & Liberal Democrats (SLD). He based his appeal on the need to rethink the party's approach, with the underlying theme that choice and individual freedoms were the entitlement of every citizen, but that with that came rights and responsibilities. Specific areas for new thinking included looking at the social security system, putting green politics at the top of the agenda, and using the market wherever possible to promote prosperity. On 28 July 1988, after a highly professional campaign in which he always seemed ahead, Ashdown was elected leader over Alan Beith, with over 70 per cent of the vote.

The characteristics he displayed during his early political career were to become ever more clear in his leadership. First, his self-belief and love of a challenge, perhaps fuelled by not thinking about it too clearly ahead of time – exemplified by deciding to fight Yeovil in the first place; as he put it later, quoting David Penhaligon, he won because 'he was too naive to know it was impossible'.[440] Second, his penchant for plans – as in his three-election strategy for the constituency. Third, his political courage, including a number of

439   Ibid., p. 162.
440   Ibid., p. 166.

instances where he took principled positions which were unpopular locally; although this caused some difficulty, they did not appear to damage his prospects in the long term, and he concluded that in general voters preferred MPs to do what they believed to be right, and respected them for it, even while disagreeing with them. He was to follow this instinct later, in supporting the Conservative government over the Maastricht Treaty of European Union. Finally, his evident love for the party and respect for its activists – which is not a universal characteristic of leaders.

It was clear even before his election to Parliament that he was a naturally gifted speaker; his first-ever speech to the Liberal assembly, in 1981, successfully opposing the deployment of US cruise missiles in the UK, won him a standing ovation. As leader he worked hard on his delivery and style, receiving assistance from, among others, Max Atkinson, author of the classic study of political speech-making, *Our Masters' Voices*.[441] Although his conference speeches could occasionally suffer from being over-rehearsed, at his best he was a powerful and inspiring speaker, with a compelling voice and distinctive turn of phrase. He was probably even better at talks with small groups of party members or ordinary citizens, taking his jacket off and turning his chair round in an easy, familiar way. He dealt effectively with the media and although at times could sound sanctimonious (something of an occupational hazard for politicians from third parties, used to criticising both government and opposition), he came over well to the public, and frequently featured in opinion polls as the most popular party leader.

His career as leader of the Liberal Democrats can be divided into three phases, following the plan he himself had mapped out on becoming leader:

> The first was survival from a point of near extinction; the second was to build a political force with the strength, policy and positions to matter again in British politics; and the third was to get on to the field and play in what I believed would become a very fluid period of politics.[442]

---

441   Max Atkinson, *Our Masters' Voices: The language and body language of politics*, London, Methuen, 1984.

442   Paddy Ashdown, *The Ashdown Diaries: Volume Two, 1997–1999*, Harmondsworth, Allen Lane / The Penguin Press, 2001, p. 494.

Strategic planning of this sort was absolutely typical of Ashdown, one of the characteristics almost everyone who worked with him remembered – he always had a plan, and a position paper, and when he achieved one objective he was often already looking ahead to the next. Other personal qualities included an apparently inexhaustible supply of energy, helped by his obvious physical fitness, and hyperactivity. He thought – and worried – about everything, ringing up party spokesmen, for example, to get them to respond to an obscure proposal in a local party's conference resolution. He was fascinated by ideas, and published a series of books and pamphlets, including *Citizen's Britain* in 1989, and *Beyond Westminster* in 1994;[443] his conference speeches often challenged party orthodoxies, particularly in the early years.

Ashdown needed all these qualities in his first phase (1988–92), that of survival. The party he inherited was demoralised, shedding members and almost bankrupt after the long-drawn-out process of merger; on the day he was elected leader, the Inland Revenue sent officials into party HQ to seize assets in lieu of unpaid national insurance contributions. Furthermore, the SLD faced challenges to its role as Britain's third party, initially from the 'continuing SDP', those followers of David Owen who had refused to join the merged party, whose high-water mark was beating the SLD, in February 1989, into third place in the Richmond by-election. Four months later the SLD ended up in a humiliating fourth place in the European parliamentary elections, scoring just 6.2 per cent and falling well behind the Green Party. It sank even further in the opinion polls thereafter and had to sack more than half its staff in response to the membership and financial crisis. As Ashdown put it, he was 'plagued by the nightmare that the party that started with Gladstone will end with Ashdown'.[444]

The financial and electoral crises of summer 1989 were bad enough, but they helped to bring to a head the third challenge faced by the party: confusion over its identity. Was the new party to be Liberal, Social Democratic or something else entirely? In practice, the argument was conducted over what the party was

---

443 Paddy Ashdown, *Citizen's Britain: A Radical Agenda for the 1990s*, London, Fourth Estate, 1989, and Paddy Ashdown, *Beyond Westminster: Finding Hope in Britain*, London, Simon & Schuster, 1994.

444 Ashdown, op. cit., 2000, p. 50 (entry for 15 June 1988).

to be called. The decision, which Ashdown backed at his first party conference, to opt for the new name of 'Democrats' to replace the clumsy merger compromise of 'Social & Liberal Democrats', proved disastrous, undermining the sense of identity and self-image that party members need, particularly in difficult times. 'Being a relative outsider compared to the older MPs,' as he put it later:

> I had, in my rush to create the new party, failed to understand that a political party is about more than plans and priorities and policies and a chromium-plated organisation. It also has a heart and a history and a soul – especially a very old party like the Liberals … I had nearly wrecked the party by becoming too attached to my own vision and ignoring the fact that political parties are, at root, human organisations and not machines.[445]

An all-member ballot in the autumn chose 'Liberal Democrats' by a clear majority. In retrospect this marked the beginnings of recovery. Party finances and membership both stabilised, and the local strength and campaigning tenacity of the core of activists who stayed true to the party ensured that it saw off the other competitors for the centre-left ground; the Greens had clearly faded by early 1990 and after humiliating by-election results the Owenites wound themselves up in May 1990. The shock Liberal Democrat by-election victory of Eastbourne, in October 1990, underlined the fact that the party had survived – and also helped signal the beginning of the end for Margaret Thatcher's premiership. The party won two further by-elections in 1991 (the victory in Ribble Valley heralding the end of the hated poll tax) and achieved 22 per cent in that year's local elections. Further local election and by-election gains, some with record swings, were to follow in the 1992–97 parliament, and in 1994 the party won its first ever seats in the European Parliament.

The fact that the party survived at all was very much due to Ashdown; it seems unlikely that had his leadership opponent Alan Beith been elected, he would have displayed the energy, drive and charisma the party needed. Ashdown also

445   Ashdown, op. cit., 2009, p. 246.

succeeded in finding positions for his party which were principled and distinctive, the constant quest for third-party leaders; as Ashdown himself said,
'I would sell my grandmother for some distinctiveness for the party'.[446] The
first of these was his championing, after the Tiananmen Square massacre of
June 1989, of the right of Hong Kong citizens to be given British passports in
advance of the colony's incorporation into China. Later on it included support
for the Maastricht Treaty of European Union in Parliament, which included
voting with John Major's government after it lost its majority following internal
rebellions, and pressing for western action on Bosnia and Kosovo; his repeated
visits to the Balkan war zones helped to build public support in Britain for the
NATO-led action that ended the Serbian attempt to destroy the Bosnian state.

Ashdown's interest in policy ideas led him to take the chairmanship of the
party's Federal Policy Committee and to use it to establish a series of key policy
positions, including a more market-oriented economic policy than the Liberal–
SDP Alliance had possessed (including the proposal for independence for the
Bank of England, later implemented by Labour), a strong environmental platform
and a pledge to invest in public services, including, most memorably, a penny
on income tax for education. By 1993, the party was coming top in opinion polls
asking which party was the best on environmental issues; it also scored relatively
well on education. Both the election manifestos produced under Ashdown's
leadership were well regarded by the media. 'The Liberal Democrat essay far
outdistances its competitors with a fizz of ideas and an absence of fudge,' stated
The Guardian in 1992.[447] In 1997, *The Independent* called the party's manifesto
the most challenging of the three, saying that politics without the Liberal Democrats would be 'intolerable'; Peter Riddell in *The Times* enjoyed its 'refreshing
candour' and admired Ashdown's willingness to leap where Tony Blair feared
to tread.[448] Ashdown was able to stamp his ideas firmly on the party largely
because of the respect and admiration he came to enjoy among its members; as

446 Ashdown, op. cit., 2001, p. 495.

447 *The Guardian*, 19 March 1992.

448 David Butler and Denis Kavanagh, *The British General Election of 1997*, Basingstoke, Macmillan, 1997, p. 178.

The Economist commented in 1991, 'Ordinary party members will take things from him for which they would have lynched David Owen.'[449]

This all meant that in the 1992 election the party was able to run an effective campaign with an attractive policy platform. The build-up to the election was nearly thrown off course, however, by the revelation of a brief affair between Ashdown and his former secretary five years earlier. The support of his wife Jane, his own willingness to face a Westminster press conference and some deft public relations saw him through this painful experience, though it cast a shadow over the campaign. Overall, however, the 1992 election was a personal success for Ashdown, establishing him as a significant voice in British politics. He was consistently described in opinion polls as the most popular party leader, and the party's policies, especially its pledge to raise income tax to spend more on education, were widely praised. The result – 17.8 per cent of the vote and twenty seats – proved that the Liberal Democrats were not going to disappear, as had seemed possible in 1989.

The second phase of the Ashdown leadership, from 1992 to 1997, centred around his attempts at realignment of the left, a common theme of previous Liberal leaders and an objective of Ashdown's since the very early days of his leadership. Although there had been some contacts with Labour politicians and sympathisers before 1992, it was Labour's fourth successive election defeat that provided the main opportunity for action. Exactly a month after the election, Ashdown delivered the 'Chard speech', given to an audience of only forty or fifty in a small town in his constituency, arguing that the party needed to 'work with others to assemble the ideas around which a non-socialist alternative to the Conservatives can be constructed'.[450] Although the speech was deeply unpopular within the parliamentary party (one hostile MP took to referring to it as a 'burnt offering'), it was to prove the opening scene of more than five years of delicate negotiations with Labour, particularly after Tony Blair took over as leader in 1994.

In due course Ashdown and Blair reached an agreement to focus their attacks

---

449 'Paddy's people', *The Economist*, 14 September 1991.

450 Paddy Ashdown, 'A broader movement dedicated to winning the battle of ideas', 9 May 1992, in Brack and Little, op. cit., p. 427.

on the Conservatives rather than each other. This included a formal abandonment of 'equidistance' by the Liberal Democrat conference in 1995, a decision reached after extensive consultation within the party by Ashdown; but since Liberal Democrat policy positions were generally much closer to Labour's than to the Tories, and since the Conservative government was deeply unpopular by 1995, this seemed mainly simple common sense. In fact, cooperation between Labour and the Liberal Democrats extended further than most realised at the time. In the run-up to the 1997 election the two parties agreed a (secret) list of Tory seats in which one party had little chance of winning and would therefore not invest resources, so as to give the other a clear run. Also as a result of joint discussions, during the election the *Daily Mirror* published a list of twenty-two seats where, if Labour voters backed the Liberal Democrats, the Conservatives would be defeated; in the event the party won twenty of them.

Blair and Ashdown also agreed to collaborate on policy areas where they hoped to work together. The key outcome was a series of talks on constitutional reform led by Robin Cook, for Labour, and Robert Maclennan, for the Liberal Democrats. In March 1997 the group reached agreement on a package of proposals including incorporation of the European Convention on Human Rights into UK law, freedom of information legislation, devolution to Scotland and Wales (and elections by proportional representation to their parliaments), an elected authority for London, removal of the hereditary peers from the House of Lords, proportional representation for the European elections, and a referendum on voting reform for Westminster elections. Most of this had been Liberal Democrat policy for years (or was a watered-down version of it), but much was new for Labour.

The Cook–Maclennan process was public, and in general was cautiously welcomed by Liberal Democrats. What was discussed in secret, however – and which would have alarmed many party members – was something much more dramatic, what Ashdown called 'the big thing': an agreement to fight the election on a common platform on at least two or three major issues. 'If, as it appears,' Ashdown confided to his diary in April 1996, 'I have more in common with Blair than he has with his left wing, surely the logical thing is for us to create a new, more powerful alternative force which would be unified around a broadly liberal agenda.'[451] Ashdown went so far as to draft successive versions of a 'Partnership for Britain's Future', covering constitutional reform, cleaning up politics (after several examples of corruption and dishonest conduct among MPs), the reform of welfare systems and economic policy reform, including investing in education, awarding independence to the Bank of England, and adherence to the criteria for entry into the single European currency. From July 1996, Blair and Ashdown started to talk about Liberal Democrat participation in a Labour government; Peter Mandelson later claimed that this would have involved including two Liberal Democrat MPs, Alan Beith and Menzies Campbell, in Blair's first Cabinet.[452] Blair even sprang on a surprised Ashdown the idea of merger between the parties; Ashdown responded by saying 'that may be a long-term destination ... that may happen, say, ten years from now, probably under someone else's leadership'.[453]

In the end, the 'big thing' was too big a step. What worried Ashdown and his colleagues was Blair's refusal to commit firmly to the introduction of proportional representation for Westminster elections – the absolute bottom line for the Liberal Democrats, who could not be expected to tie themselves to a much bigger partner without being able to survive its eventual fall. Ashdown's diaries record in painstaking detail a long series of meetings in which Blair was first educated about what PR meant and the different systems through which it could be introduced, and then prevaricated, hinting at his own possible conversion to it but stressing the opposition he would face in the Parliamentary Labour Party. By January 1997, the very small number of Liberal Democrat colleagues who were kept in the loop by Ashdown were unanimously urging him to drop the project, but he persevered, despite his advisor Richard Holme's warning that: 'You must not get carried away with the film script you have written in your head – two strong people standing up and shaping history.'[454]

---

451   Ashdown, op. cit., 2000, p. 419.

452   Peter Mandelson, *The Third Man*, London, Harper Press, 2011, p. 256.

453   Ashdown, op. cit., 2000, p. 452.

454   Ibid., p. 449.

As late as election day in May 1997, Blair and Ashdown were still talking about whether they could entertain any form of cooperation; Blair declared that he was 'absolutely determined to mend the schism that occurred in the progressive forces in British politics at the start of this century'.[455] By the next day, however, Blair had changed his tone, talking merely of a 'framework for cooperation'. Robin Cook later confirmed that Gordon Brown (Labour's shadow Chancellor) and John Prescott (its deputy leader) had both made clear to Blair overnight their virulent opposition to any role for Ashdown or his colleagues in government. In any case, the size of Labour's majority destroyed any argument for it.

The second phase of Ashdown's leadership, like his first, must be accounted a success. He successfully rode the rising tide of support for centre-left sentiment and the rejection of the Conservative government that not only swept Labour into power in 1997 but delivered the highest number of seats for a third party for seventy years. Under a less skilled leader, the Liberal Democrats could easily have been squeezed out by Blair's New Labour. Indeed, Ashdown feared this at the time, referring to the months after Blair's election as Labour leader as the most difficult period of his own leadership; the party's standing in the opinion polls sank from 25 per cent in 1993 to 12 per cent in 1996. It might have fallen further had the party not benefited from the defection of two Conservative MPs in 1996–97, helping to thrust it back into the limelight and suggesting that some at least of the departing Tory vote might prefer the Liberal Democrats to Labour.

The abandonment of equidistance can thus be seen as an – ultimately successful – attempt to become part of the movement for change rather than being swept aside by it, and the party was able to benefit from the high level of anti-Tory tactical voting in the 1997 election, winning forty-six seats on a slightly lower share of the vote (16.8 per cent) than in 1992. Without this cooperation between the voters of both parties – and, to a certain extent, between the party organisations themselves – the Conservative defeat would probably not have been so overwhelming. The election campaign itself, focused tightly around the need to improve public services, was a success, and seen as a credit to Ashdown

---

455   Ibid., p. 555.

personally; it added five points to the party's standing. And 'the project' with Labour had a direct impact in the shape of the constitutional reforms Blair implemented after 1997: probably Labour would have brought in Scottish devolution without any prompting from the Liberal Democrats, but their attachment to Welsh devolution and to proportional representation for the European elections was much weaker and may not have borne fruit in the absence of the Cook–Maclennan agreement.

In contrast, the third phase of the Ashdown leadership, 1997–99, was a failure, as the leader and his party increasingly came to differ over its future direction. Ashdown was determined to adopt a stance of 'constructive opposition' – opposing the new government where the Liberal Democrats disagreed with them, but working with Labour where they agreed, especially over constitutional reform. In place of a coalition, a Joint Cabinet Committee was established between the two parties to discuss issues where there was already agreement in principle, such as devolution or first-stage reform of the House of Lords. The announcement of the Committee came as a shock to the party, most of whom were not aware of the close relationship Blair and Ashdown had built up over the preceding three years. Ashdown freely admits that he bounced his party into accepting it – 'I am absolutely convinced that we would never have got the party into the Joint Cabinet Committee … if I had gone through a consensual process'[456] – but this was a calculated part of his strategy. As he put it later:

> I quite deliberately went round building up my popularity in the party, both
> by delivering results and also by being very consensual, conscious of the fact
> that when I started to play on the field in Stage 3, I was really going to have to
> [use up this political capital and] … make myself unpopular with the party.[457]

Being friendly to Labour was not too difficult to accept when both parties were in opposition; but maintaining this closeness when Labour was in government

---

456   Interview with Paddy Ashdown, *Journal of Liberal History*, Vol. 30, spring 2001, p. 13.
457   Ibid.

increasingly seemed less sensible to a growing portion of the party membership. Not only did this risk the Liberal Democrats being tarred with government
unpopularity, when it came, but it seemed to achieve less and less in policy outcomes. The two big unfulfilled promises of Cook–Maclennan were reform of the
House of Lords, where Blair showed no likelihood of accepting the principle of
an elected chamber, and proportional representation for Westminster elections.

Ashdown, increasingly frustrated with Blair's prevarication, suggested a deal
by which Liberal Democrats would agree to a coalition with Labour on the
basis of an agreed policy programme, including PR. But Blair would never commit firmly, and the greater the delay in forming a coalition, the less possible it
became, as the government steadily became less palatable to Liberal Democrat
sensibilities. The government's centralising approach to politics, its determination to stick to the Tories' previous spending plans, thus putting public services
under pressure, and the lack of any announcements on PR or British entry into
the European single currency were not what the Liberal Democrats had fought
the election for.

In December, the government finally announced the establishment of an
independent commission on voting reform, to be chaired by Roy Jenkins. In
practice this further weakened Ashdown's chances of getting a coalition through
his own party; if the government was doing what Liberal Democrats wanted on
constitutional reform anyway, why tie the party in to the rest of its agenda, with
an increasing proportion of which it disagreed? It was against this background
that the Liberal Democrat conference in March 1998 agreed the 'triple lock'
procedure for agreeing to 'any substantial proposal which could affect the party's independence of political action'. The support of the parliamentary party
and federal executive would be needed for any such proposal; failing a three-
quarters majority in each body, a special conference would be held; and failing
a two-thirds majority there, an all-member ballot would need to be organised.
The system was deliberately designed to tie Ashdown's hands, though in fact
it was not to be put to the test until 2010.

Throughout the summer of 1998 Ashdown attempted to nail Blair down to
a commitment to a PR referendum, and other aspects of the Cook–Maclennan

agreement. But despite a long series of meetings Blair seemed ever less likely to reach a final decision. Richard Holme described the process as like 'being condemned to attend endless repeats of *Hamlet*'; Ashdown noted in his diary that 'waiting for Blair is like waiting for Godot'.[458] In September Blair agreed with Ashdown to hold a referendum on PR before the next election, but six weeks later changed his mind yet again, feeling that he could not overcome opposition in the Cabinet and did not want to risk splitting the government. When, on 29 October, the Jenkins Report was published, advocating an additional member system of PR, Blair's response was entirely neutral, with no commitment to a referendum; later that day Jack Straw, the Home Secretary, rubbished it publicly, and did so again in a Commons debate on the report the following week.

Ashdown was forced to conclude that 'the project' had failed and that his time as leader should end. (He had already decided, before the 1997 election, that he would stand down at some point in the next parliament.) He made one final, and predictably futile, attempt to extract a promise from Blair to state publicly that he would hold a referendum on the Jenkins proposals, and in November he and Blair announced the extension of the remit of the Joint Cabinet Committee, following a review of its work and effectiveness; the remit was eventually extended to cover a number of specific European policy issues. The move roused predictable opposition within the Liberal Democrats, but Ashdown won support for it from the parliamentary party and, narrowly, from the party's committees. After this had been agreed, he announced, on 20 January 1999, his own intention to step down as leader.

Ashdown's resignation was to take effect in August, with the leadership election due to take place after the European elections in June. He therefore had the satisfaction of seeing the party do well in the first elections to the new Scottish Parliament and Welsh Assembly in May, forming a coalition with Labour in Scotland; the party also performed well in the local elections held on the same day. A month later the introduction of PR helped the party increase its representation in the European Parliament from two to ten MEPs, the largest national

---

contingent in the European Liberal group. When the leadership election concluded with Charles Kennedy's victory on 11 August, Ashdown recorded in his diary: 'I left the celebrations quietly and walked back to the House feeling just a tinge of sadness that I am no longer a leader of one of the great British political parties. But this was more than offset by the feeling of having cast off a very heavy burden ... I felt very contented.'[459]

Why did the third phase of Ashdown's leadership end in failure? He himself later blamed Blair's overriding objective in his first term, which was to get elected for a second, rather than achieve anything as fundamental as reforming the political system; Blair's overestimation of his ability to charm away opposition in his own party; and his underestimation of the strength of that opposition to any deal with the Liberal Democrats.[460] Ashdown felt that that was due in part to the fact that Blair was an outsider in Labour politics, not someone who had grown up in the tribal traditions of the party – a characteristic that Ashdown shared in relation to the Liberal Democrats, and which arguably led him to make the same error, to underestimate the strength of his own party's opposition to a deal with Labour. Ashdown believed that Blair was serious about the attempt to reach a deal, but: 'although I think he spoke the truth when he said that partnership with the Lib Dems was the big thing he wanted to do to reshape British politics, it never was the *next* thing he wanted to do. Hence the delays, which in the end killed us.'[461]

The result of the last phase of Ashdown's leadership, as Tony Greaves has observed, was that:

> Liberal Democrats loved their leader but, in so far as they sensed his strategy, most wanted none of it. The 'what if?' question must be how much more could have been achieved if all that time at the top and personal energy had been spent on something other than 'the project'.

---

459 Ibid., pp. 489–90.
460 Ashdown, op. cit., 2009, pp. 323–5.
461 Ibid.

But was there a realistic alternative? Like Grimond and Steel before him, Ashdown was driven inexorably by the logic of the realignment/cooperation strategy. However well the Liberal Democrats performed in elections – and Ashdown hardly neglected that aspect of party strategy – it never seemed remotely feasible that the party would leap straight to majority government from third position, or even replace one of the two bigger parties as the main opposition. Sooner or later the party would hold the balance of power, and in the political circumstances of the 1990s, it was inconceivable that the Liberal Democrats could have reached an arrangement with anyone other than the Labour Party. Indeed, Ashdown was not particularly aiming for a hung parliament, in which, he thought, any attempt to bring in PR would be seen as weakness on the part of the bigger coalition partner; he wanted to introduce it from a position of strength, with both parties of the left genuinely behind it. His problem was that most of the Labour Party was never committed to PR at all, and saw no point in making any concessions to Ashdown's party once they commanded a 179-seat majority in the House of Commons. But Ashdown was always going to try; he possessed neither the temperament nor the patience to sit quietly on the sidelines, snatching what chances he could to advance incrementally.

No comprehensive and objective assessment of the 'project' with Labour has yet been carried out. It is not clear what, if anything, the JCC ever achieved, but it can certainly be argued that the Cook–Maclennan agreement had a direct impact in the shape of the constitutional reforms Blair implemented after 1997. Thus, Ashdown and the Liberal Democrats contributed to permanent and profound changes in the way in which Britain is governed. And in the final analysis, if Ashdown had delivered on proportional representation, the third phase of his leadership would have been seen as a triumphant success. It was a calculated strategy, but in that respect it failed.

Ashdown stood down from the Commons at the 2001 election. From 2002 to 2006 he occupied the post of high representative and EU special representative for Bosnia & Herzegovina, reflecting his long-term advocacy of international intervention in the region. Back in British politics, he supported Nick Clegg for the leadership of the Liberal Democrats in 2007, and played a full part in the 2010 general election campaign. With some reluctance, he supported the decision to join the coalition government with the Conservatives. In 2012 he was appointed chair of the Liberal Democrats' general election campaign for the 2015 election. The characteristic energy and drive with which he took on the task could not save the party, however, from electoral catastrophe; probably, the party's fate was effectively sealed after the first year of its coalition with the Conservatives.

Paddy Ashdown is held in enormous affection in the party he once led. His leader's speeches to party conference – visionary, challenging, displaying a fascination with new ideas – have seldom been bettered, and he was just as at ease with small groups of activists. He coped well with the media and in general was an excellent party manager. He retained his energy, drive and enthusiasm, and his belief in the party and what it stood for, in the most trying circumstances. And above all, having rescued his party from near-collapse, he built it into an effective political force and did something with it. He left it with a distinctive and rigorous policy programme and, through the Cook–Maclennan constitutional reforms, he changed for good the structure of government within the UK. And whatever his disagreements with members over policy and strategy, he obviously always genuinely loved his party – which is rare among party leaders. And – which is even rarer – most of the time, they loved him too.

CHAPTER 25

CHARLES KENNEDY

GREG HURST

Before, during and even after his turbulent period as leader of the Liberal Democrats from 1999 to 2006, Charles Kennedy remained an enigma. From early adulthood, as he progressed from student prodigy to precocious parliamentarian, he was tipped as a future leader. Yet when the crown was his, he wore it uncertainly: flashes of his youthful brilliance as an orator and debater were largely extinguished. He appeared uncomfortable with the limited authority it yielded, often unhappy with the pressures it brought. Nonetheless, he emerged as a popular figure with the public, appreciated for his quick wit, self-deprecating manner, and careful understatement in an era when trust in mainstream politicians was eroding. When his tenure was brutally ended by a revolt within his parliamentary party he fought back, although unsuccessfully, with a vigour that often had been absent while his position was unchallenged.

- Charles Peter Kennedy (25 November 1959 – 1 June 2015), born in Inverness and grew up in Fort William in the West Highlands of Scotland.
- Educated at local schools and University of Glasgow (MA politics and philosophy) and Indiana University (speech communication, political rhetoric and British politics).
- Elected to Parliament in 1983, aged twenty-three, for Ross, Cromarty and Skye, representing the SDP; switched to Liberal Democrats in 1988.
- Married Sarah Gurling, a Lib Dem activist 2002–10; one son Donald (born 2005).
- SDP spokesman for health and social security; Lib Dem spokesman for trade & industry, health and agriculture; Lib Dem president 1990–94, party leader 1999–2006.

K ennedy's outlook and beliefs were heavily shaped by his upbringing in the West Highlands of Scotland. Born in November 1959, Charles Peter Kennedy was the youngest of three children in a crofting family whose ancestors had tilled the same land beneath Ben Nevis in Fort William since 1801. He attended the local comprehensive school, where he enjoying acting and excelled in debating, and continued this passion at the University of Glasgow, whose university union was renowned across Scotland for its tradition of student debating. He enrolled on a four-year honours degree to read English, but switched to read politics and philosophy and repeated a year. He thus spent five years as a student in Glasgow, one while president of the university union, and a sixth in America studying for a Master's degree in political rhetoric at the University of Indiana. After graduating from Glasgow, he spent several weeks as a temporary reporter with BBC Radio Highland in Inverness, the only job outside politics he ever had.

Despite a Liberal tradition within his family, Kennedy joined the Labour Party at fifteen and remained a member until deciding to cast his lot with the emergent SDP six years later while at university. He applied for the approved candidates' list and astounded his interviewers by declaring he wished to stand in the forthcoming general election, in 1983. 'Young Mr Kennedy', as local members called him, was – equally surprisingly – chosen as the Alliance candidate for Ross, Cromarty and Skye, where the Liberals had been in fourth place, flying back from Indiana for the selection meeting. More astonishing still, he captured the vast West Highland seat from the Conservatives with a traditional campaign addressing public meetings, often preceded by his father playing the fiddle. The result was the last of the election, declared the lunchtime after polling day, and was so unpredicted that SDP officials in London scoured a map to locate the seat and had to find out who he was.

He arrived in the House of Commons, aged twenty-three, one of just six Members of Parliament for the routed SDP. Its new leader David Owen appointed Kennedy as spokesman on health, social security and Scotland, a steep learning curve as he found his feet in the Commons. During his formative years as a parliamentarian little was expected of him in terms of policy development. Owen, a former doctor, had clear views on the National Health Service; moreover, one of the SDP's features was its use of outside 'experts' to advise on policy formation. Kennedy's role as a spokesman was, when required, to summarise the views of others.

Kennedy's key contribution to the SDP came after the 1987 general election, which the party again fought in strained alliance with the Liberals. In the traumatic aftermath, he became the only one of the five remaining SDP MPs to back a merger with the Liberal Party, breaking ranks with parliamentary colleagues to do so. Although still junior, Kennedy composed speeches to party conferences during this period that were much commented upon, and laid the ground for his election in 1990 as president of the merged party. This gave him a broader representational role in the fledgling Liberal Democrats plus a media platform, further raising his profile.

One reason for his wish to become party president was his difficult relationship with Paddy Ashdown, the leader, whose driven work ethic, structured approach and keen interest in policy stood in contrast to Kennedy's laid-back, intuitive style. Ashdown initially gave him important front-bench roles – trade and industry, then health – but in teams headed by senior colleagues. He felt Kennedy was not pulling his weight and later moved him to become spokesman on Europe and, finally, agriculture. Throughout, Ashdown kept Kennedy at a distance and never involved him in his 'project' to seek a progressive alliance with Labour under Tony Blair. Kennedy became detached from his party in the mid-1990s as, exiled under Ashdown, he pursued other interests.

As the youngest Member of Parliament, a certain celebrity attached to Kennedy on his arrival at Westminster. With his interest in broadcasting and skill in debate and repartee, he found himself in demand as a newspaper columnist and, later, guest on radio and television shows that strayed beyond the realms of politics. He earned himself the nickname 'Chat Show Charlie' and signed up to the after-dinner speaking circuit. Such appearances broadened his reputation as an approachable, quick-witted politician able to laugh at his trade, although it irked parliamentary colleagues who toiled away in the Commons while he made a name as a minor celebrity elsewhere. Intriguingly, Kennedy never developed a parallel reputation as an orator or performer in Parliament, due to a combination of lack of application, diminished interest and, later as leader, the absence of a despatch box at the Lib Dem bench to use as both prop and shield. While a younger MP he could be sharp in his occasional interventions at question time, typically using humour to soften their edges, and was a popular figure with colleagues on all sides of the House. As a frontbencher he performed parliamentary duties perfunctorily, sometimes speed-reading documents at short notice and relying on his wits rather than careful preparation. He left little of his own mark on legislation, either in amending government bills or in significant private members' bills. He was interested in Parliament; he took great satisfaction, for example, in serving on a select committee that set terms for televising the proceedings of Commons in 1988–89, later sat on the standards and procedure committee, and was associate editor of the House magazine for parliamentarians. It was the process that drew him, not legislating.

After the 1997 general election, Kennedy was a reasonably well-known figure as he took a conscious decision to re-engage with his party, sensing in the months that followed that Ashdown's position was weakening. He distanced himself from a joint consultative committee on which Labour ministers and Lib Dem nominees discussed constitutional reforms, Ashdown's consolation after Blair failed to offer him a coalition, and criticised the Lib Dems' strategy of 'constructive opposition' to the Labour government. When a review of electoral reform came to naught and Ashdown quit, Kennedy found himself front-runner to succeed him although his strength always lay in media endorsements and name recognition among inactive members rather than support from the Lib Dems' committed volunteers or colleagues. Several of Ashdown's allies contemplated standing but decided against. Over a drawn-out period, Kennedy's team ran a largely disciplined, if slightly complacent campaign but lacked boldness as, anticipating a large majority, he wished to keep all options open. From the field of five Simon Hughes, from the party's radical left, emerged as the popular choice among grassroots activists. While Kennedy won by a clear margin, in August 1999, his victory was not as convincing as many had assumed and created long-lasting suspicion in the Kennedy camp of Hughes's populist appeal within the party.

Kennedy's chief strategic challenge on becoming leader was the party's relationship with Labour. The Lib Dems were seen by commentators almost entirely
through the prism of leverage they could extract on the Blair government, whose
commanding Commons majority of 179 gave it a historic opportunity to seek a
realignment of the progressive centre-left, although entirely on Labour's own
terms. Kennedy was not opposed to working with Labour. Many of his political instincts still chimed with the party he joined in his mid-teens. He had, too,
been closely associated with attempts at cross-party dialogue amid the despair
felt by many on the centre-left at John Major's unlikely Conservative victory in
1992. Kennedy became chairman of a quarterly journal launched the following
year, *The Reformer*, which advocated preparation for a Lib–Lab coalition. Several
people involved were social democrats who re-joined Labour under Blair. The
question for Kennedy was, rather, was how to respond once Labour's majority
meant Blair did not need the Lib Dems to govern and was unable to convince
his party to forge a coalition regardless to realign the left.

Kennedy's handling of this was subtle. Blair and Ashdown had widened the
JCC's remit beyond its original focus of constitutional affairs to other policies
but its momentum had gone. Nonetheless, to allies of Ashdown it remained
a symbol of cross-party cooperation. Kennedy allowed its work to continue,
meeting twice to agree positions on European Union enlargement and United
Nations peacekeeping operations, giving it a chance and retaining the considerable goodwill on Blair's side. When, after a year, Kennedy told Blair he wished
to withdraw from the JCC before the general election, he accepted the Prime
Minister's request to suspend it instead although this made no difference. Without fuss, rancour or even much controversy, the formal inherited link between
the Lib Dems and Labour government was severed.

In his first eighteen months or so, Kennedy enjoyed a honeymoon period
within his party as he sought to establish a consensual style of leadership that
was the direct opposite of the autocratic approach of Ashdown's latter years,
that to many felt like a route-march. Kennedy consulted colleagues on endless
drafts of major speeches, although he lost something of his own voice within them
each time he did so; he asked MPs which posts they wanted before front-bench

reshuffles, although some inevitably were disappointed; and he was open and consultative with the wider voluntary party, which was initially appreciated widely. Among the wider electorate, however, he made less of an impact.

A by-election early in his tenure, in Romsey, Hampshire, gave the opportunity to test the electoral appeal of his more consensual style of leadership, with the contest given an edge as the Conservative leader William Hague laid out hard-line positions on immigration and asylum policy. The Lib Dems caused a minor sensation by taking Romsey from the Tories, boosting Kennedy's standing and self-confidence. In the general election campaign the following year, he was given a fairly easy ride. Both Labour and the Lib Dems co-ordinated their 'air war' campaign to isolate and attack the Conservatives, a strategy referred to by Blair and Kennedy's advisors as 'two against one': Charlie Falconer, a Cabinet Office minister and trusted friend of Blair, met weekly with Tim Razzall, chairman of the Lib Dems' campaign, to co-ordinate daily campaign 'grids'. There was also tacit but widespread encouragement of tactical voting among Labour and Lib Dem voters, although candidates contested seats at constituency level.

Kennedy's own image was used widely on Lib Dem election material, as the party calculated his straightforward manner would be an electoral asset, and his informal, bantering style with journalists at press conferences often created a convivial atmosphere. A common assumption had taken hold that the Lib Dems would lose ground in the 2001 election, but they exceeded expectations by emerging with fifty-two seats, a net increase of six, five from the Conservatives, one from Labour, and a higher share of the vote, up 1.5 points to 18.3 per cent.

Within months of the election came the terrorist attacks on the World Trade Center in New York, which profoundly reshaped politics in Britain as well as in America. The repercussions dominated the remainder of Kennedy's tenure as leader. The Lib Dems supported the bombing campaign that followed in Afghanistan, although Kennedy had a difficult task in marshalling widely opposing views within the party. As emergency anti-terrorism powers were fast-tracked through both Houses of Parliament, Lib Dems successfully navigated a path between responding to the changed public mood and heightened security threat while articulating legitimate questions about the curbs to individual liberty these entailed.

The key challenge came once President George Bush began making a case for military action against Iraq as Blair, seeking maximum influence for Britain, resolved to support the emerging US policy of pre-empting threats to national interests before they were realised. Ordinarily, the position of the Liberal Democrats might have been insignificant but the new Conservative leader Iain Duncan Smith, whose father had been an RAF wing commander, took a similar view to the Prime Minister and advocated attacking Iraq. With the official opposition in agreement, the Lib Dems became the only mainstream British political party opposing British troops joining America's invasion of Iraq in March 2003.

Blair's premiership was at stake and, while Kennedy was careful not to attack his integrity, relations with Labour were strained. It meant, too, taking positions on constantly evolving circumstances, as authorisation for military action was sought from the United Nations and a huge mobilisation of American and British forces began in readiness for combat. Kennedy was not naturally comfortable with military affairs but convened an informal group of advisors, including Tim Garden, a retired air vice marshal and expert in chemical, biological and nuclear weapons, to provide counsel. Kennedy was briefed on party leader's terms about Iraq's weapons capability by intelligence chiefs and faced taunts of cowardice or appeasement from Tory MPs during key debates in the Commons. His position was that, once international weapons inspectors returned to Iraq to search for biological or chemical weapons, they must finish their work and, without a fresh UN mandate, a case for war had not been made. He pressed Blair repeatedly on this in the Commons. The defining moment for Kennedy came when, after much prevarication, he agreed to address a Stop the War rally in Hyde Park that was organised by hard-left groups but swelled to attract a million protestors. Kennedy faced pressure from activists within his own party to attend this powerfully symbolic march; ever cautious, reluctant to commit, he held back. After a lunch with its journalists who challenged him, *The Guardian* ran a leading article chastising the Lib Dem leader for not going. Finally, he announced he would do so. In the Commons, Lib Dems joined growing numbers of defiant Labour MPs, and a handful of Tories, in votes refusing to sanction war. These culminated in an unprecedented debate in which Blair sought, and got, parliamentary approval for the invasion, with 139 Labour MPs, fifteen Conservatives and all fifty-three Lib Dems against.

Ahead of the 2001 general election, Kennedy made peripheral and presentational changes to the Lib Dems' manifesto but core elements remained: more spending on public services, funded by moderate increases in general taxation – a penny on income tax for education – and a higher 50p rate of tax for the biggest earners. Afterwards, Kennedy commissioned a policy review chaired by Chris Huhne, then an MEP, to look more fundamentally at the delivery and funding of public services, although its proposals were overtaken by events. After Gordon Brown's large increases in public spending, especially in the Budget of 2002, the party shifted to a fiscally neutral position for most tax-payers; only the highest earners would pay more, via a top 50p tax rate, to fund a pledge to abolish university tuition fees. Yet Kennedy's 2005 manifesto and election campaign themes lacked a coherent unifying philosophy, listing what the party was against: identity cards, student tuition fees, charges for residential care, the Iraq War. It was frustration with this approach that prompted the publication in 2004 of a collection of economically liberal essays, *The Orange Book*,[462] by MPs less hostile to the Conservatives, upsetting many on the party's left.

Kennedy was not a conventional leader. He had little interest in policy and still less in party management. He shied from taking sides when possible, avoided confrontation and preferred to operate via informal discussion within a tight circle of confidants than in formal structures, although his eventual judgement was often shrewd. Consequently, important decisions such as front-bench appointments or nominations for peerages were drawn-out or poorly handled, while meetings with the party's volunteers often left activists frustrated. Tim Razzall later claimed in his memoirs Kennedy had 'strong leadership skills', describing how he would deal with dissenting MPs:

> His skill was to invite a potential rebel to see him, to listen while the individual explained his concerns, and not say much, thereby giving the individual

---

462   Paul Marshall and David Laws, *The Orange Book: Reclaiming Liberalism*, London, Profile Books, 2004.

the impression that he really agreed with him but the political realities were pulling the other way. It invariably worked.[463]

Most people, of course, would conclude the reverse. A leader succeeds by giving definition to himself and to his party, not by appearing to agree with opposing positions. Without consciously doing so, Kennedy distanced himself from all but a handful of his MPs and peers while leader and, unpunctual and uninterested in policy detail or party affairs, did not provide good internal leadership. It created a vacuum that allowed Chris Rennard, the Lib Dems' campaigns chief who became chief executive, to become increasingly powerful. Kennedy was better at the glad-handing, representational and campaigning role with members, but inconsistent and could be a demotivating presence on an off-day.

Once Saddam Hussein was toppled, the failure to discover chemical or biological weapons in Iraq led to mounting criticism of Blair, who used the likely presence of such weapons as the legal justification for sending British troops. Lib Dems exploited a loss of faith in the Prime Minister among ethnic minority communities to make unprecedented gains from Labour in by-elections in Brent East and Leicester South and fight fierce by-election battles in Birmingham Hodge Hill and Hartlepool. Lib Dem poll ratings peaked at 24–25 per cent before dipping but remained strong. Despite tensions, and with Lib Dems targeting three or four dozen Labour seats, the two parties again agreed to coordinate campaigns in the general election itself. Sally Morgan, Blair's director of government relations, initially spoke daily with Tim Razzall until relations cooled when Kennedy refused to join an attack on the Conservatives' stance on immigration and ended when the Lib Dems made the Iraq War a campaign issue. Blair began to denounce the party in the final days, disrupting some of Kennedy's momentum. The Lib Dems won sixty-two seats, taking eleven from Labour, one from Plaid Cymru and a net loss of two to the Tories. Six million people backed Kennedy's party, 22.0 per cent of votes cast. This was substantial growth yet failed to match expectations, given the unprecedented opportunity

---

463   Tim Razzall, *Chance Encounters: Tales from a Varied Life*, London, Biteback Publishing, 2014, p. 236.

with Labour vulnerable and the Conservatives still weak: many Lib Dems, and some commentators, anticipated gaining another fifteen or twenty seats, perhaps more, especially in Tory constituencies.

Within months Kennedy was gone. Disappointment at the outcome was a strong undercurrent to his departure but not the deciding one. The reason was his alcoholism. Kennedy, whose bonhomie masked a shyness and lack of confidence, was always a heavy drinker. As his itinerant bachelor's lifestyle continued into his thirties, this developed into a drink problem. He was largely able to contain his alcoholism, aided by the fact that Liberal Democrat spokesmen attracted less public attention. Even on his election as leader, those closest to him could suppress the secret of his drink problem: there were rumours, drink-related incidents that were hushed up, but very few knew for certain.

Menzies Campbell later described his embarrassment when, at a meeting with the Palestinian leader Yasser Arafat in 2001, Kennedy arrived late, shaking violently, and managed just one question.[464] Kennedy himself sought professional help for the first time a year later, via his doctor. He decided in July 2003 to hold a press conference to acknowledge a drink problem, but changed his mind with hours to spare. After several absences and difficult performances, a delegation of the party deputy leader, chairman, Chief Whip and chief executive confronted Kennedy in 2004, forcing him to admit his alcoholism and commit to treatment in return for their continuing support.

During the 2005 general election campaign the issue returned when Kennedy, two days after the birth of his son, gave a disastrous performance at the launch of the Liberal Democrats' manifesto, stammering painfully over the detail of replacing council tax with a local income tax. He blamed lack of sleep. Others, including broadcasters who interviewed him afterwards, attributed it to alcohol.

Another episode that autumn prompted group of younger frontbenchers to act. It was a wretchedly messy episode, with a series of inconclusive confrontations, culminating in the leaking of the secret of his alcoholism. In desperation, Kennedy gave a press conference to acknowledge his drink problem and called a leadership ballot, saying he would stand again as a candidate. The following day twenty-five MPs declared they would resign from the front bench unless he quit. Left with no choice, Kennedy did so on 7 January 2006, defiantly claiming he retained the support of ordinary members and activists if not parliamentary colleagues.

He remained a backbencher thereafter, rather than return to a front-bench role such as spokesman on foreign affairs. He picked up posts that interested him, becoming Rector of Glasgow University, but was not suited to or comfortable as an elder statesman figure. When the Conservative–Lib Dem coalition was formed after the 2010 general election, he withheld support, abstaining and saying he would rather offer a confidence and supply arrangement to a minority Tory administration. He was also among the Lib Dem MPs who voted against the trebling of tuition fees but was otherwise not troublesome. He lost his seat in 2015, swept away by the Scottish National Party landslide that captured fifty-six of Scotland's fifty-nine seats, in his case with a huge swing of almost 25 per cent in Ross, Skye and Lochaber. Tragically, a month later he was found dead in his grandfather's crofter's cottage near Fort William that was his home. His family later released a statement saying he died of a major haemorrhage that 'was a consequence of his battle with alcoholism'.

As leader Kennedy delivered for the Lib Dems the largest number of MPs for a third party since the 1920s, twelve MEPs, some 4,500 councillors, seventeen MSPs in Scotland where Lib Dems remained junior coalition partners with Labour, and six AMs in Wales, where a Lab–Lib coalition proved short-lived. Yet by his own terms he failed. He wanted, and planned, to contest a third general election after which he anticipated, presciently, that the Lib Dems might hold the balance of power. Moreover, he did not prepare the party for government but did the opposite. From 2001 onwards, his stated aim for the Lib Dems was 'effective opposition', a theme writ large in his 2005 manifesto. Electorally, it yielded results: the Lib Dems began to collect a large and diverse alliance of protest votes held together by the range of issues the party pledged to resist. Yet these gains proved unsustainable, given they were built upon the sands of protest votes, not the rock of firmer, consolidated support.

What did he achieve? His lasting legacy was leading the only mainstream

UK party to oppose the Iraq invasion. The significance is not merely that he opposed the Iraq War but how he did so: measured, patient, eloquent yet resolute. To criticise military action in which large numbers of British troops are engaged is difficult, sensitive and controversial, yet in this case was constitutionally necessary: millions opposed the war or harboured deep misgivings and it was important that an opposition party articulated these in Parliament.

Kennedy certainly lacked leadership ability in the conventional sense: some Lib Dems have suggested this, not his alcoholism, was the reason his party rose to oust him.[465] Duncan Brack, a member of the party's federal policy committee, said one or two MPs used his drink problem as a pretext to act:

> Kennedy's drinking was a symptom of his problem, not a cause ... he was not
> an effective leader, drunk or sober, and he knew it; he drank partly out of recognition of his own under-performance. His basic problem was that he had
> no agenda for his leadership, no obvious reason to be leader and no idea of
> the direction he wanted the party to go in.[466]

For the principal actors in his overthrow this was not, however, a binary argument; the weaknesses and eccentricities of his leadership were intertwined with a severe concealed drink problem that, for them, was no longer tolerable.

But Kennedy deserves to be remembered for another quality, one more ephemeral yet profound in its own way. He had a rare emotional intelligence, an ability to see and articulate politics from the perspective of the ordinary person. Despite being the ultimate professional politician – he'd never done anything else – he appealed to an emerging anti-politics sentiment; another paradox. However difficult, frustrating and disempowering MPs and activists found this informal instinctive style, voters liked and felt a connection with him, which extended the Lib Dems' electoral reach. This became evident in the public reaction to his death, which dominated the day's news headlines. Many, many people appeared

465   Dennis Kavanagh and Philip Cowley, *The British General Election of 2010*, Basingstoke, Palgrave, 2010, p. 98.

466   Brack and Ingham, op. cit., p. 360.

to be personally touched, and spoke of his death as though they had known him. The *Daily Record*, a Labour-supporting tabloid, observed in its leader column: 'His death has prompted a wave of sadness because we feel he was neither elite nor remote as a politician. He was one of us.'[467]

Was he ever capable of fulfilling his youthful promise and mobilising his immense talent to become a more effective leader? We shall never know. That is the puzzle, and the tragedy, of Charles Kennedy.

---

467   *Daily Record*, 2 June 2015.

CHAPTER 26

SIR MENZIES CAMPBELL

GREG SIMPSON

Menzies Campbell, commonly known as 'Ming', came late to leadership of the Liberal Democrats. Aged sixty-four, on 2 March 2006, Campbell was elected leader of a party struggling to come to terms with the revelations of Charles Kennedy's personal problems and his removal as leader. Campbell succeeded in steadying the ship; his professional approach enabled the party to be ready for the early election anticipated when Gordon Brown replaced Tony Blair as Prime Minister. On 5 October 2007, however, Brown ruled out an early election, and, within ten days, Campbell had resigned as Liberal Democrat leader after just nineteen months in charge. Despite the progress he had made internally, Campbell's lawyerly style, his old-fashioned image and his statesman-like approach had limited his ability to connect with the public. His background as a foreign affairs spokesman ill equipped him to deal with the demands of the complex domestic agenda. Judging that he would struggle to convert a caretaker's stint as leader into a longer-term haul through to the end of the parliament, Campbell stood aside.

- Walter Menzies Campbell, born Kelvinbridge, Glasgow, 22 May 1941.
- Son of George Campbell – joiner who finished his career as general manager of the Glasgow Corporation building department – and Elizabeth – post office clerk – with one sister (Fiona).
- Educated locally; trained as a solicitor.
- Married Lady Elspeth Grant Suttie (née Urquhart) in 1970; one son James from Elspeth's previous marriage.

- Elected as Liberal MP for North East Fife in 1987, held the seat until stepping down in 2015.
- Queen's Counsel 1982, knighthood 2003, leader of the Liberal Democrats 2 March 2006 – 15 October 2007, chancellor of St Andrews University 2006, incumbent.

B orn in 1941, Campbell spent his childhood in a rented Glasgow ten-ement that was 'comfortable and commonplace for the standards of the time'.[468] The young Campbell was an accomplished sprinter, representing Great Britain at the 1964 Olympics while studying law at Glasgow University. A contemporary of John Smith and Donald Dewar, Campbell could count future luminaries of the Labour Party among his personal friends, but he rejected the industrial socialism of Scottish Labour and the iron grip it held in the west of Scotland. Captured in his teens by the radical, puckish enthusiasm of Jo Grimond, Campbell was an independent-minded Liberal. He served as the president of the Glasgow University Liberal Club, and, in the same year that he competed in the Olympics, was president of the union.

After graduation Campbell pursued the law with the same determination that he had shown on the track. He was called to the Scottish Bar in 1968, with ambitions to become a Scottish Supreme Court judge.

Encouraged by David Steel, Campbell also became an active member of the Scottish Liberals. He stood in Greenock and Port Glasgow in both general elections in 1974 and chaired the Scottish Liberal Party in 1975. He fought East Fife for the Liberals in 1979 and North East Fife, in 1983. He considered himself, however, a lawyer first and a politician second, becoming a Queen's Counsel in 1982. In 1987, he stood again for North East Fife but only after striking a deal with Steel that if successful he could continue his legal practice while an MP. At the age of forty-six, he was elected to Parliament with a majority of 1,447.

Under Steel and Ashdown, Campbell was given briefs that played to his professional strengths while allowing time for his legal pursuits: spokesperson for arts, broadcasting and sport, and shadowing the Lord Advocate and solicitor general

---

468   Campbell, op. cit., p. 18.

for Scotland. After the 1992 election, however, he requested and was given the defence brief, keen to avoid being pigeon-holed as a Scot, a lawyer or an athlete.

He was to become an established part of Paddy Ashdown's inner circle, seeing Ashdown's 'project' to foster close relations with Labour as an extension of his Liberal hero Jo Grimond's aim of a realignment of the progressive left. Enthused by the possibilities this could bring, including a possible Cabinet seat, and on the advice of his political mentor Roy Jenkins, Campbell turned down the offer of a judgeship in 1996 to concentrate on politics.

He was considered by many as a contender to succeed Ashdown, but did not stand for leader in 1999. He saw no possibility of gaining enough support to challenge Charles Kennedy successfully, and consequently threw his weight behind the front-runner. With a younger man from a different political generation now at the helm, Campbell's own ambitions to lead the Liberal Democrats seemed at an end. He stood unsuccessfully for Speaker of the House in 2000, and considered retiring from politics to pursue his legal ambitions.

The next parliament, however, rejuvenated Campbell's political career. As Liberal Democrat shadow Foreign Secretary, he played a major role in setting the party's direction after the terrorist attacks of 11 September 2001. Campbell's ardent defence of international law provided the intellectual underpinning for the Liberal Democrat opposition to UK involvement in toppling Saddam Hussein. Despite undergoing treatment for cancer at the time, Campbell became a regular face in the media, arguing with all the force of his legal training that the case for war had not been made. In February 2003, he was elected Liberal Democrat deputy leader by his fellow MPs. The role gave him first-hand experience of Kennedy's personal difficulties, as he was asked on more than one occasion to stand in at short notice when Kennedy was incapacitated.

Campbell was not a central part of the circle of MPs who ultimately pushed Kennedy out, but he understood that he was their choice to take over. Having seen the enormous pressure and impact of leadership on the three previous incumbents, Campbell no longer craved the burden, but with the relative immaturity of some other potential candidates, and the difficult task ahead of reuniting the parliamentary party, Campbell considered himself best placed to lead in the circumstances. It was duty more than residual ambition that ultimately led him to stand, and he declared on the same day Kennedy resigned.

Many of the advantages which had propelled the Liberal Democrats to their best ever showing in the general election of 2005 had dissipated. Increasingly seen by the media as ideologically incoherent and directionless, and with the salience of Iraq as a political issue rapidly diminishing, by January 2006 the party's poll rating had fallen to an average of 16 per cent.[469] With a resurgent Conservative Party under David Cameron pitching for Liberal Democrat voters, and with the prospect of the Labour government renewing itself in power as Tony Blair's premiership came to an end, whoever took over from Kennedy faced a squeeze from both left and the right.

Campbell's leadership pitch was to be 'captain and coach' and 'a bridge to the future'[470] – a safe pair of hands to steady the ship and shore up support. From the off, this laid Campbell open to being seen as a caretaker leader in the mould of the Conservative Michael Howard – taking over the party after a leadership resignation, steering it through the rough patch and fighting a quick election before handing over. Although a Howard-style coronation was not on the cards, the wide support Campbell received from the parliamentary party suggests that his pitch had been tacitly agreed. He was elected leader on 2 March 2006 by a comfortable margin, beating Simon Hughes and Chris Huhne by winning 45 per cent of the vote in the first round and 58 per cent in the final round.

Campbell's immediate challenge was to stabilise the party after disruption of the previous six months and to provide a sense of direction and momentum. He was determined that there should be no return to the bunker mentality of the leader's office under Kennedy – nor his laid-back approach to policymaking. He promoted some of the new generation of MPs to spokespeople positions, embraced the party organisation, professionalising meeting structures and chairing meetings effectively. He set in train a streamlining of the policymaking process to make it more responsive to external events. He moved to hold party HQ – in

469   Author's research based on monthly averages of UK Polling Report 2005–10 archive.

470   Leadership campaign launch speech, 19 January 2006.

particular, the fundraising operation – more closely to account after it emerged that a high-profile donor, Michael Brown, had acted fraudulently. Overall, he sought to impose a sense of purpose – getting the house in order for a possible snap election after Blair stood down.

After the 2005 election the party had begun a thorough policy review. Kennedy had signalled that he expected it to tackle some of the positions that had been considered to have held the party back, such as the commitment to raise the top tax rate, but had given little direction beyond that. Campbell, no expert outside the areas of foreign affairs and defence, was a pragmatist, not an ideologue. He did not dictate policy solutions, but empowered those driving the process to construct an agenda that was overtly of the liberal centre-left, promoting social opportunity, protecting civil liberties, adopting the green agenda and, crucially, finding methods of redistribution that were not perceived as hostile to aspiration.

He threw the weight of the leadership firmly behind the conclusions. At the 2006 autumn conference, the commitment to a higher top rate of tax was dropped in favour of a new package that was in fact more redistributive. In the spring 2007 conference, he took the unusual step, for a leader, of intervening in a debate over the UK's nuclear deterrent, successfully seeing off a proposal for the immediate scrapping of the Trident nuclear missile system. In his conferences as leader, Campbell never lost a vote or had a policy foisted on him where the leadership had expressed a preference.

By mid-2007, Campbell had largely fulfilled the terms of his leadership pitch. He had recovered the Liberal Democrat position to a point of competitiveness. Poll ratings had stabilised at an average of 18 per cent under his leadership, a respectable level at mid-term in the parliament.[471] The party organisation was in good shape to fight an election, with finance, a campaign plan and key personnel all in place and ready.

The election manifesto was approved immediately after the September conference. Entitled *Choose a Fairer and Greener Britain*, it represented significant progress from the 2005 platform, including the new tax policy package,

---

471 Author's research based on monthly averages of UK Polling Report 2005–10 archive.

a commitment to a zero-carbon Britain by 2050, a pupil premium to help children from disadvantaged backgrounds, and a new maternity income guarantee for first-time parents, alongside familiar policy positions such as local income tax and scrapping tuition fees.

With his confidence boosted by an ICM poll that showed Liberal Democrat support at 20 per cent, Campbell's speech at the 2007 autumn conference was his best: a coherent annunciation of the new policy platform and an impassioned argument for the defence of civil liberties and opportunity.[472] He left the conference in no doubt about how he had positioned the party against David Cameron's 'broken society' Conservatism and Gordon Brown's 'clunking fist' Labour Party. 'I'm a politician in the centre-left, I joined a centre-left party, I'm leading a centre-left party, I make no secret of that,' he told Michael White of *The Guardian*. 'I think the real divide is between not so much left and right but from liberal and authoritarian. And we are the anti-authoritarian party.'[473]

By this point, however, Campbell was no longer the master of his own fate. In the words of BBC political correspondent Nick Robinson: 'There was no plot this week to unseat Sir Menzies Campbell, but there were mutterings. This speech should stop them – for now.'[474] So why was Campbell's leadership in trouble?

While he had indeed proved an effective 'chairman' and 'bridge to the future', he had struggled to build a charismatic image outside the party – a key part of the role of 'captain'. Campbell saw politics as a civilised competition of ideas, in which the best contestants were sincere and honest, not to be despised but admired for their strength of argument or position. Although Campbell could play rough on his home patch, given the choice he would play the ball, never the person. Indeed, in the Commons, he would go out of his way to find opportunities to apologise publically to those whom he felt he slighted unfairly. As foreign affairs spokesman, he had cultivated the persona of an objective commentator.

472   http://www.britishpoliticalspeech.org/speech-archive.htm?speech=65

473   http://www.theguardian.com/politics/2007/sep/20/uk.libdem2007

474   http://conservativehome.blogs.com/torydiary/2007/09/blog-reactions-.html

This suited his respect for intellectual argument but ill-served him as leader. His natural tendency towards caution and reflection could give the impression of flat-footedness, and he initially struggled at Prime Minister's questions. 'It's theatre, not debate. I'm uncomfortable with that type of politics and it showed,' he later reflected.[475]

Campbell political career had been built around too narrow a front to step into the glaring sunlight as a new party leader. While he was able to take a brief and emote on principles, he was relatively unfamiliar with the complexities of education, health, and local government. As a Scottish MP, he often had no reserves to fall back on where the Scottish experience was markedly different from that of other parts of the UK. He could not instinctively recognise where the Liberal Democrats could occupy unique political space on domestic issues, as he had always been able to do on international ones.

Campbell governed in prose, but could not find the poetry to campaign in the rough-and-tumble world of political leadership. As Andrew Rawnsley put it:

> Sir Menzies, elected on the basis that a steady pair of hands was the best replacement for a shaky pair of hands, has struggled to make an impact with the public ... In the top job, he has seemed ill at ease and unsure of himself ... he has been wounded by polls suggesting that voters still preferred Kennedy drunk to Campbell sober ... He likes to think of himself as a statesman. He needs to remember that a leader also has to be a salesman.[476]

He worked hard at his communications style and was getting much better by the end of his leadership, but by then it was too late. In the media, he was lampooned cruelly for his age. The political press lobby jumped on every small reverse, weak poll rating or loose comments from Liberal Democrat MPs or Lords. From the off, he faced systematic negative briefing from within the party. Some who had supported Chris Huhne's leadership bid saw an interest in ensuring

---

475   Campbell, op. cit., p. 258.

476   Andrew Rawnsley, 'Burst out of the pinstripes and show us some passion', *The Observer*, 17 September 2006.

that Campbell's leadership did not progress beyond that of a caretaker. He was forced into defending his leadership time and again, making it more difficult to concentrate on promoting Liberal Democrat policy and values outside the party.

His leadership also suffered from the limited ambitions he had set. Since the problems were short term, his plan was short term; there was no overarching project beyond that. During the leadership campaign, David Laws MP had written a '200 days' paper of suggested initiatives, but this was filleted by the party's communications function into a dry strategy that focused on process rather than headline-grabbing announcements. His team of advisors were not deft enough to provide a platform for him that he could naturally embody and build into a coherent political narrative.

In the local elections in May 2007, the Liberal Democrats lost 246 councillors, bringing to an end several years of steady gains. The UK-wide vote share of 26 per cent was solid, but Campbell and his team had failed to manage media expectations, and the result looked bad. In Scotland, a major advance by the SNP brought the Labour–Liberal Democrat coalition to an end, adding to a growing impression that the party was losing ground.

To compound Campbell's difficulties, Gordon Brown's elevation to Prime Minister in June gave Labour a boost in the polls, up by 10 per cent, with the Liberal Democrats falling to an average of 15 per cent, or even lower in some polls.[477] By the end of July Campbell was faced with a delegation of senior peers, including three former party presidents, who urged him to consider his position. Though there was no overt plotting among MPs, the question of his leadership was on their lips.

In the end it was Brown's decision to rule out an early election that finished Campbell's leadership. The parliament would now probably run the full five years to May 2010, at which point Campbell would have been sixty-nine. He judged that he would not be able to 'trade his way' out of the position he faced, converting a caretaker stint into a longer-term haul; questions about his leadership would be a constant distraction. He had fulfilled his role, steadying the

---

477   Author's research based on monthly averages of UK Polling Report 2005–10 archive.

party after Kennedy's fall. On 15 October 2007, gracefully, and on his own terms, Menzies Campbell exited the stage.

At the general election of May 2015, after serving twenty-eight years as MP for North East Fife, Menzies Campbell retired from the House of Commons. In Parliament he will be remembered as a courteous but forensic debater, who readily made friends across party divides but gave no quarter in political argument. Most of all he will be remembered for his principled defence of international law in opposing war in Iraq in 2003. Campbell was fighting cancer at the time; if there was ever a case of putting country before self, this must count.

For Liberal Democrats, Campbell commands respect and admiration. In his early years in Parliament, his professionalism and credibility helped the Liberals overcome their amateur beard-and-sandals image. As leader, he provided much-needed stability at a crucial point after the toppling of Kennedy, and, with impeccable judgement and timing, did not overstay his welcome.

For Campbell himself, his experience as leader will have been bitter-sweet. He can point to considerable success in his management of the party and election preparations, but the mauling he received at times from the hands of the press, even for a seasoned veteran, must have been difficult for such a proud man. For a former Olympic athlete, the ambition to succeed and reach to top of his profession must have played some part in his decision to stand as leader. But just as it was his sense of duty to the party that led him to Parliament in the first place, so it was with a sense of duty that he assumed the leadership. That duty, surely, was fulfilled.

CHAPTER 27

NICK CLEGG

CHRIS BOWERS

Nick Clegg was the leader who took the Liberal tradition into government for the first time since the Second World War and the first peacetime government since the '30s. Yet he also led it to its most disastrous election result since 1970, and, in relative terms, worst ever. The team of fifty-seven Liberal Democrat MPs that held the balance of power after the 2010 election had been assembled by previous leaders, notably Ashdown and Kennedy (and the massive tactical influence of the party's chief executive Chris Rennard). Clegg profited from the hung parliament that resulted from Britain falling out of love with New Labour under Gordon Brown and failing fully to trust David Cameron's Conservatives. It is still too soon to assess Clegg's legacy in a historical context, but a provisional assessment has him as a decent and resilient man who inspired great warmth among those close to him, but whose belief in doing the right thing blinded him at times to the political fallout.

- Nicholas Peter William Clegg (b. 7 January 1967), born in Chalfont St Giles, the third of four children, to an English father and a Dutch mother.
- Educated Westminster School, Robinson College, Cambridge, plus postgraduate degrees in Minnesota and Bruges.
- Married Miriam González Durántez 2000, three sons.
- External trade official, European Commission 1994–96, member of *cabinet* of trade commissioner Leon Brittan 1996–99, MEP East Midlands 1999–2004, MP Sheffield Hallam 2005, incumbent. Liberal Democrat home affairs spokesperson 2006–07, leader of the Liberal Democrats 2007–15, Deputy Prime Minister 2010–15.

C legg knew no hint of poverty as a child. Even as the British economy nosedived in the '70s, there was never a suggestion that he and his three siblings would not go to private schools or continue to live in the affluent Home Counties. Such a small-c conservative background, and the family's familiarity with plenty of capital-c Conservatives, has led some observers to wonder whether Clegg was a closet Conservative.

While he may have grown up amid material prosperity, his broader environment was characterised by the emotional scars of displacement and suffering among his parents and grandparents. Only one of his four grandparents was British at birth – his paternal grandmother was a Russian émigré who lost everything as a child in the 1917 revolution, and his mother and maternal grandmother nearly starved to death in a Japanese prisoner-of-war camp in the Dutch East Indies. His elder two siblings initially spoke Dutch as their first language, and the family made numerous trips to mainland Europe. Much of this made him a liberal, and his guiding political lights were human rights, civil liberties, equality of opportunity and internationalism. He did not believe that the state should be any bigger than it needed to be, and, in a survey of the sixty-two Liberal Democrat MPs elected in 2005, he is believed to have been the only one not to list the environment as one of his three core topics.

Clegg's internationalism was further augmented by his natural affinity for foreign languages – he spoke Dutch and English at home, learned French and German, and perfected his Spanish after marrying Miriam González Durántez, the daughter of a Spanish senator.

The student Clegg was genuinely interested in the world but had no truck with organised politics, and never even dabbled in student politics. He was interested in political themes and had a sense of his own principles, but seems genuinely not to have consciously considered a political career until Leon Brittan suggested it to him. A former Conservative Home Secretary, Brittan was by the mid-'90s the EU trade commissioner. Given Clegg's patchy CV, Brittan took something of a gamble by appointing him, at the age of twenty-seven, to his personal *cabinet*; but Clegg justified his appointment and by all accounts cut an impressive figure, participating in various missions aimed at integrating Asian countries into the global trade framework, including some slightly dangerous trips to the southern states of the newly disintegrated USSR ('all the -stans', as Brittan describes them).

Brittan assumed that Clegg would be a Conservative, but Clegg was seriously opposed to the Tories' stance on Europe, and had been disillusioned with Margaret Thatcher. According to Brittan, Clegg 'didn't like Labour at all, and didn't like the Conservatives enough',[478] so all that was left was the Liberal Democrats – though this appeared such a poor option that Clegg remembers Brittan saying, 'Oh, for heaven's sake, joining the Liberal Democrats is like joining an NGO!'[479] However, Brittan enjoyed good relations with Paddy Ashdown, a staunch European, and in late May 1997 recommended Clegg to Ashdown as 'the brightest young man I've ever come across'.[480]

Such was Clegg's introduction to politics, and he rapidly started developing a series of key political relationships. Ashdown was one, and he was shortly to meet Chris Huhne, with whom he was bracketed for several years as the standard-bearers of the Liberal Democrats' future; but perhaps the most important was Danny Alexander, a young Scotsman as passionate about the EU and the single currency as Clegg was. Clegg and Alexander saw immense potential for the Liberal Democrats, if only the party could get its act together. As Alexander said:

> We have a shared outlook about the party, and about liberalism. As a party we felt we had a huge opportunity, because liberalism is the basic philosophy of an awful lot of people in this country, but the party has never quite managed to capitalise on that. We both felt there were possibilities in front of us, including getting into government, but we needed to be very disciplined and organised in order to take them.[481]

---

478   Chris Bowers, *Nick Clegg: The Biography*, London, Biteback Publishing, 2012, p. 84.
479   Ibid.
480   Ibid., p. 85.
481   Ibid., p. 90.

Given the dramatic nature of Clegg's fall in 2015, what happened in this period (1997–99) is important. To make the Liberal Democrats a potential party of government, Clegg and Alexander aimed to professionalise the party and make its economic policy more grounded. Although it took a while for the stresses to become visible, this approach was at odds with the slightly chaotic culture of the party. The Liberal Democrats may have grown under the ebullient Ashdown, but this was partly due to it seeming an endearingly rustic and ramshackle protest party. The new boys' professionalisation plans wouldn't be to everyone's taste.

In addition, Clegg was politically very inexperienced. He was eminently electable, but there are many who look at his phenomenal run of electoral successes as a drawback, because so much is learned in defeat that can never be learned in victory. Having become Deputy Prime Minister without ever losing an election, he was perhaps unprepared for the slings and arrows that come with being in government.

Having agreed to throw himself into the 1999 European elections, he made a beeline for the East Midlands, an unprepossessing area in Liberal Democrat electoral terms. He finished top of the regional list, which in the UK's first European election to be conducted under proportional representation was enough to get him elected. The biggest achievement of his five years as an MEP was in shepherding through a piece of legislation on 'unbundling the local loop' – in effect opening up the final stage of telephone networks to competition, thereby allowing a choice of landline providers.

But Clegg found the work of an MEP unsatisfying in its failure to give him meaningful contact with those he represented, and it became clear after a couple of years that his future lay at Westminster. He was known to the movers and shakers at party HQ as a rising star, so was alerted when a vacancy in a winnable seat came up. When Richard Allan, who had wrested Sheffield Hallam from the Conservatives in 1997, announced in 2003 that he was standing down, Clegg applied to be his successor and was selected in a four-way contest that included the future MP Jo Swinson. He was elected in 2005.

Throughout the eight years between throwing his hat in with the Liberal Democrats and becoming an MP, Clegg had impressed with his charm and down-to-earthness. Many saw him as a potential leader, most people who met him were genuinely impressed with him, and he seemed to encapsulate what politics had been missing. But he was not scared to reject plaudits from directions he considered unwelcome. At a conference in 2002, Allan recalls Clegg being greeted by an enthusiastic supporter who said the Liberal Democrats were 'a true left-wing alternative to Labour', to which Clegg replied: 'Look, if that's what you think the party is, you're wrong. You can join this party, but you need to understand that we're not the left-wing socialist alternative to Labour, we're a liberal and democratic party.'[482] In 2004 he was among the authors of *The Orange Book: Reclaiming Liberalism*, the publication that scandalised the party's social liberal wing as it seemed to be taking the party to the right. (Clegg wrote the – largely uncontroversial – chapter on Europe.)

Clegg was one of sixty-two MPs elected in 2005, the party's best result since 1923, and was appointed Europe spokesperson by Charles Kennedy. But he still had the temerity to suggest in an internal meeting shortly after the election that the party's manifesto had been 'technocratic mush'. He had been alarmed at its lack of an effective message and its long list of spending pledges. Although not a front-line architect of Kennedy's downfall eight months later, Clegg was active behind the scenes in pushing for an end to the constant fear that Kennedy's alcoholism would soon embarrass the party.

Clegg decided it was too early for him to stand for the leadership, but was arguably outflanked by the more politically astute Chris Huhne, who had given him the impression that he would not stand – but then put himself forward as the candidate of the new generation. Huhne failed to beat Menzies Campbell, but the team he assembled gave him a massive advantage in the leadership election twenty-one months later when Campbell resigned. Campbell saw Clegg as his natural successor, and appointed him home affairs spokesperson. It was a role in which Clegg was able to shine, although he spent much of the ensuing nineteen months on the local party dinner circuit, preparing for a leadership election that everyone knew would come.

---

482   Ibid., p. 129.

Campbell's resignation on 15 October 2007 triggered the leadership election that many in the party had been talking about for several years: Clegg versus Huhne. It was an ill-tempered campaign, with the two candidates clashing on the BBC's *Politics Show* over a leaked dossier from the Huhne camp entitled 'Calamity Clegg', purporting to detail Clegg's changes of mind on various issues. Clegg kept his dignity and scraped home by the narrowest of margins – just 511 votes out of 41,465, winning 50.6 per cent of the total – but on a lacklustre and disorganised campaign that even his greatest admirers felt was poor.

Clegg's first couple of years as leader were remarkably low-profile. Such was the impact that Vince Cable had made in his two months as acting leader after Campbell's resignation that Cable had the higher profile. That gave Clegg the chance to stay largely under the radar as he settled into the job, which proved useful when he was less than discreet about the party's pensions expert Steve Webb while chatting to Danny Alexander on a plane, and when he got the politics of a vote on the Lisbon Treaty all wrong and ended up splitting the parliamentary party three ways. But he did have some notable successes. He broke with parliamentary tradition by becoming the first party leader to call on the Speaker of the House of Commons, Michael Martin, to resign (over his weak response to the revelations of MPs' abuse of their expenses), and he teamed up with the actor Joanna Lumley in successfully campaigning for Gurkha soldiers to earn the right to live in Britain.

Clegg took over the leadership as the British – and global – economy was going through massive convulsions; Gordon Brown had had to bail out several British banks with large-scale public spending. It was clear that there would be much less money in the state kitty when the parties drew up their manifestos for the next general election. This plunged the Liberal Democrats into a round of soul-searching, in which a compromise between Liberalism and financial reality led to one of the biggest disasters of their period in government.

The onset of the economic recession threw into doubt the affordability of the party's opposition to university tuition fees. Introduced by the Labour government in 1998 and increased in 2004 (despite a 2001 election promise not to), by 2008 fees stood at £3,000 a year. Clegg, and others, believed the party's wish to offer free tuition was desirable but unaffordable. Their arguments put them on a collision course with those who believed that free education was a core principle of equality of opportunity that should not be negotiated away, whatever the economic reality, and also those who pointed to the success of the policy in helping to win a string of university seats in 2005.

A compromise policy was worked out for the 2010 manifesto that proposed phasing out tuition fees for first degrees over six years. Clegg accepted the compromise, but it took on a life of its own when he signed a pledge drawn up by the National Union of Students committing him (and in reality all Liberal Democrat candidates) 'to vote against any increase in fees'. He had no regrets about signing it because it was consistent with the manifesto, but the pledge created a rod for his own back, which was to come back to beat him in the first months of the 2010–15 coalition.

When Clegg appeared on the UK's first ever televised leaders' debate on 15 April 2010, few people knew him. Yet he seemed to encapsulate what many had been seeking. He spoke directly to the camera, he used the names of those asking questions, he looked relaxed with his jacket open and his hand in his pocket, and he talked about 'a new politics'. One comment on his opponents was particularly effective: 'The more they attack each other, the more they sound the same.' After two years of economic fumbling to manage the recession, peppered with a massive scandal about MPs' expenses, the fresh-faced, straight-talking Clegg seemed exactly what the British electorate was looking for.

The aftermath of the ninety-minute debate was one of the most extraordinary episodes in the history of Liberalism. In the period of 'Cleggmania', T-shirts appeared with 'I agree with Nick' emblazoned on them (after Brown used the phrase rather too often during the debate), and the Liberal Democrats' opinion poll ratings climbed into the low thirties. Yet it was too good to last; on election day the party polled 23 per cent, just one point higher than in 2005, and the number of seats fell from sixty-two to fifty-seven.

It was a dejected Clegg who arrived at party HQ the morning after polling day, and yet the Liberal Democrats held the balance of power. The party could not form a majority government with Labour, but it could come very close, and it could form a majority government with the Conservatives. Despondency over the result, particularly after the hopes raised by Cleggmania, soon gave way to the excitement of opportunity. The Liberal Democrats really did have influence.

The decisions Clegg and the party took in those heady days of May 2010 will continue to be pored over in the aftermath of the Liberal Democrats' cataclysmic election showing of 2015. There were many reasons why the Lib Dems ended up with the Conservatives, not least the parliamentary arithmetic, plus the far greater readiness and commitment of the Conservative negotiating team compared to the Labour team. But the fact that Clegg was thought to be more comfortable with the Tories added to the sense that he had made his party an easier fit with the Conservatives than it would have been in 2005, with its spending pledges that pitched it in many respects to the left of Labour.

Clegg was very much a behind-the-scenes general. The negotiations were carried out by a team of four, headed by his closest ally Danny Alexander, with David Laws, Chris Huhne and the local council specialist Andrew Stunell. Clegg was always on the end of a telephone and met both Cameron and Brown at various stages, but the coalition agreement was negotiated by his lieutenants. On the Tuesday morning after polling day, the Conservatives offered the missing piece in the coalition puzzle, a referendum on electoral reform, and by the end of the day Britain's first post-war coalition government had been announced.

The next day Clegg and Cameron appeared side by side in the Downing Street Rose Garden, smiling and joking. It proved an image the Liberal Democrats spent the next five years regretting, but at the time it seemed vital as a show of unity. A week earlier, the Greek debt crisis had spooked the European markets, and with the British election ending inconclusively, both partners felt they needed to offer a public gesture that the coalition would last.

The show of unity worked for the markets, but it created an image that did not help the Liberal Democrats. A feature of the coalition was that the old custom of collegiality in government remained, and Clegg insisted the Liberal Democrats had to 'own everything'. So even when Liberal Democrat MPs voted for policies they had campaigned against, they had to stand four-square behind the government instead of saying they were solely respecting the coalition agreement. The image of the Rose Garden meant that it was easy for people to believe the party was too comfortable with the Tories, which angered those who had voted Liberal Democrat to keep the Tories out.

'Do you think the party membership will wear a coalition with the Conservatives?' Clegg is said to have asked his senior colleagues, showing that, for all his own ease with the Conservatives, he still had sufficient sense of his own party to wonder if a special party conference would approve working with the enemy. It did, overwhelmingly. Ultimately, even those on the left of the party felt he had no choice. As Paddy Ashdown colourfully put it, 'We had three choices: we could be shot in the morning if we went in with Labour, we could be shot in the autumn if we let the Tories govern on a minority basis, or we *might* be shot in four or five years if we went into coalition with the Conservatives. So it was the only thing to do.'[483]

The fact that Clegg and his party were shot five years later confirms the reservations of another former leader, Charles Kennedy. He was one of just seven of the fifty-seven Liberal Democrat MPs who abstained when asked to approve the coalition. A few months later he explained:

> The coalition agreement is excellent. You're never going to get everything you want, but as deals go, that was fine. My concern is more historic, that every time the Liberal tradition has hooked up with the Conservative tradition, funnily enough the long-term gainers tend to be the Conservatives, and that remains my strategic anxiety.[484]

Kennedy was one of the casualties, his perception failing to save him from losing his seat in 2015.

History is likely to judge the five years of coalition – and the role the Liberal Democrats played in it – more favourably than the electoral outcome of 2015. For a party that had no experience of government, the Liberal Democrats offered discipline, quality ministers and an influence on government that went beyond their 20

---

483   Ibid., pp. 237–38.
484   Ibid., p. 239.

per cent of coalition MPs, indeed beyond the 23 per cent of the popular vote they had gained in 2010, compared with the Conservatives' 36 per cent. The flagship £10,000 income tax threshold was reached ahead of schedule, the pupil premium and index-linking of state pensions were achieved on time, the world's first Green Investment Bank was established and support for renewable energy maintained, and the party stopped several right-wing policies, from the renewal of the Trident nuclear weapons system to a law allowing employers to fire employees at will.

Yet the public perception of the Liberal Democrats as a party of government never overcame a disastrous first 100 days. During the coalition negotiations, civil servants and Bank of England officials had convinced Liberal Democrat negotiators that the Greek debt crisis had strengthened the need for immediate financial tightening, so Liberal Democrat ministers agreed a rise in the rate of VAT from 17.5 per cent to 20 per cent, despite having campaigned against the Conservatives' 'VAT bombshell', and they approved £6 billion of initial spending cuts which they had also vociferously opposed. Two dossiers, in particular, were to cause massive political difficulties: NHS reform and higher education funding.

Unlike many mainland European coalitions, Clegg chose breadth over depth, opting for a Liberal Democrat minister in most departments rather than taking over a couple of ministries and making them Liberal Democrat strongholds. He himself opted not to take on a ministry but to carve out the Deputy Prime Minister's role as a filter through which all initiatives had to pass. This gave him massive influence behind the scenes, where he and Danny Alexander negotiated as equals with Cameron and George Osborne in 'the quad'. But the public saw little of this influence, which may have cost the party dear. His calculation, that the public wanted a new politics and would respond to a senior figure just getting on with the role of government without a media fanfare, assumed that the public would recognise what it had wanted and respond positively to it. This was a flawed assumption; and the Liberal Democrats' popularity was eroded, in particular, by a trio of troublesome major issues.

To what extent the Liberal Democrats were sold the weapon of their downfall by the Conservatives is open to debate. Some believe Cameron's decision to offer Cable the Business, Innovation and Skills department was very smart, as it forced a Liberal Democrat minister to reform higher education funding after the party had campaigned for abolishing tuition fees. When the Browne Report on higher education funding came out in October 2010 it recommended there should be no cap on university fees. As both Labour and the Conservatives had committed to implementing Browne's recommendations, it left the Liberal Democrats in a precarious position.

The coalition agreement had given the Liberal Democrats the option of abstaining on the tuition fees vote because of the NUS pledge, an odd concession for a party whose minister was proposing the legislation. Even though abstaining would not have avoided breaking the pledge (it had called for signatories to vote against an increase in fees), at one stage it was hoped that all Liberal Democrat MPs would abstain. But a handful of MPs were determined to vote against the proposals, which meant if Clegg and his ministers had abstained, the legislation would have been defeated and the Liberal Democrats would have broken the coalition agreement. Clegg was determined for this not to happen so early in the government, so used his influence to broker a much better deal for students than Browne had advocated. Yet the fact that he ended up voting for a package of legislation that included a rise in tuition fees went against his highly publicised pledge, which created an issue of trust with the electorate. As a charging model, the new higher education funding package had some successes, notably in enhancing access to university for youngsters from low-income families, but in political terms it failed spectacularly.

Even after the enormity of the political damage became clear, Clegg was adamant that he had not been wrong to sign the NUS pledge. He believed its wording was consistent with the manifesto, so it would have been disingenuous not to sign it. He also believed – perhaps because of his family and European background – that the British people would understand the difference between policies campaigned for before an election and the post-election compromises required in coalition. But since the Liberal Democrats had campaigned for a new politics, in part under the slogan 'no more broken promises', the media and NUS majored on the change in direction, widely labelling it a 'U-turn', and the public ended up seeing it as a betrayal of their hope of a better politics rather than as a necessary compromise of coalition. And that proved catastrophic for the Liberal Democrats. The party had already fallen in the opinion polls to below 20 per cent immediately after the coalition was announced; after the tuition fees legislation was voted through, it sank a further 7 per cent. Clegg eventually, in 2012, apologised for having made a promise he could not then deliver, yet this did no good, and the issue was still being raised on the doorsteps in the 2015 election, despite the new system's advantages.

The tuition fees issue is largely blamed for the resounding defeat of the referendum on the alternative vote in May 2011. Private polling for Clegg in summer 2010 suggested that the public might well vote yes, but by the spring of 2011 it was clear that the referendum was being used more as a stick with which to beat the Liberal Democrats. The campaign was particularly vicious, with the 'No' side bringing out literature that depicted Clegg as doing shady deals if AV were approved; the fact that such literature was funded by Conservative donors (whose party Clegg's 'shady deal' in 2010 had put into government) angered Clegg intensely. AV was defeated by 68 per cent to 32 per cent.

There was one spin-off from the AV referendum, however, that came back to bite the Conservatives. The Tories had agreed to the referendum in return for a redrawing of the constituency boundaries, which tended to favour Labour over the Tories. With electoral reform lost, Clegg was apparently at the mercy of his coalition partners, but they voted against the coalition commitment to reform the House of Lords, which allowed him to jettison the boundary review, which at the time looked like saving the Liberal Democrats from losing an estimated ten to twenty seats. Behind the scenes, Clegg made no secret of the fact that Cameron's tactics on the AV referendum had hardened his resolve.

Andrew Lansley's reforms of the NHS were a further blow, costing the Liberal Democrats public support and members – but were not as damaging as tuition fees. Despite the coalition agreement specifying a stop to 'top-down reorganisations' of the NHS, a document proposing just that appeared on the Cabinet table barely six weeks into the coalition. The Liberal Democrats were clearly ambushed by it, and as it arrived in the early months – a period Clegg had designated as the time to show that coalition worked – they tried to run with it. By the time they realised the enormity, much of it had already taken place, with senior NHS personnel moving jobs in anticipation of the reforms. Despite this, the widespread opposition to the reforms – fuelled partly by Liberal Democrat rebels – led to a pause in the legislative process, which in turn led to several significant changes to the original legislation. Yet little of this was picked up by the public, and with the Labour Party and the pressure group 38 Degrees campaigning against the 'privatisation' and 'marketisation' of the NHS in 2015, the Liberal Democrats were tarred with the coalition's brush, further eroding their credibility among left-of-centre voters.

Throughout the first two years of the coalition, Clegg showed considerable resilience. Effigies of him were burnt at hysterical public demonstrations, dog excrement was put through the door of his constituency office, and protesters outside a building where he was speaking chanted 'Nick Clegg must die'. After four successive years of dreadful results in local, Scottish, Welsh and European elections, in 2014 he seriously considered resigning as leader, but colleagues talked him out of it, arguing that he had to stay in post and fight to defend the cause of Liberalism at the general election.[485] His staff say that he showed a remarkable ability to be cheerful amid these stresses and venomous personal attacks, and Liberal Democrat strategists calculated that such resilience would morph into a grudging respect by the 2015 election.

But there were no signs of it. As the Liberal Democrats' poll ratings failed to shift from either side of 10 per cent, Clegg tried to become more visible. In 2013 he agreed to a weekly half hour on the London independent radio station LBC in which he took questions from listeners. It seemed to put a spring in his step, and his party conference speech in September 2014 had more passion than some of his more colourless speeches of the previous three years. He pitched the Liberal Democrats as the party that could 'anchor the government in the centre ground', and as the election approached, he rammed home his split-the-difference message that the Liberal Democrats would borrow less than Labour and cut less than the Tories. It was a natural progression from the 'stronger economy, fairer society' mantra that characterised the Clegg era, pushing the notion that the Conservatives had no heart and Labour no brain. It was calculated to keep open the options of

---

485   Patrick Wintour and Nicholas Watt, 'Nick Clegg offered to resign as Lib Dem leader a year before 2015 election', *The Guardian*, 24 June 2015.

a post-2015 coalition with either Labour or the Tories; yet, critics said, it was the victory of focus groups over conviction, and of caution over risk, as there was little in it that could inspire an image of what Liberalism actually meant.

In the 2015 election campaign, Clegg performed reasonably well in the potentially chaotic seven-leader televised debate, and with David Dimbleby and a BBC audience a week before polling day. But whether he lacked the spark of 2010 or whether the public were simply less disposed to hear his message, he could not make the impact in the polls he had done five years earlier. Although arguing that the Liberal Democrats were 'the great Houdini of British politics',[486] on election night the party's fifty-seven seats became just eight. A pale and drawn Clegg hinted that he was on the point of quitting when he made his winner's speech after scraping home in Sheffield Hallam (thanks to a concerted effort among Tory supporters to see him survive), and later that morning he resigned the leadership, taking 'full responsibility' for 'a cruel defeat'.

His resignation speech was for many the kind of impassioned address that might have made a difference during the campaign; it helped fuel a surge in Liberal Democrat membership in the weeks after the polls closed. It was a rallying cry against the demise of Liberalism in spite of the crushing losses. He said:

> The cruellest irony of all is that it is exactly at this time that British Liberalism – that fine, noble tradition that believes that we are stronger together and weaker apart – is more needed than ever before. Fear and grievance have won, Liberalism has lost, but it is more precious than ever, and we must keep fighting for it. That is both the great challenge and the great cause that my successor will have to face. There is no path to a fairer, greener, freer Britain without British Liberalism showing the way. This is a very dark hour for our party, but we cannot and will not let decent Liberal values be extinguished overnight. Our party will come back, our party will win again.[487]

---

486   Andrew Grice, 'I've had bumps and scrapes but I want to carry on doing it' – interview with Nick Clegg, *The Independent*, 10 April 2015.

487   'Nick Clegg resigns as leader', *Lib Dem Voice*, 8 May 2015 (http://www.libdemvoice.org/nick-clegg-resigns-as-leader-45834.html).

Clegg's demise was a bitter blow for the Liberal tradition. If he had been uned-
ifying as a person or had proved inept in government, it could have been put
down to incompetence. But just about everyone who came into contact with
him said that he was a decent and amenable man who epitomised Liberalism;
he was open about his privileged background but never spoke like a toff, he was
an internationalist with a total lack of prejudice, and even allowing for some mistakes (however 'mistakes' are defined) the Liberal Democrats proved themselves
competent in government. Machiavelli suggested that it is effectively impossible
to be a good politician and a good person: it is possible to see Clegg as too good
a man to have been a good political operator, especially with his relative lack of
political education before becoming an MEP – but this too is a blow to the Liberal tradition's belief that 'goodness' can triumph through politics.

Some said he was too much of an economic liberal who took the party too
far from its social-liberal roots. He clearly wasn't everyone's cup of tea within
the party, but he had his own view of 'Liberalism as an optimistic creed', and
few ever seriously questioned that he belonged in the Liberal tent. 'I'm a liberal
interventionist,' he said. 'The Liberal view starts from the premise that there's
something wonderful about every person, there's something marvellous about
their potential and talents, and you've got to do everything you possibly can in
politics to emancipate individuals.'[488] Inevitably some say his biggest mistake
was entering into government with the Conservatives, but a Lib–Lab government
was not realistic in 2010, and the only other option was staying in opposition,
which might have been equally damaging.

Another blow was that Clegg had led the Liberal Democrats to exactly what
they had craved – an opportunity to be in government born from a hung parliament. They had seized the opportunity and done well, but there was no electoral
reward. The more sanguine Liberal Democrat strategists had always known that
the party's vote would go down if ever they went into coalition, but the calculation was that PR would save the party; losing the AV referendum meant there
was no cushion to the unpopularity that followed (under PR the party could

488 Bowers, op. cit., p. 340.

have won about fifty seats in 2015, only a few less than its fifty-seven seats in 2010 – though AV is not proportional).

Could Clegg have acted differently over tuition fees? In an interview with *The Independent* a month before polling day, he accepted: 'We could have explained the invidious choices and unpalatable decisions rather than done things at such a breathtaking pace.'[489] He was perhaps also unlucky with the media's fixation on the tuition fees pledge, relishing talk of 'U-turns', 'betrayals' and 'broken promises', conveniently overlooking the two dozen or so other pledges in circulation at the 2010 election. But if it hadn't been tuition fees, might it have been something else, like the U-turn on raising VAT? There were plenty of U-turns by both the Liberal Democrats and the Tories to allow the coalition to happen, so why did the media and public focus on that one?

Perhaps he was always doomed? The Liberals' popularity had plummeted during the Lib–Lab pact of 1977–78 despite it being successful in its aims (of steering the economy into calmer waters), and it only salvaged eleven of its fourteen seats in 1979 because David Steel took the party out of the arrangement before the election. Clegg had little option to do this, and there is no guarantee that it would have worked if he had. One of the issues raised during the leadership contest to replace Clegg was that perhaps the damage was done before 2010, through the party's failure to prepare the electorate for the compromises necessary in a coalition. This fuels the theory that Clegg may not have fully believed that the 2010 election would deliver a hung parliament and that he and the party were therefore less prepared for coalition than it seemed.

Ultimately, Clegg's default questions were: 'What's the right thing to do? What's the Liberal thing to do?' Historians may come to view many of his acts in government as good Liberal policies, if not always good Liberal politics. He had devoted energy to professionalise the party precisely to be a credible party of government, and he felt that he was doing the right thing by adding a strong Liberal seam to a government led by an increasingly right-wing Conservative Party. The fact that he gained no reward politically suggests that Liberal idealism

---

489   Grice, op. cit.

on its own is not enough, and that political nous is always required, even if it does not always sit easily with Liberalism.

Clegg may yet have bequeathed a meaningful legacy to the Liberal Democrats. He showed that coalition can work and deliver stable government, and the memory of the 2010–15 coalition could prove useful to the party at future elections. Both candidates in the election to replace him, Tim Farron and Norman Lamb, emphasised in their campaigns that the party was not wrong to go into coalition with the Conservatives in 2010. But historically, for all his successes on policy – including same-sex marriage, the Green Investment Bank, free school meals, funding for renewable energy, and much more – Nick Clegg was ultimately disastrous on the politics.

PART III

LEADERSHIP PERSPECTIVES

CHAPTER 28

DAVID STEEL ON POLITICAL LEADERSHIP AND THE LIBERAL PARTY[490]

DAVID STEEL, TOBY S. JAMES AND DUNCAN BRACK

TOBY JAMES: Why did you first set out into politics? Did you have something particular that you wanted to achieve?

DAVID STEEL: Well, I came into politics through a rather unusual route. I'd been brought up at school in Kenya for the first four years of my parents' time there; for the second four years I was sent home to a school in Edinburgh, and not being any good at sports I had to take up something, so I took up debating – and I suppose that was the start. George Watson's College in Edinburgh had quite a good track record because both the Speaker of the House of Commons, W. S. Morrison, and the Lord Chancellor and Home Secretary, David Maxwell Fyfe, were both former pupils; in fact, I invited David Maxwell Fyfe to come back and speak to us and he and Morrison were both there in the year that I was president of the Literary and Debating Society.

So with that background I went up to university. It was just at the time of the Sharpeville massacre in South Africa, and because of my background in Kenya I joined the anti-apartheid movement right away. I also joined the Liberal Club, not because I knew very much about the Liberal Party but simply because I was anti the Conservatives because of their policy in Africa, and I wasn't a socialist, so by default I joined the Liberal Club – though people join political clubs at university without any real sense of commitment. But then what happened was that I

---

490   This interview took place on Thursday 18 June 2015 in the House of Lords.

became president of the Liberal Club and spoke in Union debates and won them on Liberal policy. Jo Grimond became Rector of the university and, just listening to visiting speakers I became more and more committed to the Liberal Party; I felt it was the right one to join and be active in. At the time the party had only five or six MPs, so I wasn't expecting a political career. It was very much under the influence of Jo Grimond that I became involved. When I finished at university with a law degree I decided I really didn't want to be a lawyer and the Scottish Liberal Party offered me a job for a year as assistant secretary leading up to the election.

I always say to people that there's a word you don't read in any political science textbook which is very important in politics: it's 'luck'. I had a bit of luck because first of all Harold Macmillan retired as Prime Minister, so instead of a job for a year it became a job for two years, and in the meantime the Liberal candidate in the Borders fell out with the local party and resigned. Jo Grimond was insistent that this seat had to be fought. Remember, in those days we didn't fight every seat, but the Borders seat had always had a second place, so we couldn't possibly not fight it. But they didn't have a candidate, so I was moved from Edinburgh where I was going to be the candidate in Edinburgh Pentlands, where my main ambition was to save my deposit, to the Borders where there was at least a chance. I remember going to the adoption meeting and saying, 'Well, yes, I'll come and do it, but it'll take two elections so you've got to be willing to have me as candidate for both.' I fought the 1964 election and got the Tory majority down from nearly 10,000 to just under 2,000, which was better than we expected. I got all my pals from university to come down and deliver leaflets and canvass and so on, so we did quite well. The Tory MP was pretty much an absentee: he lived in London and visited the constituency reasonably regularly but he wasn't a local. And then, another bit of luck – though bad luck for him! – he pegged out on the operating table about a month after the election during some minor surgery. He was only sixty-three, so it was totally unexpected. There was a by-election, and of course we were well placed to win it.

So that was that. My background in the Liberal Party was to do with African policy and nothing to do with domestic policy, which is a bit unusual, but there we are.

TOBY JAMES: Having been elected as an MP, when did you develop aspirations to be leader?

DAVID STEEL: I had no aspirations to be leader. I was the baby of the House in '65. I was actually up doing a dinner for Jo Grimond in Orkney when he told me he was going to stand down as leader – that was in January '67 – and I was really very shocked. Grimond was my guru, and I just thought, 'I can't imagine the Liberal Party without him as leader'. It was a terrible blow. So then I supported Jeremy Thorpe, and he was elected leader. He had helped me a lot in the by-election campaign: he came up many times and actually drove me around on polling day. But obviously at that stage one just assumed because Jeremy was quite young that he would be leader for a long time. So your question is a little odd because I had no aspirations to be party leader; it just happened because Jeremy fell on his sword. Up to that point I would never have thought about being party leader.

TOBY JAMES: Having become leader, what did you then want to achieve and to what extent do you feel that you achieved it?

DAVID STEEL: Apart from foreign affairs I had become more and more interested in some of the domestic policies of the party. The two big ones were Scottish home rule, about which I'd spoken a lot at university, and co-ownership and co-determination in industry. I was keen to push those as leader, but I think probably the most important thing I did was to change the party's attitude toward coalition. During the Thorpe/Heath discussions in '74, I remember everybody at a meeting the MPs had in a basement room agreeing that there was no question of doing a coalition with Ted Heath; but Jo Grimond was quite worried at the tone of some of the statements round the table, and said: 'Come on, be realistic, we are a small party. If we ever hope to be in government – and we believe in electoral reform – coalition must be an inevitable route forward.' That was always my view as well, and so in my first speech as leader I made that quite a central part of the strategy that we would pursue, which was to work with others in promoting Liberalism, which could possibly include coalition.

TOBY JAMES: So it was always your aim at some point to try to get into government?

DAVID STEEL: Yes. So when the opportunity arose for the Lib–Lab pact, that was the motivation behind it.

DUNCAN BRACK: But weren't you critical of the decision to enter coalition in 2010?

DAVID STEEL: I wasn't publicly critical. I was very unhappy about it, but I didn't oppose it. Maybe I should have done, but I had the view all along that a former party leader shouldn't be trying to tell the current party leader what to do, and although I've been very critical since, at the time I just thought, you've just got to shut up and support it and get on with it. But I thought it was completely unnatural, because every single leader from Jo Grimond on – me, Paddy, Jeremy Thorpe, Charles Kennedy, Ming Campbell – had all seen ourselves as being left of centre and possibly ready to cooperate with the Labour Party in different shapes and forms; Paddy probably got closest with 'the project'. That was a consistent view that had been pursued by every party leader and then suddenly we were doing the opposite. It was a very difficult time.

TOBY JAMES: By what criteria do you think we should evaluate Liberal leaders?

DAVID STEEL: Well I think there can only be one criterion and that is: how successful were they? And by any estimate, therefore, the most successful of all the recent ones was Charles Kennedy, because he produced the goods. I think they were all successful in different ways but Charles was the one who reached the highest point.

TOBY JAMES: Successful in what way?

DAVID STEEL: Number of seats.

DUNCAN BRACK: So it's purely about the number of seats? That's the only thing that counts?

DAVID STEEL: Well, I wouldn't say it's the only thing. Obviously people were critical of Charles' leadership in other areas, but if you look outside the party, which I think is the important thing if you're looking at political leaders, you have to ask, what did the public think? And the fact is that the public reacted more positively to Charles than to any of the rest of us – and that must be a plus.

TOBY JAMES: A key theme across the three books is to look closely at the electoral record of party leaders. To what extent are leaders successful in terms of winning seats at Westminster and moving towards part of government? Is that a fair method, do you think?

DAVID STEEL: Obviously you'll also have to look at to what extent they were able to move public opinion in their direction. Last night, I was at the inaugural Edward Heath Lecture, with John Major speaking, and, you know, if you were considering Ted Heath as party leader, you would have to say that, probably, taking us into Europe was the single most important thing he did. The fact that he won or lost an election was relatively minor; that's what history will remember him by. So it's not just elections; it's also what you do.

DUNCAN BRACK: For Liberal leaders, isn't it also about just creating an image for the party? We always tend to have a rather indistinct image among the electorate, so the more you can sharpen it up, the better.

DAVID STEEL: Exactly. The strange thing is that Nick, for example, was very effective in creating an image for the party, and I would argue that he will be treated differently by history than by the electorate in terms of his activities as Deputy Prime Minister. I think he was very effective in government. Unfortunately, he was not effective in terms of party leadership. The two things were at a disjunction, really.

TOBY JAMES: Do you think that leaders feel a particular pressure to deliver in terms of results at election time? It's often said that a leader who doesn't either win an election or at least show progress has their position under threat.

DAVID STEEL: Well, I remember that the 1979 election was a very difficult one for us when I was leader; in the aftermath of the Thorpe affair our poll ratings were abysmal, we had lost lots of councillors, we were in deep trouble and the forecast was that we would only hold two seats – Orkney and Shetland and Montgomery, the rest would all be gone. I remember making a bet with Ian Mikardo, who was the House bookie! The '79 election in some ways was the most effective one that I've led because it snatched survival out of defeat. We increased the percentage vote and lost just three seats – which was different from coming back with two; we heaved a great sigh of relief! I felt very bad about the loss of John Pardoe, though; he had been effectively deputy leader (although we didn't have such a post), and he was particularly strong on economic issues, where I was very weak, so we proved to be a very good partnership. Montgomery's a funny place – I don't know quite why we lost that one.

TOBY JAMES: What were your overall electoral strategies? Were there particular seats you were looking to win, or particular segments of the population that you were trying to target?

DAVID STEEL: We really didn't have as effective a targeting strategy as we have nowadays. There were seats that we hoped to win, but there was no particular mechanism for doing that as there has been ever since. In that first election it was pretty hand-to-mouth.

DUNCAN BRACK: The party seemed to rely very much on strong local characters getting in in their seats.

DAVID STEEL: That was the criticism of the party at the time – that we had Clay Freud and Cyril Smith and people who were larger-than-life characters in their own field and therefore were not easily moulded together as a team. That was true, it was quite difficult. But if you didn't have strong characters then you tended not to win the seats.

TOBY JAMES: Did you have a view about who your core voters could be? Were they from a particular class, or gender or geographical area?

DAVID STEEL: We didn't, no. Before this last election we had endless presentations in wonderful detail on which sections of the electorate were going to support us and which seats we would target, and all the rest of it – all of which of course totally collapsed. We didn't have that in my time as leader.

DUNCAN BRACK: Not even during the Alliance years?

DAVID STEEL: Not even then. The '83 election was a 'bubbly' one, you know; we would have done very much better if it hadn't been for the Falklands War, because that wiped domestic politics off the map. Margaret Thatcher, who had been a very unpopular Prime Minister, suddenly became Britannia and Boadicea rolled into one. So we had bad luck there, but that's life, you just have to accept that things can happen; in Macmillan's famous phrase, 'events, dear boy, events', and there's not much you can do about it.

TOBY JAMES: What challenges do you think that you faced in terms of managing your own party, and how successful do you think you were in dealing with them?

DAVID STEEL: I don't think I get full marks for managing the party. One of the real problems that I had was that I had a very big constituency: there were eight towns, eight town councils and three county councils. If you turned up in one town one weekend you had not been in any of the other seven, so it was a very demanding constituency. Lovely to represent – I really enjoyed it, but it was very time-consuming. On top of that I was expected to do regional tours around the country about once a month or six weeks, at the weekend, and I had a family. On top of all that, to attend the party executive on a Saturday was just not on. I remember saying to them, 'You make the bullets and I'll fire them, but don't expect me to come to the executive or the council or the policy committee.' Now, Paddy took a very different view and – full marks to him – he got involved in the party machine, and also at some point they stopped meeting at weekends, which made a big difference because it enabled the leader and the parliamentary group to be much more involved in the party. I left the management of the party to the party chairman and the party president.

DUNCAN BRACK: Did you try to identify people who could do those roles or did you just let them be elected?

DAVID STEEL: No, the party chose them. I was very lucky, they all seemed to be good people, but I had no say in the choice of them.

DUNCAN BRACK: During the Alliance years, there was perhaps a perception that you gave priority to trying to lead the Alliance, to be an effective co-leader of the Alliance, whereas David Owen was always much more interested in just being leader of the SDP, and getting SDP positions through, come what may. Do you think that's a fair observation?

DAVID STEEL: Yes, I think that is probably true. Funnily enough, David and I had lunch together just before the election (at his invitation) and we were reminiscing about what had gone right and what had gone wrong and I think that was the way he saw himself. To be fair to him he was the one of the Gang of Four who never liked the joint approach with the Liberals from the beginning. His view was quite consistent, that the SDP should be a new party, and there might be a need for some sort of quiet agreement with the Liberals. The other three saw the need to work together, but he didn't, and he continued to think that right the way through to the end when his party conference voted against him. Our personal relations were always good, but we weren't as close as I had been with Roy Jenkins, because Roy was totally committed to the concept of the Alliance.

DUNCAN BRACK: Do you think it would have been very different if Roy Jenkins had joined the Liberal Party and brought in people like Shirley Williams and others?

DAVID STEEL: I go back to the discussion I had with him in Brussels after '79. A lot of people, including, I remember, John Pardoe, were very cross with me because, they said, 'You should have just got him to join the Liberal Party!' – but I remember very clearly what he said to me which was that he wanted to see a break-out from the existing party structure. He said: 'If it fails, I would think about joining the Liberal Party, but just as an ordinary member, I wouldn't be taking an active part.' I thought: 'Well, what's the point in that?' – we've had other people, maybe less distinguished, like Chris Mayhew, for example, joining the party and you get a bit of a boost from it for a while but it doesn't have any long-term effect. So I wasn't in any way attempting to persuade him to join the Liberal Party; I said, 'No, I think you're right, I think you've got to lead a break-out from the Labour Party and we must work together.' That was a view I took consistently, and he shared it.

TOBY JAMES: Obviously there were lengthy discussions and disagreements about the merger. Were there particular policy issues on which there was division within your own party as well?

DAVID STEEL: There wasn't. In the initial coming together of the Alliance there were no real policy issues. Looking back on merger, I think we handled it extremely badly, because the negotiating teams were far too large. It was madness to have sixteen a side or something, nearly thirty-two people negotiating the merger. I blame myself partly, but I should have had a firmer grip on the process and had a small group of people doing the actual nitty-gritty and then putting it democratically to the party. As it was, everybody was able to nitpick from the thirty-two people in the room about this clause and that clause and it went on and on and on and we lost support during the merger process because I think it was so badly handled. So if I had my time all over again I think I would have pressed for a different route.

But I don't think there were any major policy differences until we got to defence. That was David Owen's particular brief, coming from the Labour Party where they'd had to fight unilateralists. But as for the Liberal Party I kept pointing out that 'we're not unilateralists, but we've never supported the independent nuclear deterrent' – we didn't support Polaris, we didn't support Trident, though somewhere along the line we muddied the waters. I can remember the debates in the early '60s, before I was an MP, with Jo Grimond and people like John Bannerman in Scotland arguing against the Polaris base. We were an integral part of NATO, we could provide NATO bases, but why go down the expense and proliferation avenue of having an independent nuclear deterrent? So there was a difference of opinion there which kept surfacing every now and again, particularly at party conferences!

TOBY JAMES: How successful do you think you were at changing, and winning, the elite debates across Parliament on particular issues? Did your positions begin to change the views of other politicians and other parties?

DAVID STEEL: It was always very difficult for the leader of the Liberal Party in my time, when you were a small party and you are speaking basically to a hostile audience. I think I managed to get some sympathy because of the Lib–Lab pact; I can remember when Kinnock became leader of the Labour Party he used to sit and nod when I was speaking, which was unusual! Normally you are up against it as a minority party. I remember Roy Jenkins found it very difficult. I don't know whether we influenced the general debate; I'm not sure that the House of Commons was a place where you do influence people very much.

DUNCAN BRACK: And do you think we had an influence on the public, more broadly?

DAVID STEEL: Yes.

DUNCAN BRACK: On any particular issues, or just the general stance?

DAVID STEEL: I think the public liked the idea of the Alliance; if you remember, at one stage we were up to 51 per cent in the opinion polls. They liked the concept of people from different political backgrounds working together, and they liked the novelty of it and it was very attractive. As I say, it was derailed by General Galtieri, but the momentum was there and the capture of public imagination was there.

TOBY JAMES: Obviously the Liberal Party would always, in modern times anyway, have gained from a different electoral system at Westminster. Did you have a strategy about how you could try to influence debate and bring one about?

DAVID STEEL: Well, in the Scottish constitutional convention we did manage to come up with a compromise proposal based on the German electoral system, which has been reasonably successful, I wouldn't say it's perfect. We also managed to get proper PR for local government in Scotland and eventually for Europe, so I think we just have to keep pushing for electoral reform. I've noticed over the years that there's always a demand for it immediately after an election, but then it sort of withers away, it's happened every single time the momentum is not kept up. I don't think the AV referendum was a great success; I think it was probably a mistake, it wasn't a PR policy and the public didn't react well to it at all.

TOBY JAMES: Ultimately, because of the position that Labour and Conservatives will naturally take to defending it, reforming the electoral system was always going to be too difficult to achieve?

DAVID STEEL: Well, if you look back over the time I've been in Parliament the mood in the other parties has changed and fluctuated quite a lot. At one time I was counting on about 100 Tory MPs who might vote for PR because they did so in one of the debates – I can't remember which one it was, it might have been the early Scotland and Wales Bill. But when it came to the vote for the system for the European elections, of course, because it was part of the Lib–Lab pact the 100 Tory MPs melted away and we never got it! That was definitely a misjudgement on my part. I doubt if you'd get 100 now, but you might get 100 Labour MPs – but, you know, it just fluctuates. Quite a large number of people were talking about electoral reform in the debate on the Queen's Speech in the Lords – now that they're not in the Commons and having to deal with it.

TOBY JAMES: Are there personal characteristics that you think leaders need to have in order to be successful?

DAVID STEEL: Nowadays you certainly need to be at ease with television. I think each of the modern leaders in our party has been. I was lucky because I actually worked in television briefly before I came into Parliament so I was quite at ease with it, but Jo Grimond wasn't, quite. I can remember recording a party broadcast with him and getting quite cross that he wasn't sticking to the script, and he said: 'But I can't read the autocue! I would need glasses to read the autocue and I don't wear glasses now.' I gave up on that one; but all the others – Jeremy Thorpe and myself, Paddy, Charles, Nick – were all quite good on the box. The Tories really had difficulties because I don't think that Hague, or Howard, or Duncan Smith, were very good, and that was a major defect.

TOBY JAMES: Are there any other particular characteristics, personal characteristics, that make for a good leader?

DAVID STEEL: I think you just have to be thought to be reachable, and in contact with real life.

DUNCAN BRACK: Looking back over your leadership period, what are you most proud of achieving?

DAVID STEEL: I do think the Alliance with the SDP was a major change. I think it probably led to the changes in the Labour Party.

Funnily enough, only this weekend I was talking to Gordon Brown, who I always thought of as a very tribal Labour politician, and he was saying: 'You know, in the aftermath of what's happened in Scotland, our parties should really get together and discuss a common strategy.' I thought: 'Well, this is completely new, coming from him!' But I could see the point he was making. He said: 'You should fight the rural seats in Scotland, leave us to the industrial ones' – I don't think it's as simple as that, but the fact that it was coming from him was quite remarkable.

CHAPTER 29

PADDY ASHDOWN ON POLITICAL LEADERSHIP AND THE LIBERAL DEMOCRATS[491]

PADDY ASHDOWN, TOBY S. JAMES AND DUNCAN BRACK

TOBY JAMES: Why did you first set out into politics? Did you have had an idea then about something particular you wanted to achieve?

PADDY ASHDOWN: I don't think you can do anything important in life unless you know what you want to achieve. As is often the case, at least in my life – which is why I called my autobiography *A Fortunate Life* – it often happens by coincidence or circumstance. So here I am in 1974, about to go out to Geneva to be a member of the Foreign Service, and I'm packing to go. I was a member of the Labour Party until I gave it up over *In Place of Strife* – I thought, 'Maybe it's always going to be the child of the trade unions.' So I'd given them up and I wasn't going to be in politics.

Then a little man came and knocked on my door, it must have been during the general election of February '74. He probably didn't have a bobble hat, I don't think he had a beard, he may not have been wearing sandals but he was certainly wearing an anorak, and he said, 'Hello, I'm the local Liberal, are you going to vote Liberal?' And I said, 'Go away! I'm not going to vote at all.' He said, 'Well, are you sure?' And I don't know why but, for some bizarre reason, I said, 'Come in and sit down. Tell me why I should be a Liberal.' We must have talked for a couple of hours, and I discovered that actually I'd been a Liberal all my life, I

---

491   This interview took place on Thursday 18 June 2015 in the House of Lords.

wasn't a socialist at all. It was as if, as I sometimes say, I'd found this old coat hanging in the cloakroom, and I put it on and it's never felt uncomfortable since.

So then I went out to Geneva and I saw my country falling apart – it was the sick man of Europe, two elections, the three-day week and all that. My wife and I had a lovely life; we lived beside the shores of Lake Geneva, we took the kids yachting in the summer and skiing in the winter and walking in the mountains. It was an idyllic life and a great job, but it was pointless if your country was falling apart. It sounds very self-righteous and pompous but actually that's what we did – we decided to return home and get involved in politics. My friends thought, 'You're mad!', and I was mad, because Yeovil had been Tory since 1910 – they didn't count their majorities, they bloody weighed them, and we were in third place in the second election of '74. It was a mad thing to do, with a wife and two children, but sometimes the maddest things are the best. Everyone, except for two people, thought I was mad. One was the Swedish ambassador, a lovely man, who said, 'Yes, you should do this.' The other person was my boss at the time, Colin McColl; he subsequently became the head of MI6 and he was one of the real guiding lights of my life. He said, 'Yes, Paddy, go on, do it. You should always take these risks at one stage in your life.' The people I was working for at the time said that I could come back in four years. So anyway, I went off and did this.

It took me eight years to win the seat. And from that moment onwards, although I've profoundly disagreed with the Liberals from time to time and had rows with them, I've never felt uncomfortable about being a Liberal. I am absolutely comfortable with this. It is the only philosophy at all that makes any sense of the conundrums of our age. And while it was the most stupid, the most irresponsible, the most difficult thing, my greatest achievement undoubtedly is winning Yeovil after eight years, after losing once, in '79, being unemployed twice, being a youth worker. If someone said to me, 'If you could have one thing on your gravestone, what would it be?' It would be 'Member of Parliament for Yeovil'. Politics was more fun, then. It was more straightforward, more black and white. And I had no other ambition in life, I promise you. I didn't get elected in order to be leader of the party.

I think I was a truculent and difficult Liberal MP, in the 1983–87 parliament. I'm basically a radical liberal at heart. I misjudged the SDP; I said, 'We shouldn't sell our Liberal birthright for this mess of pottage,' but then I suddenly realised that actually this was the process of realignment, which I thought was the only way to make sense of politics, because manifestly people were in the wrong party given the things they believed in. So, after '88, I'm not sure I was the first, but I was nearly the first – because I did it on *Question Time* straight after the election – to argue that these parties have got to get together to form the Liberal Democrats. And then when David Steel stood down, I was very sure that I was going to stand as leader.

DUNCAN BRACK: When did you think you might have a chance to be the next leader? It must have been before David actually stood down.

PADDY ASHDOWN: Yes, it was. I was very confident. I wasn't rushing it, but I was very confident and I had a little group of people around me who would help to plan the campaign if and when David stood down. It was his choice; we didn't want him to go early. If he stood down, I would have a go. I thought there would be three people in the running: Alan Beith, myself and David Penhaligon, and my own view was that it would be very tough to beat David Penhaligon, I wasn't sure it could be done. And I wrote a book, called *After the Alliance*, in '87. I've always written. I think one of the things that is really missing about our leaders today is that they don't write. They don't write articles. I love doing a thousand words for *The Independent*, or *The Guardian*, or *The Times*. And then of course there's my books, which have almost become my hobby.

So yes, it was all planned beforehand. And I was very, very clear on what I wanted to do. There is no point in being a leader and then wallow in the bubble bath of being a leader. You've got to have a clear idea of what you want to achieve, and I think I had a very clear idea of that. And so in '88, in order to put that idea forward, I wrote *Citizen's Britain*, which I still think is one of my best books; certainly the most prophetic book I've written. It laid out the whole agenda, about entitlements, civil benefits, and choice for the citizen and so on.

That agenda was pretty much lock, stock and barrel picked up by Blair, who then subsequently messed it up.

TOBY JAMES: I've touched on this already, but what you were seeking at achieve as leader? And to what extent did you achieve it?

PADDY ASHDOWN: Duncan was very close to me at the time so he can remember, but what I saw was an opening on the left of British politics (at no point in my life could I have been a Conservative) for a party that believed in social justice, but also believed that inequality should be dealt with not by engineering outcomes but by engineering opportunity for those who are at the bottom. If you try that and it doesn't work, you have to think of engineering outcomes, but the first instinct of a true Liberal should always be to provide opportunity. I could see an opening for an egalitarian, meritocratic, environmentally conscious, civil liberties-based and opportunity-centred, internationalist agenda. One of the key things I did in those early days was to get Ralf Dahrendorf to run a commission to answer the question of how can you have social justice *and* a strong economy. I believe that's still one of the key questions that confronts us

I could see this opening and I knew that's where the party should be. And this is what I think differentiates me from others – maybe it's because I'm an impatient kind of guy, but I could see no point in this great philosophy of Liberalism if you are content with being a furry little animal on the edges of British politics, proposing good ideas that other people borrow, or if you are satisfied with simply opposing. The party had to be prepared to take the risk of being in government in order to implement the things we believed in, to change the condition of people's lives. I've always wanted to move the party towards power and away from just opportunism and oppositionalism.

That was of course impossible in '92; we had to be satisfied with survival (probably have to be satisfied with it now too). But I was really excited about post-'92 because, (a) we survived, and (b) Labour had failed. (I do think, oddly enough, that this country will always need Liberalism but it doesn't necessarily always need socialism. I think it's beginning to discover that now. Socialism has no traction in the modern age. My own view is that the present circumstances are very similar to the early decades of the twentieth century when Liberals lost their traction because it was the age of corporatism and mass movements. Now the reverse is true.)

I have to say that I thought John Smith was a terrible leader of the Labour Party. He was a lovely, lovely man and a wonderful speaker and a great parliamentarian; a very decent man and quintessentially a Scot. But he made the same mistake as Miliband; he was prepared to sit where Labour was and not take them any further. And I just thought, 'Now, this is the moment for us.' I thought we could get in there and occupy that space on the centre-left, until of course, Smith died, and along came Anthony Lynton Blair, who, as Duncan and I remember, simply moved Labour with all its power – the power of his personality and charisma, but also all the power of the Labour machine – straight on to our ground. So then there was no alternative but to abandon equidistance and become part of the movement that would change Britain – part of the movement that, above all, would bring an end to the Conservative government – rather than risk being taken to be part of the movement that stood against that change. I think that was the key strategic decision I took, and the right one – although it was, as you remember with the Chard speech, not at all welcome to many of our members. It delivered, in the end, twice the number of seats in '97, but I don't think that was the key thing. It delivered so much that was on the Liberal Democrat agenda, the Liberal agenda: self-government for Scotland, which Blair, I know, delivered only because he had loyalty to John Smith, and to keep us on board; proportional representation for the European elections, the Freedom of Information Act, the Bill of Rights etc. Blair was totally uninterested in all that. The paradox is that the biggest things Blair did – that is, changing the way Britain is governed – were things that he was completely uninterested in doing.

DUNCAN BRACK: Do you think you could have achieved coalition if you had pushed for it harder right after the '97 election?

PADDY ASHDOWN: No. I remember speaking to Blair the morning of polling day; I was at a school in Somerset, and it was the first time that Blair admitted to me that he could win. Roy Jenkins had this wonderful saying that 'Blair was like a man carrying a cut-glass crystal bowl across a very slippery floor; his job was to get to the end, get across the floor without dropping it.' He could never believe that he could win – but he knew it then, and he suddenly said, 'Well, I think we're going to win very big, Paddy.' And I said, 'Well, I think you are too.' Then we spoke that evening, and I could already hear him beginning to shift. And then there was the baleful influence of just about the worst constitutional mechanism that Britain has, the Downing Street removal van, which forces you to take decisions which have very long-term consequences, even though you are knackered, tired, with your bloodstream awash with testosterone and adrenalin. I met Roy Jenkins that morning, and both of us thought that there was something illegitimate about creating an even larger majority for the government; it would have been a wrong judgement. Blair obviously felt the same thing.

However, I think if we'd grabbed that moment and said, 'No, we'll stick with it,' we'd have created the first coalition formed from a position of strength rather than a position of weakness – and I allow myself the luxury of thinking that it would have been a better government if we'd been there. I don't say necessarily that it would not have suffered the fate of all governments, which in the end collapse into hubris and self-belief, but I do think that we would have challenged them more on key issues. I'm very confident that if we'd been there the first parliament wouldn't have been such a wasted opportunity; it was dedicated utterly to getting elected for a second parliament instead of taking the opportunity to do the things that were necessary. But that is one of the 'what would have happened if…'s of history.

So then, consistent with the belief that we had to be in power, or close to power, we went into the Joint Cabinet Committee. I never thought it would deliver very much, but it was a useful framework to keep Blair on board with us, in order to be able to deliver some of the other stuff we wanted – devolution to Scotland and Wales, a Freedom of Information Act, PR for Europe, the Human Rights Act etc. At this stage he was in his 'big tent' phase and the committee was an expression of that. But then it became plain to me, on the night that Blair ditched PR and the Jenkins Report, that the committee had run its course and there was no

point in continuing with it. That was the end. (Personally I would have closed
the committee down quicker than Charles actually did, but I think he probably rightly decided that we could just let it dribble away into the sand, because
there was no point in having a fuss.) But at that moment it was evident to me
that my strategy had reached its end and it was time for a new leader. Anyway
I was tired, and I was fractious with the party and they were fractious with me.

TOBY JAMES: Could you talk through your thinking behind the electoral
strategy that you devised for the Liberal Democrats? For example, where were
you looking to gain seats or retain seats?

PADDY ASHDOWN: Whatever I tried to do, I tried to get the party used to
governing. I wanted to change the culture of the party towards one that was prepared to handle power. I couldn't do it at Westminster so we did it through local
government. We began to run some of the big cities, we got used to the idea of
coalition, we got used to the idea of taking tough decisions in government. You
know, many people said that the 2010–15 coalition was a remarkable thing, but I
don't think it was. We had built a culture in the party that was used to coalitions.
I don't say there were many of them, but there were senior people who had run
coalitions in local government and were perfectly used to this idea.

The other part of the strategy was targeting – very much the Chris Rennard
strategy. He was right about that: win by-elections to get yourself relevant and
then concentrate your forces on the winnable seats.

TOBY JAMES: What were the key challenges do you think you faced in terms
of devising that strategy?

PADDY ASHDOWN: Funnily enough they were cultural. The thing that was
similar between me and Blair is we were both outsiders in our own parties, we
were not born out of the womb of the party in the way that others were. That
meant that you have a sort of pure vision of what a party is: it's just an organisation, you can make it do things. That led to the biggest mistake I made; it

nearly wrecked the party completely because I failed to realise that a political party is not the same as an organisation, an industrial company, because its key resource is human beings. You know that great line from Immanuel Kant: 'Out of the crooked timber of humanity, no straight thing can ever be made.' That's absolutely true; I can think of no exception to it. My idea was visionary, the party was going to be called the 'Democrats'. But what I forgot was that the party had a soul, and the soul was called 'Liberal'. And I nearly wrecked it until I understood that I had to incorporate that. I just had to sit down one night and say to myself, 'Paddy, you can't go on like this, you're wrong. You've got to change position.' And we did change position.

So the first thing I had to do – *we* had to do; it was very much a team effort – was to create a culture and identity for the Liberal Democrats, which was slightly different from both the Liberals and the SDP; it had to be a genuine amalgam. One of the things I did was to have people in my office who had been opposed to the merger because I wanted to hear their voices, because I knew that unless I could persuade those who had been opposed to it, we weren't going to succeed. And it worked. That was the most difficult thing. I would always say from my Bosnia days that changing laws, changing institutions is easy, but changing a culture is very, very difficult and takes a long time. And I messed that up initially, until I got the hang of it.

The second thing was there was quite a strong antipathy to any closer relationship with Blair. I won that quite marginally; there were key debates, which we wouldn't win by very big majorities. I understand that; these were the purists in the party – I don't say this in any way pejoratively, we need people in the party who are pure Liberals of heart and spirit, otherwise we would just be another party prepared to do anything for power.

Third, there was quite a lot of antagonism, especially in the early days, among the MPs, particularly the older MPs, because I'd only been in Parliament for five years when I became leader.

Events played into my hands quite a lot. I think the proudest vote that I have ever cast – and it wasn't easy – was to vote in favour of Maastricht. (By the way, Charles had many qualities, but he was one of the ones most firmly opposed to voting with Major on Maastricht. It was very difficult to get over that because he had quite a lot of clout.) Everybody said that we could bring down the Major government, though I don't think we could have done. In the end we were prepared to stand up for what we believed in; I think that's best vote we've ever cast.

My most depressed moment was when Blair came in, because I knew precisely what he was going to do. He had the potential to undermine my strategy for the previous five or six years.

DUNCAN BRACK: You gave an example of where it was a drawback for you to have been an outsider; do you think there are any advantages to being an outsider?

PADDY ASHDOWN: Yes, huge advantages. A leader has to be able to stand outside the circle. You know that phenomenon which happens at party conferences. Everyone goes round saying, 'Aren't we having a great conference?' Then you go home and emerge from the bubble and realise it had been an absolute train wreck. The leader has to have the ability to stand outside that and not simply be the creature of the party. As an outsider you could see more clearly what needed to be done than an insider. I was always looking for new ideas; I'm obsessive about new ideas, as you know. *Citizen's Britain* was an example of that. The other book I wrote, *Beyond Westminster*, was another. I wanted to bring in ideas from the outside. Then – and perhaps even more now – if we are not a party of intellectual debate and ferment about ideas, we are nothing. So, yes, it was an advantage.

DUNCAN BRACK: Do you think overall you would rate yourself as a good party manager?

PADDY ASHDOWN: No, I don't think so – though I think one of the key qualities of the leader is to know their deficiencies, and therefore to compensate for them in the people they have around them. That was a lesson that probably took me a long time to learn. But I do know my deficiencies. One of them is that party management bores me, it really bores me, but I had some very good party managers to help me: Archy Kirkwood was my Chief Whip and he was very good at that; Chris Rennard, in his way, a good party manager; Richard Holme, a good party manager and he had a lot of other gifts as well – no one liked being managed much by Richard Holme but he nevertheless managed to do it quite well!

The second failure I have is that I am very impatient, though I think that in politics the sins of impatience are always forgivable, whereas the sins of sloth are not. Sometimes I get so enthusiastic that I grab at things. So I needed people who would act as a counterweight. The most important people in my office, and I learned that in the days of the leadership, and again in Bosnia, were those who simply disagreed with me. Julian Astle did it brilliantly for me in Bosnia; he would just stand there and say, 'No, Paddy, you're wrong.' Sometimes, after hours of discussion, I had to say, 'Fuck off, this is what we're going to do,' but mostly the business of answering his objections massively improved whatever plan I had.

So no, I don't think I was very good at party management. I think where I'm quite good, though, is doing that second-lieutenant-army-training thing of saying thank you to people afterwards – always saying, 'I'm really grateful' when people did good things or helped me in some ways, those little skills (by the way, Thatcher was brilliant at this). This has the effect of tying people to you with bonds of loyalty because they'd had a hard time and you'd recognised it.

TOBY JAMES: To what extent do you think you changed the elite debate on particular policy issues, on both sides of the aisle, across the party spectrum? Were there areas where you felt your imprint?

PADDY ASHDOWN: I don't think so very much. In the end, Blair occupied the ground we had been developing and it was his horsepower, I suppose, that was more important in winning the arguments – though I supposed that I played a bit in it.

I think that there is one big case where I won it, which is the case of Bosnia. This was like the Hong Kong passports issue in being recognised, at least afterwards, for being the right thing to do. I think we made an impact on Hong

Kong passports. It was a breakthrough for the party because suddenly people said, 'Ah! That's what they're for.'

I think also the first Iraq War had an impact – I think leaders become understood when people realise who they are and where they come from, and the Iraq War illuminated me as a leader because people said, 'Ah, I see! *That's* who he is. So he's Liberal but he's also quite sensible at the business of foreign affairs and conflict.' And then of course you start playing up to that – which is the deadly thing and no doubt I've done that too. I think the least important thing about me, genuinely, is the fact that I was a soldier for eleven years – although no one ever lets me forget it. So what else? Did we alter the climate on the environment? Possibly a bit. That was very much a feature of the 1992–97 period – a key issue we were pushing forward.

DUNCAN BRACK: How about the Cook–Maclennan agreement?

PADDY ASHDOWN: Ah, yes, very interesting. The Cook–Maclennan agreement was certainly very important, that's true. What the Cook–Maclennan agreement did was to shape the climate for the debate between ourselves and Labour, and with the country. It was the framework that enabled the coalition to follow – it placed coalition on the agenda.

TOBY JAMES: Obviously, the Liberal Democrats lost out significantly from the first-past-the-post electoral system in Westminster. What was your strategy for trying to change that? What were the key challenges you faced?

PADDY ASHDOWN: In those days you could scratch a Liberal Democrat and, whatever the subject was, in the end the debate would get back to proportional representation. That's where we'd end up: 'Oh, if only we had proportional representation!' But I believed that we would never get proportional representation in Britain unless and until we could prove that we could use the coalition to constructive effect. So if proportional representation leads to coalitions, you must show that coalition can work before you get to proportional representation. We've just shown that coalition can work and I think proportional representation now is pretty well inevitable – I don't say under this government, but it's pretty well inevitable. So, much though I am attached to the case of PR – of course – I thought we were a bit obsessive about it, to be honest with you; which is why I also think – forgive me, I can say this now – I also think there's a battle on PR between the absolute purists, political scientists who say, 'STV is the only answer', and people like myself who are slightly more practical politicians who say, 'Actually I'm not sure.' The only bit of the political system that people like is the link between themselves and the MP representing their area. I think you're not likely to get PR if you ask them to abandon the one bit of the political system they like. So I would trade a bit of purity for a greater degree of practicality – which is why I was prepared to think of 'AV plus' under Jenkins. If we had gone to pure AV, I'm not sure Blair wouldn't have given it to us then.

The important part of constitutional change, for me, is not the theoretical bit. The really important part – it's where I think we didn't succeed in the last government as effectively as we might – is the central Liberal idea of the empowered citizen. I do not believe in a strong state. I believe in the empowered citizen. Constitutional reform is only the means within the political system by which the citizen can be empowered. You can also do this by by encouraging enterprise and small business, to empower people economically. This is my central belief as a Liberal.

TOBY JAMES: How should we assess Liberal leaders? One of the key things across the three books, of which this is one volume, is focusing on the electoral record and using that as a proxy test.

PADDY ASHDOWN: There's only one answer I can give you on that, which is how close did they get to power? To what extent did they achieve the ultimate goal of politics, which is enabling people to benefit in their lives from the power of governance exercised according to Liberal values? That is the single judgement. I don't rate political leaders highly who, say, double the number of seats they hold but avoid the possibility of influencing events in the nation we serve because they will not take the risks of governing. You've got to take those risks; you've got to take those chances. So that's the way I'd judge it.

Secondly, I think one of Nick's really extraordinary achievements is in holding the party together, because usually if you go into coalition the party splits. It was the Tories who split – we did not – and that is one of Nick's greatest achievements. I think leaders have a real duty in managing a party to hold it together; in the end you have to remember that a political party is a club of spirits who can only work if they hold together. If you lose that unity, you lose the lot. That's why, after courage, I rate loyalty as the prime political virtue. This is not one gift that I'm especially good at, by the way; I have a habit of confronting people! I hope I don't manage by confrontation but I'm not afraid of it. Sometimes you have to create a crisis to solve things – but you should do so with care, realising how dangerous it can be.

DUNCAN BRACK: Most Liberal leaders, really since the 1920s, haven't been anywhere near power. Are there other ways we should evaluate whether they're successful?

PADDY ASHDOWN: No, but I think they all had a strategy to move us closer to power. The ones that I admire did. Grimond did; Grimond talked about the realignment of the left; Steel did; Thorpe, in a slightly different way – he was prepared to consider coalition with Heath in 1974. All of them were wrestling with the issue of how I get this great idea with this rather minimal force into a position where we can influence affairs for the things we believe in.

David Steel's answer to that was always manoeuvre; he was a brilliant politician at positioning. I think politicians, leaders, come in two forms: position-takers and positioners. I'm a position-taker. Owen is a position-taker. Thatcher is a position-taker. Nick is a position-taker. Steel was a positioner, a brilliant positioner; brilliant at positioning the party at just the right point between the two great forces to gain advantage. Charles was a positioner. All of them moved our party forward towards greater influence, and therefore in the end, greater power.

DUNCAN BRACK: Presumably that's consistent across all leaders of any party?

PADDY ASHDOWN: Yes, because the great democratic carnival of the election day is the ultimate mechanism by which you are judged, fairly or unfairly – unfairly in the case of the last election, we would claim. But that is the mechanism you're judged by. What else is the purpose? It doesn't say you can't influence things outside that. If you can't have power, influence will have to do. Jo Grimond, for instance influenced very significantly by the position he took on Suez; and he was the man who brought me into the party.

TOBY JAMES: Are there personal characteristics that leaders need in order to be able to achieve that?

PADDY ASHDOWN: There is this great idea that you can do leadership by numbers; I don't believe that. I don't think you can teach leadership, either. In the end, there are two great qualities for human beings, and for leaders in particular. The first is courage. You have to have courage, otherwise any other gift you have vanishes in the morning dew. And the second is loyalty. I rate loyalty far higher than most people do. The great Liberal Prime Minister Lord Melbourne once said, 'It's more important that you support your friends when they are wrong than when they are right.' He was right. Because human beings are herd animals and therefore loyalty – not, obviously, ridiculous loyalty, not loyalty to the extent that you'd put Jews in the gas chambers because you're loyal to the Führer – but loyalty to the tribe is a quintessential human characteristic, just as much as egotism and selfishness is. This is particularly so in British politics. In American politics, David Owen could have been President. But British politics is a team affair. Here you need to play the team, have loyalty to the team. So I think loyalty is an extremely important quality. And that means loyalty of leaders to their members as well, rather than just of members to their leaders. I am not sure parties have to love their leaders – probably respect will do. But leaders must love their parties – otherwise why would you put up with it?

DUNCAN BRACK: I think I disagree with you that you were a bad party manager.

PADDY ASHDOWN: I don't think you'd disagree that I managed by confrontation!

DUNCAN BRACK: No, I agree with that. But that was often the good thing, you did it pretty sensitively.

PADDY ASHDOWN: Well, that is kind of you. The thing I can do is have flaming rows with people, when I shout insults at them – and completely forget about it five minutes later. I meet them three weeks later and they're not talking to me and cutting me dead. And I say, 'What's wrong?' And they say, 'Don't you realise what you said to me?' I don't like rows, but some times a good row clears the tubes!

DUNCAN BRACK: But you spent a lot of time on party management, chairing the Policy Committee, going out to local parties, dealing with the party's near-bankruptcy, and so on.

PADDY ASHDOWN: Ah! Yes, maybe that's true. Maybe I was better than I thought.

CHAPTER 30

NICK CLEGG ON POLITICAL LEADERSHIP AND THE LIBERAL DEMOCRATS[492]

NICK CLEGG, TOBY S. JAMES AND DUNCAN BRACK

TOBY JAMES: Going back to the beginning, why did you first set out into politics? Did you have an idea then of what you wanted to achieve?

NICK CLEGG: There wasn't a blinding-light moment of epiphany where I suddenly decided my vocation in life was to go into politics, let alone become the leader of the Liberal Democrats, or the Deputy Prime Minister in a coalition. It crept up on me a bit more than that.

I think I can fairly say that I came from a family that was very interested in politics and had a great deal of respect for politics, but not in a party-political way. I think that was partly because of the somewhat unusual history of my family, on both sides. My mum was Dutch. She was born in Indonesia and spent time in a Japanese prisoner-of-war camp; she was a teacher by profession, by training, a Montessori teacher, and she had a sort of low-church, Dutch approach. Looking back on it – of course I wouldn't have described it like this as a child – but my mum had a very pronounced influence on me, and on my brothers and my sister, a very pronounced egalitarian view. She was always and remains utterly nonplussed by the British class system. So I had a very strong sense that other countries did things differently and maybe even, on occasions, better; that was instilled at a very early age. And – again I wouldn't have thought of it like this as a child and maybe I'm remembering it through the filter of hindsight – but I

---

492   This interview took place on Monday 15 June 2015 in the House of Commons.

was instilled with quite a strong sense that politics matters and that politics can lead to big, good things, but also big, bad things as well. My dad's side of the family was very much marked by the fact that my grandmother was Russian, she was a White Russian; she lost her family, then she moved here and was part of the White Russian diaspora in London. I used to toddle along with my brothers and my sister from time to time, to the Russian Orthodox church in central London, and you were acutely aware that people had moved big distances, and great big things had ripped their communities and their families apart. That has an impact on a child. It doesn't make you interested in day-to-day politics, but it does make you think: 'Wow, actually, ideas matter and what people believe matters.' So, looking back on it, the idea that history matters, that ideas matter, that politics matter and was to be taken seriously, was, I think, instilled in me – though not in the sombre way I've just described it! – and with that came an innate, intuitive internationalism.

For the rest I was very typical of my generation. I'm forty-eight, so I was at university in the mid-1980s. Like many people of my generation I was appalled by Margaret Thatcher's time in government. The thing that I remember most distinctly was the harshness of the language, her sink-or-swim language, which for most idealistic youngsters was of course utterly offputting, because it celebrated an eat-or-be-eaten ethos. That's the way it came across; I'm sure biographers of Margaret Thatcher would say it was more subtle than that, but it certainly didn't come across as if it was. I remember once moaning to my dad about how dispiriting I found it to be told as a youngster that 'there was no such thing as society' (I know she claims she never said it – but that's the way it came across).

Also what I found particularly offputting was the way in which the Tory Party just gorged themselves on their obsession about Europe. So it was quite a natural step for me, after I left Cambridge and spent time at the University of Minnesota, to become pretty left-wing, or at least desperate to find an alternative to 1980s conservatism. I was very impressed at the time by writers like Christopher Hitchens, for whom I was for a short period of time a fact-checker; I worked as a glorified tea boy at *The Nation* magazine. I wrote a small dissertation on deep green philosophy and that provided a window for me to look at classic philosophical tomes, from Locke to Rawls and all the rest of it. I remember distinctly at that time looking at the debate in the UK over the country's place in Europe and just being appalled by the parochialism and the blinkered manner of that debate.

So, put all those things together, and I came out thinking I was going to try to find my feet in Europe. I did an internship and one thing led to the next. The next catalyst was when I was employed as an official for Leon Brittan, who was then the vice-president of the European Commission working on trade. As I ranted about how ghastly I thought the government was, and how poorly they were serving Britain in the debates about Europe, he was probably the first person who turned round and said: 'Instead of constantly shouting at the television, why don't you actually put your own neck on the line?' That was the moment that really stopped me in my tracks and stumped me for words – uncharacteristically! – because I'd always looked at politicians as a different species from another planet, another galaxy – no doubt that's how people view me now. I never thought there was any connection. So those were the things that came together: growing up under Thatcher, the upbringing I had – very internationalist, small-'l' liberal – and the nudge from an individual. Looking back on it, the internationalism, the belief that Britain needs to remain open and engaged, was very strong right from the outset.

TOBY JAMES: Having begun to look at parliamentary politics did you always have aspirations to become leader of the party? When did that emerge?

NICK CLEGG: No, I didn't at all. It was much more incremental than that. Paddy made a huge impression on me when he was leader, though I'm not going to pretend I took a forensic interest and followed his every utterance. I just have images in my mind of rather brave interviews, after whatever ghastly election he'd just endured, speaking with a courage and resilience which I admired and I liked. I obviously liked the values that he articulated, and what he was saying about Hong Kong. And also, like any Liberal admirer, I just found the whole bully-boy domination of politics by these two machines, the Conservative and the Labour Party, very unappealing – as I do now, just as much as I did then. Coincidentally, Paddy Ashdown asked to see Leon Brittan at the height of the EU/US banana trade dispute, and I asked Brittan if he could put in a good word for me – so I touched the hem of the great man that way. I didn't have some great scheme in my head, no.

DUNCAN BRACK: Did you think you might want to be leader when you were elected to Parliament in 2005?

NICK CLEGG: At quite an early stage people would say about me, 'Oh, he might be leader' – including a somewhat breathless Paddy, after we'd just done a white-water rafting stunt for no apparent reason when I was standing for the European Parliament in the East Midlands. So almost by osmosis, when I look back on it, it became an assumption that I might want to do it. But I was just acutely aware, as well, of people like Ed Davey and David Laws and lots of other people of my generation who I thought were tremendously good, as well as people of an older generation who clearly wore their ambition on their sleeve (I don't think this is a criticism): Chris Huhne, obviously, from the moment I met him – one of his both less and more attractive qualities was that he didn't hide his ambition.

I don't want to sound falsely modest. Did people suggest it to me? Of course they did, and it would have been silly of me not to have thought about it when I had the then leader of the party, who I admired tremendously, saying: 'Do you know, you could be leader?' But I never had a scheme or a timetable or an organisation, and actually when Charles was forced to stand down I was very resistant to suggestions at the time that I should throw my hat in the ring. I actively didn't want to, I thought for what I hope were obvious reasons that it was just too early. In the end I was very relieved that I wasn't forced to do something I would have felt very uncomfortable with.

TOBY JAMES: When you did become leader, what did you aim to achieve? And to what extent do you think you achieved it?

NICK CLEGG: That is the key question. From the beginning I felt then, and I still feel now, that party politics is the marriage of ideals and dreams with the grubby and sometimes brutal practice of trying to put those ideals into effect. I've always been a politician who believes that in politics you've got to grab the opportunity to put your views and your values into practice. I still feel that very strongly. So I was unambiguously of the view that the Liberal Democrats should seek to make the journey from opposition into government, if it became available to us. It's something we'd done to great effect in local government and Scotland and Wales before (with the downside electoral effects too) so it wasn't entirely alien to our party. I didn't find attractive the idea that we could just be a strong parliamentary force but with no ability to effect change; I always thought that surely we have to do this for a reason. That was important to me. I also felt, right from the beginning, that maybe our Liberal identity could be crisper and clearer and more coherent. Maybe those two things became associated in my mind: if you have to put what you've talked about in opposition into practice, then along with that comes the need to make certain choices about what you can and can't do, or what you don't think is an absolute priority.

Now, how much have we succeeded? Well, clearly under my time as leader, we have succeeded far, far more in shaping the real world than in promoting our own electoral interests. I think only the most unfair commentator would do anything other than acknowledge that we have made a massive imprint on a lot of people's daily lives. I couldn't give you a whole list but it's quite a remarkable exercise, I think, of translating in many cases quite radical policies into practice with only 8 per cent of the MPs in Parliament. I genuinely can't think an example of a party which has punched so solidly and courageously above its weight. But clearly it has been accompanied by – or caused by, that's the great debate, which I'm very happy to go into – a catastrophic loss of electoral support. I can't pretend that that side of the ledger was anything other than pretty poor. But the other side of the ledger is unprecedented for us as a party, we've never got so much done.

DUNCAN BRACK: Do you think it's a fair characterisation of you that you took the party in an economic-liberal, 'Orange Book', direction?

NICK CLEGG: I think it's fair and unfair. I think it's fair to say that I had no problem, and still have no problem at all, with the idea that it is in line with liberal progressive values to make sure that over time the burden of debt is shared equitably and sensibly across the generations (therein lies a lot of detail, by the way, a stark difference from what Osborne is now doing). I've always felt that and that man [pointing at a picture of Gladstone on his office wall] would have certainly felt that. In that sense I never found it 'Orange Book', or 'Pink Book', or whatever; I've always felt strong public finances are a necessary means to a fair liberal end. To that extent I was never ideologically hung up about the idea that after the catastrophe in 2008 the repair job needed to be done. I totally accept that there are lots of very interesting debates about how precisely you do that, about the pace and about how you divvy it up between taxes and all the rest of it. You're right to say, in light of the 2008 crash, that I never had any qualms over the idea that whoever was in government at the time, including Liberals, would have to oversee a fiscal adjustment. I personally think that the fiscal adjustment that we oversaw was not perfect, but it was a hell of a lot more balanced and fairer than it would have been if we had not been there. I'm very proud of that. So that is fair.

But it's also an unfair characterisation. My own view is that the whole 'Orange Book' taxonomy – the way we divvy people up between right and left, state and market, private sector and public sector, high tax and lower tax, is being supplanted by completely different sets of distinctions – which is partly why politics is in crisis, partly why Liberalism is possibly in crisis, not just here but across the world. The key distinctions are now between open and closed, 'them and us'; they're about tribal politics, nationalism, chauvinism, identity politics. In a way, the right/left and state/market debates – you know, 'Do you reform public services a lot? Do you have the market a little bit or a lot in health?' – all the things that used to inflame and obsess the Liberal Democrats feel very anachronistic now. And I think that the case for Liberalism – evidence-based, rational, empirical, trying to strike the right balance between economic credibility and social justice – is clearly now, in many ways, more needed than before, but is more challenged than before by the visceral nature of identity politics which is now sweeping all before it. I think part of our problem – not just in our party but in this place [Parliament] – is we're still operating on the basis of distinctions that are no longer the engine which is driving politics. The fact that figures such as Steve Webb and Vince Cable – not known to be fiscal hawks – also contributed to the 'Orange Book' suggest that the subsequent caricature of the book was not entirely fair either.

TOBY JAMES: By what criteria do you think we should evaluate party leaders of the main three political parties?

NICK CLEGG: Lots of different things. Votes and seats is one perfectly sensible way to start, but I think there are plenty of other things as well. I think what you get done, the change that you are able to introduce in the real world, is not a bad place to start either, given that all politics is about change, rival visions of change.

In terms of the party, one of the things that I like to think I was very diligent at, and certainly very conscious of, was the need to keep the party as united as possible. Partly because I had made the obvious observation that every time Liberals in the past had gone anywhere near the other parties, like a moth to a flame they had always suffered – but where suffering would have turned into semi-terminal catastrophe would be if the party had split. I have many flaws but I was assiduous at trying to keep people on board. I would be at every week's parliamentary party meeting, I would constantly try to absorb all the narkiness and bitchiness, the backbiting that you constantly get in politics, not least from your own side. I always felt that one of the jobs of a leader is not to react to people who constantly want to have a go at you. One of the great privileges of being a leader is you can try to set the direction for the party, and one of the duties and obligations is that you take the rap when things go wrong. Also you just have to accept that you are trying to corral a bunch of people of very different characters, very different instincts, very different qualities, very different strengths and weaknesses, and you just have to be generous – generous to people who don't always have your interests at heart, to put it very politely. I feel that, broadly speaking, I've always tried to do that. I've always tried to reach out to people to keep the lines of communication going even though I know that they may dislike me on a personal level, or disagree with me on a political level. I like to think that's been borne out by the leadership contest we're now in the middle of which has displayed remarkably little rancour. One thing I would like to have in my modest epitaph is that I always tried to minimise rancour. I would be quite clear when I disagreed with people, and I always tried to lead in a strong way, but I always tried to make clear that I was doing what I did because I believed in it, and I would treat people fairly – for instance in reshuffles. Reshuffles are awful because you upset everybody: you upset the people who want an elevation who don't get it, you upset the people you're asking to make way for others. I always tried to do it with the minimum amount of rancour, by being tough with my friends and generous towards my opponents, as much as anything else.

DUNCAN BRACK: Do you think Liberal leaders are different from those of the other two main parties; that actually one of our main challenges is just to get noticed?

NICK CLEGG: I think the thing which is so tough for us is that even when we did get noticed, we still got hammered. I'm absolutely convinced that one of the reasons why we got so badly hammered in this last election is because towards the end of the election campaign the overriding emotion among English voters was fear, fear of what might happen if Miliband and Salmond did a deal. And of course what you don't do if you're fearful is to turn to a party that has been so remorselessly typecast as weak. So we are either ignored or mocked, as we have been in opposition; or, when we were in government, we were ruthlessly and successfully typecast as somehow being weak, having lost our souls, sold out our principles, turned in on ourselves and all the rest of it. In fact, the truth was that we had been remarkably strong and resilient over a long period of time.

There's a real issue here. The vested interests in the press ignore and mock you when you're in opposition. I had thought that by the time we were in government, and got our hands on the levers of power, we would at least get a fairer hearing – but the reverse happened. With hindsight, logically, if you are the editor of the *Daily Mail*, or the *Daily Mirror* or whatever, you can afford to ignore us when we are nowhere near power. When we're near power, we are deeply offensive to their business model, so they have to turn on us – and boy, did they. Then, of course, that was supplemented by the endearing, if somewhat slightly unwelcome, tendency of Liberal Democrats to, when any critic said anything about us, instead of doing what the other parties do, which is to reject them outright, we'd say: 'Well, they might have a point actually!' What I tried to do about halfway through this last parliament, was to accept that there were these big vested interests in the papers, so not to waste any time on them; I would try any possible way I could to work around them. So I did the LBC thing, I went on late-night chat shows, I did Twitter, town halls, our traditional way of delivering messages through letterboxes – anything I could think of. The way I visualised it was to think: 'OK, we've got these massive vested interests, who are telling millions of people every day, as they read their papers over their egg and bacon, how ghastly we are. We've got to try to provide a countervailing story.' I couldn't think of any other logical way than trying to work round this great big obstacle. It is a huge problem.

One other thing which has occurred to me, and I see this inevitably through the prism of tuition fees: I'm pretty sure that if one of the other party leaders had had to commit the decision on tuition fees, they would have had significant vested interests who would have tried to cover their backs for them. They would have explained; they would have provided the narrative which at least would have tried to explain to the public why we did it. We had none of that. We literally had no echo chamber that would say good things, positive things about what we did or seek to explain rationally the choices that we were forced to make. If we did things which were controversial, there was just no buffer. It was an incredibly vulnerable position, a very exposed position, to be in. It will be a big, big challenge for my successors, and I will do everything I can to try to help them through it because it's remorseless. The SNP have got their vested interests now, their outriders, their echo chambers.

Even UKIP has now; it has a sort of in-house newspaper in the *Daily Express*. We still don't have that and it's a big impediment for us.

TOBY JAMES: Was this because of the alignment of the national press or because of the party machinery?

NICK CLEGG: The alignment of the press. I personally don't think that the level of vitriol and vituperation that was levelled at us, and me personally, over the past five years can be rationally explained by the normal conduct of politics. This was something else. I would see these hysterical red-faced Labour MPs screaming that we were quislings; or the loopy stuff you read in the *Daily Mail*. I was held responsible for stuff that I wasn't even aware was happening! I think that part of it is just that I underestimated – maybe we all underestimated – that if people have a mental map made up of reassuring opposites, with this reassuring pendulum swing, where the left might get terribly angry with the right, and the right may get terribly angry with the left, but they need each other to define each other; and if you suddenly mess that mental map up, I think it elicits a very visceral reaction from people because they can't say, 'We've won for a while before the pendulum swings back.' You're messing up the basic transmission mechanism that people are used to. I just think those vested interests hated that with an absolute passion. If you are a newspaper editor from the right, you hate the Liberal Democrats in government more than you hate the Labour Party. You need the Labour Party to hate because that makes you feel good, but you have to *destroy* the Liberal Democrats to return to business as usual. I can't think of another explanation. The individual decisions, even the highly controversial ones like tuition fees, cannot explain the level of vituperation that was levelled at us. I've heard a lot of seasoned politicians from other parties saying that this was just off the radar screen compared to what politicians normally contend with.

TOBY JAMES: One of the key things in the book is evaluating leaders in terms of their electoral record, the number of seats and those things, about their movement towards office. Is that a fair method? Or is that too narrow?

NICK CLEGG: You obviously need to look at it from different angles. Of course, we have an electoral system which provides a rather warped measuring stick. In 2010, we got about a million more votes than in 2005, but we went from sixty-two to fifty-seven seats. We got a million more votes than the SNP in this election but we ended up with eight seats, down from fifty-seven. So obviously you need to look at votes as well seats.

But you have to look at it more widely too. I remain bullish about our record because I think that what we achieved in government was genuinely remarkable. I now see David Cameron going around, espousing so-called 'blue-collar Conservatism', with a bunch of policies that he was entirely uninterested in when we pushed them in government: childcare, apprenticeships and so on. I think in terms of shaping the ideas that drive politics, we've done incredibly well. But there's a massive asymmetry in being a party of ideas in coalition with a party of power. The Conservative Party is a party of power; it's not a party of ideas. It is a remarkably effective opportunistic party and our virtues lie elsewhere. We are very diligent about developing our ideas and sticking to them, but poor at the kind of ducking and weaving and the tactics of politics in order to make sure we get the credit for those ideas. From pensions to tax reform to education to the environment and a whole bunch of things besides, we really were the pocket-sized engine room for the best ideas. But the Tories won the politics of power hands down.

DUNCAN BRACK: Do you think that what we achieved was all worth it? Did it outweigh the damage that the election inflicted on us?

NICK CLEGG: I'm not convinced that if we had been out of government over the last five years we would have had a stomping great big victory at the last election. For the reasons we've already dwelt on – being in coalition and being vilified – we lost a lot of the 2010 voters who came to us from the left; clearly that was damaging enough. I happen to believe, however, that even if we had languished in opposition for the last five years, we still wouldn't have been the answer to those very profound English fears that were driving people's voting behaviour, when push came to shove, on 7 May. If you want to really understand what happened in the election a month ago, you need to look at what happened in Scotland more than what happened in Whitehall. In my political life I have never seen the English heart gripped with quite such a cold fear that I saw in that last week or so of the election campaign. And if we'd been in opposition we still wouldn't have been the answer. The Conservatives were always going to be the antidote to Scottish nationalism, and of course they ruthlessly exploited it. So I stand by this idea that if we hadn't been in coalition we still would have lost quite a lot of seats – though clearly not on the scale that we did. So I don't make such a stark comparison, I think it would be glib of me to say, 'Yes, it was all worth it,' because clearly I feel, like everybody else, deeply battered and bruised and very, very sad. We lost so many colleagues. But the rational side of my brain tells me that it's false to somehow suggest that opposition would have delivered us sweet victory. I doubt very much it would.

TOBY JAMES: One reason why the electoral record is thought to be so important is that those that do not do well in elections are not leaders for long. Did you feel this pressure to deliver at election time as leader? How did it affect your actions?

NICK CLEGG: Of course, the challenge of doing well at election time is very important to any party leader. It was a source of great pride to me that we won a million more votes in 2010 than we had at the previous election – achieving the highest vote for the Liberal Democrats since the party was founded – and, equally, a source of great sadness that we did so poorly in 2015. Obviously, one can't judge a leader solely on seats and votes won, but it is critical. One reason I resigned immediately after the 2015 election was that I judged it unsustainable to remain leader of a party that had had such an electoral setback.

TOBY JAMES: Could you talk through your thinking behind the electoral strategy that you devised throughout your time as leader? In terms of where you were looking to win seats or retain seats, some of the challenges you faced.

NICK CLEGG: I expressed it poorly when I was once held to imply that the loss of some of the people who voted for us in 2010 was something to be relaxed about; I didn't mean it like that. What I meant was that the moment we went into coalition in 2010, we walked through a door through which you couldn't walk back. So my whole electoral strategy was based on not trying to hanker for a past which I felt we couldn't recapture, but in trying to expand our appeal to some people who hadn't previously voted for us. I always thought to myself, OK, so you lose some people who never wanted to be associated with a party which was in government in the first place. There are some people like that, it's a perfectly respectable position in a democracy – they vote for people who can act as a balance, but outside government.

Then there was a hefty chunk of people who just loathe the Conservatives, who couldn't cope with the idea that we went into coalition with them. I always thought, well, OK, they're lost for the time being, they might come back eventually but most of them are not going to be recaptured in this electoral cycle. But I'd always assumed there would be rich pickings for us, particularly among the small-'l', liberal-minded folk – broadly, but not exclusively, professional types, the educated middle class, who I thought we could now appeal to over and above the Labour or Conservative parties.

To understand why that was my electoral strategy you've got to understand how disappointed I was that we lost seats in 2010. A lot of my thinking was shaped by the very bitter disappointment that, despite all the hype and frothy optimism about our chances in 2010, we went backwards in terms of seats. One of the things that I learned, partly intuitively, partly through hearing what people said, partly through what our candidates were telling us, was that the reason why we didn't do as well in 2010 as I'd hoped was because the public was very fearful about the economy, above and beyond anything else in 2010. They saw the crash in 2008, they were unconvinced that Labour had the answers, and they felt that we were not tested enough, that we were not somehow gritty enough, we were not a party of government. We were, almost, a party for the good times but not for the tough times.

So I thought, logically, that the way to deliver that electoral appeal to those people who hadn't voted for us in the past but were inclined to do so was to show that we could not only retain our heart but also come with a hard head to the task of fixing the economy. For me, it wasn't just a sense of national duty that, at a time of outright economic emergency, someone needed to step up to the plate; it was a view that this might also reap electoral benefits – because that's where I felt our weakness lay. Clearly, it hasn't turned out like that, and one of the reasons for that, which I've gone on about earlier, is that we didn't foresee quite how successfully we would be vilified by our opponents, and how some of the coalition's policies were, while rational, especially offensive to some of our core voters – universities, public-sector workers and others – for which we, not the Tories, got all the blame.

Thirdly, because the dynamic of coalition in our majoritarian political culture, where only one person rather than two can stand on the steps of No. 10, is that the bigger party gets all the credit and the smaller party gets all the grief. I don't think any of us could have predicted the extent of that – though with hindsight, I realised when you look round Europe that seems to be the case, from the FDP to the Liberals in Sweden and elsewhere.

Anyway, that was, I thought, a logical electoral strategy. From that flowed a perfectly reasonable belief that in the early stages of the government we needed to show, above and beyond anything else, that we could govern, and that was more important than talking to ourselves or to our core vote. Then, over time, particularly after the terrible elections in May 2011 and the failure of the AV referendum, there was a turning of the page, in the sense that I understood that we also needed to show not just what the sausage was from coalition government but also how the sausage was made. So we went through various iterations, revealing and illuminating the differences with the Conservatives, but the electoral strategy remained to try to be the authentic voice of small-'l' liberal middle-ground political opinion.

I know many people would disagree, but my own view is that at the outset of this recent campaign, our electoral strategy and our electoral refrain made a lot of sense. The beginning of the campaign was shaping up to be quite a conventional right/left argument. Is Osborne going to hurt the poor? Was Ed Balls going to screw up the economy again? We were, at that stage, at least, a plausible centre-ground alternative to that choice. We may or may not have succeeded, but I was saying there was a Liberal alternative, which in one shape or form has always been our refrain, that the other two present a false choice. We were saying that you could both sort out the economy and have a fair society – and not be forced to choose between the two. Then what happened, about a week or ten days before the election, it was a bit like doing an exam in school, and the examiner coming up to you while you're busily finishing your essay and gently pulling away the paper you're working on and just slipping in a completely different question. Suddenly the question became, in England: 'How can we stop Miliband and Salmond?' To which suddenly we were not the answer. Head, heart and all this stuff, strong economy, fair society, was an irrelevant answer to the much more visceral question of 'we just don't want Miliband dancing to Salmond's tune'.

I remain of the view that it would have been very, very difficult for us to have dealt with this other than through making one major strategic choice – which I never seriously considered, but I knew was the only other choice we could have taken – which was to present ourselves to the British public basically as a continuation of the coalition. I remember saying to my team a week before the election – after we'd tried all this 'Blukip' stuff, to counter this groundswell shift to the Tories – that the only thing we could have done to change the weather at that stage would have been to say that under no circumstances whatsoever would the Liberal Democrats ever enter into a coalition with Labour. That would have helped stem the flight of voters to the Tories, but it would have been inconsistent with our identity as an independent party.

The fundamental choice in any election campaign at the end of the day always comes down to one lot saying 'stick with us', and the other lot saying 'time for a change'. If we'd made that choice we'd basically have said we're going to choose 'stick with us' – but we ended up, of course, saying neither, or a little bit of both. It allowed the Tories to ring up our voters, as they did in huge numbers, and say: 'Nick Clegg hasn't ruled out a coalition with Labour, you know.' As, of course, I couldn't – it would have been the end of the identity of the Liberal Democrats if I had. It was the only thing that would have made a difference, electorally, at the end, and I'm pretty convinced it would have been the surest way to have saved more seats, but it would have been a Pyrrhic victory for the Liberal Democrats in the long run. The only way we could have saved our seats was to say something which is absolutely the antithesis of what Liberalism should be about – to say that we were only really hitched to one wagon, the Conservative wagon and no one else's. It would have saved our seats but I think it would have damaged our soul. We've been very badly damaged electorally but at least our soul is still intact. And at the end of the day, that matters, because it means there is a route forward.

DUNCAN BRACK: Going back to something you said – to the extent that we had a core vote in 2010, people like graduates, people in education, public-sector professionals, we almost seemed to go out of our way in the coalition to piss them all off. Do you think that is fair? Do you think we could have done things differently?

NICK CLEGG: I tell you what I think is fair – and I direct this to myself and actually to all of us – that what I think is a great strength and a great weakness of the Liberal Democrats is while other parties are very aware of their interests, we are not. I noticed this when having policy discussions with the Tories; suddenly, the debate was closed down and they said, 'We're not going to do that to our people, we just won't do it.' I remember a conversation about property taxation – the way in which we tax property in this country is clearly bonkers, and at the end of lengthy discussions, when at one point George Osborne was tempted to accept a mansion tax in return for other things we would concede to him – the answer I got from David Cameron was, 'No, I won't do that because my people won't like it,' full stop, end of story. What was rather touching, but also flawed, in our approach is that we are quite an intellectual party. We have a very intellectual machinery, which you know better than almost anyone. We labour over policy, but we forget at the end of the day that voters are not policy entities, they are people who worry about their own interests and the interests of their family and their community. We think with the head, most people vote with the heart. I think the other parties are much more attuned to the idea that they are representing certain interests and they're in office to defend those interests – even, frankly, when it bumps up against rational policymaking. We always allow rational policymaking to trump interest. I think that is very admirable because it means we are a party of values and policies, rather than vested interests, but it's not electorally always the smartest way to conduct business. So I do accept the criticism.

The really big question, I would suggest, is that we need to be quite careful in the next phase, as we rebuild, that we are quite clear about *who* we are seeking to speak for. I think that if you look at the 20,000-odd people who have joined our party since the election, these are people who are not interested in raking over the past and not interested in beating ourselves up about tuition fees and all the rest of it. They are people who seemed to respond very powerfully to what they thought was a decent and dignified attempt to cling to the centre ground. They're generally young, tech-savvy, open-minded reformist folk. I tried but clearly failed to reach out to a new electoral base. I think that there is a very fundamental decision to be made about whether we try to recoup what we lost or try to capture new ground. I think that we have an opportunity to capture new ground, but that is for other people to decide.

TOBY JAMES: You've touched a little bit on this already, but the next question is about the challenges you faced in managing your party and how successfully you dealt with them.

NICK CLEGG: Much though I've wrestled with the arcane comitology we have in our party, and while I still think we can sometimes move with a sloth-like grace under the pressure of the 24-hour media demands, I genuinely think that the open, deliberative, collective way of making decisions remains an overwhelming strength rather than a weakness. I really wouldn't want to see it replaced. I think you do need sometimes to cut through it, taking rapid decisions and all the rest of it, but I think on the whole it has been the secret weapon for the

Liberal Democrats, given the pressure we've been under. So I wouldn't mess too much with that.

The only thing I would say as a leader – and I'll be very careful to say this in a way which doesn't sound whingey, because I'm not – but I have noticed that in other parties, perhaps most particularly the Tory Party, they understand intuitively that you have to protect the leader when he or she is under pressure, so the leader can speak in as undamaged a way to the public. They'll circle the wagons, they'll create diversions, they'll get other people to carry the can for things that have gone wrong – until they no longer want them and then they ruthlessly decapitate them! I did at times slightly feel that when the Liberal Democrats were under pressure people would say, 'Well, it's nothing to do with us, what's the leader got to say about it?' I think we do need to understand that under the remorseless pressure of the 24-hour media, if you have a spokesperson – the leader – it makes sense for the rest of the cast to allow that person to continue to speak loudly and clearly from the pulpit you've given them. Don't give a leader a pulpit and then, in a sense, expect them to also carry the can for all the difficult stuff.

To be fair, Paddy did that for me in the latter stages of my leadership. You've no idea what a difference it made to me when I felt I didn't *always* need to be the person on the *Today* programme, to have to defend difficult stuff. Malcolm Bruce was brilliant as well, he would just get on with it. You have that in politics, you've got difficult stuff to deal with, but don't ask the leader always to be the person who fronts up the rubbish – because then the public associate the leader with negative news. In the latter stages I felt we'd got it right. The fact we hadn't earlier is my failing, not anybody else's. The next leader needs to have people around them who are just prepared to act as a diversion or to carry bad news.

DUNCAN BRACK: Do you think there is tension between being a strong leader and a leader who listens to their party?

NICK CLEGG: I don't think they are inconsistent. There's a tension with people who feel the leader takes a decision they don't like, but as long as one takes decisions which are preceded by debate, discussion and rational thought, and as much consultation as you can manage, that's OK – though sometimes it's just impossible for you to do that.

I take quite an old-fashioned view. For instance, I don't think that strong leadership is expressed by being rude or aggressive towards your opponents. I think strength is often better expressed by civility. In the same way, I think there is plenty of strength in being prepared to listen to countervailing views, arguing your side and then sticking with your own decision. I think the great danger of any organisation, particularly political parties, is that the sheer volume of decisions you have to take each day is just so overwhelming; I certainly found that when I was leader of the Liberal Democrats and I was in charge of certain issues in government and I was Deputy Prime Minister. Then, just for pragmatic reasons, you end up consulting with people who are closest to you, literally who were physically close to you, who of course would end up being your advisors. Then you do get this tension in any political party, including ours, between the leader's closest advisors and the rest of the party. I always think it's incredibly unfair on those advisors when they're blamed for the leader not consulting the wider party – sometimes it's because the leader fails to do so, but sometimes it's just because the sheer pace and velocity of decision-making is such that you can't consult. I got that balance wrong sometimes and right at other times.

TOBY JAMES: Again this is a question that you've touched on already – what is the extent to which you felt that you won or changed the elite debate on some of the policy issues within Parliament?

NICK CLEGG: I think we've made a massive difference. Look at the debate now about surveillance. This David Anderson report [*A Question of Trust – Report of the Investigatory Powers Review*] only happened because of us. We've changed the debate completely, for example around the idea of an international treaty, which is the most radical thing in Anderson's report, or having judge-led decisions on warrants. This is a total change, and it was something Tim Colbourne [special advisor] and I came up with in government, speaking to people in the industry and on the other side of the Atlantic who said that at the end of the day, the internet is global, you can't have this balkanised approach to surveillance. That's just a current example from this week.

I think we had a massive impact in the early stages in favour of devolution to cities across the country; George Osborne wasn't the slightest bit interested in it when I first went on about it five years ago. On education, you heard this morning the stuff on social mobility, stuff from Alan Milburn, who was appointed to chair a commission [the Social Mobility and Child Poverty Commission] which I established in the teeth of Conservative opposition, because they quite rightly predicted it would spend a lot of its time criticising the way in which the pecking order is sustained. The list goes on: the fact that the raising of the personal allowance is now by a long chalk the public's favourite policy in any domain at all; we'd been going on about it for ten years.

But as well as wanting to oversee the transition of a party which had been in opposition ever since we were founded to a party that proves it can govern, I also hoped that the coalition would be a way in which we could finally break the mould, finally break the duopoly of British politics. It seemed obvious to me that the coalition was as subversive of the established political order as any amount of campaigning on the streets; it could demolish overnight the claim that government had to be run by one party or another. So it saddens me massively that this election result will now allow a lot of people to claim that coalitions are the wrong route for political change. I think people will inevitably say that, but I think it's a misdiagnosis of exactly what happened, in the latter stages of the election campaign; as I say, I think nationalism, Scottish nationalism and the English reaction to it, were the big drivers behind the final result. But I accept that in the rubble of all this, I suspect that no one else is going to try coalition for a long time – and that saddens me immensely. I think that if you're a Liberal, you're a pluralist, and that means embracing the reality of coalitions.

The Roy Jenkins view espoused by Adonis, Ashdown, Blair and others was always that the Conservative Party dominated British politics across the twentieth century because the centre-left allowed itself to be split. So the assertion was – and still is, and I think will become resurgent again – that to provide balance and choice in British politics, the centre-left needs to re-congregate, basically through a Labour and Liberal Democrat merger. But I always thought, and I still do think, that, hang on, we don't have to be like America, we don't have to have a Republican block and a Democrat block. There has to be room in a society as complex as ours for genuine pluralism. I always thought, what's wrong with more choice? It's a pretty old-fashioned Liberal idea. That's why for me, ideologically, being in coalition with the Conservatives when no one won a majority, was never a heinous crime – it's a logical consequence if you take a Liberal, pluralist view. But of course because now people will deem that it was an electoral failure, I think what they will say is that the experiment in pluralism rather than realignment has failed. I fully anticipate the push for realignment will now re-emerge, which, by the way, might well be the right thing to do in order to pose a challenge to the Conservatives. But it's still for me a bitter-sweet realisation, because I'd always dreamt that we could not only be a party of power but that we could be a party that showed that pluralism worked, and that Liberalism could be a permanent part of the menu of choices available to the British people.

DUNCAN BRACK: Tim Farron argued in a speech last week that a precondition for us to enter another coalition – not that that will be an issue for a long time – ought to be proportional representation.

NICK CLEGG: I agree, basically. I think that's a totally coherent conclusion from what's happened to us. With hindsight, the failure of AV was an even bigger problem for us than I realised at the time. Because, it removed the escape hatch, if I can put it that way. If we'd had AV we would have had fifty-odd seats now, it would have been completely different. Once that was closed, and closed in such a shamelessly, cynical manner by the Conservatives and the Tory-supporting press, it was really just closing the escape hatch for the smaller party in the coalition. *How* to make proportional representation a precondition is another matter, because guaranteeing it will happen without any votes or caveats is not as straightforward as it sounds.

TOBY JAMES: Could you expand on this answer a little? In retrospect, do you think you could have achieved more on electoral reform, either in the coalition negotiations or in government?

NICK CLEGG: I don't think we could have secured more in the coalition negotiations, not least because any plausible option, including those we were tentatively exploring in our talks with the Labour Party, would have required a referendum. I don't think we could have ended up with any proposed system without a referendum, partly because of the practical politics of the issue but also because I think it is the right thing to do as a matter of principle; for very large constitutional changes it's right to seek the consent of the British people. I don't think there was any shortcut to electoral reform under any coalition scenario at the time.

In terms of the referendum itself, there's a perfectly legitimate debate – which one can enter into with the wonderful benefit of hindsight – about whether the timing was the most propitious for a positive outcome. In the wake of tuition fees, the comprehensive spending review, and so on, it was very easy for our opponents to turn it into an anti-Liberal Democrat referendum rather than engage on the merits of the issue. But there was huge pressure at the time to show that the Liberal Democrats meant business by holding the referendum as fast as possible. I harboured some doubts myself, but I remember endless editorials putting pressure on us to hold it quickly, and I judged that delay would not have been acceptable to our supporters.

Is AV the best form of PR? No, of course not. Would a different acronym – STV – on the ballot paper have made any difference? No. Did we opt for AV in the hope of getting Labour support? Yes, absolutely. It's clear that as a smaller party we couldn't achieve electoral reform on our own; we had to persuade one of the larger parties to support it too. Since AV was in the Labour manifesto, this seemed a sensible move. But, in practice, far from seeking to implement their manifesto, some in the Labour Party put themselves at the forefront of denigrating any change.

TOBY JAMES: What personal characteristics do you think leaders need to have?

NICK CLEGG: Physical resilience. Seriously. Do not underestimate how physical front-line politics is. It is an unbelievably physical job; it was one of the things that surprised me the most. I learned the hard way, because I didn't look after myself for the first year or so, and my health suffered. I then got fit, ate better, did exercise, kickboxing regularly, and so on. Physical resilience is unbelievably important.

Secondly, infinite amounts of patience: patience in the sense that so much of politics now is breathless, hyperbolic, who's up, who's down, nasty backstabbing and all the rest of it. You just have to keep a sense of patience and perspective – and then be clear in your own mind about what you're trying to do, and go for it, just go for it. If you fail, at least you've given it your best shot. That's always the philosophy I've taken. Clearly, electorally, what I tried to do did not work for one reason and another, but I think that it's better to go for something rather than constantly hedge your bets. I don't personally think there is much point being a leader of any organisation just to be the leader. In my view it's much better to go for something, which is at least worthwhile pursuing, to take chances and to succeed or fail. I think the worst thing to do is to want to be leader just because you want to be leader.

So, physical resilience, patience and perspective – and a willingness to set out the values that you care about, go for it, go for broke and then be big enough to accept the consequences of success or failure.

DUNCAN BRACK: Do you think you need to have a strategy that you stick to?

NICK CLEGG: Yes, that's basically what I meant. People would talk endlessly about strategy and tactics – I never know quite where one ends and the other begins – but you need to have an aim. To have an aim in politics is incredibly important, because otherwise you just get knocked about so much. You need a lodestar and you go for it, and people will follow you or they won't follow you. You need a lodestar, you need a sense of bearing, because it's all so noisy; people get too pumped up by the here and now. For me the lodestar was to establish the position of the party, to be true to my liberal values, to do the right things by the country, try to do my bit to break the mould – and I stuck with it and I went for it. I certainly stuck with it and went for it for much longer than many people anticipated. Then you let other people – like yourselves – judge how you did!

FURTHER READING

For those readers interested in knowing more about the leaders covered in this book, we recommend the following.

OVERVIEWS

Duncan Brack, 'Liberal Democrat Leadership', *Journal of Liberal History*, Vol. 83, summer 2014.

Duncan Brack and Robert Ingham eds, *Peace, Reform and Liberation: Liberal Politics in Britain, 1679–2011*, London, Biteback Publishing, 2011.

David Dutton, *A History of the Liberal Party Since 1900*, Basingstoke, Palgrave, 2013.

Jonathan Parry, *The Rise and Fall of Liberal Government in Victorian Britain*, New Haven and London, Yale University Press, 1993.

Geoffrey Searle, *The Liberal Party: Triumph and Disintegration, 1886–1929*, Basingstoke, Palgrave, 2001.

CHAPTER 4: GREY

Austin Mitchell, *The Whigs in Opposition, 1815–1830*, Oxford, Clarendon Press, 1967.

Ian Newbould, *Whiggery and Reform, 1830–41: The Politics of Government*, Stanford, Stanford University Press, 1990.

E. A. Smith, *Lord Grey, 1764–1845*, Oxford, Clarendon, 1990.

George Trevelyan, *Lord Grey of the Reform Bill*, London, Longmans & Co., 1920.

CHAPTER 5: RUSSELL

Angus Hawkins, *Parliament, Party and the Art of Politics in Britain, 1855–59*, Stanford, Stanford University Press, 1987.

T. A. Jenkins, *The Liberal Ascendancy, 1830–1886*, Basingstoke, Macmillan, 1994.

Jonathan Parry, 'Past and Future in the Later Career of Lord John Russell', in T. C. W. Blanning and David Cannadine eds, *History & Biography: Essays in Honour of Derek Beales*, Cambridge, Cambridge University Press, 1996.

John Prest, *Lord John Russell*, Basingstoke, Macmillan, 1972.

CHAPTER 6: MELBOURNE

Abraham D. Kriegel ed., *The Holland House Diaries, 1831–1840* [Lord Holland], London, Routledge, 1977.

Peter Mandler, *Aristocratic Government in the Age of Reform: Whigs and Liberals 1830–1852*, Oxford, Clarendon, 1990.

L. G. Mitchell, *Lord Melbourne, 1779–1848*, Oxford, Oxford University Press, 1997.

Jonathan Parry, *The Rise and Fall of Liberal Government in Victorian Britain*, New Haven and London, Yale University Press, 1993.

CHAPTER 7: PALMERSTON

David Brown, *Palmerston: A Biography*, New Haven and London, Yale University Press, 2010.

Kenneth Bourne, *Palmerston: The Early Years, 1784–1841*, London, Allen Lane, 1982.

Joseph Coohill, *Ideas of the Liberal Party; Perceptions, Agendas and Liberal Politics in the House of Commons, 1832–52*, Oxford, Wiley-Blackwell, 2011.

Jonathan Parry, *The Rise and Fall of Liberal Government in Victorian Britain*, New Haven and London, Yale University Press, 1993.

E. D. Steele, *Palmerston and Liberalism, 1855–1865*, Cambridge, Cambridge University Press, 1991.

CHAPTER 8: GLADSTONE

Roy Jenkins, *Gladstone*, Basingstoke, Macmillan, 1995.

H. C. G. Matthew, *Gladstone 1809–1898*, Oxford, Oxford University Press, 1998.

John Morley, *The Life of William Ewart Gladstone*, London, Macmillan, 1903.

Richard Shannon, *Gladstone: God and Politics*, London, Hambledon Continuum, 2008.

CHAPTER 9: HARTINGTON AND GRANVILLE

Lord Edmond Fitzmaurice, *The Life of the Second Earl Granville*, London, Longmans, Green, 1905.

Bernard Holland, *The Life of the Eighth Duke of Devonshire*, London, Longmans, Green, 1911.

Patrick Jackson, *The Last of the Whigs*, London, Associated University Presses, 1994.

T. A. Jenkins, *Gladstone, Whiggery and the Liberal Party 1874–1886*, Oxford, Oxford University Press, 1988.

John P. Rossi, 'The Transformation of the British Liberal Party: A Study of the Tactics of the Liberal Opposition, 1874–1880', *Transactions of the American Philosophical Society* Vol. 68, December 1978.

Henry Vane, *Affair of State: A Biography of the 8th Duke & Duchess of Devonshire*, London, Peter Owen, 2004.

CHAPTER 10: ROSEBERY

David Brooks ed., *The Destruction of Lord Rosebery: From the Diary of Sir Edward Walter Hamilton 1894–1895*, London, Historians' Press, 1986.

Leo McKinstry, *Rosebery: Statesman in Turmoil*, London, John Murray, 2005.

Peter Stansky, *Ambitions and Strategies: the Struggle for the Leadership of the Liberal Party in the 1890s*, Oxford, Clarendon Press, 1964.

CHAPTER 11: HARCOURT

A. G. Gardiner, *The Life of Sir William Harcourt*, London, Constable, 1923.

Patrick Jackson, *Harcourt and Son*, Madison NJ, Fairleigh Dickinson University Press, 2004.

Roy Jenkins, 'Sir William Harcourt', in *The Chancellors*, Basingstoke, Macmillan, 1998.

CHAPTER 12: CAMPBELL-BANNERMAN

Ewen Cameron, 'Maistly Scotch: Campbell-Bannerman and Liberal Leadership', *Journal of Liberal History* Vol. 54, spring 2007.

Roy Hattersley, *Campbell-Bannerman*, London, Haus, 2006.

John Wilson, *CB: A Life of Sir Henry Campbell-Bannerman*, London, Constable, 1973.

CHAPTER 13: ASQUITH

George H. Cassar, *Asquith as War Leader*, London, Hambledon Continuum, 1994.

Colin Clifford, *The Asquiths*, London, John Murray, 2003.

Roy Jenkins, *Asquith*, London, Collins, 1988.

CHAPTER 14: LLOYD GEORGE

Travis L. Crosby, *The Unknown Lloyd George*, London, I. B. Tauris, 2014.

John Grigg, *Lloyd George: From Peace to War, 1912–16*, London, Methuen, 1985.

Cameron Hazlehurst, *Politicians at War, July 1914 to May 1915*, London, Jonathan Cape, 1971.

Kenneth O. Morgan, *Consensus and Disunity: The Lloyd George Coalition Government 1918–1922*, Oxford, Clarendon Press, 1979.

Richard Toye, *Lloyd George and Churchill: Rivals for Greatness*, Basingstoke, Macmillan, 2007.

CHAPTER 15: SAMUEL

Herbert Samuel, *Memoirs*, London, Cresset Press, 1945.

Bernard Wasserstein, *Herbert Samuel – A Political Life*, Oxford, Oxford University Press, 1992.

John Bowle, *Viscount Samuel – A Biography*, London, Victor Gollancz, 1957.

CHAPTER 16: SINCLAIR

G. de Groot, *Liberal Crusader: The Life of Sir Archibald Sinclair*, London, Hurst & Co., 1993.

R. Grayson, *Liberals, International Relations and Appeasement*, London, Frank Cass, 2001.

I. Hunter ed., *Winston and Archie: The Collected Correspondence of Winston Churchill and Archibald Sinclair 1915–1960*, London, Politico's, 2005.

A. Thorpe, *Parties at War: Political Organisation in Second World War Britain*, Oxford, Oxford University Press, 2009.

CHAPTER 17: DAVIES

Emlyn Hooson, 'Clement Davies: an underestimated Welshman and politician', *Journal of Liberal Democrat History*, Vol. 24, autumn 1999.

Geoffrey Sell, 'A sad business – an examination of Clement Davies's resignation from the leadership in 1956', *Journal of Liberal Democrat History*, Vol. 24, autumn 1999.

Alun Wyburn-Powell, *Clement Davies – Liberal Leader*, London, Politico's, 2003.

CHAPTER 18: GRIMOND

Peter Barberis, *Liberal Lion – Jo Grimond: a Political Life*, London, I. B. Tauris, 2005.

Jo Grimond, *Memoirs*, London, Heinemann, 1979.

Michael McManus, *Jo Grimond: Towards the Sound of Gunfire*, Edinburgh, Birlinn, 2001.

CHAPTER 19: THORPE

Michael Bloch, *Jeremy Thorpe*, London, Little, Brown, 2014.

Jeremy Thorpe, *In My Own Time*, London, Politico's, 1999.

Simon Freeman and Barrie Penrose, *Rinkagate: The Rise and Fall of Jeremy Thorpe*, London, Bloomsbury, 1996.

CHAPTER 20: STEEL

David Steel, *A House Divided: The Lib–Lab Pact and the Future of British Politics*, London, Weidenfeld & Nicolson, 1980.

David Steel, *Against Goliath: David Steel's Story*, London, Weidenfeld & Nicolson, 1989.

David Torrance, *David Steel: Rising Hope to Elder Statesman*, London, Biteback Publishing, 2012.

CHAPTER 21: JENKINS

Andrew Adonis and Keith Thomas eds, *Roy Jenkins: A Retrospective*, Oxford, Oxford University Press, 2004.

John Campbell, *Roy Jenkins: A Well-Rounded Life*, London, Jonathan Cape, 2014.

Ivor Crewe and Anthony King, *SDP: The Birth, Life and Death of the Social Democratic Party*, Oxford, Oxford University Press, 1995.

Roy Jenkins, *A Life at the Centre*, Basingstoke, Macmillan, 1991.

CHAPTER 22: OWEN

Ivor Crewe and Anthony King, *SDP: The Birth, Life and Death of the Social Democratic Party*, Oxford, Oxford University Press, 1995.

Tudor Jones, *The Revival of British Liberalism: From Grimond to Clegg*, Basingstoke, Palgrave, 2011.

David Owen, *A Future That Will Work*, Harmondsworth, Penguin, 1984.

David Owen, *Time to Declare*, London, Michael Joseph, 1991.

CHAPTER 23: MACLENNAN

Helen Bailey, 'Robert MacLennan MP', in Duncan Brack ed., *Dictionary of Liberal Biography*, London, Politico's, 1998.

Bill Rodgers, *Fourth Among Equals*, London, Politico's, 2000.

CHAPTER 24: ASHDOWN

Paddy Ashdown, *A Fortunate Life*, London, Aurum Press, 2009.

Paddy Ashdown, *The Ashdown Diaries*, Vol. 1, 1988–97, Vol. 2, 1997–99, Harmondsworth, Allen Lane / The Penguin Press, 2000 and 2001.

Interview with Paddy Ashdown, *Journal of Liberal History*, Vol. 30, spring 2001.

CHAPTER 25: KENNEDY

Paddy Ashdown, *The Ashdown Diaries*, Vol. 1 1988–97, Harmondsworth, Allen Lane / The Penguin Press, 2000.

Greg Hurst, *Charles Kennedy: A Tragic Flaw*, London, Politico's, 2006.

Charles Kennedy, *The Future of Politics*, London, HarperCollins, 2000.

CHAPTER 26: CAMPBELL

Menzies Campbell, *My Autobiography*, London, Hodder & Stoughton, 2008.

Interview with Menzies Campbell, *Journal of Liberal History*, Vol. 60, autumn
2008.

CHAPTER 27: CLEGG

Chris Bowers, *Nick Clegg: The Biography*, London, Biteback Publishing, 2012.

Nick Clegg, *The Liberal Moment*, London, Demos, 2009.

Robert Hazell and Ben Yong, *The Politics of Coalition: How the Conservative–Liberal Democrat Government Works*, Oxford, Hart Publishing, 2012.

INDEX

early life and career 143–9
under Viscount Palmerston 147
as Prime Minister 149–53, 156–61, 173–4, 180, 207, 208
resigns from leadership 153–5, 161–2, 171
parliamentary reform 158–9
1885 general election 159
and Lord Granville and Lord Hartington 170–71, 173–5
and H. H. Asquith 219
admired by David Lloyd George 240
Glasgow Hillhead by-election (1982) 341
Goderich, Lord 95
Gordon, Charles 157, 174
governing competence 38–41
Granville, Edgar 292
Granville, Lord 12, 137, 152, 156, 179, 194
communication and campaigning skills 22
vision development 22
objectives of Liberalism 23
party management 23
party success 23
overall assessment 24
and general elections 53
as joint leader 154, 170, 171–6
early life and career 167–71
Great Reform Act (1832) 6, 45, 50, 87–90, 94–5, 96–7, 111–12, 131
Greaves, Tony 387
Green, T. H. 218, 310
Greenwood, Arthur 290
Grey, Charles Earl 6, 210, 213
becomes leader 12, 83
party management 19, 23
objectives of Liberalism 19, 23, 83
communication and campaigning skills 22
vision development 22
party success 23, 90–91
overall assessment 24
performance in general elections 57
early life and career 81–3
as leader of Whig opposition 83–7
support for parliamentary reform 86–7, 87–90
as Prime Minister 87–91, 110–11
1831 general election 88

1832 general election 90
and Lord John Russell 96
retirement of 98
Grey, Sir Charles 82, 83
Grey, Edward 220, 229, 235
Grimond, Joseph 9, 292, 296, 313, 337, 406, 436, 437, 444
becomes leader 14, 298
objectives of Liberalism 20, 23
communication and campaigning skills 22, 299–300
vision development 22, 300–304
party management 23, 304–5
party success 23, 299, 300, 308–9
overall assessment 24, 309–10
performance in general elections 56, 58, 60, 61, 62, 64, 65, 67, 68, 70, 73, 74
early life and career 295–8
as leader of Liberal Party 298–306
later life 306–8
Guardian, The 379
Guedalla, Philip 135, 138
Guest, Freddie 251, 254

Hague, William 396
Haldane, Richard 204, 210, 213, 218, 220, 221, 231, 246
Hamilton, Sir Edward 186
Hankey, Colonel 233
Hankey, Maurice 252
Harcourt, Lewis (Loulou)181, 192
Harcourt, Sir William 7, 162, 178, 180–81
as leader 13, 198–9, 208–9
communication and campaigning skills 22
vision development 22
party management 23
objectives of Liberalism 23
party success 23
overall assessment 24
and general elections 50, 53
under Lord Rosebery 182–3, 184, 185, 186, 193–6
early life and career 191–6
under William Gladstone 193–6
under Lord Rosebery 196–8
and H. H. Asquith 219

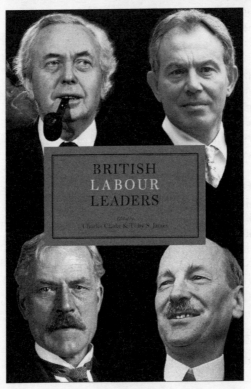

416PP HARDBACK, £25

As the party that championed trade union rights, the creation of the NHS and the establishment of a national minimum wage, Labour has played a crucial role in the shaping of contemporary British society.

And yet, the leaders who have stood at its helm – from Keir Hardie to Ed Miliband, via Ramsay MacDonald, Clement Attlee and Tony Blair – have steered the party vessel with enormously varying degrees of success.

This comprehensive and enlightening book considers the attributes and achievements of each leader in the context of their respective time and diplomatic landscape, offering a compelling analytical framework by which they may be judged, detailed personal biographies from some of the country's foremost political critics, and exclusive interviews with former leaders themselves.

An indispensable contribution to the study of party leadership, *British Labour Leaders* is the essential guide to understanding British political history and governance.

— AVAILABLE FROM ALL GOOD BOOKSHOPS —

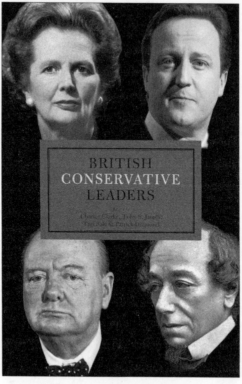

496PP HARDBACK, £25

As the party that has won wars, reversed recessions and held prime ministerial power more times than any other, the Conservatives have played a crucial role in the shaping of contemporary British society.

And yet, the leaders who have stood at its helm – from Sir Robert Peel to David Cameron, via Benjamin Disraeli, Winston Churchill and Margaret Thatcher – have steered the party vessel with enormously varying degrees of success.

This comprehensive and enlightening book considers the attributes and achievements of each leader in the context of their respective time and diplomatic landscape, offering a compelling analytical framework by which they may be judged, detailed personal biographies from some of the country's foremost political critics, and exclusive interviews with former leaders themselves.

An indispensable contribution to the study of party leadership, *British Conservative Leaders* is the essential guide to understanding British political history and governance.

— AVAILABLE FROM ALL GOOD BOOKSHOPS —